SIXTEEN MINOR

SMṚTIS

(With an Introduction, Original Sanskrit Text and English Translation)

PARIMAL SANSKRIT SERIES NO. 88

SIXTEEN MINOR SMṚTIS

(With An Introduction, Original Sanskrit Text and English Translation)

Vol. 2

(Hārīta-Smṛti, Bṛhaspati-Smṛti, Dakṣa-Smṛti, Śātātapa-Smṛti, Śaṅkha-Smṛti, Likhita-Smṛti, Vyāsa-Smṛti, Gautama-Smṛti, Vasiṭha-Smṛti)

Translated into English with notes
by
Manmatha Nath Dutt (Shastri)

Edited By
K. L. Joshi
M.A. B.Ed. Shastri, Vedalankar,
Sahitya-Ayurveda Ratna

PARIMAL PUBLICATIONS
DELHI (INDIA)

Published by

PARIMAL PUBLICATIONS

27/28, SHAKTI NAGAR

DELHI 110007 (INDIA)

Ph. : 011-2384 5456, 55441516

E-mail : parimal@ndf.vsnl.net.in

URL : http://www.parimalpublication.com

First Edition 2006

ISBN : 81-7110-279-4 (Set)

81-7110-281-6 (Vol.2)

PRICE : Rs. 500.00 (Each Volume)

Rs. 1000.00 (Set)

Printed by

Himanshu Printers

14, Maujpur, Yamuna Vihar Main Road

Delhi - 110 091

Editor's Note

In the year 1908, a collection of 20 Smṛtis was translated into English by M.N. Dutt and published under the collective name of Dharma-Śāstra in which some of the Smṛtis such as Manusmṛti, Yājñavalkyasmriti, Viṣṇusmṛti etc.. are compratively major in size as far as their subject-matter are concerned than the remaining sixteen smṛtis which are relatively minor in size.

In this edition, I have made an attempt to collect these sixteen minor smṛtis and bring out them separately in 2 volumes. The remaining 4 major smṛtis have been already published separately. I have put the Sanskrit Text and English Translation side by side for the benefit and quick reference of the readers. Further, is has been tried by me to correct the flaws in the Sanskrit Text of the earlier edition as far as possible. Also, the older usage of English words such as thee, thou, ye etc. has been replaced by their corresponding modern English equivalents. The incorrect and older diacritical notations has also been corrected and replaced respectively at various places in the English Translation portion.

K.L. Joshi

CONTENTS

8. Hārīta Smṛti

Subject	Ślokas	Page
Chapter 1		
Creation of the universe, etc.	1-14	1
The duties of a Brāhmaṇa	15-32	3
Chapter 2		
The duties of the Kṣatriyas, Vaiśyas and the Śūdras	1-15	6
Chapter 3		
Religious studentship	1-16	9
Chapter 4		
The domestic mode of life	1-17	12
Chapter 5		
The Vānaprastha mode of life	1-10	25
Chapter 6		
Sannyāsa	1-23	28
Chapter 7		
Essence of Yoga	1-21	32

9. Bṛhaspati Smṛti

Subject	Ślokas	Page
Various gifts and their fruits	1-6	36
Measurement of lands	7-8	37
Various other gifts	9-34	41
Penance for various sins	35-45	41
Penance for the theft of a Brāhmaṇa's property	46-54	43
Worthy recipients	55-61	44
Fruits of various other gifts	62-66	45
The destroyer of a Brāhmaṇa	67-69	46
Sin for obstructing marriage, etc.	70	47
The rewards of taking fruits, etc., and abstention from injury, etc.	71-72	47
The fruits of other deeds	73-80	47

10. Dakṣa Smṛti

Subject	Ślokas	Page
Chapter 1		
Four modes of life : description of a religious student	1-15	49
Chapter 2		
The daily rites of a twice-born person	1-58	51
Chapter 3		
The nine acts and objects : the nine Sudhās	1-5	62
Minor gifts of a house-holder	6-7	63
The nine sacred works	8-14	63
Fruitful and fruitless gifts	15-16	64
The nine articles which should never be given away	17-18	64
Other regulations about gifts	19-31	65
Chapter 4		
Duties towards a wife	1-20	67
Chapter 5		
Means of purification, external and internal	1-13	70
Chapter 6		
Birth and death impurity	1-19	73
Chapter 7		
Yoga	1-54	76

11. Śātātapa Smṛti

Subject	Ślokas	Page
Chapter 1		
Sin indicating signs : diseases the outcome of crimes	1-11	86
Gifts : The penance for sins	12-31	87
Chapter 2		
Penitential rites	1-57	91
Chapter 3		
The punishment for drinking spirituous liquor	1-3	101
Punishment for drinking forbidden food	4-8	101
The condition in another birth for various sins	9-22	102
Chapter 4		
The punishment of the various forms of theft	1-32	105

Chapter 5
Punishment for knowing mother and a Cāṇḍāla woman 1-23 110
Diseases originating from cohabiting with women relations other than one's own wife 24-38 114
Chapter 6
The penance for various forms of death and man slaughter 1-51 116

12. Śaṅkha Smṛti

Subject	Ślokas	Page
Chapter 1		
Duties of various castes	1-8	126
Chapter 2		
The purificatory rites	1-12	127
Chapter 3		
Rules of study	1-14	130
Chapter 4		
Rules of marriage, duties of a married couple	1-16	132
Chapter 5		
The duties of a householder	1-18	135
Chapter 6		
The duties of a forest recluse	1-7	138
Chapter 7		
The duties of Yati	1-33	139
Chapter 8		
Ceremonial ablution	1-15	145
Chapter 9		
Rules of Ācamana	1-20	148
Chapter 10		
The various Vedic Mantras	1-10	151
Chapter 11		
Detailed account of the Sāvitrī mantra	1-19	152
Chapter 12		
Rules relating to libations of water	1-4	157
Chapter 13		
Qualification of Brāhmaṇas who may be invited at a Śrāddha	1-8	158

Rules of feasting at a Śrāddha	9-25	160
Chapter 14		
Gifts made at sacred places	1-7	163
Chapter 15		
Periods of uncleanness consequent on birth and death	1-24	164
Chapter 16		
Purification of articles	1-23	168
Chapter 17		
Various penances	1-62	172
Chapter 18		
Various other Vratas or purificatory rites	1-13	183

13. Likhita Smṛti

Subject	Ślokas	Page
Fruits for digging tanks, planting trees etc. (Purtta acts.)	1-4	186
Iṣṭa acts, adoration of fine etc. : those entitled to them	5-6	186
The offering of water and other forms of piṇḍa	7-13	187
Definition of a Neela bull	14	188
Various forms of Śrāddha	15-23	188
Śrāddha regulations for women	24-27	189
Other regulations about oblation	28-39	190
Rules about holding Kuśa	40-45	192
Viśvadeva worship and other oblations	46-50	193
Marriage Regulations	51-52	195
Feeding of Brāhmaṇas on the occasion of a Śrāddha	53-58	195
Sandhyā rite	59-60	196
Rules of Japa and Homa	61	197
Cāndrāyaṇa Vrata	62-63	197
Death that does not demand Śrāddha	64	197
Other forms of Penance	65-82	198
Forms of uncleanliness	83-92	201

14. Vyāsa Smṛti

Subject	Ślokas	Page
Chapter 1		
The various castes, orders and rites	1-41	204

Chapter 2

The order of the house-holders : marriage : Duties of husband and wife.	1-56	212

Chapter 3

The various rites of house-holder	1-73	222

Chapter 4

The merits of a dutiful house-holder	1-4	235
Sin of theft and coveting others' wives and riches	5	236
Merit of Hospitality	6-9	236
Pre-eminence of Brāhmaṇas	10-12	236
Merit of self control	13-14	237
Virtue of Charity	15-40	237
Superiority of Brāhmaṇas	41-57	242
Pre-eminence of charitable man	57-59	244
A really heroic and wise man	60	245
Rules for making gifts	61-63	245
Rules about taking boiled rice and food	64-71	246

15. Gautama Smṛti

Subject	Page
Chapter 1	
Investiture with sacred thread	248
Rules of purification	250
Regulation about studies	251
Chapter 2	
Duties of a preceptor and a student	252
Chapter 3	
Other modes of life : a general account	255
Chapter 4	
Various forms of marriage and the status of issues therefrom	257
Chapter 5	
The duties of a householder towards his wife, preceptor, guests, Brāhmaṇas and others	259
Chapter 6	
Various forms of reverence and courtesy : forms of address	262

Chapter 7
Occasions when any caste may follow an interdicted calling 264
Chapter 8
The vows of a Brāhmaṇa 265
Chapter 9
Further duties of a Brāhmaṇa : General duties of others 267
Chapter 10
Duties of a king, a Vaiśya and a Śūdra 271
Chapter 11
The royal duties of a king 275
Chapter 12
Punishment for abusing a Brāhmaṇa 277
Law about capital and interest 280
Law about payment of debt 280
Law about theft 281
Chapter 13
Law of evidence 281
Chapter 14
Uncleanness consequent on birth and death 283
Chapter 15
Regulations about Śrāddhas 285
Chapter 16
Regulations about the study of the Vedas 288
Chapter 17
Regulations about the various articles of food and drink 291
Chapter 18
The position of women : their marriage and children
Gifts 293
Chapter 19
Sinful deeds 295
Chapter 20
Effects of sinful deeds 297
Chapter 21
Position of regicide and of an insulter of the Veda 299

Chapter 22

Definition of degraded persons 301

Chapter 23

Punishment for Brahmanicide 302

Atonement for various other murders and for destruction of animals 304

Chapter 24

Penance for drinking wine and other interdicted articles 305

Chapter 25

Penance for receiving an interdicted article 307

Chapter 26

The vow of an Avakīrṇi 308

Chapter 27

Kṛcha penance 310

Chapter 28

Cāndrāyaṇa penance 312

Chapter 29

Partition of a property amongst sons : law of succession 313

16. Vasiṣṭha Smṛti

Subject	Page
Chapter 1	
Sources of the sacred Laws– Practices of Siddhas, and religious practices and usages obtaining in countries between the Vindhya and the Himālaya	318
Geographical limits, and physical features, of Āryāvarta and Brahmāvarta	318
Sinners and the five heinous crimes	319
Obligation of the three castes to remain under the control of Brāhmaṇas– Exemption of Brāhmaṇas from the liability of paying king's revenue	320
Chapter 2	
Nomenclature of the four castes– reasons for calling the first three castes "twice-born"	321
Sons of twice-born castes are equal to Śūdras before initiation with the holy thread	322
Discourse between the sacred learning and the	

Brāhmaṇa– duty of obeying and honouring a preceptor obligatory on a disciple 322
Duties of Brāhmaṇas, Kṣatriyas and Vaiśyas 323
No regulation as to the duties of Śūdras, who are prohibited from lying up the tufts of hair on their crowns into knots. 324
Specific injunction as to the adoption of an honest mode of living by one, on the failure of earning a livelihood by means, proper to one's caste 324
Things prohibited to be sold for money or gain 325
Chapter 3
Factors which tend to degrade a Brāhmaṇa to the status of a Śūdra 327
No sin attaches to the insulter of a degraded Brāhmaṇa 328
Sixth part of a treasure-find goes to the king; Brāhmaṇas exempted from paying such sixth parts 329
Six kinds of Ātatāyins (assasins) 329
Sanctifiers of Rows and Snātakas 330
Constitution of a Pariṣad (legal assembly) 330
Definitions of Ācāryas, Upādhyāyas, etc., and conditions under which Vaiśyas and Brāhmaṇas may take up arms 331
The rite of Ācamana described 331
Enumeration of articles, pure and impure 333
Purification of articles defiled by foul touch, etc. 334
Chapter 4
Origin of the four castes from the different limbs of Brahmā 335
Manner of offering hospitality to a Brāhmaṇa, or to a Kṣatriya guest 336
Birth and Death-impurities 336
Chapter 5
Perpetual dependent status of women 338
Uncleanness of women during their menses 339
Chapter 6
Irretrievable spiritual loss of a man of vile conduct 340
Rules of voiding stool and urine, and rites of purification to be performed thereafter 342

Meals of the different orders of Brāhmaṇas 344
Characteristic traits of Brāhmaṇas 344
Definition of a Brahma-Cāṇḍāla 345
Degraded condition of a Brāhmaṇa who partakes of food given by a Śūdra 345
Worthy recipients of gifts 346
Chapter 7
The four orders of life (Āśramas) 347
Chapter 8
Definition of an Atithi 349
Duties of householders 349
The order of householders is the best of all the Āśramas 350
Chapter 9
Duties of a Vānaprastha hermit 350
Chapter 10
Duties of religious mendicants and ascetics 351
Chapter 11
Daily offering made by a Brāhmaṇa house-holder and the feeling of guests etc. 354
Mode of offering oblations to one's departed manes 355
Mode of feeding Brāhmaṇas at a Śrāddha ceremony 357
Staffs of students of the three twice-born castes 360
Uddālaka penance 361
Chapter 12
Duties of a Snātaka 361
Conduct which kills one's soul 364
Acts prohibited in respect of Brāhmaṇas 364
Chapter 13
Performance of Upākarman rites 364
Circumstances under which the Vedas should not be studied 365
Severance with one's contaminated relations 367
Presents which may be accepted by a Brāhmana– Precedence given to men of learning, age and wealth, and to Snātakas 367
Chapter 14
Things which may be eaten and which may not be eaten 368

Persons from whom gifts may be taken and the circumstances under which they may be accepted 369
Mode of purifying defiled food 371
Penances for eating forbidden articles of fare 372
Animals whose flesh may or may not be eaten 372
Chapter 15
Right of parents to give away a son in adoption 373
Sons who can not be given in adoption 373
Mode of taking a son in adoption by a man, or a woman 374
The share of a begotten son born after the adoption 374
Mode of excommunicating divulgers of Veda to unworthy persons 374
Penitential rites in connection with the redemption of such excommunicated persons 374
Chapter 16
Duties of a king in matters of adjudicating law suits 375
Administration of properties of minors by kings 375
The three kinds of proof, recognised in law courts 375
Procedure in disputes relating to fields, boundaries, interpretations of gifts, etc. 375
Properties that can not be alienated 376
Persons who may be cited as witnesses 377
Instances where a son's obligation to repay the debts of his deceased father ceases 377
Why truthful testimony obligatory 377
Occasions where a lie is not sinful 378
Chapter 17
Spiritual benefits derived by a father from his son 379
Twelve kinds of sons recognised by the Smṛti, and their status and definitions 380
Determination of shares of different sons in the paternal property 382
Mode of procreating sons under appointment 383
Obligation of a father to marry his daughter before the age of puberty 384
Circumstances under which a married, or betrothed maiden may be married again 385

Periods for which Brāhmaṇa, Kṣatriya, Vaiśya and Śūdra wives shall wait for their lost or absent husbands 385

Persons who may procreate sons on such wives 385

Comparison of a Brāhmaṇa's property with poison 386

Chapter 18

Status of sons who are called Cāṇḍālas, Anta-Vyavasāyins, Ramakas, etc. 386

Penalty for explaining sacred laws etc., to Śūdras 387

Chapter 19

Duties of king 389

Persons exempted from paying taxes 390

Penance in cases of miscarriage of justice 391

Chapter 20

Different kinds of sin (crimes) and their expiating penance described 392

Rites to be omitted on re-initiation of a twice born person 393

Penances for wine-drinkers, procurers of abortions of pregnancy and murderers 393

Penance's for killing Kṣatriyas, Vaiśyas and Śūdras 395

Congenital diseases and deformities, and sins for which men are visited with them 396

Penance for associating with the out caste 396

Chapter 21

Procedure in cases where Kṣatriyas, Vaiśyas or Śūdras carnally know Brāhmaṇa women 397

Penance for a faithless wife 398

८. हारीतस्मृति:

8. Hārīta Smṛti

Chapter-1

The Duties of Brāhmaṇa

[The King Ambarīṣa puts the question to the Ṛṣi Mārkaṇḍeya]

ये वर्णाश्रमधर्मस्थास्ते भुक्त्वा केशवं प्रति।

इति पूर्वं त्वया प्रोक्तं भूर्भुव:स्वर्द्विजोत्तमा:॥१॥

It has, before, been said by you that the foremost of the twice-born ones,– residing on the earth, the atmospheric and the celestial regions, performing the duties laid down [in the ordinances] for the various castes and order,– are [said to be] devoted to Keśava.

वर्णानामाश्रमाणाञ्च धर्मान् नो ब्रूहि सत्तम।

येन सन्तुष्यते देवो नारसिंह: सनातन:॥२॥

O foremost of the good, do you describe unto us the duties of castes and orders by which the eternal Deity Nara-Simha (Man-Lion) is gratified.

अत्राहं कथयिष्यामि पुरावृत्तमनुत्तमम्।

ऋषिभि: सह संवादं हारीतस्य महात्मन:॥३॥

Mārkaṇḍeya said:– I shall here recount the ancient and the most excellent conversation that took place between the high-souled Hārīta and the Ṛsis.

हारीतं सर्वधर्मज्ञमासीनमिव पावकम्।

प्रणिपत्याब्रुवन् सर्वे मुनयो धर्मकाङ्क्षिण:॥४॥

Having saluted Hārīta, conversant with all forms of religion and effulgent like fire, all the ascetics, desirous of questioning about religion, said–

भगवन् सर्वधर्मज्ञ सर्वधर्मप्रवर्त्तक।
वर्णानामाश्रमाणाञ्च धर्मान् नो ब्रूहि भार्गव॥५॥

"O you endued with lordly powers, O you conversant with all [forms of] religion and the institutor of all religions, do you, O son of Bhṛgu, describe unto us the duties of various castes and orders.

समासाद्योगशास्त्रञ्च विष्णुभक्तिकरं परम्।
एतच्चान्यच्च भगवन् ब्रूहि नः परमो गुरुः॥६॥

O you endued with lordly powers, do you describe unto us, in brief, the Yoga-Śāstra and every thing else that goes to create firm faith in Viṣṇu. You are our great preceptor."

हारीतस्तानुवाचाथ तैरेवं चोदितो मुनिः।
शृण्वन्तु मुनयः सर्वे धर्मान् वक्ष्यामि शाश्वतान्॥७॥

Having been thus accosted by them, the ascetic Hārīta said to them:– Hear, O you all ascetics, I shall describe the eternal duties.

वर्णानामाश्रमाणाञ्च योगशास्त्रञ्च सत्तमाः।
सन्ध्यार्य मुच्यते मर्त्यो जन्मसंसारबन्धनात्॥८॥

O foremost ones, by following the duties of castes and orders, as well as [the precepts of] the Yoga-Śāstra, a mortal is freed from the fetters of birth and Saṁsāra (mundane existence).

पुरा देवो जगत्स्रष्टा परमात्मा जलोपरि।
सुष्वाप भोगिपर्यङ्के शयने तु श्रिया सह॥९॥

Formerly (*i.e.,* before the creation) the Divine creator of the Universe, the Great Soul [Viṣṇu] was laying asleep with [His Consort] Śrī (the Goddess of Prosperity) on a bed of serpent in water.

तस्य सुप्तस्य नाभौ तु महत् पद्ममभूत् किल।
पद्ममध्येऽभवद् ब्रह्मा वेदवेदाङ्गभूषणः॥१०॥

From the navel of that Deity, lying asleep, originated a huge

Lotus. Within that lotus sprang into existence Brahmā having Vedas and the Vedāṅgas for his ornaments.

स चोक्तो देवदेवेन जगत् सृज पुनः पुनः।
सोऽपि सृष्ट्वा जगत् सर्वं सदेवासुरमानुषम्।।११।।
यज्ञसिद्ध्यर्थमनघान् ब्राह्मणान् मुखतोऽसृजत्।
असृजत् क्षत्रियान् बाह्वोर्वैश्यानप्यूरूदेशतः।।१२।।

He (Brahmā) was, again and again, asked by the god of gods, saying:– "Create the universe." He, too, having created the entire universe consisting of the Celestials, Asurās and the human beings, brought out from his mouth the sinless Brāhmaṇas for successfully performing sacrifices; the Kṣatriyas, from his arms; and the Vaiśyas, from his thighs.

शूद्रांश्च पादयोः सृष्ट्वा तेषाञ्चैवानुपूर्वशः।
यथा प्रोवाच भगवान् ब्रह्मयोनिः पितामहः।।१३।।
तद्वचः सम्प्रवक्ष्यामि शृणुत द्विजसत्तमाः।
धनं यशस्यमायुष्यं स्वर्ग्यं मोक्षफलप्रदम्।।१४।।

Hear, O you foremost of the twice-born, I shall describe the words,– capable of giving wealth, fame, long life, the celestial region and the fruit of emancipation,– which the Divine Grand Father Brahmā addressed to them all, in order of succession, after having created the Śūdras.

ब्राह्मण्यां ब्राह्मणेनैवमुत्पन्नो ब्राह्मणः स्मृतः।
तस्य धर्मं प्रवक्ष्यामि तद्योग्यं देशमेव च।।१५।।

Those begotten by the Brāhmaṇas on Brāhmaṇa-woman are known in the Smṛtis as the Brāhmaṇas. I shall describe their duties and the country worthy of being inhabited by them.

कृष्णसारो मृगो यत्र स्वभावेन प्रवर्त्तते।
तस्मिन् देशे वसेद्धर्माः सिद्ध्यन्ति द्विजसत्तमाः।।१६।।

O you foremost of the twice-born, [a Brāhmaṇa] should live in a country where the antelope moves about freely by nature, [for there only] religious practices become successful.

षट्कर्माणि निजान्याहुर्ब्राह्मणस्य महात्मनः।
तैरेव सततं यस्तु वर्तयेत्सुखमेधते॥१७॥

Sixfold works have been laid down for a high-souled Brāhmaṇa. He, who always lives with them (*i.e.,* performs them) attains to happiness.

अध्यापनञ्चाध्ययनं याजनं यजनं तथा।
दानं प्रतिग्रहश्चेति षट्कर्माणीति प्रोच्यते॥१८॥

Teaching, religious study, officiating as a priest a sacrifices, celebrating sacrifices, making gifts, and accepting gifts are mentioned as the sixfold duties of a Brāhmaṇa.

अध्यापनञ्च त्रिविधं धर्मार्थमृक्थकारणात्।
शुश्रूषाकरणञ्चेति त्रिविधं परिकीर्त्तितम्॥१९॥

Teaching is threefold, [namely,] for virtue or wealth, and service is described as the third [object.]

एषामन्यतमाभावे वृषाचारो भवेद्द्विजः।
तत्र विद्या न दातव्या पुरुषेण हितैषिणा॥२०॥

In the absence, of at least one, of these works, a Brāhmaṇa becomes a Vṛṣācāra, (i.e., one acting like a bull). Learning should not be bestowed, by a person, on him who seeks [only] his [own] advancement.

योग्यानध्यापयेच्छिष्यानयोग्यानपि वर्जयेत्।
विदितात् प्रतिगृह्णीयाद्गृहे धर्मप्रसिद्धये॥२१॥

One should teach a worthy disciple and discard an unworthy one. For successfully performing a religious rite, one should accept a gift from a householder who is known as being freed from sins.

वेदञ्चैवाभ्यसेन्नित्यं शुचौ देशे समाहितः।
धर्मशास्त्रं तथा पाठ्यं ब्राह्मणैः शुद्धमानसैः॥२२॥

One should, in a purified place, daily attentively study any

Veda. Dharma-Śāstras should be [similarly] studies by the pure-minded Brāhmaṇas.

वेदवत् पठितव्यञ्च श्रोतव्यञ्च दिवा निशि।
स्मृतिहीनाय विप्राय श्रुतिहीने तथैव च॥२३॥
दानं भोजनमन्यच्च दत्तं कुलविनाशनम्।
तस्मात् सर्वप्रयत्नेन धर्मशास्त्रं पठेद्द्विजः॥२४॥

They should be daily and nightly studies and listened to like the Vedas. To make a gift and offer food unto a Brāhmaṇa who is ignorant of the Śruti and the Smṛti, encompasses the destruction of the giver's family. Therefore a Brāhmaṇa, with all care, should study the Dharma-Śāstras.

श्रुतिस्मृती च विप्राणां चक्षुषी देवनिर्मिते।
काणस्तत्रैकया हीनो द्वाभ्यामन्धः प्रकीर्तितः॥२५॥

The Śruti and the Smṛti are the two eyes of the Brāhmaṇas created by God. If deprived [of the knowledge] of the one, [a person] is called one-eyed; and if of the two, a blind.

गुरुशुश्रूषणञ्चैव यथान्यायमतन्द्रितः।
सायं प्रातरुपासीत विवाहाग्निं द्विजोत्तमः॥२६॥

A good Brāhmaṇa should zealously attend upon his preceptor and worship the Vivāha-Fire, morning and evening.

सुस्नातस्तु प्रकुर्वीत वैश्वदेवं दिने दिने।
अतिथीनागताञ्छक्त्या पूजयेदविचारतः॥२७॥

Having bathed properly, he should offer, every day, oblations to the Vaiśvadevas, and adore the in-coming guests, to the best of his power, and without any distinction.

अन्यानभ्यागतान् विप्रान्पूजयेच्छक्तितो गृही।
स्वदारनिरतो नित्यं परदारविवर्जितः॥२८॥

A person, leading the domestic mode of life, who is always devoted to his wife, and shuns other peoples' wives, should also, adore other in-coming Brāhmaṇa-guests to the best of his power.

कृतहोमस्तु भुञ्जीत सायं प्रातरुदारधी:।
सत्यवादी जितक्रोधो नाधर्मे वर्त्तयेन्मतिम्॥२९॥

An intelligent person should take his meal in the evening, after having performed the Homa. He should be truthful, have control over his passion, and never fix his mind on irreligion.

स्वकर्मणि च सम्प्राप्ते प्रमादान्न निवर्त्तते।
सत्यां हितां वदेद्वाचं परलोकहितैषणीम्॥३०॥

Having undertaken the performance of his own duty, he should not neglect it form carelessness. He should always speak truthful words conducive to the well-being of all and in the next world.

एष धर्म: समुद्दिष्टो ब्राह्मणस्य समासत:।
धर्ममेव हि य: कुर्यात्स याति ब्रह्मण: पदम्॥३१॥

This is the duty of a Brāhmaṇa described in brief. He, who performs this duty, attains to the station of Brāhmaṇa, (i.e., emancipation).

इत्येष धर्म: कथित मयायं पृष्टो भवद्भिस्त्वखिलाघहारी।
वदामि राज्ञामपि चैव धर्मान्पृथक्पृथग्बोधत विप्रवर्या:॥३२॥

O you foremost of the Brāhmaṇas, as accosted by you, thus the Code of Religious Regulations, which dissipates the entire multitude of sins, has been described by me. Hear, I shall now describe the duties of the Kṣatriyas and severally of other castes.

इति हारीते धर्मशास्त्रे प्रथमोऽध्याय:॥१॥

Chapter-2

[The duties of the Kṣatriya's Vaiśya's and Śūdra's]

क्षत्रादीनां प्रवक्ष्यामि यथावदनुपूर्वश:।
येषु प्रवृत्ता विधिना सर्वे यान्ति परां गतिम्॥१॥

I shall, describe, in order, from the beginning to the end, [the duties of] the Kṣatriyas and others, by following which regulations all come by most excellent condition.

राज्यस्थ: क्षत्रियश्चापि प्रजा धर्मेण पालयन्।
कुर्यादध्ययनं सम्यग्यजेद्यज्ञान्यथाविधि॥२॥

When placed in [charge of] a kingdom, a Kṣatriya should protect his subjects righteously, be devoted to study, and should duly celebrate sacrifices.

दद्याद्दानं द्विजातिभ्यो धर्मबुद्धिसमन्वित:।
स्वभार्यानिरतो नित्यं षड्भागार्ह: सदा नृप:॥३॥

A king, endued with a righteous understanding, should always make gifts unto the twice-born, (*i.e,* the Brāhmaṇas), be always devoted unto his own wife and take a sixth part [of the income of his subjects as revenue.]

नीतिशास्त्रार्थकुशल: सन्धिविग्रहतत्त्ववित्।
देवब्राह्मणभक्तश्च पितृकार्यपरिवर्जनम्॥४॥

He should be proficient in the Laws of Polity, well-informed in the true spirit of making peace and dissension, devoted to the Deities and the Brāhmaṇas, and be intent on performing rites for the Pitṛs (the departed manes).

धर्मेण यजनं कार्यमधर्मपरिवर्जनम्।
उत्तमां गतिमाप्नोति क्षत्रियोऽप्येवमाचरन्॥५॥

He should perform sacrifices righteously and shun irreligious works. By acting thus a Kṣatriya attains to the most excellent condition [in after like].

गोरक्षां कृषिवाणिज्यं कुर्याद्वैश्यो यथाविधि।
दानं देयं यथाशक्ति ब्राह्मणानाञ्च भोजनम्॥६॥

A Vaiśya should duly tend cattle, drive trade and agriculture, make charities and feed the Brāhmaṇas according to his power.

दम्भमोहविनिर्मुक्तस्तथा वागनसूयक:।
स्वदारनिरतो दान्त: परदारविवर्जित:॥७॥

He should be shorn of pride and stupefaction, [and] even by words he should not injure others, be devoted to his own wife and self-restrained, and avoid other people's wives.

धनैर्विप्रान्भोजयित्वा यज्ञकाले तु याजकान्।
अप्रभुत्वञ्च वर्तेत धर्मे चादेहपातनात्॥८॥

Having fed with his money, the Brāhmaṇas, and the priests at the time of sacrifice, he should live, without lording over, in religious matters till the fall of his body (*i.e.,* till his death).

यज्ञाध्ययनदानानि कुर्यान्नित्यमतन्द्रितः।
पितृकार्यपरश्चैव नरसिंहार्चनापरः॥९॥

He should zealously celebrate sacrifices, study religious books, make charities, perform the rite for the Pitṛs and worship the Man-Lion, (i.e, Viṣṇu).

एतद्वैश्यस्य धर्मोऽयं स्वधर्ममनुतिष्ठति।
एतदाचरते यो हि स स्वर्गो नात्र संशयः॥१०॥

This is the duty of a Vaiśya. He who follows the duty of his own caste, and acts thus, forsooth, repairs to the celestial region.

वर्णत्रयस्य शुश्रूषां कुर्याच्छूद्रः प्रयत्नतः।
दासवद्ब्राह्मणानाञ्च विशेषेण समाचरेत्॥११॥

A Śūdra should, with care, serve the three Varṇas and particularly act like a servant unto the Brāhmaṇas.

अयाचितप्रदाता च कष्टं वृत्त्यर्थमाचरेत्।
पाकयज्ञविधानेन यजेद्देवमतन्द्रितः॥१२॥

He should make gifts without being solicited, earn his livelihood by hardship, and zealously worship the Deity according to the rules of Pāka-Yajña (a simple or domestic sacrifice).

शूद्राणामधिकं कुर्यादर्चनं न्यायवर्तिनाम्।
धारणं जीर्णवस्त्रस्य विप्रस्योच्छिष्टभोजनम्।
स्वदारेषु रतिश्चैव परदारविवर्जनम्॥१३॥

Furthermore he should adore the Śūdras, who wend righteous

and just ways. He should put on a tattered cloth, eat the remnant of a Brāhmaṇa's food, find pleasure only in his own wife and avoid another's wife.

इत्थं कुर्यात् सदा शूद्रो मनोवाक्कायकर्मभिः।
स्थानमैन्द्रमवाप्नोति नष्टपापः सुपुण्यकृत्॥१४॥

A Śūdra should always do this with his mind, words and deeds. Having performed righteous deeds and having his sins dissipated [thereby], he attains to the dignity of Indra.

वर्णेषु धर्मा विविधा मयोक्ता
यथा तथा ब्रह्ममुखेरिताः पुरा।
शृणुध्वमत्राश्रमधर्ममाद्यं
मयोच्यमानं क्रमशो मुनीन्द्राः॥१५॥

The duties of the various Varṇas have, thus, been described by me, as they formerly emitted from the mouth of Brahmā. O you lords of ascetics, listen now to the duties of the first Āśrama (i.e., the order of religious students) as I go on narrating them one after the other.

इति हारीते धर्मशास्त्रे द्वितीयोऽध्यायः॥२॥

Chapter-3

[Brahmacarya, or Religious studentship]

उपनीतो माणवको वसेद्गुरुकुलेषु च।
गुरो कुले प्रियं कुर्यात् कर्मणा मनसा गिरा॥१॥

Having been invested with the sacred thread, a person (i.e., one of the three castes) should live in the family of his preceptor and do good unto it by deeds, mind and words.

ब्रह्मचर्यमधःशय्या तथा वह्नेरुपासना।
उदकुम्भान् गुरोर्दद्याद्गोग्रासञ्चेन्धनानि च॥२॥

[He should] lead a life of celibacy, sleep on [the bare] earth, adore the Fire, and offer, unto his preceptor, pitchers full of water, sacrificial fuels and go-grāsa (i.e., morsels of grass for his cow).

कुर्यादध्ययनञ्चैव ब्रह्मचारी यथाविधि।
विधिं त्यक्त्वा प्रकुर्वाणो न स्वाध्यायफलं लभेत्।।३।।

A Brahmacārin should study [the Vedas] with propriety without which he does not attain the fruit of Vedic studies.

यः कश्चित् कुरुते धर्मं विधिं हित्वा दुरात्मवान्।
न तत्फलमवाप्नोति कुर्वाणोऽपि विधिच्युतः।।४।।

A wicked-souled person, divorced from regulations, even when he performs righteous deeds, disregarding the proper rules, does not attain the fruits thereof.

तस्माद्वेदव्रतानीह चरेत् स्वाध्यायसिद्धये।
शौचाचारमशेषं तु शिक्षयेद्गुरुसन्निधौ।।५।।

Therefore for attaining success in his Vedic study, he should perform the rites laid down in the Vedas. He should learn, from his preceptor, the many and varied rules [for attaining] purification.

अजिनं दण्डकाष्ठञ्च मेखलाञ्चोपवीतकम्।
धारयेदप्रमत्तश्च ब्रह्मचारी समाहितः।।६।।

Being careful and attentive, a Brahmacārin should use a deer-skin [for his waist cloth] a piece of wood for cleansing the teeth, *mekhalā* (i.e., the triple girdle worn by the first three castes), and the sacrificial thread.

सायं प्रातश्चरेद्भैक्षं भोज्यार्थं संयतेन्द्रियः।
आचम्य प्रयतो नित्यं न कुर्याद्दन्तधावनम्।।७।।

For procuring food, he should, having restrained his senses, beg alms in the morning and evening. Rinsing his mouth carefully every day, he should not cleanse his teeth.[1]

---

1. i.e., He should not rub his teeth with wood, after having rinsed his mouth at the time of bathing.

छत्रञ्चोपानहञ्चैव गन्धमाल्यादि वर्जयेत्।
नृत्यं गीतमथालापं मैथुनञ्च विवर्जयेत्॥८॥

He should renounce umbrella, shoes, scents and garlands; and must, also abstain from dancing and singing, useless conversation and sexual intercourse.

हस्त्यश्वारोहणं चैव सन्त्यजेत् संयतेन्द्रियः।
सन्ध्योपास्ति प्रकुर्वीत ब्रह्मचारी व्रतस्थितः॥९॥

Having restrained his senses, he should abstain from riding on elephants and horses. Observing his vow, a Brahmacārin should perform his evening adoration.

अभिवाद्य गुरोः पादौ सन्ध्याकर्मावसानतः।
तथा योगं प्रकुर्वीत मातापित्रोश्च भक्तितः॥१०॥

After the termination of the evening adoration, he should salute the feet of his preceptor and reverentially meditate upon his parents (i.e., adore them mentally).

एतेषु त्रिषु नष्टेषु नष्टाः स्युः सर्वदेवताः।
एतेषां शासने तिष्ठेद्ब्रह्मचारी विमत्सरः॥११॥

These three (i.e., the preceptor, the father and the mother) being lost (becoming displeased) all the Deities are displeased. Shorn of pride a Brahmacārin should abide by the commands of all these.

अधीत्य च गुरोर्वेदान् वेदो वा वेदमेव वा।
गुरवे दक्षिणां दद्यात्संयमी ग्राममावसेत्॥१२॥

Having studied either the one, two or the three Vedas from the preceptor, he should make the usual present to him, and then being self-controlled, [he should] live in his village.

यस्यैतानि सुगुप्तानि जिह्वोपस्थोदरं करः।
संन्यासमयं कृत्वा ब्राह्मणो ब्रह्मचर्यया॥१३॥
तस्मिन्नेव नयेत्कालमाचार्य्ये यावदायुषम्।

तदभावे च तत्पुत्रे तच्छिष्येऽप्यथवा कुले।
न विवाहो न संन्यासो नैष्ठिकस्य विधीयते॥१४॥

A Brāhmaṇa, whose tongue, generative organ, belly and hands, have all been controlled, should, resorting to Sannyāsa (renunciation), lead a celibate life near the same preceptor, as long as he lives; in his absence, near his (preceptor's) son; [in the latter's absence] near his disciple or in his family. Neither marriage nor [absolute] renunciation is laid down for the Naiṣṭhika.[1]

इमं यो विधिमास्थाय त्यजेद्देहमतन्द्रितः।
नेह भूयोऽपि जायेत ब्रह्मचारी दृढव्रतः॥१५॥

A Brahmacārin, of firm vows, who, carefully following this regulation, renounces his body, is not born again in this world.

यो ब्रह्मचारी विधिना समाहित-
श्चरेत् पृथिव्यां गुरुसेवने रतः।
सम्प्राप्य विद्यामतिदुर्लभां शिवां
फलञ्च तस्याः सुलभन्तु विन्दति॥१६॥

A Brahmacārin, who, being self-controlled an devoted to the service of his preceptor, moves about on this earth, acquires an auspicious learning, so difficult of attainment, and comes by its fruit (i.e., virtue, worldly profit, desire and emancipation) so easily attainable [by such a person].

इति हारीते धर्मशास्त्रे तृतीयोऽध्यायः॥३॥

Chapter-4

[Gārhastya, or The Domestic Mode of Life]

गृहीतवेदाध्ययनः श्रुतशास्त्रार्थतत्त्ववित्।
असमानर्षिगोत्रां हि कन्यां सभ्रातृकां शुभाम्॥१॥

---

1. A perpetual religious student, who continues with his spiritual preceptor even after the prescribed period, and vows life-long abstinence and chastity.

सर्वावयवसम्पूर्णां सुवृत्तामुद्वहेन्नरः।
ब्राह्मेण विधिना कुर्यात्प्रशस्तेन द्विजोत्तमः॥२॥

After having completed his Vedic studies and being acquainted with the true import of Dharma-Śāstras, a person should wed a maiden of a different family, having a brother, endued with auspicious marks, perfect limbs and a good character. That foremost of the twice-born must do so according to the most excellent rite of Brāhma.

तथान्ये बहवः प्रोक्ता विवाहा वर्णधर्मतः।
औपासनञ्च विधिवदाहृत्य द्विजपुङ्गवाः॥३॥
सायं प्रातश्च जुहुयात् सर्वकालमतन्द्रितः।
स्नानं कार्यं ततो नित्यं दन्तधावनपूर्वकम्॥४॥

Various other forms of marriage, according to caste and order, have been spoken of. Having duly collected sacrificial fuels, the foremost of the twice-born, being all the while wide awake, should offer oblations [to the Fire] in the morning and evening. Thereupon [he] should daily bathe after having previously cleansed his teeth.

उषःकाले समुत्थाय कृतशौचो यथाविधि।
मुखे पर्युषिते नित्यं भवत्यप्रयतो नरः॥५॥

Having got up from bed at dawn he should duly perform [all] the purifying operations. The mouth remaining stale (*i.e.,* not washed) every day, a person loses control over his own self.

तस्माच्छुष्कमथार्द्रं वा भक्षयेद्दन्तकाष्ठकम्।
करञ्जं खादिरं वापि कदम्बं कुरवं तथा॥६॥
सप्तपर्णपृश्निपर्णीजम्बुनिम्बं तथैव च।
अपामार्गं च बिल्वञ्चार्कञ्चोदुम्बरमेव च॥७॥
एते प्रशस्ताः कथिता दन्तधावनकर्मणि।
दन्तकाष्ठस्य भक्षश्च समासेन प्रकीर्तितः॥८॥

Therefore one should eat (use) a piece of wood, dry or wet,

for cleaning the teeth. Karañja,[1] Khadira, Kadamba, Kurava, Saptaparṇī, Pṛśniparṇī, Jambu, Nimba, Apāmārga, Bilva, Arka, Udumbara,– these are mentioned as the most suitable wood in the operation of tooth rubbing. Thus is described, in brief, the wood which should be used for rubbing the tooth.

सर्वे कण्टकिनः पुण्याः क्षीरिणश्च यशस्विनः।
अष्टाङ्गुलेन मानेन दण्डकाष्ठमिहोच्यते।
प्रादेशमात्रमथवा तेन दन्तान् विशोधयेत्॥९॥

All thorny woods yield virtue; and milky ones, fame. It is said that the wood, for rubbing the tooth, should be of the measure of eight fingers. Or it should be of the size of a span, measured from the tip of the thumb to that of the forefinger. With such [a piece of wood] one should cleanse one's teeth.

प्रतिपत्पर्वषष्ठीषु नवम्याञ्चैव सुत्तमाः।
दन्तानां काष्ठसंयोगाद्दहत्यासप्तमं कुलम्॥१०॥

If the teeth are touched with a twig on the first day of a lunar fortnight, the fifteenth day of the dark fortnight the fullmoon day, the sixth and the ninth lunar day, one's seven generations are consumed.

अभावे दन्तकाष्ठानां प्रतिषिद्धदिनेषु च।
अपां द्वादशगण्डूषैर्मुखशुद्धिं समाचरेत्॥११॥

On the interdicted days, the mouth should be rinsed with twelve handfuls of water instead of a twig.

स्नात्वा मंत्रवदाचम्य पुनराचमनं चरेत्।
मन्त्रवत् प्रोक्ष्य चात्मानं प्रक्षिपेदुदकाञ्जलिम्॥१२॥

Having rinsed the mouth, as laid down in the *Mantra*, one should again rinse it. Then sprinkling one's own self with water, as described in the Mantra, one should throw palmfuls of water.

आदित्येन सं प्रातर्मन्देहा नाम राक्षसाः।
युध्यति वरदानेन ब्रह्मणोऽव्यक्तजन्मनः॥१३॥

---

1. Name of a tree used in medicinal preparations.

By virtue of the boon conferred by Brahmā, whose birth is not known, the Rākṣasas Mandeha fight every morning with the Sun.

उदकाञ्जलिनिक्षेपाद् गायत्र्या चाभिमन्त्रिताः।
निघ्नन्ति राक्षसान् सर्वान् मन्देहाख्यान् द्विजेरिताः॥१४॥

The handfuls of water, thrown by the Brāhmaṇās and inspired with the mystic verse Gāyatrī, destroy all the Rākṣasas passing under the appellation of Mandeha.

ततः प्रयाति सविता ब्राह्मणैरभिरक्षितः।
मरीच्याद्यैर्महाभागैः सनकाद्यैश्च योगिभिः॥१५॥

Thereupon protected by the Brāhmaṇas, the Sun proceeds along with the Yogins headed by the great Marīci and Sanaka.

तस्मान्न लङ्घयेत् सन्ध्यां सायं प्रातः समाहितः।
उल्लङ्घयति यो मोहात् स याति नरकं ध्रुवम्॥१६॥

Therefore one should not studiously neglect the morning and evening adorations. One, who neglects the same out of stupefaction, forsooth, goes to [the infernal region of] hell.

सायं मन्त्रवदाचम्य प्रोक्ष्य सूर्यस्य चाञ्जलिम्।
दत्त्वा प्रदक्षिणं कुर्याज्जलं स्पृष्ट्वा विशुध्यति॥१७॥

Having rinsed one's mouth sprinkled one's own self with water, according to the Mantra, and offered handfuls of water in honour of the Sun, one should perform the rite of circumambulation and then purify one's self by touching water.

पूर्वां सन्ध्यां सनक्षत्रामुपासीत यथाविधि।
गायत्रीमभ्यसेत्तावद्यावदादित्यदर्शनात्॥१८॥

Even when the stars are visible, one should duly perform the first Sandhyā adoration and recite the *Gāyatrī* till the Sun is not seen.

उपास्य पश्चिमां सन्ध्यां सादित्याञ्च यथाविधि।
गायत्रीमभ्यसेत्तावद्यावत्तारां न पश्यति॥१९॥

Then having duly performed the evening *Sandhyā*, even when the Sun remains, visible, one should recite the *Gāyatrī* till the stars are not seen.

ततश्चावसथं प्राप्य कृत्वा होमं स्वयं बुधः।
सञ्चिन्त्य पोष्यवर्गस्य भरणार्थं विचक्षणः॥२०॥

Thereupon reaching the house and performing the *Homa*, a learned and sage person should think of measures for supporting those who depend on him.

ततः शिष्यहितार्थाय स्वाध्यायं किञ्चिदाचरेत्।
ईश्वरञ्चैव कार्यार्थमभिगच्छेद्द्विजोत्तमः॥२१॥

Thereupon, for the behoof of his disciples, he should conduct Vedic studies for a little while; then a good Brāhmaṇa should approach his king of business.

कुशपुष्पेन्धनादीनि गत्वा दूरं समाहरेत्।
ततो मध्याह्निकं कुर्याच्छुचौ देशे मनोरमे॥२२॥

Then repairing to a distant place, he should fetch Kuśa, flowers and sacrificial fuels. Then he should perform the midday adoration at a holy and charming place.

विधिं तस्य प्रवक्ष्यामि समासात् पापनाशनम्।
स्नात्वा येन विधानेन मुच्यते सर्वकिल्विषात्॥२३॥

I shall [now] describe, in brief, the regulations, destructive of sins, [of that form of bath] by bathing according to which, one is freed from all sins.

स्नानार्थं मृदमानीय शुद्धाक्षततिलैः सह।
सुमनाश्च ततो गच्छेन्नदीं शुद्धजलाधिकाम्॥२४॥

Having brought, for bathing, earth, together with pure rice and sesame, one should then, with a careful mind, go to river having profuse pure water.

नद्यान्तु विद्यमानायां न स्नायादन्यवारिणि।
न स्नायादल्पतोयेषु विद्यमाने बहूदके॥२५॥

A river existing, one should not bathe in another water. One should not bathe in little water while there exists a profusion of it.

सरिद्वरं नदीस्नानं प्रतिस्रोत: स्थितश्चरेत्।
तडागादिषु तोयेषु स्नायाच्च तदभावत:।।२६।।

The water of a river is the best. One should bathe in the river, standing against the current. In its absence, one should bathe in a tank or in others pools.

शुचिदेशं समभ्युक्ष्य स्थापयेत् सकलाम्बरम्।
मृत्तोयेन स्वकं देहं लिम्पेत् प्रक्षाल्य यत्नत:।।२७।।

Sprinkling a pure spot with water, one should place one's all clothes there. Then carefully washing one's own body, one should rub it with earth and water.

स्नानादिकं समाप्यैव कुर्यादाचमनं बुध:।
सोऽन्तर्जलं प्रविश्याथ वाग्यतो नियमेन हि।
हरिं संस्मृत्य मनसा मज्जयेच्चोरुमज्जले।।२८।।

Just before bathing, a learned person should rinse his mouth. Then entering into water, controlling his speech duly, and mentally thinking of Hari, he should immerse himself in thigh-deep water.

ततस्तीरं समासाद्य आचम्याप: समंत्रत:।
प्रोक्ष्येद्वारुणैर्मन्त्रै: पावमानीभिरेव च।।२९।।

Then returning to the bank and rinsing his mouth according to the Mantra, he should sprinkle his body with water (reciting) the *Vāruṇa-Mantra* and the Pāvamānī Ṛk.

कुशाग्रकृततोयेन प्रोक्ष्यात्मानं प्रयत्नत:।
स्योनापृथ्वीति मृद्गात्रे इदंविष्णुरिति द्विजा:।।३०।।

Then having carefully sprinkled his own body, with the water taken by the tips of Kuśa-grass, [and reciting the *Mantra*,–] "*Syona prithivī*," the twice-born should rub it [his body] with earth [reciting the Mantra,–] " *Idam Viṣṇu.*"

ततो नारायणं देवं संस्मरेत् प्रतिमज्जनम्।
निमज्जयांतर्जले सम्यक् क्रियते चाघमर्षणम्।।३१।।

Then, when immersing in water again, he should meditate on the divine Nārāyaṇa. Then entering into water properly, he should recite [the Mantra,–] *"Aghamarṣaṇam"*.

स्नात्वाक्षततिलैस्तद्वद्देवर्षिपितृभिः सह।
तर्पयित्वा जलं तस्मान्निष्पीड्य च समाहितः।।३२।।
जलतीरं समासाद्य तत्र शुक्ले च वाससी।
परिधायोत्तरीयञ्च कुर्यात् केशान्न धूनयेत्।।३३।।

Having bathed, he should offer, as usual, oblations, of water with rice and sesame, to the celestial saints and the departed manes; then pressing out water [from his cloth] and reaching the bank, being self-controlled, he should put on two pieces of white cloth and *Uttarīya* (cloth to cover the body). He should not shake his hairs.

न रक्तमुल्बणं वासो न नीलञ्च प्रशस्यते।
मलाक्तं गन्धहीनञ्च वर्जयेदम्बरं बुधः।।३४।।

A dark-blue or a blue cloth is not preferable. A learned person should always avoid a dirty cloth [and one] that doe not emit a good smell.

ततः प्रक्षालयेत् पादौ मृत्तोयेन विचक्षणः।
दक्षिणन्तु करं कृत्वा गोकर्णाकृतिवत् पुनः।।३५।।
त्रिः पिबेदीक्षितं तोयमास्यं द्विः परिमार्जयेत्।
पादौ शिरस्ततोऽभ्युक्ष्य त्रिभिरास्यमुपस्पृशेत्।।३६।।

Thereupon a learned person should wash his feet with clay water. Then, again, converting the right palm into the shape of a cow's ear, he should see the water inside, drink it thrice and rinse the mouth twice therewith. Then sprinkling his head and feet with water, he should touch his mouth with three fingers.

अङ्गुष्ठानामिकाभ्याञ्च चक्षुषी समुपस्पृशेत्।
तथैव पञ्चभिर्मूर्ध्नि स्पृशेदेवं समाहितः।।३७।।

With the thumb and nameless finger, he should touch the two eyes. Then being self-restrained, he should touch his head with five fingers.

अनेन विधिनाचम्य ब्राह्मणः शुद्धमानसः।

कुर्वीत दर्भपाणिस्तूदङ्मुखः प्राङ्मुखोऽपि वा॥३८॥

प्राणायामत्रयं धीमान् यथान्यायमतन्द्रितः।

जपयज्ञं ततः कुर्याद्गायत्रीं वेदमातरम्॥३९॥

Having rinsed his mouth, according to this regulation, a pure-minded Brāhmaṇa, shorn of idleness, should, with Kuśa in hands and his face directed towards the east or the north, perform the Prāṇāyāma thrice, and thereafter perform the sacrifice of the recitation of the Gāyatrī, the mother of the Vedas.

त्रिविधो जपयज्ञः स्यात्तस्य तत्त्वं निबोधत।

वाचिकश्चाप्युपांशुश्च मानसश्च त्रिधाकृतिः॥४०॥

There are three kinds of Japa– Yajña; understand their secret meaning. Vācika, Upāmśu and Mānasa are the three forms.

त्रयाणामपि यज्ञानां श्रेष्ठः स्यादुत्तरोत्तरः॥४१॥

Of these three forms of Yajña, each succeeding one is superior to the preceding one.

यदुच्चनीचोच्चरितैः शब्दैः स्पष्टपदाक्षरैः।

मन्त्रमुच्चारयन् वाचो जपयज्ञस्तु वाचिकः॥४२॥

What is performed by reciting the *Mantras* the various parts and letters being distinctly sounded either high or low, is called *Vācika Japa-Yajña.*

शनैरुच्चारयन्मंत्रं किञ्चिदोष्ठौ प्रचालयेत्।

किञ्चिच्छ्रवणयोग्यः स्यात् स उपांशुर्जपः स्मृतः॥४३॥

That, in which the Mantras are recited slowly, the lips, quiver a little, and the sound becomes audible to a slight extent, is known as Upāmśu-Japa.

धिया पदाक्षरश्रेण्या अवर्णमपदाक्षरम्।

शब्दार्थचिन्तनाभ्यान्तु तदुक्तं मानसं स्मृतम्॥४४॥

That, in which the words and letters [of the Mantras] are comprehensible by the intellect, [though the words and letters are not audible,] and the meaning of the words is meditated on, is called Mānasa.

जपेन देवता नित्यं स्तूयमाना प्रसीदति।

प्रसन्ने विपुलान् गोत्रान् प्राप्नुवन्ति मनीषिण:॥४५॥

Being daily lauded with recitation, the Deities become propitiated. They being pleased, the sages acquire a large family.

राक्षसाश्च पिशाचाश्च महासर्पाश्च भीषणा:।

जपितान्नोपसर्पन्ति दूरादेव प्रयान्ति ते॥४६॥

When the recitation is performed, the Rākṣasas, Piśācas, and the dreadful huge serpents do not come near but fly away from a distance.

छन्द ऋष्यादि विज्ञाय जपेन्मन्त्रमतन्द्रित:।

जपेदहरहर्ज्ञात्वा गायत्रीं मनसा द्विज:॥४७॥

Knowing the metre and the Ṛṣi (saintly author), one should zealously recite the Mantras. And knowing their meaning, a twice-born one should mentally recite the Gāyatrī, day and night.

सहस्रपरमां देवीं शतमध्यां दशावराम्।

गायत्रीं यो जपेन्नित्यं स न पापेन लिप्यते॥४८॥

He,-- who daily recites the Divine Gāyatrī, the highest [form of recitation] being a thousand times; the middling, a hundred times; and the lowest, ten times;– is not sullied by sin.

अथ पष्पाञ्जलिं कृत्वा भानवे चोर्ध्वबाहुक:।

उदुत्यञ्च जपेत् सूक्तं तच्चक्षुरिति चापरम्॥४९॥

Then offering, with upraised arms, handfuls of flowers to the Sun, he should recite the Sūkta,– *Udutyam* etc., and *Taccakṣu*.

प्रदक्षिणमुपावृत्य नमस्कुर्य्याद्दिवाकरम्।

ततस्तीर्थेन देवादीनद्भि: सन्तर्पयेद्द्विज:॥५०॥

Performing the rite of circumambulation and covering [his face] with hands, a twice-born one should bow unto the Sun and then propitiate the other Deities with the Tīrtha-water.

स्नानवस्त्रन्तु निष्पीड्य पुनराचमनं चरेत्।
तद्वद्भक्तजनस्येह स्नानं दानं प्रकीर्त्तितम्।।५१।।

Then pressing water out of the cloth with which he had bathed, he should rinse his mouth again. Bathing and making gift by a devout follower has been described here like that (*i.e.*, they should be accompanied with the rinsing of mouth).

दर्भासीनो दर्भपाणिर्ब्रह्मयज्ञविधानतः।
प्राङ्मुखो ब्रह्मयज्ञन्तु कुर्याच्छ्रद्धासमन्वितः।।५२।।

Seated on Kuśa-grass, with Kuśā-grass is hands and with his face directed towards the east, a person should reverentially perform *Brahma-Yajña*, according to the rites thereof.

ततोऽर्घं भानवे दद्यात्तिलपुष्पाक्षतान्वितम्।
उत्थाय मूर्द्धपर्यन्तं हंसः शुचिषदित्यृचा।।५३।।

Thereupon having got up and place his joined hands on his head, he should reciting the *Ṛk,– Śuciṣadi*, offer *Arghya* of sesame, flowers and rice to the Sun.

ततो देवं नमस्कृत्य गृहं गच्छेत्ततः पुनः।
विधिना पुरुषसूक्तस्य गत्वा विष्णुं समर्च्चयेत्।।५४।।

Thereupon having saluted the Sun-God he should again return to his house. And, going there, he should adore Viṣṇu, according to the rite laid down in the *Puruṣa-Sūkta*.

वैश्वदेवं ततः कुर्य्याद्बलिकर्म विधानतः।
गोदाहमात्रमाकाङ्क्षेदतिथिं प्रति वै गृही।।५५।।

Thereafter he should offer *Bali* (offerings of food) to the *Vaiśvadevas* according to the rite thereof. A house-holder should wait for a guest till the hour of milching the cow.

अदृष्टपूर्वमज्ञातमतिथिं प्राप्तमर्च्चयेत्।
स्वागतसनदानेन प्रत्युत्थानेन चाम्बुना।।५६।।

If a guest, not seen or known before, comes, he should, rising up, adore him with a welcome, offer of water and a seat.

स्वागतेनाग्नयस्तुष्टा भवन्ति गृहमेधिनः।

आसनेन तु दत्तेन प्रीतो भवति देवराट्॥५७॥

[On a guest] being welcomed, the Fires of a house-holder become gratified. On a seat being offered, the King of the Celestials becomes pleased.

पादशौचेन पितरः प्रीतिमायान्ति दुर्लभाम्।

अन्नदानेन युक्तेन तृप्यते हि प्रजापतिः॥५८॥

Water, for washing the feet, being offered, the departed manes attain to gratification which it is so difficult to secure. On food being offered, Prajāpati is pleased.

तस्मादतिथये कार्यं पूजनं गृहमेधिना।

भक्त्या च शक्तितो नित्यं विष्णोरर्च्चादनन्तरम्॥५९॥

Therefore, after the adoration of Viṣṇu, the guests should be daily worshipped by a householder with respect and according to his might.

भिक्षाञ्च भिक्षवे दद्यात् परिव्राड्ब्रह्मचारिणे।

अकल्पितान्नमुद्धृत्य सव्यञ्जनसमन्वितम्॥६०॥

He should give unto the beggars and the mendicant Brahmacārins alms consisting of undedicated curry and rice.

अकृते वैश्वदेवेऽपि भिक्षौ च गृहमागते।

उद्धृत्य वैश्वदेवार्थं भिक्षां दत्त्वा विसर्जयेत्॥६१॥

If a mendicant arrives at a house before food is offered to the Vaiśvadevas, then keeping a part thereof for them, one should dismiss him by giving him alms.

वैश्वदेवकृतान् दोषाञ्छक्तो भिक्षुर्व्यपोहितुम्।

न हि भिक्षुकृतान् दोषान् वैश्वदेवो व्यपोहति॥६२॥

A mendicant, being fed, can remove the mischief done by the Vaiśvadevas. But the Vaiśvadevas can never remove the mischief done by the mendicants.

तस्मात् प्राप्ताय यतये भिक्षां दद्यात् समाहित:।
विष्णुरेव यतिच्छाय इति निश्चित्य भावयेत्॥६३॥

Therefore when Yatins arrive at a house, one should respectfully offer them alms, for he should think without a shadow of doubt that Viṣṇu is himself a Yatin.

सुवासिनी कुमारीश्च भोजयित्वा नरानपि।
वालवृद्धांस्तत: शेषं स्वयं भुञ्जीत वा गृही॥६४॥

After having fed well-dressed maidens, aged persons and children, a householder should then take his meal.

प्राङ्मुखोदङ्मुखो वापि मौनी च मितभाषक:।
अन्नमादौ नमस्कृत्य प्रहृष्टेनान्तरात्मना॥६५॥

With his face directed either towards the east or the north, abstaining entirely from speaking or controlling his speech, he should, with a delighted heart, salute the boiled rice in the beginning.

एवं प्राणाहुतिं कुर्य्यान्मन्त्रेण च पृथक् पृथक्।
तत: स्वादुकरान्नञ्च भुञ्जीत सुसमाहित:॥६६॥

Then offering oblations to the vital airs with different Mantras, he should, being self-restrained, take sweet food.

आचम्य देवतामिष्टां संस्मरन्नुदरं स्पृशेत्।
इतिहासपुराणाभ्यां कञ्चित् कालं नयेद्‌बुध:॥६७॥

Then rinsing his mouth and remembering his Tutelary Deity, he should touch his belly. Then a wise person should spend his time in the study of history and the Purāṇas.

तत: सन्ध्यामुपासीत वहिर्गत्वा विधानत:।
कृतहोमस्तु भुञ्जीत रात्रौ चातिथिभोजनम्॥६८॥

Then going out, he should duly perform the evening adoration. Then performing the *Homa* and feeding the guests, he should take his meal in the night.

सायं प्रातर्द्विजातीनामशनं श्रुतिचोदितम्।
नान्तरा भोजनं कुर्यादग्निहोत्रसायं विधिः॥६९॥

Eating in the morning and evening has been sanctioned by the Śruti for the twice-born. But they cannot take any intermediate meal. The rule for the *Agnihotrins* is [to take meals only in] the evening.

शिष्यानध्यापयेच्चापि अनध्याये विसर्जयेत्।
स्मृत्युक्तानखिलांश्चापि पुराणोक्तानपि द्विजः॥७०॥

A Brāhmaṇa should teach his disciples but dismiss them on those days on which no religious studies are to be prosecuted. All the days mentioned in the Smṛtis and the Purāṇas [are to be accepted].

महानवम्यां द्वादश्यां भरण्यामपि पर्वसु।
तथाक्षयतृतीयायां शिष्यान् नाध्यापयेद्द्विजः॥७१॥

On the *Mahānavamī* (the ninth day in the bright half of the month of *Āśvin*, sacred to the worship of Durgā), the twelfth day of the fortnight, *Bharaṇī*, the *Parva*-days (Fullmoon, and the last day of the dark fortnight, and the third day of the bright half of *Vaiśākha*, a Brāhmaṇa should not teach his disciples.

माघमासे तु सप्तम्यां रथ्याख्यायान्तु वर्जयेत्।
अध्यापनं समभ्यञ्चन् स्नानकाले च वर्जयेत्॥७२॥

On the seventh day of the fortnight in the month of *Māgha*, on *Rathyā Saptamī*, while rubbing oil, and at the time of bathing, one should avoid teaching.

नीयमानं शवं दृष्ट्वा महीस्थं वा द्विजोत्तमाः।
न पठेद्रुदितं श्रुत्वा सन्ध्यायान्तु द्विजोत्तमाः॥७३॥

Seeing a dead body carried or placed on earth and hearing the sound of weeping in the evening, the foremost of the twice-born should not study [the Vedas].

दानानि च प्रदेयानि गृहस्थेन द्विजोत्तमाः।
हिरण्यदानं गोदानं पृथिवीदानमेव च॥७४॥

O you the leading twice-born ones, charities must be made by a householder– the gift of gold, cow and earth.

एवं धर्मो गृहस्थस्त सारभूत उदाहृतः।
य एवं श्रद्धया कुर्य्यात् स याति ब्रह्मणः पदम्।।७५।।

This is the essence of the duties of a householder described [by me]. He, who satisfies them with reverence, attains to the dignity of Brahma.

ज्ञानोत्कर्यश्च तस्य स्यान्नारसिंहप्रसादतः।
तस्मान्मुक्तिवाप्नोति ब्राह्मणों द्विजसत्तमाः।।७६।।

By the favour of the Man-Lion, he acquires the most excellent knowledge. And, by it, a Brāhmaṇa attains emancipation, O you twice-born ones.

एवं हि विप्राः कथितो मया वः
समासतः शाश्वतधर्मराशिः।
गृही गृहस्थस्य सतो हि धर्मं
कुर्वन् प्रयत्नाद्धरिमिते युक्तम्।।७७।।

O you Viprās, thus the eternal Code of Duties has been described, in brief by me, to you. If a householder carefully performs the duties laid down for the domestic mode of life, he becomes united with [the God] Hari.

इति हारीते धर्मशास्त्रे चतुर्थोऽध्यायः।।४।।

Chapter- 5

[The Duties of the Vānaprastha Mode of Life]

अतः परं प्रवक्ष्यामि वानप्रस्थस्य सत्तमाः।
धर्माश्रमं महाभागाः कथ्यमानं निबोधतः।।१।।

O you great and most excellent Ṛṣis, hear, I shall, hereafter, describe the duties of a Vānaprastha or a hermit.

गृहस्थः पुत्रपौत्रादीन् दृष्ट्वा पलितमात्मनः।
भार्यां पुत्रेषु निक्षिप्य सह वा प्रविशेद्वनम्।।२।।

Having seen sons and grandsons and his hairs grow grey, a householder, consigning the care of his wife to his sons or with her, should enter into a forest.

नखरोमाणि च तथा सितगात्रत्वगादि च।
धारयन् जुहुयादग्निं वनस्थो विधिमाश्रित:॥३॥

Having nails, hairs of the body and white skin covering the body, a hermit, living in a forest, should duly offer oblations to Fire.

धान्यैश्च वनसम्भूतैर्नीवाराद्यैरनिन्दितै:।
शाकमूलफलैर्वापि कुर्यान्नित्यं प्रयत्नत:॥४॥

He should carefully daily offer oblations with paddy grown in the forest, unimpeachable rice growing without cultivation, leaves, roots and fruits.

त्रिकूलस्नानयुक्तस्तु कुर्यातीव्रं तपस्तदा।
पक्षान्ते वा समश्नीयान्मासान्ते वा स्वपक्वभुक्॥५॥

Having bathed thrice, he should practise austere penances. Either after a fortnight or a month, he should take his meals, cooking the food himself.

यथा चतुर्थकाले तु भुञ्जीयादष्टमेऽथवा।
षष्ठे च कालेऽप्यथवा वायुभक्षोऽथवा भवेत्॥६॥

Or he should take his meals at the fourth, eighth, or the sixth period;[1] or he should sustain himself with air.

धर्मे पञ्चाग्निमध्यस्थस्तथा वर्षे निराश्रय:।
हेमन्ते च जले स्थित्वा नयेत् कालं तपश्चरन्॥७॥

Stationed in the midst of five fires in the summer, living without shelter in the rainy season and remaining inside the water in the dewy season, he should spend his time practising penances.

---

1. The fourth period is the evening of the second day, after fasting for a day; the eighth period is the evening of the fourth day, after fasting for three days; and so forth.

एवञ्च कुर्वता येन कृतबुद्धिर्यथाक्रमम्।
अग्निं स्वात्मनि कृत्वा तु प्रव्रजेदुत्तरां दिशम्॥८॥

That person of well-formed religious understanding, who performs these rites in order, shall, taking his own Fire, repair to the northern quarter.

आदेहपातं वनगो मौनमास्थाय तापसः।
स्मरन्नतीन्द्रियं ब्रह्मं ब्रह्मलोके महीयते॥९॥

An ascetic, going to a forest, who, abstaining from speech, meditates on Brahman– who is beyond the ken of senses– till the destruction of his body, becomes glorified in the region of Brahmā.

तपो हि यः सेवति वन्यवासः
समाधियुक्त प्रयतान्तरात्मा।
विमुक्तपापो विमलः प्रशान्तः
स याति दिव्यं पुरुषं पुराणम्॥१०॥

He,– who, living in a forest and being endued with mental abstraction and self-restraint, practises penances,– goes, freed from sins, purified and endued with a quiet mind to the ancient, divine Puruṣa.

इति हारीते धर्मशास्त्रे पञ्चमोऽध्यायः॥५॥

Chapter-6

[The Duties of the four order, Sannyāsa]

अतः परं प्रवक्ष्यामि चतुर्थाश्रममुत्तमम्।
श्रद्धया तदनुष्ठाय तिष्ठन् मुच्येत बन्धनात्॥१॥

I shall, hereafter, describe the most excellent fourth Āśrama or order, by following which with reverence, one is released from the fetters [of worldly existence].

एवं वनाश्रमे तिष्ठन् पातयश्चैव किल्विषम्।
चतुर्थमाश्रमं गच्छेत् संन्यासविधिना द्विजः॥२॥

Living in the Vānaprastha Āśrama as mentioned before and dissipating all his sins, s twice-born one should enter upon the fourth order according to the rules of Sannyāsa (renunciation).

दत्त्वा पितृभ्यो देवेभ्यः मानुषेभ्यश्च यत्नतः।
दत्त्वा श्राद्धं पितृभ्यश्च मानुषेभ्यस्तथात्मनः।।३।।
इष्टिं वैश्वानरीं कृत्वा प्राङ्मुखोदङ्मुखोऽपि वा।
अग्निं स्वात्मनि संरोप्य मंत्रवत्प्रव्रजेत् पुनः।।४।।

Having carefully made gifts unto the departed manes, the celestials and the human beings, performed Śrāddha for the departed manes and the human relations and performed the funeral rites of his own self, and taking the Sacred Fire with his own self, one, knowing the Mantra, should again enter upon the life of mendicancy.

ततः प्रभृति पुत्रादौ स्नेहालापादि वर्जयेत्।
बन्धूनामभयं दद्यात् सर्वभूताभयं तथा।।५।।

Since then he should desist from cherishing attachment for sons and conversing with them. He should give assurance of safety unto his kinsmen and all creatures.

त्रिदण्डं वैष्णवं सम्यक् सन्ततं समपर्वकम्।
वेष्टितं कृष्णगोवालरज्जुमच्चतुरङ्गुलम्।।६।।
शौचार्थं मानसार्थञ्च मुनिभिः समुदाहृतम्।
कौपीनाच्छादनं वासः कन्थां शीतनिवारिणीम्।।७।।

A triple staff, made of bamboo, of equal knots, measuring four fingers and covered with the down of a black calf, has been highly spoken of by the ascetics for physical and mental purification. A small strip of cloth [is allowed] for covering the body and a wallet for protection against cold.

पादुके चापि गृह्णीयात् कुर्यान्नान्यस्य संग्रहम्।
एतानि तस्य लिङ्गानि यतेः प्रोक्तानि सर्वदा।।८।।

He should also take a pair of sandals and must not collect any thing else. These all, that have been described, are always his marks.

संगृह्य कृतसन्न्यासो गत्वा तीर्थमनुत्तमम्।
स्नात्वाचम्य च विधिवद्वस्त्रपूतेन वारिणा॥९॥

Collecting all these, leading a life of renunciation and going to a most excellent shrine, [he should] bathe there and rinse his mouth with water inspired with the Mantras.

तर्पयित्वा तु देवांश्च मन्त्रवद्भास्करं नमेत्।
आत्मन: प्राङ्मुखो मौनी प्राणायामत्रयं चरेत्॥१०॥

Then offering oblations to the Deities, he should bow unto the Sun according to the Mantra. Then with his face directed towards the east and abstaining from speech, he should perform the Prāṇāyāma thrice.

गायत्रीञ्च यथाशक्ति जप्त्वा ध्यायेत् परं पदम्।
स्थित्यर्थमात्मनो नित्यं भिक्षाटनमथाचरेत्॥११॥

Having recited the *Gāyatrī* according to his might, he should meditate on the *Para-Brahman*. And for supporting his own self, he should daily go out for receiving alms.

सायंकाले तु विप्राणां गृहाण्यभ्यवपद्य तु।
सम्यन् याचेच्च कवलं दक्षिणेन करेण वै॥१२॥

Having arrive in the evening at the residence of the Brāhmaṇas, he should, with his right hand, beg for a mouthful of food.

पात्रं वामकरे स्थाप्य दक्षिणेन तु शेषयेत्।
यावतान्नेन तृप्ति: स्यात्तावद्भैक्षं समाचरेत्॥१३॥

Having taken up the bowl with his left hand, he should collect alms with his right one. He should receive alms so long as food, capable of gratifying him, is not secured.

ततो निवृत्य तत्पात्रं संस्थाप्यान्यत्र संयमी।
चतुर्भिरङ्गुलैश्छाद्य ग्रासमात्रं समाहित:॥१४॥

सर्वव्यञ्जनसंयुक्तं पृथक्पात्रे नियोजयेत्।
सूर्य्यादिभूतदेवेभ्यो दत्त्वा सम्प्रोक्ष्य वारिणा॥१५॥

भुञ्जीत पात्रपुटके पात्रे वा वाग्यतो यतिः।
वटकाश्वत्थपर्णेषु कुम्भीतैन्दुकपात्रके॥१६॥
कोविदारकदम्बेषु न भुञ्जीयात् कदाचन।
मलाक्ताः सर्व उच्यन्ते यतयः कांस्यभोजिनः॥१७॥

Then returning, the self-controlled [mendicant] should place the bowl elsewhere. Then being self-controlled, he should take rice, containing all sorts of curries with four fingers and keep it in another vessel. Then sprinkling it with water and offering it to the elemental Deities headed by the Sun, the Yatin should take his meal either in two vessels or in one. He should never eat from a vessel made of fig-leaves, or one made of *Kumbhī*, *Tainduka*, *Kovidāra* and *Kadamba*. The Yatins, who eat from vessels made of belmetal, are all described as being covered with dirt.

कांस्यभाण्डेषु यत् पाको गृहस्थस्य तथैव च।
कांस्ये भोजयतः सर्वं किल्विषं प्राप्नुयात्तयोः॥१८॥

The Yatins, [who take their meals from a belmetal vessel], are visited by the sins of the householder, who cooks food in a belmetal vessel, as well as of all those [persons] who make others eat from the same.

भुक्त्वा पात्रे यतिर्नित्यं क्षालयेन्मन्त्रपूर्वकम्।
न दुष्यते च तत्पात्रं यज्ञेषु चमसा इव॥१९॥

A Yatin should daily wash the vessel, with Mantras, in which he takes his meal. Like the *Camasa*-vessel (ladle), of sacrifice that vessel in never sullied.

अथाचम्य निदिध्यास्य उपतिष्ठेच्च भास्करम्।
जपध्यानेतिहासैश्च दिनशेषं नयेद्बुधः॥२०॥

Thereupon having rinsed his mouth and performed deep meditation, he should adore the Sun. A sage man should then spend his day in recitation, meditation, and the study of history.

कृतसन्ध्यस्ततो रात्रिं नयेद्देवगृहादिषु।
हृत्पुण्डरीकनिलये ध्यायेदात्मानमव्ययम्॥२१॥

Then performing the evening adoration, he should spend the night in a temple and meditate on the eternal Brahman in the lotus of his heart.

यदि धर्मरतिः शान्तः सर्वभूतसमो वशी।
प्राप्नोति परमं स्थानं यत्प्राप्य न निवर्तते॥२२॥

If [a Sannyāsin] be thus religiously bent, be of a quiescent soul, impartial unto all creatures and self restrained, he attains to the highest station from which he does not return.

त्रिदण्डभृद्यो हि पृथक्समाचरे
च्छनैः शनैर्यस्तु बहिर्मुखाक्षः।
सम्मुच्य संसारसमस्तबन्धनात्
स यातिविष्णोरमृतात्मनःपदम्॥२३॥

The holder of the triple staff,– who, withholding the senses from the external objects, gradually acts thus,– attains to the most exalted station of Viṣṇu, freed from the fetters of worldly existence.

इति हारीते धर्मशास्त्रे षष्ठोऽध्यायः॥६॥

Chapter-7
[Essence of Yoga]

वर्णानामाश्रमाणां कथितं धर्मलक्षणम्।
येन स्वर्गापवर्गं च प्राप्नुवन्ति द्विजातयः॥१॥

I have described the duties of various Varṇas and Āśramas, by following which men attain to emancipation and the celestial region.

योगशास्त्रं प्रवक्ष्यामि सङ्क्षेपात्सारमुत्तमम्।
यस्य च श्रवणद्यान्ति मोक्षञ्चैव मुमुक्षवः॥२॥

I shall now describe, in brief, the most essential and excellent Yoga-Śāstra by listening to which, persons, desirous of acquiring emancipation, attain to it.

योगाभ्यासबलेनैव नश्येयुः पातकानि तु।
तस्माद्योगपरो भूत्वा ध्यायेन्नित्यं क्रियापरः॥३॥

All the sins are dissipated by the practice of Yoga. Therefore, resorting to Yoga and performing all religious rites, one should daily perform meditation.

प्राणायामेन वचनं प्रत्याहारेण चेन्द्रियम्।
धारणाभिर्वशे कृत्वा पूर्वं दुर्धर्षणं मनः॥४॥

Having brought first the mind, difficult of being restrained, under control, by *dhāraṇā* (steady abstraction), one should control one's speech by *prāṇāyāma*; and the senses, by withholding them from their objects.

एकाकारमना मन्दं बुधरूपमनामयम्।
सक्ष्मात् सूक्ष्मतरं ध्यायेज्जगदाधारमुच्यते॥५॥

Considering the individual soul as identical with the Great Soul, he should meditate on Brahman, that is all knowledge, freed from diseases, subtler than the subtle and described as the stay of the universe.

आत्मानं बहिरन्तस्थं शुद्धचामीकरप्रभम्।
रहस्येकान्तमासीनो ध्यायेदामरणान्तिकम्॥६॥

Seated in a solitary place with a concentrated mind, he should, till death, meditate on the Ātman, that is situated both in the mind and the external world, and effulgent like gold.

यत् सर्वप्राणिहृदयं सर्वेवाञ्च हृदिस्थितम्।
यच्च सर्वजनैर्ज्ञेयं सोऽहमस्मीति चिन्तयेत्॥७॥

He should think,– "I am that which is the heart of all creatures, which is situated in the hearts of all and which is worthy of being known by all."

आत्मलाभसुखं यावत्तपोध्यानमुदीरितम्।
श्रुतिस्मृत्यादिकं धर्मं तद्विरुद्धं न चाचरेत्॥८॥

So long one enjoys the pleasure of seeing the ātman, he

should not act against the religious practices mentioned in the Śruti and the Smṛti (such as penances, meditation, etc.)

यथा रथोऽश्वहीनस्तु यथाश्वो रथिहीनकः।
एवं तपश्च विद्या च संयुतं भैषजं भवेत्॥९॥

As a car without a horse and a horse without a charioteer [are of no use], so is penance and learning. They become useful when [they are] united.

यथान्नं मधुसंयुक्तं मधुरान्नेन संयुतम्।
उभाभ्यामपि पक्षाभ्यां यता खे पक्षिणां गतिः॥१०॥
तथैव ज्ञानकर्मस्थां प्राप्यते ब्रह्म शाश्वतम्।
विद्यातपोभ्यां संपन्नो ब्राह्मणो योगतत्परः॥११॥
देहद्वयं विहायाशु मुक्तो भवति बन्धनात्।
न तथा क्षीणदेहस्य विनाशो विद्यते क्वचित्॥१२॥

As food united with sweet juice, and sweet juice united with food, [are useful]; as birds, with two wings, fly in the sky; so one, by *jñāna* (knowledge) and *karma* (action), attains to the eternal Brahman. A Brāhmaṇa endued with learning and penance and given to the practice of yoga– having cast off the two bodies (the material and the subtle), becomes freed from fetters. There is no destruction of the soul when the material body is destroyed.

मया ते कथितः सर्वो वर्णाश्रमविभागशः।
सङ्क्षेपेण द्विजश्रेष्ठा धर्मस्तेषां सनातनः॥१३॥

O you foremost of the twice-born ones, all the divisions of castes and orders and their duties have been described unto you, in brief, by me.

श्रुत्वैवं मुनयो धर्मं स्वर्गमोक्षफलप्रदम्।
प्रणम्य तमृषिं जग्मुर्मुदिताः स्वं स्वमाश्रमम्॥१४॥

Hearing of religious duties, which yield, as fruits, the celestial region and emancipation, the ascetics, saluted the Ṛṣi, and delighted, repaired to their respective habitations.

धर्मशास्त्रमिदं सर्वं हारीतमुखनिःसृतम।
अधीत्य कुरूते धर्मं स याति परमां गतिम्॥१५॥

Mārkaṇḍeya said– Having studied this Religious Code, in full, emanating from the mouth of Hārīta, he, who follows its religious teachings, comes by the most excellent state.

ब्राह्मणस्य तु यत् कर्म कथितं बाहुजस्य च।
ऊरूजस्यापि यत्कर्म कथितं पादजस्य च॥१६॥
अन्यथा वर्त्तमानस्तु सद्यः पतति जातितः।
यो यस्याभिहितो धर्मः स तु तस्य तथैव च।
तस्मात् स्वधर्मं कुर्वीत द्विजो नित्यमनापदि॥१७॥

By acting against the duties laid down for the Brāhmaṇas, those laid down for the Kṣatriyas (sprung from the arms of Brahmā), those laid down for the Vaiśyas (thigh-begotten), and those laid down for the Śūdras (foot-sprung), one is immediately degraded from his caste. Every one should perform the duty laid down for him (*i.e.*, for his caste). The twice-born should, therefore, carefully satisfy their respective duties.

वर्णाश्चत्वारो राजेन्द्र चत्वारश्चापि चाश्रमाः।
स्वधर्मं ये तु तिष्ठन्ति ते यान्ति परमां गतिम्॥१८॥

Thus, O king, there are four Varṇas, and four Āśramas. Those, who abide by their own duties, come by the most excellent condition.

स्वधर्मेण यथा नॄणां नारसिंहः प्रसीदति।
न तुष्यति तथान्येन कर्मणा मधुसूदनः॥१९॥

The slayer of Madhu is not so much pleased with any other work, as the Man-Lion is gratified with the discharge of their respective duties by men.

अतः कुर्वन् निजं कर्म यथाकालमतन्द्रितः।
सहस्रानीकदेवेशं नारसिंहञ्च सालयम्॥२०॥

Therefore performing one's own duty in proper time and vigilantly, a person acquires habitation with the thousand-eyed King of the Celestials and the Man-Lion (Viṣṇu).

उत्पन्नवैराग्यवलेन योगी ध्यायेत् परं ब्रह्म सदाक्रियावान्।
सत्यं सुखं रूपमनन्तमाद्यं विहाय देहं पदमेति विष्णोः॥२१॥

By the power of the spirit of disassociation sprung in him, a Yogin, always, performing religious rites, should meditate on *Para-Brahman*. Then casting off his body, he shall attain to the eternal and the ever-blissful station of Viṣṇu, which is without beginning or end.

इति हारीते धर्मशास्त्रे सप्तमोऽध्याय:॥७॥

९. बृहस्पतिस्मृति:

9. Bṛhaspati Smṛti

इष्ट्वा क्रतुशतं राजा समाप्तवरदक्षिणम्।
मघवान् वाग्विदां श्रेष्ठं पर्यपृच्छद् बृहस्पतिम्॥१॥

Having celebrated a hundred sacrifices [and] completed [them] with profuse presents, King Indra accosted Bṛhaspati, the foremost of orators, saying–

भगवन् केन दानेन सर्वतः सुखमेधते।
यद्दत्तं यन्महार्घञ्च तन्मे ब्रूहि महातपः॥२॥

O lord! By what gift happiness is always multiplied? Tell me, O you of great asceticism, of that, which, being given, yields most precious fruits.

एवमिन्द्रेण पृष्टोऽसौ देवदेवपुरोहितः।
वाचस्पतिर्महाप्राज्ञो बृहस्पतिरुवाच ह॥३॥

Being thus accosted by Indra, the greatly wise Bṛhaspati, the master of speech and the priest of the Celestials, said–

सुवर्णदानं गोदानं भूमिदानञ्च वासव।
एतत् प्रयच्छमानस्तु सर्वपापैः प्रमुच्यते॥४॥

O Vāsava! He, who makes gifts of gold, cow and lands, is freed from all sins.

सुवर्णं रजतं वस्त्रं मणिरत्नञ्च वासव।
सर्वमेव भवेद्दत्तं वसुधां यः प्रयच्छति॥५॥

Gold, silver, raiment, diamond and precious stones, are all given by him who gives away lands.

फालाकृष्टां महीं दत्त्वा सबीजां शस्य शालिनीम्।
यावत् सूर्यकरा लोकास्तावत् स्वर्गे महीयते॥६।

By giving away furrowed lands, capable of germinating seeds

and filled with corns, one lives gloriously in the celestials region, so long as the solar rays remain in the three regions.

यत् किंचित् कुरुते पापं पुरुषो वृत्तिकर्षितः।
अपि गोचर्ममात्रेण भूमिदानेन शुध्यति।।७।।

By making a gift of land, even of the measurement of a *Gocarma*, one is purged of any sin he commits under the distressing pressure of limited means of livelihood.

दशहस्तेन दण्डेन त्रिंशद्दण्डानि वर्त्तनम्।
दश तान्येव विस्तारा गोचर्मैतन्महाफलम्।।८।।

A plot of land, thirty rods of ten cubits in length and ten such in breadth, is called *Gocarma*. [The gift of such a land yields] great fruits.

सवृषं गोसहस्रञ्च यत्र तिष्ठत्यतन्द्रितम्।
बालवत्साप्रसूतानां तद्गोचर्म इति स्मृतम्।।९।।

Or the plot of land where a thousand kine, having given birth to young ones, may live comfortably, is called *Gocarma* in the *Smṛti*.

विप्राय दद्याच्च गुणान्विताय तपोऽनियुक्ताय जितेन्द्रियाय।
यावन्मही तिष्ठति सागरान्ता तावत् फलं तस्य भवेदनन्तम्।।१०।।

By making gift of a land unto a Vipra, endued with accomplishments, asceticism and self-controlled, one enjoys the unending fruits thereof, so long as the earth girt by the ocean exists.

यथा बीजानि रोहन्ति प्रकीर्णानि महीतले।
एवं पुण्याः प्ररोहन्ति भूमिदानसमार्ज्जिताः।।११।।

As seeds, scattered on the surface of the earth germinate; so virtue, acquired by the gift of lands, multiplies.

यथाऽप्सु पतितः सद्यस्तैलबिन्दुः प्रसर्पति।
एवं भूमिकृतं दानं शस्ये शस्ये प्ररोहति।।१२।।

As a drop of oil, thrown into water, spreads itself; so the

virtue of the gift of lands, multiplies itself in every corn.

अन्नदाः सुखिनो नित्यं वस्त्रदश्चैव रूपवान्॥
स नरः सर्वदो भूपो यो ददाति वसुन्धराम्॥१३॥

The giver of rice becomes ever happy; and that of raiments, beautiful. The man, who makes gifts of lands, becomes always like a king.

यथा गौर्भरते वत्सं क्षीरमुत्सृज्य क्षीरिणी।
एवं दत्ता सहस्राक्ष, भूमिर्भरति भूमिदम्॥१४॥

As a milch-cow rears its calf by discharging milk, so, O thousand-eyed Deity! The land, given away, multiplies the prosperity of the giver.

शङ्खं भद्रासनं छत्रं चरस्थावरवारणाः।
भूमिदानस्य पुण्येन फलं स्वर्गः पुरन्दर॥१५॥

[By giving away lands, one comes by the fruits of the gifts of] conch-shell, house, umbrella, animate and inanimate objects and elephants. The fruit of the gift of lands, O Purandara! Comprises various virtues and the celestial region.

आदित्यो वरुणो विष्णुर्ब्रह्मा सोमो हुताशनः।
शूलपाणिश्च भगवानभिनन्दति भूमिदम्॥ १६॥

The Sun, Varuṇa, Viṣṇu, Soma, Fire-God, and the Divine Holder of the Trident (Śiva), gratify the giver of lands.

आस्फोटयन्ति पितरः प्रहर्षन्ति पितामहाः।
भूमिदाता कुले जातः स नस्त्राता भविष्यति॥१७॥

The fathers vaunt and the grandfathers become gratified, [and say–] A giver of lands is born in our family. He will become our rescuer.

त्रीण्याहुरतिदानानि गावः पृथ्वी सरस्वती।
तारयन्ति हि दातारं सर्वात् पापादसंशयम्॥१८॥

The gifts of kine, lands and learning, are spoken of as supreme gifts. They, forsooth, rescue the giver from all sins.

प्रावृता वस्त्रदा यान्ति नग्ना यान्ति त्ववस्त्रदाः।
तृप्ता यान्त्यन्नदातारः क्षुधिता यान्त्यनन्नदाः॥१९॥

The givers of clothes go [to the other region], being covered therewith. And those, who fail to do so, go nude. The givers of food, go there, gratified [with food]. And those, who do not make gifts of food, go hungry.

काङ्क्षन्ति पितरः सर्वे नरकाद्भयभीरवः।
गयां यो यास्यति पुत्रः स नस्त्राता भविष्यति॥२०॥

All the departed Manes, afraid of hell, seek it, thinking, 'The son who will go to Gayā would be our rescuer.

एष्टव्या बहवः पुत्राः यद्येकोऽपि गयां व्रजेत्।
यजेत वाऽश्वमेधेन नीलं वा वृषमुत्सृजेत्॥२१॥

One should desire for many sons, for if one happens to go to Gayā, or one happens perform a Horse-Sacrifice, or to dedicate a *Nīla*-bull.

लोहितो यस्तु वर्णेन पुच्छाग्रे यस्तु पाण्डुरः।
श्वेतः खुरविषाणाभ्यां स नीलो वृष उच्यते॥२२॥

The one, the upper part of whose tail is dark-blue in colour, whose hoops are tawny-coloured, and whose horns are white, is called a *Nīla*-bull.

नीलः पाण्डुरलाङ्गूलस्तृणमुद्धरते तु यः।
षष्टिर्वर्षसहस्राणि पितरस्तेन तर्पिताः॥२३॥

If that *Nīla*-bull, having a tawny-coloured tail, goes about eating grass, the departed Manes [of the giver], remain gratified for sixty thousand years.

यच्च शृङ्गगतं पङ्कं कूलात्तिष्ठति चोद्धृतम्।
पितरस्तस्य गच्छन्ति सोमलोकं शुभाद्युतिम्॥२४॥

If the mud, upraised from the bank, exists on its horns, the departed Manes of the dedicator repair to the most beautiful region of *Soma*.

पृथ्वी यदोर्दिलीपस्य नृगस्य नहुषस्य च।
अन्येषाञ्च नरेन्द्राणां पुनरन्या भविष्यति॥२५॥

Formerly [this earth] [belonged] to Yadu, Dilīpa, Nṛga, Nahuṣa and other kings; and in future it will go to others.

बहुभिर्वसुधा दत्ता राजभिः सगरादिभिः।
यस्य यस्य यदा भूमिस्तस्य तस्य तदा फलम्॥२६॥

This earth was given away by many kings, Sagara, and others. But the fruit belongs to him in whose possession the land exists.

यस्तु ब्रह्मघ्नः स्त्रीघ्नो वा यस्तु वै पितृघातकः।
गवां शतसहस्त्राणां हन्ता भवति दुष्कृती॥२७॥
स्वदत्तां परदत्तां वा यो हरेच्च वसुन्धराम्।
स्वविष्ठायां क्रिमिर्भूत्वा पितृभिः सह पच्यते॥२८॥

The perpetrator of sinful deeds, he, who kills a Brāhmaṇa, who kills a woman, who kills his father, who kills a hundred or a thousand kine, who seizes lands given away by his own self or by another,- rots with his departed Manes by becoming a vermin in his own excreta.

आक्षेप्ता वानुमन्ता च तमेव नरकं व्रजेत्॥२९॥

He, who speaks ill of the gift of lands, and he, who gives permission for stealing the same, goes to hell.

भूमिदो भूमिहर्ता च नापरं पुण्यपापयोः।
ऊर्ध्वाधो वावतिष्ठेत यावदाभूतसम्प्लवम्॥३०॥

The giver of land and the stealer of the same, reap the virtue or the sin and no one else. Till the dissolution of the universe, [the giver] remains upwards (*i.e.*, in the celestial region); and the stealer, downwards (*i.e.*, in hell).

अग्नेरपत्यं प्रथमं हिरण्यं भूर्वैष्णवी सूर्यसूताश्च गावः।
लोकास्त्रयस्तेन भवन्ति दत्ता यः काञ्चनं गाञ्च महीञ्च दद्यात्॥३१॥

The first offspring of the Fire, is gold. The daughter of Viṣṇu, is the earth. A cow is the daughter of the Sun. He, who gives away gold, cow, or the earth, becomes the giver of the threefold regions (*i.e.*, enjoys the fruits of such a gift).

षडशीतिसहस्राणां योजनानां वसुन्धराम्।
स्वतो दत्ता तु सर्वत्र सर्वकामप्रदायिनी॥३२॥

[A part of] the earth, extending over eighty-six thousand *Yojanas*, being given away by one of one's own accord, it gives everywhere all sorts of desired for objects.

भूमिं यः प्रतिगृह्णाति भूमिं यस्तु प्रयच्छति।
उभौ तौ पुण्यकर्माणौ नियतं स्वर्गगामिनौ॥३३॥

Both he,- who accepts the gifts of land, and he,- who makes such a gift, are the performers of pious deeds. And they, forsooth, repair to the celestial region.

सर्वेषामेव दानानामेकजन्मानुगं फलम्।
हाटकक्षितिगौरीणां सप्तजन्मानुगं फलम्॥३४॥

The fruits of all the [other] gifts, follow one birth, but those of the gifts of gold, lands and a seven years old maiden, follow seven births.

यो न हिंस्यादहं ह्यात्मा भूतग्रामं चतुर्विधम्।
तस्य देहाद्वियुक्तस्य भयं नास्ति कदाचन॥३५॥

Thinking that I am the soul, he, who does no injury to the fourfold creations (those born of perspiration, those born of eggs, the vegetables, and those born of the uterus), has nothing to fear of, even when he is alienated from his body.

अन्यायेन हृता भूमिर्यैर्नरैरपहारिता।
हरन्तो हारयन्तश्च हन्युस्ते सप्तमं कुलम्॥३६॥

Those men, by whom a land is improperly stolen, or those by whom it is made to be stolen, both the stealer and the orderer, destroy their seven generations.

हरते हारयेद्यस्तु मन्दबुद्धिस्तमोवृतः।
स वध्यो वारुणैः पाशैस्तिर्यग्योनिषु जायते॥३७॥

That wicked-minded person, stupefied by *Tamas* (disorganizing tendency), pilfers a land or makes another do the same, is killed by Varuṇas noose, and is born in the species of the feathery tribe.

अश्रुभिः पतितैस्तेषां दानानामवकीर्तनम्।
ब्राह्मणस्य हृते क्षेत्रे हन्ति त्रिपुरुषं कुलम्॥३८॥

If denying the gift, one pilfers a land belonging to Brāhmaṇa, his three generations are destroyed by tears shed [by such a Brāhmaṇa].

वापीकूपसहस्रेण अश्वमेधशतेन च।
गवां कोटिप्रदानेन भूमिहर्ता न शुध्यति॥३९॥

The stealer of lands, is not purified by [the gift of] a thousand of wells and tanks, by [the celebration of] a hundred Horse-Sacrifices, and by the gift of a *Koṭi* (ten millions) of kine.

गामेकां स्वर्णमेकं वा भूमेरप्यर्द्धमङ्गुलम्।
रुन्धन्नरकमायाति यावदाभूतसम्प्लवम्॥४०॥

He, who wrongly possesses a cow, a piece of gold, or a plot of land half a cubit in measurement, lives in hell till the hour of final dissolution.

अर्द्धङ्गुलस्य सीमाया हरणेन प्रणश्यति।
गोवीथीं ग्रामरथ्याश्च श्मशानं गोकुलं तथा॥४१॥
सम्पीड्य नरकं याति यावदाभूतसम्प्लवम्।
ऊषरे निर्ज्जले स्थाने प्रोस्तं शस्यं विसर्ज्जयेत्॥४२॥
जलाधरश्च कर्त्तव्यो व्यासस्य वचनं यथा।
पञ्च कन्याऽनृते हन्ति दश हन्ति गवानृते॥४३॥

One meets with destruction by wrongfully possessing a boundary land, measuring even half a cubit. By obstructing a road trodden by kine, or the village-road, or the cremation-ground and striking the kine, one remains in hell till the final dissolution. Vyāsas deliverance is that one should sow corns in a barren place, dig wells in a waterless place. The false accusation of a maiden, destroys five generations; and that of a cow, ten.

शतमश्वानृते हन्ति सहस्रं पुरुषानृते।
हन्ति जातानजातांश्च हिरण्यार्थेऽनृतं वदन्।।४४।।

The false accusation of a horse, destroys a hundred generations; that of men (*i.e.*, servants), a thousand. Those born and those who will be born in the family of one who utters a falsehood for gold, are destroyed.

सर्वं भूम्यनृते हन्ति मास्म भूम्यनृतं वदीः।
ब्रह्मस्वे मा रतिं कुर्याः प्राणैः कण्ठगतैरपि।।४५।।

To speak false for land, destroys all. Therefore, one should never utter a falsehood for land. One should never cherish an inclination for a Brāhmaṇas property, even if his vital breath comes up to the throat.

अनौषधमभेषजः विषमं तद्धलाहलम्।
न विषं विषमित्याहुर्ब्रह्मस्वं विषमुच्यते।।४६।।

That dreadful poison has no medicine and no physician. Poison is no poison; but a Brāhmaṇas property [verily] is spoken of as poison.

विषमेकाकिनं हन्ति ब्रह्मस्वं पुत्रपौत्रकम्।
लौहखण्डश्मचूर्णञ्च विषञ्च जरयेन्नरः।।४७।।

Poison kills only one man [who takes it], but a Brāhmaṇas property destroys even his son and grandson. One can digest iron, powdered stone and even poison.

ब्रह्मस्वं त्रिषु लोकेषु कः पुमान् जरयिष्यति।
मन्युप्रहरणं विप्रा राजानः शस्त्रपाणयः।।४८।।

What man, in the three regions, can digest a Brāhmaṇas property? A Brāhmaṇas anger is a weapon, a kings hand is a weapon.

शस्त्रमेकाकिनं हन्ति विप्रमन्युः कुलक्षयम्।
मन्युप्रहरणा विप्राश्चक्रप्रहरणो हरिः।।४९।।

A weapon destroys only one man; but a Brāhmaṇas anger, the entire family. The Brāhmaṇas have thus ire for their weapons; and Hari (Viṣṇu) has the discus for his weapon.

चक्रात् तीव्रतरो मन्युस्तस्माद्विप्रं न कोपयेत्।
अग्निदग्धाः प्ररोहन्ति सूर्यदग्धास्तथैव च॥५०॥

[A Brāhmaṇas] anger is fiercer than the discus; one should not, therefore, make a Brāhmaṇa irate. Those destroyed by fire or the Sun, may grow again.

मन्युदग्धस्य विप्राणामङ्कुरो न प्ररोहति ।
अग्निर्दहति तेजसा सूर्यो दहति रश्मिभिः॥५१॥

But there is no re-growth for him, who has been destroyed by a Brāhmaṇas ire. Fire destroys [an article] by its power; and the Sun, by its rays.

राजा दहति दण्डेन विप्रो दहति मन्युना।
ब्रह्मस्वेन तु यत् सौख्यं देवस्वेन तु या रतिः॥५२॥
तद्धनं कुलनाशाय भवत्यात्मविनाशकम्।
ब्रह्मस्वं ब्रह्महत्या च दरिद्रस्य च यद्धनम्॥५३॥
गुरुमित्रहिरण्ये च स्वर्गस्थमपि पीडयेत्।
ब्रह्मस्वेन तु यच्छिद्रं तच्छिद्रं न प्ररोहति॥५४॥

The king consumes [a person] with the rod of chastisement; and a Vipra, with anger. That wealth which creates a desire for a Brāhmaṇas property and hankering for what is dedicated to a Deity, leads to the destruction of ones family and self. The theft of a Brāhmaṇas property, Brahmanicide, the pilfering of a poor mans wealth and that of a preceptors or a friends gold, afflicts one, even if one is stationed in the celestial region. The sin, attached to the stealth of a Brāhmaṇas property, is never dissipated.

प्रच्छादयति तच्छिद्रमन्यत्र तु विसर्पति।
ब्रह्मस्वेन तु पुष्टानि साधनानि बलानि च॥५५॥

संग्रामे तानि लीयन्ते सिकतासु यथोदकम्।
श्रोत्रियाय कुलीनाय दरिद्राय च वासव॥५६॥
सन्तुष्टाय विनीताय सर्वभूतहिताय च।
वेदाभ्यासस्तपो ज्ञानमिन्द्रियाणाञ्च संयमः॥५७॥
ईदृशाय सुरश्रेष्ठ यद्दत्तं हि तदक्षयम्।
आमपात्रे यथा न्यस्तं क्षीरं दधि घृतं मधु॥५८॥
विनश्येत् पात्रदौर्बल्यात् तच्च पात्रं विनश्यति।
एवं गाञ्च हिरण्यञ्च वस्त्रमन्नं महीं तिलान्॥५९॥
अविद्वान् प्रतिगृह्णाति भस्मीभवति काष्ठवत्।
यस्य चैव गृहे मूर्खो दूरे चापि बहुश्रुतः॥६०॥
बहुश्रुताय दातव्यं नास्ति मूर्खे व्यतिक्रमः।
कुलं तारयते धीरः सप्त सप्त च वासव॥६१॥

If one hides that sin, it will get wind elsewhere. The weapons [bought] and the soldiers fed by a Brāhmaṇas wealth, are destroyed in a battle like water in sands. O Vāsava, O foremost of the Celestials, eternal is the gift that is made unto a person who is well-read in the Vedas, born in a good family, poor, contented, humble, given to the well-being of all creatures, who studies the Vedas, performs penances, has acquired knowledge and controlled the senses. As milk, curd, clarified butter and honey, placed in a raw earthen vessel, are destroyed for the defect of the vessel, so an ignorant man, who accepts cows, gold, raiment, food, land and sesame, is consumed like a wood. If an ignorant person lives in ones own house and one vastly read in the *Śruti* at a distance, presents should be made unto the one who is master of the Veda. There is no sin in superseding the ignorant wight. A learned person, O Vāsava, rescues the family by seven and seven (*i.e.*, seven generations upwards and seven downwards).

यस्तटाकं नवं कुर्यात् पुराणं वाऽपि खानयेत्।
स सर्वं कुलमुद्धृत्य स्वर्गे लोके महीयते॥६२॥

He, who excavates a new tank, or reclaims an old one, lives gloriously in the celestial region after rescuing his entire family.

वापीकूपतडागानि उद्यानोपवनानि च।
पुनःसंस्कारकर्त्ता च लभते मौलिकं फलम्॥६३॥

He, who reclaims old tanks, wells, pools, forests and gardens, enjoys the same fruits of the original maker.

निदाघकाले पानीयं यस्य तिष्ठति वासव।
स दुर्गं विषमं कृत्स्नं न कदाचिदवाप्नुयात्॥६४॥

The person, O Vāsava, in whose tank, water exists even in the summer season, never comes by any distressing condition.

एकाहन्तु स्थितं तोयं पृथिव्यां राजसत्तम।
कुलानि तारयेत् तस्य सप्त सप्त पराण्यपि॥६५॥

O foremost of the kings, the person, in whose tank on this earth, water exists even for a day, rescues seven generations upwards and downwards.

दीपालोकप्रदानेन वपुष्मान् स भवेन्नरः।
प्रोक्षणीयप्रदानेन स्मृतिं मेधाञ्च विन्दति॥६६॥

By making gifts of lamp, one becomes of a handsome body. By making gifts of edibles, one acquires memory and intellect.

कृत्वाऽपि पापकर्माणि यो दद्यादन्नमर्थिने।
ब्राह्मणाय विशेषेण न स पापेन लिप्यते ॥६७॥

If, after perpetrating iniquitous deeds, one gives food unto one soliciting the same and especially unto a Brāhmaṇa, one is to affected by the sin [thereof].

भूमिर्गावस्तथा दाराः प्रसह्य ह्रियते यदा।
न चावेदयते यस्तु तमाहुर्ब्रह्मघातकम्॥६८॥

[The sages] call him the destroyer of a Brāhmaṇa, who, when seeing lands, kine and wives of one, forcibly taken by another, does not communicate [the matter unto the master].

निवेदितस्तु राजा वै ब्राह्मणैर्मन्युपीडितैः।
तं न तारयते यस्तु तमाहुर्ब्रह्मघातकम्॥६९॥

If a king, on being communicated by the Brāhmaṇas, oppressed by anger, does not save them, him also, they call the destroyer of a Brāhmaṇa.

उपस्थिते विवाहे च यज्ञे दाने च वासव।
मोहाच्चलति विघ्नं यः स मृतो जायते कृमिः॥७०॥

He, who, out of stupefaction, puts impediments in an impending marriage, sacrifice or gift, O Vāsava, is born as a vermin after death.

धनं फलति दानेन जीवितं जीवरक्षणात्।
रूपमैश्वर्यमारोग्यमहिंसाफलमश्नुते ॥७१॥

Wealth is multiplied by a gift; and life [is prolonged] by the protection of lives. By abstention from injury, one enjoys the fruits [thereof in the shape of] beauty, prosperity and freedom from diseases.

फलमूलाशनात् पूज्यं स्वर्गः खस्तेन लभ्यते।
प्रायोपवेशनाद्राज्यं सर्वत्र सुखमश्नुते॥७२॥

By partaking of fruits and roots, one attains to the adorable celestial region along with the dwellers therein. By fasting, one enjoys a kingdom and happiness everywhere.

गवाद्यः शक्र दीक्षायाः स्वर्गगामी तृणाशनः।
स्त्रियस्त्रिषवणस्नायी वायुं पीत्वा क्रतुं लभेत्॥ ७३॥

[The acquisition of] kine, etc., [is the fruit of] initiation. One, by living on grass, attains to the celestial region. One, by bathing three times [a day], acquires women and by drinking air only [and dying thereby], one reaps the fruit of a sacrifice.

नित्यस्नायी भवेदर्क सन्ध्ये द्वे च जपन् द्विजः।
न तत् साधयते राज्यं नाकपृष्ठमनाशके॥७४॥

A kingdom does not accomplish what [is gained by] a twice-born person, who bathes daily, adores the Sun, and recites the *Mantras* at the two periods of junction. One attains to the celestial region by meeting with death while fasting.

अग्निप्रवेशे नियतं ब्रह्मलोके महीयते।
रत्नानां प्रतिसंहारे पशून् पुत्रांश्च विन्दति॥७५॥

Entering into a fire by being self-restrained, one lives gloriously in the region of Brahmā. He, who returns precious stones, comes by creature-comforts and sons.

नाके चिरं स वसते उपवासी च यो भवेत्।
सततञ्चैकशायी यः स लभेदीप्सितां गतिम्॥७६॥

He, who fasts, lives, for good, in the celestial region. He, who always lies down on one side, comes by a desired for condition.

वीरासनं वीरशय्यां वीरस्थानमुपाश्रितः।
अक्षयास्तस्य लोकाः स्युः सर्वकामगमास्तथा॥७७॥

He, who resorts to a heroes seat, a heroes bed and a heroes place, has eternal regions and desired for objects.

उपवासञ्च दीक्षाञ्च अभिषेकञ्च वासव।
कृत्वा द्वादश वर्षाणि वीरस्थानाद्विशिष्यते॥७८॥

By performing fasting, initiation and water-sprinkling for twelve years, one attains to a region superior to that of heroes.

अधीत्य सर्ववेदान् वै सद्यो दुःखात्प्रमुच्यते।
पावनं चरते धर्मं स्वर्गे लोके महीयते॥७९॥

By studying all the Vedas, one is immediately freed from sorrow. He, who performs sanctifying religious rites, lives gloriously in the celestial region.

बृहस्पतिमतं पुण्यं ये पठन्ति द्विजातयः।
चत्वारि तेषां वर्द्धन्ते आयुर्विद्या यशो बलम्॥८०॥

The twice-born, who study the holy deliverance of Bṛhaspati, have these four, viz.– longevity, learning, fame and strength, multiplied.

॥ बृहस्पतिस्मृतिः समाप्ता॥

१०. दक्षस्मृतिः

10. Dakṣa Smṛti

Chapter 1

सर्वधर्मार्थतत्त्वज्ञः सर्ववेदविदां वरः।

पारगः सर्वविद्यानां दक्षो नाम प्रजापतिः॥१॥

There was a patriarch named Dakṣa, who was acquainted with the true import of *Dharma* (religion), *Artha* (worldly profit), the foremost of all those conversant with the Vedas, and a perfect master of all forms of learning.

उत्पत्तिः प्रलयश्चैव स्थितिः संहार एव च।

आत्मा चात्मनि तिष्ठेत आत्मा ब्रह्मण्यवस्थितः॥२॥

Creation, universal dissolution, preservation and destruction take place of themselves and the soul abides in Brahman.

ब्रह्मचारी गृहस्थश्च वानप्रस्थो यतिस्तथा।

एतेषान्तु हितार्थाय दक्षःशास्त्रमकल्पयत्॥३॥

A *Brahmacārin* (religious student), a *Gṛhastha* (householder), a *Vānaprastha* (forest-recluse) and a *Yatin* (hermit)– for all these, Dakṣa, wrote his Institutes.

जातमात्रः शिशुस्तावद्यावदृष्टौ समा वयः।

स हि गर्भसमो ज्ञेये व्यक्तिमात्रप्रदर्शितः॥४॥

As long as a boy does not attain to the age of eight, [he is known] as a new-born babe. He is to be known as an embryo, the difference [only] being that of his individuality.

भक्ष्याभक्ष्ये तथा पेये वाच्यावाच्ये तथानृते।

तस्मिन् काले न दोषोस्ति स यावन्नोपनीयते॥५॥

In the period [that is during the period] that he is not invested with the sacred thread, there is no sin in a food and an interdicted edible, in drink, in what should be spoken or not, and in falsehood.

उपनीतस्य दोषोऽस्ति क्रियमाणैर्विगर्हितैः।
अप्राप्तव्यवहारोऽसौ यावत् षोडशवार्षिकः॥६॥

By doing forbidden deeds, after being invested with the sacred thread, one commits a sin. As long as he is not sixteen years old, he is not entitled to follow an established rule or practice.

स्वीकरोति यदा वेदं चरेद्वेदव्रतानि च।
ब्रह्मचारी भवेत् तावदूर्ध्वं स्नातो भवेद्गृही॥७॥

As long as one studies the Vedas and follows the Vedic observances, he is called a *Brahmacārin*. Thereafter, on being bathed, he becomes a householder.

द्विविद्यो ब्रह्मचारी तु स्मृतः शास्त्रे मनीषिभिः।
उपकुर्वाणकस्त्वाद्यो द्वितीयो नैष्ठिकः स्मृतः॥८॥

Two classes of *Brahmacārin* have been mentioned by the wise in the *Smṛti*. The first is *Upakurvāṇaka* (a Brāhmaṇa, in a state of pupil age, who wishes to pass on to the state of a householder); the second is *Naiṣṭhika* (one who leads a life of perpetual celibacy).

यो गृहाश्रममास्थाय ब्रह्मचारी भवेत् पुनः।
न यतिर्न वनस्थश्च सर्वाश्रमविवर्ज्जितः॥९॥

He, who after having adopted the life of a householder, becomes a religious student again, is neither a *Yatin* nor a *Vānaprastha* but he is divorced from all the *Āśramas*.

अनाश्रमी न तिष्ठत्तु दिनमेकमपि द्विजः।
आश्रमेण विना तिष्ठन् प्रायश्चित्तीयते हि सः॥१०॥

A twice-born person should not live, even for a day without following any order. If he lives without following an order, he is required to perform a penitential rite.

जपे होमे तथा दाने स्वाध्याये चरतेस्तु यः।
नासौ तत्फलमाप्नोति कुर्वाणोऽप्याश्रमाच्च्युतः।
त्रयाणामानुलोम्यं हि प्रातिलोम्यं न विद्यते।।११।।

He, who, divorced from an order, engages himself in recitation, or in the performance of *Homa*, or in making gifts, or in Vedic study,- does not reap the fruit thereof.

प्रातिलोम्येन यो यानि न तस्मात् पापकृत्तमः।
मेखलाजिनदण्डेन ब्रह्मचारी तु लक्ष्यते।।१२।।
गृहस्थो देवयज्ञाद्यैर्नखलाम्ना वनाश्रितः।
त्रिदण्डेन यतिश्चैव लक्षणानि पृथक्-पृथक्।।१३।।

The three orders should be followed in due succession, and not in a reverse course. There is none more sinful than he who follows them in a reverse order. A *Brahmacārin* is marked by a girdle, a black antelope skin and a staff; a householder, by the sacrifices for the Deities, etc.; and a forest-recluse, by the presence of nails and hairs. And a *Yatin* [is known] by a threefold staff. These are the different characteristic marks.

यस्य तल्लक्षणं नास्ति प्रायश्चित्ती न चाश्रमी।
उक्तकर्मक्रमेणोक्ता न कालो मुनिभिः स्मृतः।।१४।।
द्विजानान्तु हितार्थाय दक्षस्तु स्वयमब्रवीत्।।१५।।

He, who has none of these marks, is no follower of an order; and he is required to perform a penitential rite. The order of the above-mentioned rites has not been spoken of, nor has the time [of those rites] been recorded, in the *Smṛti*, by the Sages. For the behoof of the twice-born, Dakṣa himself has spoken of [all those rites].

।। इति दक्षस्मृतौ प्रथमोऽध्यायः।।१।।

Chapter 2

प्रातरुत्थाय कर्तव्यं यद् द्विजेन दिने दिने।
तत् सर्वं संप्रवक्ष्यामि द्विजानामुपकारकम्।।१।।

I shall now describe all those rites, which, being conducive to their well-being, should be performed by the twice-born every day, after getting up from the bed early in the morning.

उदयास्तमयं यावन्न विप्रः क्षणिको भवेत्।
नित्यनैमित्तिकैर्मुक्तः काम्यैश्चान्यैरगर्हितः॥२॥

From sunrise to sunset, a Vipra should not remain, even for a moment, without performing the daily and the obligatory rites, as also those performed with an end in view and those, not censurable.

यः स्वकर्म परित्यज्य यदन्यत् कुरुते द्विजः।
अज्ञानाद्यदि वा मोहात् स तेन पतिता भवेत्॥३॥

If a twice-born person, abandoning his own rite, performs those of another caste, either unwittingly or out of stupefaction, he becomes degraded thereby.

दिवसस्याद्यभागे तु कृत्यं तस्योपदिश्यते।
द्वितीये च तृतीये च चतुर्थे पञ्चमे तथा॥४॥
षष्ठे च सप्तमे चैव अष्टमे च पृथक् पृथक्॥
विभागेष्वेषु यत् कर्म तत् प्रवक्ष्याम्यशेषतः॥५॥

Instructions would [now] be delivered by me about what should be performed in the first part of the day. I would [also] describe in full all those different rites which should be performed in the various divisions of the day, the second, third, fourth, fifth, sixth, seventh and the eighth.

उषःकाले तु संप्राप्ते शौचं कृत्वा यथार्थवत्।
ततः स्नानं प्रकुर्वीत दन्तधावनपूर्वकम्॥६॥

When the dawn arrives, one should, after duly performing the purificatory works (*i.e.*, passing urine and excreta) and cleansing the teeth, bathe in the morning.

अत्यन्तमलिनः कायो नवच्छिद्रसमन्वितः।
स्रवत्येष दिवारात्रौ प्रातःस्नानं विशोधनम्॥७॥

Bathing in the morning is the purifier of the highly dirty body, having nine apertures, [and] passing [urine and excreta] day and night.

क्लिद्यन्ति हि प्रसुप्तस्य इन्द्रियाणि स्रवन्ति च।
अङ्गानि समतां यान्ति उत्तमान्यधमैः सह॥८॥

The organs of a sleeping person become moistened and pass discharges. The superior organs thereby come to the level of the inferior ones.

नानास्वेदसमाकीर्णः शयनादुस्थितः पुमान्।
अस्नात्वा नाचरेत् कर्म जपहोमादि किञ्चन॥९॥

Besmeared with sweat and perspiration, one gets up from the bed. Therefore without bathing, one must not perform any religious rite, such as, the recitation of the *Mantras*, the celebration of *Homa*, etc.

प्रातरुत्थाय यो विप्र प्रातःस्नायी भवेत् सदा।
समस्तजन्मजं पापं त्रिभिर्वर्षैर्व्यपोहति॥१०॥

If a Vipra, getting up from the bed at dawn, takes his daily bath early in the morning for three years, he has the sins of his entire birth dissipated.

उषस्युषसि यत् स्नानं सन्ध्यायामुदिते रवौ।
प्राजापत्येन तत्तुल्यं महापातकनाशनम्॥११॥

Bathing in the morning, at the period of conjunction when the Sun rises, is equal to the [penitential rite of] *Prājāpatya* in the destruction even of mighty iniquities.

प्रातःस्नानं प्रशंसन्ति दृष्टादृष्टकरं हि तत्।
सर्वमर्हति पूतात्मा प्रातःस्नायी जपादिकम्॥१२॥

The *Ṛṣis* highly speak of early bathing in the morning; for it yields fruits seen and unseen. One who bathes in the morning with his soul purified is entitled to perform all, such as, the recitation of the *Mantras*, etc.

स्नानादनन्तरं तावदुपस्पर्शनमुच्यते।
अनेन तु विधानेन आचान्तः शुचितामियात्॥१३॥

It is said that one should rinse the mouth after bathing. By performing the *Ācamanam* (rinsing), according to the following regulations, one attains to purification.

प्रक्षाल्य पादौ हस्तौ च त्रिः पिबेदम्बु वीक्षितम्।
संवृत्याङ्गुष्ठमूलेन द्विः प्रमृज्यात्ततो मुखम्॥१४॥

Having washed both the hands and feet, one should drink water thrice, after seeing it carefully. Then one should rub the mouth twice, with the thumb curved a little.

संहत्य तिसृभिः पूर्वमास्यमेवमुपस्पृशेत्।
ततः पादौ समभ्यक्ष्य अङ्गानि समुस्पृशेत्॥१५॥

Having sprinkled his two feet completely with water, one should touch ones limbs with the fingers. Thereafter, one should touch the two nostrils with the thumb and the forefinger. Sprinkling water thrice, one should touch ones face. Then sprinkling the feet completely with water, one should touch the limbs.

अङ्गुष्ठेन प्रदेशिन्या घ्राणं पश्चादनन्तरम्।
अङ्गुष्ठानामिकाभ्याञ्च चक्षुःश्रोत्रे पुनः पुनः॥१६॥

Thereafter, one should touch the nose with the thumb and the forefinger. And with the thumb and the nameless one, one should repeatedly touch the eyes and the ears.

कनिष्ठाऽङ्गुष्ठाया नाभिं हृदयञ्च तलेन वै।
सर्वाभिस्तु शिरः पश्चाद्बाहू चाग्रेण संस्पृशेत्॥१७॥

Then one should touch the navel with the thumb and the little finger; the breast, with the right palm; then the head, with all the fingers; and the arms, with the tops of all the fingers.

सन्ध्यायाञ्च प्रभाते च मध्याह्ने च ततः पुनः।
सन्ध्यां नोपासते यस्तु ब्राह्मणो हि विशेषतः।
स जीवन्नेव शूद्रः स्यान्मृतः श्वा चैव जायते॥१८॥

That Brāhmaṇa in particular, who does not perform his *Sandhyā*-adorations, in the evening, morning and the noon, becomes in his lifetime like a Śūdra. After his death, he is born as a dog.

सन्ध्याहीनोऽशुचिर्नित्यमनर्हः सर्वकर्मसु।
यदन्यत् कुरुते कर्म न तस्य फलमश्नुते॥१९॥

One, who does not perform the *Sandhyā*-adorations, is always impure and is unworthy of all religious rites. The fruit, of any religious rite that he may perform, goes not to him.

सन्ध्याकर्मावसाने तु स्वयं होमो विधीयते।
स्वयं होमे फलं यत्तु तदन्येन न जायते॥२०॥

After the termination of the *Sandhyā*-adoration, one should himself perform a *Homa*. The fruit, which one reaps by himself performing the *Homa*, is not attained if it is performed by another.

ऋत्विक्पुत्रो गुरुर्भ्राता भागिनेयोऽथ विट्पतिः।
एभिरेव हुतं यत्तु तद्धुतं स्वयमेव हि॥२१॥

When a *Homa* is performed by any of these– a *Ṛtvik*, a son, the preceptor, a brother, a daughters son, and a son-in-law, it is equal to that performed by ones own self.

देवकार्यं ततः कृत्वा गुरुमङ्गलवीक्षणम्।
देवकार्याणि पूर्वाह्ने मनुष्याणाञ्च मध्यमे॥२२॥
पितृणामपराह्ने च कार्याण्येतानि यत्नतः॥२३॥

Having performed the sacrifice for the Deities, one should, thereafter, adore the preceptor and look at the auspicious articles. The rites for the Deities should be performed in the first part of the day; that for men, in the middle part; that for the departed Manes, in the afternoon; all these rites are to be performed with great care.

पौर्वाह्निकं तु यत् कर्म यदि तत् सायमाचरेत्।
न तस्य फलमाप्नोति वन्ध्यास्त्रीमैथुनं यथा॥२४॥

If one performs a rite in the evening which should be performed in the morning, he reaps no fruit thereby as a barren woman by sexual intercourse.

दिवस्याद्यभागे तु सर्वमेतद्विधीयते।
द्वितीये च तथा भागे वेदाभ्यासो विधीयते॥२५॥

It is laid down that all the rites should be performed in the first part of the day. And the Vedas, it is laid down should be studied in the second part.

वेदाभ्यासो हि विप्राणां परमं तप उच्यते।
ब्रह्मयज्ञः स विज्ञेयः षडङ्गसहितस्तु सः॥२६॥

The study of the Vedas is spoken of as the highest austerity for the Vipras. The study of the Vedas with its six auxiliaries is to be known as *Brahma-Yajña*.

वेदस्वीकरणं पूर्वं विचारोऽभ्यसनं जपः।
ततो दानश्च शिष्येभ्यो वेदाभ्यासो हि पञ्चधा॥२७॥

The first is the admission [of the superiority] of the Vedas; then discussion [on the Vedas], then the study, then the recitation [of the Vedas], and then the deliverance of instructions unto the disciples. This is the fivefold practice of the Vedas.

समित् पुष्पकुशादीनां स कालः समुदाहृतः।
तृतीये चैव भागे तु पोष्यवर्गार्थसाधनम्॥२८॥

This time (*i.e.*, the second part of the day) is also spoken of as the fittest time for the gathering of sacrificial fuels, flowers, *Kuśa*, etc. In the third part of the day, means, for acquiring riches and supporting the dependants, should be thought of.

पिता माता गुरुर्भार्या प्रजा दीनाः समाश्रिताः।
अभ्यागतोऽतिथिश्चान्यः पोष्यवर्ग उदाहृतः॥२९॥

The father, the mother, the preceptor, the wife, the children, the poor people, the dependants, the incomers and the guests, are spoken of as the *Poṣyas* (*i.e.*, those who should be supported).

ज्ञातिर्बन्धुजनः क्षीणस्तथानाथः समाश्रितः।
अन्येऽप्यधनयुक्ताश्च पोष्यवर्ग उदाहृतः॥३०॥

Kinsmen, relatives, those suffering from diseases, who have none to look after them, those who seek refuge and others having no means, are also spoken of as the *Posyas*.

भरणं पोष्यवर्गस्य प्रशस्तं स्वर्गसाधनम्।
नरकः पीडने चास्य तस्माद्यत्नेन तं भरेत्॥३१॥

To support the *Posyas*, is the most excellent expedient for attaining to the celestial region. By oppressing them, one goes to hell. Therefore one should support them with care.

सार्वभौतिकमन्नाद्यं कर्त्तव्यन्तु विशेषतः।
ज्ञानविद्भ्यः प्रदातव्यमन्यथा नरकं व्रजेत्॥३२॥

One should especially offer boiled rice unto all creatures. One should make presents unto the learned, or else he would go to hell.

स जीवति य एवैको बहुभिश्चोपजीव्यते।
जीवन्तो मृतकाश्चान्ये य आत्मम्भरयो नराः॥३३॥

Blessed is his life, who alone is the instrument of support unto many. Those men are like the dead, although alive, who live for themselves only.

बह्वर्थे जीव्यते कश्चित् कुटुम्बार्थे तथा पराः।
आत्मार्थेऽन्यो न शक्नोति स्वोदरेणापि दुःखितः॥३४॥

Some live for many; others live for their kith and kin; others [only] for themselves. And some cannot, with difficulty [even], support themselves.

दीनानाथविशिष्टेभ्यो दातव्यं भूतिमिच्छता।
अदत्तदाना जायन्ते परभाग्योपजीविनः॥३५॥

One desiring for lordly powers, should make gifts unto the poor, the helpless and the learned. By making gifts unto unworthy persons, people are born dependant on anothers fortune.

यद्ददाति विशिष्टेभ्यो यज्जुहोति दिने दिने।
तत्तु वित्तमहं मन्ये शेषं कस्यापि रक्षति।
चतुर्थे च तथा भागे स्नानार्थं मृदमाहरेत्॥३६॥

I consider that wealth, which one presents unto worthy persons and which one offers every day in *Homa*, as the true wealth. The rest belongs to some body else which one merely protects. In the fourth part of the day, one should fetch earth for bathing.

तिलपुष्पकुशादीनि स्नानञ्चाकृत्रिमे जले।
नित्यं नैमित्तिकं काम्यं त्रिविधं स्नानमुच्यते॥३७॥

[One should in the same part of the day, collect] sesame, flowers, *Kuśa*, etc. One should bathe in the natural water. Bathing has been spoken of as being threefold, viz., *Nitya* (daily), *Naimittika* (obligatory, as in the solar or lunar eclipse), and *Kāmya* (having an end, such as the attainment of the celestial region in view).

तेषां मध्ये तु यन्नित्यं तत् पुनर्भिद्यते त्रिधा।
मलापहरणं पश्चान्मन्त्रवत्तु जले स्मृतम्॥३८॥

Of them that which is *Nitya* (daily), divides itself again into three :– (1) *malāpaharaṇam* (that which removes the dirt of the body); (2) the next is the one which is done after reciting the *Mantras*.

सन्ध्यास्नानमुभाभ्याञ्च स्नानभेदाः प्रकीर्त्तिताः।
मार्ज्जनं जलमध्ये तु प्राणायामो यतस्ततः॥३९॥

[The third] is the bathing at the two periods of junction. These are the divisions of bathing described. *Mārjanam* (sprinkling the person with water by means of the hands) should be made in the water. *Prāṇāyāma* may be practised anywhere.

उपस्थानं ततः पश्चात् सावित्र्या जप उच्यते।
सविता देवता यस्या मुखमग्निस्त्रिधा स्थितः॥४०॥

Then adorations should be offered to the Sun; afterwards the recitation of the *Gāyatrī* is spoken of. The Sun is the Deity of the

Gāyatrī at whose mouth the threefold Fire is stationed.

विश्वामित्र ऋषिश्छन्दो गायत्री सा विशिष्यते।
पञ्चमे च तथा भागे संविभागो यथाऽर्हत:।।४१।।

The *Ṛsis* (Saintly Author) is Viśvāmitra and the metre is *Gāyatrī*. Sāvitrī is thus qualified. In the fifth part of the day, due divisions should be made.

पितृदेवमनुष्याणां कीटानाश्चोपदिश्यते।
देवैश्चैव मनुष्यैश्च तिर्यग्भिश्चोपजीव्यते।।४२।।
गृहस्थ: प्रत्यहं यस्मात्तस्माज्ज्येष्ठाश्रमी गृही।
त्रयाणामाश्रमाणान्तु गृहस्थी योनिरुच्यते।।४३।।

[Divisions of food should be made] for the departed Manes, the Deities, the mankind and the insects etc. Such is the deliverance [of Dakṣa]. Since a house holder gives daily sustenance unto the Deities, the human beings and the bipeds, the order of a *Gṛhastha* is, therefore the foremost of all *Āśramas*. The order of a householder is spoken of, as the source of the three other *Āśramas*.

तेनैव सीदमानेन सीदन्तीहेतरे त्रय:।
मूलप्राणो भवेत् स्कन्ध: स्कन्धाच्छाखा: सपल्लवा:।।४४।।

That being deteriorated, the other three also become subject to decay. A trunk has the root for its life, the branches have the trunk, and the leaves have the branches, [for their life].

मूलेनैव विनष्टेन सर्वमेतद्विनश्यति।
तस्मात् सर्वप्रयत्नेन रक्षितव्यो गृहाश्रमी।।४५।।

The root being destroyed, all these meet with destruction. A householder should therefore be protected with every case.

राजा चान्यैस्त्रिभि: पूज्यो माननीयश्च सर्वदा।
गृहस्थोऽपि क्रियायुक्तो न गृहेण गृहाश्रमी।।४६।।

He is to be reverenced and adored by the king and the three other castes, [except the Brāhmaṇa[. He is called a householder who performs the duties of the order. A householder [does not become a householder] by [merely possessing] a house.

न चैव पुत्रदारेण स्वकर्मपरिवर्जितः।
अस्नात्वा चाप्यहुत्वा चाजप्त्वादत्त्वा च मानवः॥४७॥

A man, neglecting his own duties and failing to bathe, offer oblations to the Fire, recite the *Mantras* and make gifts, does not become [a householder] by [merely having] a son and a wife.

देवादीनामृणी भूत्वा नरकं प्रतिपद्यते।
एक एव हि भुङ्क्तेऽन्नमपरोऽन्नेन भुज्यते॥४८॥

By being indebted to the Deities and others,[1] one goes to hell. One who eats alone, is the taker of food, while the other [who shares it with many], is the feeder of others.

न भुज्यते स एवैको यो भुङ्क्तेऽन्नं स साक्षिणा।
विभागशीलो यो नित्यं क्षमायुक्तो दयापरः॥४९॥
देवतातिथिभक्तश्च गृहस्थः स तु धार्मिकः।
दया लज्जा क्षमा श्रद्धा प्रज्ञा योगः कृतज्ञता॥५०॥
एते यस्य गुणाः सन्ति स गृही मुख्य उच्यते॥
संविभागं ततः कृत्वा गृहस्थः शेषभुग्भवेत्॥५१॥

[The difference between these two, is :-] He, who only takes food for himself, [lives alone for himself and] does not feed others. He, who makes allotments [of food unto the guests], is forgiving, compassionate, devoted to the Deities and guests, is a pious householder. He is spoken as the leading householder in whom exists these accomplishments, viz.,- mercy, bashfulness, forgiveness, reverential faith, discriminative knowledge, practice of Yoga and gratitude. Having made an allotment [of the food], a householder should partake of the residue.

---

1. This refers to the various debts which a man is to satisfy. The debt to the Deities; one satisfies by performing religious rites; the debt to the departed Manes, one satisfies by performing the *Śrāddha*; the debt to the *Ṛṣis*, one satisfies by making religious studies; and the debt to mankind, one satisfies by feeding them.

भुक्त्वा तु सुखमास्थाय तदन्नं परिणामयेत्।
इतिहासपुराणाद्यैः षष्ठञ्च सप्तमं नयेत्॥५२॥

Having partaken of the food and sat at ease, he should digest the same. He should then spend the sixth and seventh parts of the day in the study of the *Itihāsas* and the *Purāṇas*.

अष्टमे लोकयात्रा तु बहिः सन्ध्या ततः पुनः।
होमं भोजनकञ्चैव यच्चान्यद्गृहकृत्यकम्॥५३॥

In the eighth part [of the day], temporal affairs should be attended to. Then, again, he should adore the fire in the evening. He should next perform *Homa*, take meals and finish other household works.

कृत्वा चैवं ततः पश्चात् स्वाध्यायं किंचिदाहरेत्।
प्रदोषपश्चिमौ यामौ वेदाभ्यासेन तौ नयेत्॥७१॥

Having performed [all the duties] , one should, afterwards, study the Vedas a little. One should spend the two periods of time after *Pradoṣa* (nightfall) in the study of the Vedas.

यामद्वयं शयानो हि ब्रह्मभूयाय कल्पते।
नैमित्तिकानि काम्यानि निपतन्ति यथा यथा॥५५॥
तथा तथैव कार्याणि न कालस्तु विधीयते।
अस्मिन्नेव प्रयुञ्जानो ह्यस्मिन्नेव तु लीयते॥५६॥

He, who then sleeps for the next two periods, is competent to attain to Brāhmaṇa. Occasional rites and those undertaken with a particular aim, one may perform at any time whatsoever when the necessity arises. No fixed time is laid down for them. One, being born in this world, shall have to meet with death here.

तस्मात् सर्वप्रयत्नेन कर्त्तव्यं सुखमिच्छता।
सर्वत्र मध्यमौ यामौ हुतशेषं हविश्च यत्॥५७॥
भुञ्जानश्च शयानश्च ब्राह्मणो नावसीदति।

One wishing for happiness, should, therefore, perform all the duties with every care. The middle period is the best for all the rites. By partaking of the clarified butter left as raiment of the offering of oblation, and going to sleep in due time, a Brāhmaṇa has never to suffer from any physical disabilities.

॥ इति दाक्षस्मृतौ द्वितीयोऽध्याय:॥२॥

Chapter 3

सुधा नव गृहस्थस्य शब्दयामि नवैव तु।
तथैव नव कर्माणि विकर्माणि तथा नव॥१॥

A householder has nine *Sudhās*. I shall express these nine in words. Similarly there are nine [proper] acts and nine [improper] acts.

प्रच्छन्नानि नवान्यानि प्रकाश्यानि तथा नव।
सफलानि नवान्यानि निष्फलानि नवैव तु॥२॥

Secret deeds are nine; open works are nine; successful works are nine; and unsuccessful works are also nine.

अदेयानि नवान्यानि वस्तुजातानि सर्वदा।
नवका नव निर्दिष्टा गृहस्थोन्नतिकारका:॥४॥

There are nine objects which are never to be given away [by a householder]. These groups of nine always lead to the aggrandisement of a householder.

सुधावस्तूनि वक्ष्यामि विशिष्टे च गृहमागते।
मनश्चक्षुर्मुखं वाक्यं सौम्यं दद्याच्चतुष्टयम्॥४॥
अभ्युत्थानमिहागच्छ पृच्छालापप्रियान्वित:।
उपासनमनुव्रज्या कार्याण्येतानि यत्नत:॥५॥

I shall now describe the *Sudhā*-articles. When any distinguished person comes to the house, one should gently offer these four,- the mind, the eye, the face and the words. One should rise up and say, "come here'', carry on a pleasant conversation, saying, "welcome''; treat him with food; and follow him. [All] these works should be carefully [performed].

ईषद्दानानि चान्यानि भूमिरापस्तृणानि च।

पादशौचं तथाऽभ्यङ्गमाश्रयः शयनं तथा॥६॥
किञ्चिद्यान्नं यथाशक्ति नास्यानश्नन् गृहे वसेत्।
मृज्जलश्चार्थिने देयमेतान्यपि सदा गृहे॥७॥

Other minor gifts [are:]– [pointing out of] a place [for sitting]; [offering of] water [for washing the feet]; [offering of] a *Kuśa*-seat; washing the feet; [offering of] oil for rubbing the body; [offering of] a bed; [and offering of] food, according to ones might. A householder should not take his food before his guest is fed, the offering of earth and water; all these, a householder should always perform.

सन्ध्या स्नानं जपो होमः स्वाध्यायो देवताऽर्च्चनम्।
वैश्वदेवं तथातिथ्यमुद्धतश्चापि शक्तितः॥८॥
पितृदेवमनुष्याणां दीनानाथतपस्विनाम्।
मातापितृगुरूणाञ्च संविभागो यथार्हतः॥९॥
एतानि नव कर्माणि विकर्माणि तथा पुनः।
अनृतं पारदार्यं तथाभक्षस्य भक्षणम्।॥१०॥
अगम्यागभनापेयपानं स्तेयञ्च हिंसनम्।
अश्रौतकर्माचरणं मित्रधर्मबहिष्कृतम्॥११॥
नवैतानि विकर्माणि तानि सर्वाणि वर्ज्जयेत्।
आयुर्वित्तं गृहच्छिद्रं मन्त्रमैथुनभेषजम्॥१२॥
तपो दानावमानौ च नव गोप्यानि यत्नतः।
आरोग्यमृणशुद्धिश्च दानाध्ययनविक्रयाः॥१३॥
कन्यादानं वृषोत्सर्गो रहःपापमकुत्सनम्।
प्रकाश्यानि नवैतानि गृहस्थाश्रमिणस्तथा॥१४॥

Sandhyā-adorations, bathing, recitation of the *Gāyatrī, Homa*, Vedic study, adorations of the Deities, adoration of the *Vaiśvadevas,* hospitable treatment extended to the guests, according to ones own might, proper allotment of food for the departed Manes, Deities, human beings, the poor, the helpless, the ascetics, the father, the mother and the preceptor,- these are the nine [sacred] works. Iniquitous deeds are, again, [the following:–] Falsehood, knowing anothers wife, taking forbidden food, knowing a woman who should not be known, drinking what should not be drunk, theft, committing injury, doing works not sanctioned in the *Śruti*, transgression of a friends duty,- these are nine improper deeds. One should avoid them all. Longevity, wealth, weakness of a house, counsel, sexual intercourse, medicine, austerity, charity and honour,- these nine should be carefully kept secret. Freedom from a disease, satisfaction of a debt, gift, study, sale, giving away a daughter in marriage, dedication of a bull, secret sin and the act of not being censured by others, these nine should be publicly done by a householder.

मातापित्रोर्गुरौ मित्रे विनीते चोपकारिणि।
दीनानाथविशिष्टेभ्यो दत्तन्तु सफलं भवेत्॥१५॥

What is presented as a gift to the father, to the mother, to the preceptor, to a friend, to a humble person, to one who has done any good, to the poor, to the helpless and to distinguished persons, yields fruits.

धूर्ते वन्दिनि मन्दे च कुवैद्ये कितवे शठे।
चाटुचारणचौरेभ्यो दत्तं भवति निष्फलम्॥१६॥

What is given as a present to a wicked person, to a panegyrist, to an ignorant wight, to a bad physician, to a liar, to a cheat, to a flatterer, to a wandering actor and to a thief, becomes fruitless.

सामान्यं याजितं न्यास आधिर्द्दाराश्च तद्धनम्।
क्रमायातञ्च निक्षेप: सर्वस्वञ्चान्वये सति॥१७॥
आपत्स्वपि न देयानि नव वस्तूनि सर्वदा।
यो ददाति स मूढात्मा प्रायश्चित्तीयते नर:॥१८॥

A small property, what is gained by begging, what is kept as a security, trust-money, a woman, a woman's personal property, what is inherited, whole estate and public property,- these nine articles should never be given away even in a calamity, if there is any living member in the family. That foolish wight who gives them away, is required to perform a penitential rite.

नवनवकवेत्तारमनुष्ठानपरं नरम्।
इह लोके परे च श्रीः स्वर्गस्थञ्च न मुञ्चति॥१९॥

The Goddess of Prosperity in this world and in the celestial region in the next, does not forsake a person who knows these groups of nine and performs the rites mentioned therein.

यथैवात्मा परस्तद्वद्द्रष्टव्यः सुखमिच्छता।
सुखदुःखानि तुल्यानि यथात्मनि तथा परे॥२०॥

Others should be looked upon as his own self by a person desiring for happiness. Happiness and sorrow are equal both unto ones ownself and unto others.

सुखं वा यदि वा दुःखं यत् किंचित् क्रियते परे।
ततस्तत्तु पुनः पश्चात् सर्वमात्मनि जायते॥२१॥

Happiness or sorrow, which should be afforded unto others, would afterwards again arise in ones own self.

न क्लेशेन विना द्रव्यं द्रव्यहीने कृतः क्रिया।
क्रियाहीने न धर्मः स्याद्धर्महीने कुतः सुखम्॥२२॥

No article is procurable without trouble. How can any religious rite be performed in the absence of [proper] articles? There is no religion in the absence of rites. And where is happiness in the absence of religion?

सुखं वाञ्छन्ति सर्वे हि तच्च धर्मसमुद्भवम्।
तस्माद्धर्मः सदा कार्यः सर्ववर्णैः प्रयत्नतः॥२३॥

All persons seek happiness; but that originates from religion. Therefore religion should always be carefully practised by all the castes.

न्यायागतेन द्रव्येण कर्तव्यं पारलौकिकम्।
दानञ्च विधिना देयं काले पात्रे गुणान्विते॥२४॥

A rite for the next world should be performed by articles

acquired by fair means. A gift should be duly made unto an accomplished person in proper time.

समद्विगुणसाहस्रमानन्त्यञ्च यथाक्रमम्।
दाने फलविशेषः स्याद्‌हिंसायां तावदेव तु॥२५॥

In making a gift, the particular fruit multiplies, in order, in equal number, twofold, thousand-fold and endlessly. Similar [is the fruit] in committing injury.

सममब्राह्मणे दानं द्विगुणं ब्राह्मणब्रुवे।
सहस्रगुणमाचार्ये त्वनन्तं वेदपारगे॥२६॥

Equal [is the fruit] when a gift is made unto a Brāhmaṇa,[1] a thousand-fold [when it is made unto] a preceptor; and endless, [when it is made unto] one who has mastered the Vedas.

विधिहीने तथा पात्रे यो ददाति प्रतिग्रहम्।
न केवलं तद्विनश्येच्छेषमप्यस्य नश्यति॥२७॥

Not only that which one gives unto an unworthy person who neglects all injunctions, becomes futile, but the remaining virtue is also destroyed [thereby].

व्यसनप्रतिकाराय कुटुम्बार्थञ्च याचते।
एवमन्विष्य दातव्यमन्यथा न फलं भवेत्॥२८॥

Finding out one who solicits a gift for preventing a calamity or for maintaining his relatives, one should make a gift; otherwise it would yield no fruit.

मातापितृविहीनन्तु संस्कारोद्वहनादिभिः।
यः स्थापयति तस्येह पुण्यसंख्या न विद्यते॥२९॥

The virtue of a person, who establishes an orphan by performing the rite of investiture with the sacred thread, marriage, etc., for him, cannot be enumerated.

---

1. The Text has Brāhmaṇa *Vruve, i.e.*, one who pretends to be a Brāhmaṇa but neglects the duties of the caste. It is, however, curious how may the fruit be twofold in this case4. But we have rendered the Text literally. Perhaps the Author means Brāhmaṇa-*Śreṣthaḥ*.

न तच्छ्रेयाऽग्निहोत्रेण नाग्निष्टोमेन लभ्यते।
यच्छ्रेयः प्राप्यते पुंसा विप्रेण स्थापितेन तु॥३०॥

The well-being, which is attained by a person for settling down a Vipra, is not acquired by an *Agnihotra*, or an *Agniṣṭoma* rite.

यद्यदिष्टतमं लोके यच्चापि दयितं गृहे।
तत्तद्गुणवते देयं तदेवाक्षयमिच्छता॥३१॥

Whatever is greatly prized, whatever is the most favourite article in the house, should be given away unto a qualified person by one seeking an endless possession of all those articles.

॥ इति दाक्षस्मृतौ तृतीयोऽध्यायः॥३॥

Chapter 4

पत्नीमूलं गृहं पुंसां यदि च्छन्दोऽनुवर्त्तिनी।
गृहाश्रमसमं नास्ति यदि भार्या वशानुगा॥१॥

The household of men has the wife for its root, if she follows the Vedas; there is none equal to the domestic mode of life, if a wife is under the control of her husband.

तथा धर्मार्थकामानां त्रिवर्गफलमश्नुते।
प्राकाम्ये वर्त्तमाना तु स्नेहान्न तु निवारिता॥२॥
अवश्या सा भवेत् पश्चाद्यथा व्याधिरुपेक्षितः।
अनुकूला न वाग्दुष्टा दक्षा साध्वी प्रियंवदा॥३॥
आत्मगुप्ता स्वामिभक्ता देवता सा न मानुषी॥४॥

With her, one reaps the fruits of the threefold objects of life, namely, *Dharma* (virtue), *Artha* (worldly profit) and *Kāma* (desire). If she follows her own will and is not curbed [by her husband] out of love, she becomes uncontrollable afterwards like unto a disease neglected. She who follows the will of her lord, does not give vent to evil words, is an expert, is chaste, speaks pleasant words, is protected by her own self and is devoted to her consort, is a goddess and not a woman.

अनुकूलकलत्रो यस्तस्य स्वर्ग इहैव हि।
प्रतिकूलकलत्रस्य नरको नात्र संशयः॥५॥

This world is like a celestial region unto him whose wife follows him obediently. It is like a hell unto him whose wife is against him. There is no doubt in it.

स्वर्गेऽपि दुर्लभं ह्येतदनुरागः परस्परम्।
रक्त एको विरक्ताऽन्यस्तस्मात् कष्टतरं नु किम्॥६॥

Mutual attachment [between a husband and a wife] is rare even in the celestial region. There is nothing more painful than the fact that one is attached to, and another is unfavourably disposed towards, [the other].

गृहवासः सुखार्थाय पत्नीमूलं गृहे सुखम्।
सा पत्नी या विनीता स्याच्चित्तज्ञा वशवर्त्तिनी॥७॥

The domestic mode of life is for happiness; and happiness is dependent on a wife in the house. She, who is humble, knows the mind and is under the control [of her husband], is a [real] wife.

दुःखा ह्यन्ना सदा खिन्ना चित्तभेदः परस्परम्।
प्रतिकूलकलत्रस्य द्विदारस्य विशेषतः॥८॥

Otherwise she always becomes miserable and disappointed. Disagreement of the mind always takes place when a person has a wife always going against him and specially when he has two wives.

योषित् सर्वा जलौकैव भूषणाच्छादनाशनैः।
सुभूत्यापि कृता नित्यं पुरुषं ह्यपकर्षति॥९॥

All wives are like leeches. Even if daily gratified with ornaments, dresses and food, they never cease to extort a man.

जलौका रक्तमादत्ते केवलं सा तपस्विनी।
इतरा तु धनं वित्तं मांसं वीर्यं बलं सुखम्॥१०॥

That small leecher merely sucks the blood while the other draws the wealth, property, flesh, energy, strength and the happiness of a man.

सशङ्का बालभावे तु यौवने विमुखी भवेत्।
भृत्यवन्मन्यते पश्चाद्वृद्धभावे स्वकं पितम्॥११॥

In childhood, she always remains afraid; in youth, she becomes disobedient; and afterwards in old age, she considers her own husband as a servant.

अनुकूला न वाग्दुष्टा दक्षा साध्वी पतिव्रता।
एभिरेव गुणैर्युक्ता श्रीरेव स्त्री न संशयः॥१२॥

Obedient, unsullied by harsh speech, expert, chaste and devoted to her husband, a wife, endued with all these accomplishments, is forsooth, the Goddess of Prosperity personified.

या हृष्टमनसा नित्यं स्थानमानविचक्षणा।
भर्तुः प्रीतिकरौ नित्यं सा भार्या हीतरा जरा॥१३।

She, who is always of a delighted mind, acquainted with the position and number of household articles, and always affords satisfaction unto her husband, is the [real] wife; others are like decrepitude.

शिष्यो भार्या, शिशुर्भ्राता पुत्रो दासः समाश्रितः।
यस्यैतानि विनीतानि तस्य लोके हि गौरवम्॥१४॥

Glory is for that person in this world, whose disciple, wife, little child, brothers, grown up son, servants and dependants are all humble.

प्रथमा धर्मपत्नी च द्वितीया रतिवर्धिनी।
दृष्टमेव फलं तत्र नादृष्टमुपजायते॥१५॥

The first is the *Dharmapatnī* (*i.e.*, a wife helping in the acquisition of virtue); the second is for increasing lust. In the latter, originates the fruit that is seen, but not what is not seen (*i.e.*, virtue).

धर्मपत्नी समाख्याता निर्दोषा यदि सा भवेत्।
दोषे सति न दोषः स्यादन्या भार्या गुणान्विता॥१६॥

If she (*i.e.*, the first wife) be freed from any short-comings, she is called *Dharmapatnī*. If she suffers from any defect, there would be no sin in accepting a second one [for as such], if she happens to be endued with accomplishments.

अदुष्टांपतितां भार्यां यौवने यः परित्यजेत्।

स जीवनान्ते स्त्रीत्वं च वन्ध्यत्वं च समाप्नुयात्॥१७॥

He, who renounces, in youth, a wife who is free from any fault and is not degraded, will attain, after death, to womanhood and become barren.

दरिद्रं व्याधितश्चैव भर्तारं यावमन्यते।

शुनी गृध्री च मकरी जायते सा पुनः पुनः॥१८॥

A woman who forsakes her poor or diseased husband, is repeatedly born either as a bitch, a vulture, or a shark.

मृते भर्त्तरि या नारी समारोहेदधुताशनम्।

सा भवेत् तु शुभाचारा स्वर्गलोके महीयते॥१९॥

A woman, who, after the demise of her husband, ascends the funeral pyre, becomes of good conduct and lives gloriously in the celestial region.

व्यालग्राही यथा व्यालं बलादुद्धरते विलात्।

तथा सा पतिमुद्धृत्य तेनैव सह मोदते॥२०॥

As a snake-catcher forcibly takes out a snake from a hole, so she, rescuing her husband [from hell, lives happily with him].

॥ इति दक्षस्मृतौ चतुर्थोऽध्यायः॥४॥

Chapter 5

उक्तं शौचमशौचञ्च कार्यं त्याज्यं मनीषिभिः।

विशेषार्थं तयोः किञ्चिद्वक्ष्यामि हितकाम्यया॥१॥

What is pure and what is impure have been spoken of; [what is pure], should be done; [and what is impure], should be avoided by intelligent men. Wishing for your good, I shall speak a little on their significance.

शौचे यत्नः सदा कार्यः शौचमूलो द्विजः स्मृतः।
शौचाचारविहीनस्य समस्ता निष्फलाः क्रियाः॥२॥

Care should always be bestowed on the purificatory rites. The purificatory rite has been described in the *Smṛti* as the root of the twice-born. All the rites of a person, who is divorced from the purity of conduct, become futile.

शौचञ्च द्विविधं प्रोक्तं बाह्यमाभ्यन्तरं तथा।
मृज्जलाभ्यां स्मृतं बाह्यं भावशुद्धिस्तथान्तरम्॥३।

Purity is being spoken of as being twofold,- external and internal. It is said in the *Smṛti* that external purity [is effected] by earth, water, etc. Purity of thought is internal [purity].

आशौचाद्धि वरं बाह्यं तस्मादाभ्यन्तरं वरम्।
उभाभ्याञ्च शुचिर्यस्तु स शुचिर्नेतरः शुचिः॥४॥

External purity is superior to impurity; and internal purity is superior to that (*i.e.*, external purity). He who is pure in both (*i.e.*, externally and internally), is [said to be] in a state of purity and no one else.

एका लिङ्गे गुदे तिस्रो दश वामकरे तथा।
उभयोः सप्त दातव्या मृदस्तिस्रस्तु पादयोः॥५॥

Earth should be given once in the generative organ; thrice, in the anus; ten times, in the left palm; seven times, in both the palms, and thrice, on the feet.

गृहस्थे शौचमाख्यातं त्रिष्वन्येषु यथाक्रमम्।
द्विगुणं त्रिगुणञ्चैव चतुर्थस्य चतुर्गुणम्॥६॥

This is the purification, spoken of, for a householder; for [the followers of] the other three [orders], it is, in order, twofold, threefold and fourfold for the fourth [order].

अर्द्धप्रसृतिमात्रन्तु प्रथमा मृत्तिका स्मृता।
द्वितीया च तृतीया च तदर्द्धं परिकीर्तिता॥७॥

The earth [that is to be applied to the] first (*i.e.*, the generative organ) should be half-a-handful as described in the *Smṛti*; for the second and the third, it has been described half of each.

लिङ्गेऽप्यत्र समाख्याता त्रिपर्वी पूर्यते यथा।
एतच्छौचं गृहस्थानां द्विगुणं ब्रह्मचारिणाम्॥८॥
त्रिगुणन्तु वनस्थानां यतीनाञ्च चतुर्गुणम्।
दातव्यमुदकं तावन्मृदभावो यथा भवेत्॥९॥

The earth with which three knots of a finger are filled up, has been described for being applied to the generative organ. This purification is for the householders. Twice as much is for the *Brahmacārins*. Threefold is for the forest-recluses and fourfold for the *Yatins*. Water should be used as long as the earth is not washed off.

मृदा जलेन शुद्धिः स्यान्न क्लेशो न धनव्ययः।
यस्य शौचेऽपि शैथिल्यं चित्तं तस्य परीक्षितम्॥१०॥

Purification is effected by earth and water. There is no trouble nor [is there any] expenditure of money. His mind has been examined[1] who is lax in the matter of purification.

एतदेव दिवा शौचः रात्रवन्यद्विधीयते।
अन्यदापत्सु विप्राणामन्यदेव ह्यनापदि॥११॥

This is the purification for the day-time. Another is laid down for the night. One method obtains for the Vipras at the time of calamity, and another when they are at ease.

दिवोदितस्य शौचस्य रात्रावर्द्धं विधीयते।
तदर्द्धमातुरस्याहुस्त्वरायामर्द्धमध्वनि॥१२॥

A half of the purification which is necessary in the day-time, is laid down for the night. Half of it, is for a diseased person; and a half of it, for him who is in a hurry to go in the middle of a road.

---

1. *i.e.*, He who is not inclined to undergo the purifying process, for it is neither troublesome nor expensive.

न्यूनाधिकं न कर्तव्यं शौचं शुद्धिमभीप्सता।
प्रायश्चित्तं न युज्येत विहतातिक्रमे कृते॥१३॥

More or less should not be done, in the matter of purification, by him who wishes for purity. There is no penance for the transgression of the established practice.

॥ इति दक्षस्मृतौ पञ्चमोऽध्यायः॥५॥

Chapter 6

सूतकन्तु प्रवक्ष्यामि जन्ममृत्युसमुद्भवम्।
यावज्जीवं तृतीयन्तु यथावदनुपूर्वशः॥१॥

I shall now describe, fully and in order of precedence, the impurity arising from birth or death, as well as that which lasts for life.

सद्यः शौचं तथैकाहो द्वित्रिचतुरहस्तथा।
दशाहो द्वादशाहश्च पक्षो मासस्तथैव च॥२॥
मरणान्तं तथा चान्यद्दशपक्षन्तु सूतके।
उपन्यस्तक्रमेणैव वक्ष्याम्यहमशेषतः॥३॥

Immediate purification, one lasting for a day; those for two, three, four, ten and twelve, days; that for a fortnight; that for a month; and that terminating with death; these ten form the fixed time of impurity. I shall, in due order, describe them fully.

ग्रन्थार्थतो विजानाति वेदमङ्गैः समन्वितम्।
संकल्पं सरहस्यञ्च क्रियावांश्चेन्न सूतकी॥४॥

He, who is acquainted with the exposition of the Vedas together with their *Aṅgas* (six auxiliaries), *Kalpas* (Codes of Law), and their *Rahasya* (their gnostic portions) and who performs the rites laid down therein, suffers from no impurity.

राजर्त्विग्दीक्षितानाञ्च बाले देशान्तरे तथा।
व्रतिनां सत्रिणाञ्चैव सद्यःशौचं विधीयते॥५॥

Immediate purification is laid down for kings, sacrificial

priests, those initiated, children, for a death in a foreign country, for those engaged in a religious observance and for those engaged in a sacrifice.

एकाहस्तु समाख्यातो योऽग्निवेदसमन्वितः।
हीने हीनतरे चैव द्वित्रिचतुरहस्तथा॥६॥

One day is spoken of for him who maintains the Sacred Five and studies the Vedas. Two, three and four days, are for those who are inferior and more inferior.

जातिविप्रो दशाहेन द्वादशाहेन भूमिपः।
वैश्यः पञ्चदशाहेन शूद्रो मासेन शुध्यति॥७॥

A Brāhmaṇa, by caste, is purified in ten days; a Kṣatriya, in twelve days; a Vaiśya, in fifteen days; and a Śūdra, in a month.

अस्नात्वा चाप्यहुत्वा च भुङ्क्ते दत्वा च यः पुनः।
एवंविधस्य सर्वस्य सूतकं समुदाहृतम्॥८॥

Perpetual impurity is spoken of for all of them, who, without bathing, offering oblations to the Fire and making gifts, partake of [their] meals.

व्याधितस्य कदर्यस्य ऋणग्रस्तस्य सर्वदा।
क्रियाहीनस्य मूर्खस्य स्त्रीजितस्य विशेषतः॥९॥

Perpetual impurity is for a diseased person, a miser, one laden with debts, one who does not perform religious rites, an illiterate person, and especially for a hen-pecked person.

व्यसनासक्तचित्तस्य पराधीनस्य नित्यशः।
श्रद्धात्यागविहीनस्य भस्मान्तं सूतकं भवेत्॥१०॥

Daily impurity is for one who is addicted to gambling, etc., and for a dependant. The impurity of a person, who does not perform the *Śrāddhas*, ends with his ashes (*i.e.*, death).

न सूतकं कदाचित् स्याद्यावज्जीवन्तु सूतकम्।
एवं गुणविशेषेण सूतकं समुदाहृतम्॥११॥

Temporary impurity is not for them, but a lifelong one. Thus impurity, according to the differentiation of merits has been spoken of.

सूतके मृतके चैव तथा च मृतसूतके।

एतत्संहतशौचानां मृतशौचेन शुध्यति।।१२।।

If an impurity, consequent on birth, takes place with that of one arising from death; or if an impurity, originating from death, happens with that of birth– in a case of such a combined impurity, one is purified with [the end of the] impurity consequent on death.

दानं प्रतिग्रहो होमः स्वाध्यायश्च निवर्तते।

दशाहात्तु परं शौचं विप्रोऽर्हति च धर्मवित्।।१३।।

To make gifts, to accept presents, *Homa* and Vedic study are stopped in a state of impurity. A Vipra, conversant with sacrifices, deserves purification after the tenth day.

दानञ्च विधिना देयमशुभात्तारकं हि तत्।

मृतकान्ते मृतो यस्तु सूतकान्ते च सूतकम्।।१४।।

एतत् संहतशौचानां पूर्वाशौचेन शुध्यति।

उभयत्र दशाहानि कुलस्यान्नं न भुज्यते।।१५।।

Gifts should be duly made, for it saves one from inauspiciousness. If any impurity, consequent on death, takes place within the time of a similar one, and that arising from birth happens in the course of a like one, in cases of such combined impurities, one is purified at the end of the previous one. In both the cases, within ten days, one should not partake of any food of the family [laden with such an impurity].

चतुर्थेऽहनि कर्त्तव्यमस्थिसंचयनं द्विजैः।

ततः संचयनादूर्ध्वमङ्गस्पर्शो विधीयते।।

On the fourth day, the bones should be deposited by the twice-born. The touching of the limbs is laid down after the depositing of the bones.

वर्णानामानुलोम्येन स्त्रीणामेको यदा पतिः।
दशषट्त्र्यहमेकाहः प्रसवे सूतकं भवेत्॥१७॥

If one husband takes wives from all the castes in their natural order, then on the occasion of the child-birth, impurity extends over ten, six, three and one, days respectively.

यज्ञकाले विवाहे च देशभङ्गे तथैव च।
हूयमाने तथाग्नौ च नाशौचं मृतसूतके॥१८॥

There would be no impurity, consequent on a birth or death, when a sacrifice is being performed, or a marriage is being solemnized, when there is a revolution in the country, or a *Homa* is being performed.

सुस्थकाले त्विदं सर्वमशौचं परिकीर्त्तितम्।
आपद्गतस्य सर्वस्य सूतके न तु सूतकम्॥१९॥

All these impurities have been spoken of for the time, place and case. There is no impurity for a person who is visited with a calamity.

॥ इति दक्षस्मृतौ षष्ठोऽध्यायः॥६॥

Chapter 7

लोको वशीकृतो येन येन चात्मा वशीकृतः।
इन्द्रियार्थो जितो येन तं योगं प्रब्रवीम्यहम्॥१॥

I shall now describe that Yoga by which the universe, the soul and the senses are brought under control.

प्राणायामस्तथा ध्यानं प्रत्याहारस्तु धारणा।
तर्कश्चैव समाधिश्च षडङ्गो योग उच्यते॥२॥

Prāṇāyāma (suspension of the breath), *Dhyāna* (meditation), *Pratyāhāra* (withdrawal of the mind from external objects), *Dhāraṇā* (concentration), *Tarka* (abstract reasoning) and *Samādhi* (absorption of thought into the Supreme Spirit), are called the six *Aṅgas* (steps) of Yoga.

नारण्यसेवनाद्योगो नानेकग्रन्थचिन्तनात्।
व्रतैर्यज्ञैस्तपोभिश्च न योगः कस्यचिद्भवेत्।।३।।

Yoga does not consist in resorting to a forest; nor does it consist in thinking of many literary works; nor does Yoga is performed by religious observances, sacrifices and ascetic austerities.

न च पथ्याशनाद्योगो न नासाऽग्रनिरीक्षणात्।
न च शास्त्रातिरिक्तेन शौचेन स भवेत् क्वचित्।।४।।

Yoga does not consist in taking any particular food or in fixing ones looks on the tip of the nose. Nor does it originate from the observance of purity, more than what is mentioned in the *Śāstras*.

न मौनं मन्त्रकुहकैरनेकैः सुकृतैस्तथा।
लोकयात्राऽवियुक्तस्य योगो भवति कस्यचित्।।५।।

Nor is Yoga done by the abstention from speech, the recitation of the *Mantras* and the clever performance of the many illusory feats. Sometimes Yoga is attained by one who has disassociated himself from worldly concerns.

अभियोगात्तथाऽभ्यासात्तस्मिन्नेव तु निश्चयात्।
पुनः पुनश्च निर्वेदाद्योगः सिध्यति नान्यथा।।६।।

Yoga arises from strict concentration, practice, firm resolution, continued disgust in worldly affairs, and not by any other means.

आत्मचिन्ताविनोदेन शौचक्रीडनकेन च।
सर्वभूतसमत्वेन योगः सिध्यति नान्यथा।।७।।

Yoga is accomplished by finding pleasure in the meditation of self, by the toy of purity and by the consideration of all creatures as equal and not by any other means.

यश्चात्मनिरतो नित्यमात्मक्रीडस्तथैव च।
आत्मनिष्ठश्च सततमात्मन्येव स्वभावतः।।८।।

रतश्चैव स्वयं तुष्टः सन्तुष्टो नान्यमानसः।

आत्मन्येव सुतृप्तोऽसौ योगस्तस्य प्रसिध्यति॥९॥

He, who is devoted to self; who daily sports in self- who is given to the culture of self; who is always engaged in the meditation of self; who is by nature fond of self; who is contented; who has not his mind attached to any other object; and who is well-satisfied with self; succeeds in attaining to Yoga.

सुप्तोऽपि योगयुक्तः स्याज्जाग्रच्चापि विशेषतः।

ईदृक्चेष्टः स्मृतः श्रेष्ठो गरिष्ठो ब्रह्मवादिनाम्॥१०॥

One should be engaged in Yoga even when asleep specially when awake. In the *Smṛti,* a person, who displays such an exertion, is described as he foremost of those conversant with Brahman.

य आत्मव्यतिरेकेण द्वितीयं नैव पश्यति।

ब्रह्मभूतः स एवेह दक्षपक्ष उदाहृतः॥११॥

He, who does not see a self, is like unto Brahman. This is the deliverance of Dakṣa.

विषयासक्तचित्तो हि यतिर्मोक्षं न विन्दति।

यत्नेन विषयासक्तिं तस्माद्योगी विवर्ज्जयेत्॥१२॥

The *Yatin*, who has his mind attached to worldly objects, does not attain to *Mokṣa* (liberation); therefore a *Yogin* should carefully renounce attachment for things earthly.

विषयेन्द्रियसंयोगं केचिद्योगं वदन्ति हि।

अधर्मा धर्मरूपेण गृहीतस्तैरपण्डितैः॥१३॥

Some say that the attachment of the senses to their objects in Yoga. Irreligious is accepted as religion by these ignorant people.

मनसश्चात्मनश्चैव संयोगञ्च तथापरे।

उक्तानामधिका ह्येते केवलं योगवञ्चिताः॥१४॥

Others say that the union of the mind and the soul is Yoga. These are greater dunces than the first and are simply deprived of Yoga.

वृत्तिहीनं मनः कृत्वा क्षेत्रज्ञं परमात्मनि।
एकीकृत्य विमुच्यते योगोऽयं मुख्य उच्यते॥१५॥

By dissevering the mind from [all] its faculties and unifying the individual soul with the Supreme One, liberation is to be attained. This is spoken of as the highest Yoga.

कषायमोहविक्षेपलज्जाशङ्कादिचेतसः।
व्यापारास्तु समाख्यातास्तान् जित्वा वशमानयेत्॥१६॥

Attachment, stupefaction, distraction, bashfulness and fear, are spoken of as the operations of the mind. One should bring these under subjection.

कुटुम्बैः पञ्चभिर्ग्रामः षष्ठस्तत्र महत्तरः।
देवासुरमनुष्यैस्तु स जेतुं नैव शक्यते॥१७॥

He, who has controlled the five ordinary senses together with the higher six (*i.e.*, the mind) is incapable of being defeated by the Celestials, Asuras and the mankind.

बलेन परराष्ट्रानि गृह्णन् शूरस्तु नोच्यते।
जितो येनेन्द्रियग्रामः स शूरः कथ्यते बुधैः॥१८॥

A hero is not spoken of as one, who has forcibly taken possession of anothers kingdom; he, who has controlled all the senses, is described by the learned as a hero.

बहिर्मुखानि सर्वाणि कृत्वा चाभिमुखानि वै।
सर्वञ्चैवेन्द्रियग्रामं मनश्चात्मनि योजयेत्॥१९॥

By making all the senses, which run towards the external objects, operate internally, one should engage the mind in [the meditation of] the *Ātman* (self).

सर्वभावविनिर्मुक्तः क्षेत्रज्ञं ब्रह्मणि न्यसेत्।
एतद्ध्यानञ्च योगश्च शेषाः स्युर्ग्रन्थविस्तराः॥२०॥

Being freed from all distracting thoughts, one should consign the individual soul to the Brahman. This is *Dhyāna*, this is Yoga; the remnant is nothing but the amplification of a book.

त्यक्त्वा विषयभोगाश्च मनो निश्चलतां गतम्।
आत्मशक्तिस्वरूपेण समाधिः परिकीर्त्तितः॥२१॥

Renouncing attachment for earthly objects, where the mind becomes steadied in the form of the power of the soul, it is called *Samādhi*.

चतुर्णां सन्निकर्षेण पदं यत्तदशाश्वतम्।
द्वयोस्तु संनिकर्षेण शाश्वतं ध्रुवमक्षयम्॥२२॥

Temporary is the position that is attained by the unification of the four (viz., corporal body, subtle body, individual soul and the Supreme Soul). But eternal, real and unending is what is acquired by the union of the two (*i.e.*, the individual soul and the Supreme Soul).

यन्नास्ति सर्वलोकस्य तदस्तीति विरुध्यते।
कथ्यमानं तथान्यस्य हृदये नावतिष्ठते॥२३॥

It is a contradiction when what does not exist for all, is spoken of as existent. Therefore, that does not exist in the heart of another.

स्वसंवेद्यं हि तद्ब्रह्म कुमारी मैथुनं यथा।
अयोगी नैव जानाति जातोऽन्धो हि यथा घटम्॥२४॥

Brahma is to be known by ones own self, like cohabitation with a maiden. One, who is not a *Yogin* does not known (Brahman); as one, born blind, does not know a pitcher.

नित्याभ्यसनशीलस्य सुसंवेद्य हि तद्भवेत्।
तत् सूक्ष्मत्वादनिर्द्देश्यं परं ब्रह्म सनातनम्॥२५॥

Brahma is completely knowable by him who daily practises Yoga. The Eternal Para-Brahma is not ascertainable on account of subtleness.

बुधस्त्वाभरणं भावं मनसालोचनं यथा।
मन्यन्ते स्त्री च मूर्खश्च तदेव बहु मन्यते॥२६॥

Like mental thoughts, the learned know It (Brahman) as one.

Women and illiterate people consider it as manifold.

सत्त्वोत्कटाः सुराश्चापि विषयेण वशीकृताः।

प्रमादिभिः क्षुद्रसत्त्वैर्मानुषैरत्र का कथा॥२७॥

Even the Celestials, who are possessed of *Sattva* (harmonising tendency), are under the control of the object of the senses, what to speak of men in this respect who are under the influence of stupefaction and possessed of a very small portion of the *Sattva-guṇa*.

तस्मात् त्यक्तकषायेण कर्तव्यं दण्डधारणम्।

इतरस्तु न शक्नोति विषयैरभिभूयते॥२८॥

Therefore casting off the impurities of the mind, one should take up the staff [of a *Yogin*]; others cannot do it and become subject to the objects of the senses.

न स्थिरं क्षणमप्येकमुदकं हि यथोर्मिभिः।

वाताहतं तथा चित्तं तस्मात् तस्य न विश्वसेत्॥२९॥

The water, driven by the wind and converted into waves, does not stand still even for a moment. Therefore, one should not place confidence in any.

त्रिदण्डव्यपदेशेन जीवन्ति बहवो नराः।

यो हि ब्रह्म न जानाति न त्रिदण्डार्हं एव सः॥३०॥

Many persons drive their livelihood under the umbrage of a triple staff [*i.e.*, of being a *Sannyāsin*]; he, who does not know Brahman, is not worthy of holding the triple staff.

ब्रह्मचर्यं सदा रक्षेदष्टधा मैथुनं पृथक्

स्मरणं कीर्त्तनं केलिः प्रेक्षणं गुह्यभाषणम्॥३१॥

सङ्कल्पोऽध्यवसायश्च क्रियानिष्पत्तिरेव च।

एतन्मैथुनमष्टाङ्गं प्रवदन्ति मनीषिणः॥३२॥

[A *Yogin*] should always preserve his *Brahmacarya* [celibacy]. Sexual intercourse is of eight sorts :– viz., thinking of a woman, talking [about it], dalliance with a woman, looking [at a woman with an impure desire], speaking to her secretly, determination [for holding a sexual congress], persistent endeavour [for doing it] and the actual deed. The learned hold that these are the eight divisions of sexual intercourse.

न ध्यातव्यं न वक्तव्यं न कर्त्तव्यं कदाचन।
एतैः सर्वैः सुसम्पन्नो यतिर्भवति नेतरः॥३३॥

This should never be thought or spoken of, nor should it ever be done. One, who has mastered all these propensities, is a *Yatin*, and none else.

पारिव्राज्यं गृहीत्वा च यो धर्मे नावतिष्ठति।
श्वपदेनाङ्कयित्वा तं राजा शीघ्रं प्रवासयेत्॥३४॥

Branding him as an outcaste, the king should speedily turn him, who, having adopted the life of mendicancy, does not observe its regulations, out of his kingdom.

एको भिक्षुर्यथोक्तस्तु द्वौ चैव मिथुनं स्मृतम्।
त्रयो ग्रामस्तथा ख्यात ऊर्ध्वन्तु नगरायते॥३५॥

One [mendicant] is a *Bhikṣu*; two are called *Mithuna* in the *Smṛti*; three are called *Grāma*; and more than that, *Nagara.*

नगरं हि न कर्त्तव्यं ग्रामो वा मिथुनं तथा।
एतत्त्रयं प्रकुर्वाणः स्वधर्माच्च्यवते यतिः॥३६॥

A *Nagara, Grāma* or a *Mithuna* should not be formed [by a *Yatin*]. By doing these three, a *Yatin* transgresses his own duty.

राजवार्त्तादि तेषान्तु भिक्षावार्ता परस्परम्।
स्नेहपैशुन्यमात्सर्यं सन्निकर्षादसंशयम्॥३७॥

If they would thus come to live together, their conversation would [naturally] tend towards begging, the king, the objects of their affection, slandering and jealousy.

लाभपूजानिमित्तं हि व्याख्यानं शिष्यसंग्रहः।
एते चान्ये च बहवः प्रपञ्चाः कुतपस्विनाम्॥३८॥

The exposition of the Scriptures for lucre and adoration, the collection of disciples and many other similar displays are [in vogue] amongst the bad ascetics.

ध्यानं शौचं तथा भिक्षा नित्यमेकान्तशीलता।
भिक्षोश्चत्वारि कर्माणि पञ्चमो नोपपद्यते॥३९॥

Meditation, purification, begging alms and always living in a solitary place, these four are the duties of a *Bhikṣu*. He must not follow the fifth.

तपोजपैः कृशीभूतो व्याधितोऽवसथावहः।
वृद्धो ग्रहगृहीताश्च यश्चान्यो विकलेन्द्रियाः॥४०॥

[A Bhikṣu], emaciated by ascetic austerities and the recitation of the *Mantras*, disabled by interruptions of health, age, infirmity or decrepitude, possessed by an evil planet, deranged in intellect [may seek refuge in a house].

नीरुजश्च युवा चैव भिक्षुर्नावसथाबहः।
स दूषयति तत् स्थानं पशून् पीडयतीति च॥४१॥

But a healthy and youthful *Bhikṣu* cannot betake to a home-life; he would thereby vitiate that place and injure the learned.

नीरुजश्च युवा चैव ब्रह्मचर्यद्विनश्यति।
ब्रह्मचर्याविनष्टन्तु कुलश्चैव तु नाशयेत्॥४२॥

Such a healthy and youthful person destroys his *Brahmacarya*; when *Brahmacarya* is destroyed, his family also meets with destruction.

वसन्नावसथे भिक्षुर्मैथुनं यदि सेवते।
तस्यावसथनाथस्य मूलान्यपि निकृन्तति॥४३॥

If while living in a house, a *Bhikṣu* holds sexual intercourse then the root of the master of that house is cut off.

आश्रमे तु यतिर्यस्य मुहूर्तमपि विश्रमेत्।
किं तस्यान्येन धर्मेण कृतकृत्योऽभिजायते॥४४॥

What is the use of any other religious rite for him in whose house a *Yatin* finds shelter even for a moment? He becomes blessed thereby.

सञ्चितं यद्गृहस्थेन पापमामरणान्तिकम्।
स निर्दहति तत् सर्वमेकरात्रोषितो यतिः॥४५॥

Living even for one night, a *Yatin* consumes all the sins that are collected by a householder till his death.

योगाश्रमपरिश्रान्तं यस्तु भोजयते यतिम्।
निखिलं भोजितं तेन त्रैलोक्यं सचराचरम्॥४६॥

The three worlds, consisting of animate and inanimate creations, are fed by him who feeds a *Yatin*, laden with toil, in the order of hermitage, by the practices of Yoga.

यस्मिन् देशे वसेद्योगी ध्यानयोगविचक्षणः।
सोऽपि देशो भवेत् पूतः किं पुनस्तस्य बान्धवाः॥४७॥

The country, in which a *Yogin*, well-versed in meditation, resides, becomes purified, what to speak of his relatives?

द्वैतञ्चैव तथाद्वैतं द्वैताद्वैतं तथैव च।
न द्वैतं नापि चाद्वैतमितो तत् परमार्थिकम्॥४८॥

The thought of dualism, monism, dualism-and-monism, no-dualism and no-monism, leads to the highest acquisition.

नाहं नैवान्यसम्बन्धो ब्रह्मभावेण भावितः।
ईदृशायामवस्थायामवाप्यं परमं पदम्॥४९॥

Permeated by the thought of Brahman, one should neither think of ones self nor of his relationship with another. Obtaining such a stage, one comes by the most excellent station.

द्वैतपक्षे समाख्या ये अद्वैते तु व्यवस्थिताः।
अद्वैतानां प्रवक्ष्यामि यथा धर्मः सुनिश्चितः॥५०॥

Some firmly, believe in dualism; and some, in monism. I would describe the firmly-formed tenets of the monists.

तत्रात्मव्यतिरेकेण द्वितीयं यदि पश्यति।
ततः शास्त्राण्यधीयन्ते श्रूयन्ते ग्रन्थसञ्चयाः॥५१॥

If one sees a second object except the self, then he should study the *Śāstras* and listen to [the views contained] in innumerable books.

दक्षशास्त्रं यथा प्रोक्तमशेषाश्रममुत्तमम्।

अधीयन्ते तु ये विप्रास्ते यान्त्यमरलोकताम्।।५२।।

The Vipras, who study the Institutes of Dakṣa, containing an account of the most excellent duties of all the orders as spoken of duly, repair to the celestial religion.

इदन्तु यः पठेद्भक्त्या शृणुयादधमोऽपि वा।

स पुत्रपौत्रपशुमान् कीर्त्तिञ्च समवाप्नुयात्।।५३।।

Even if an inferior person studies and listens to it reverentially, he comes by son, grandson, animals and fame.

श्रावयित्वा त्विदं शास्त्रं श्राद्धकालेऽपि वा द्विजः।

अक्षयं भवति श्राद्धं पितृभ्यश्चोपजायते।।५४।।

If a twice-born person makes this *Dharma Śāstra* listened to by others at the time of a *Śrāddha*, it yields endless fruits and comes to the departed Manes.

।। इति दक्षस्मृतौ सप्तमोऽध्यायः।।७।।

।। दक्षस्मृतिः समाप्ता ।।

११. शातातपस्मृतिः

11. Śātātapa Smṛti

Chapter 1

प्रायश्चित्तविहीनानां महापातकिनां नृणाम्।
नरकान्ते भवेज्जन्म चिह्नाङ्कितशरीरिणाम्॥१॥

The *Mahāpātakins* who do not perform the penitentiary rites, are born, after their sufferings in hell, with bodies disfigured with the signs [of their crimes].

प्रतिजन्म भवेत्तेषां चिह्नं तत्पापसूचितम्।
प्रायश्चित्ते कृते याति पश्चात्तापवतां पुनः॥२॥

The sin-indicating signs appear in every birth but, with the performance of the penitential rites and repentance [for the commission of the sins] they disappear.

महापातकजं चिह्नं सप्तजन्मनि जायते।
उपपापोद्भवं पञ्च त्रीणि पापसमुद्भवम्॥३॥

The marks of heinous crimes appear for seven births [consecutively]; those of the *Upapātaks* (minor sins), for five; and those of other sins, for three.

दुष्कर्मजा नृणां रोगी यान्ति चोपक्रमैः शमम्।
जपैः सुरार्च्चनैर्होमैर्दानैस्तेषां शमी भवेत्॥४॥

The diseases, begotten of the iniquitous deeds of mankind, disappear with proper treatment. They are cured by the recitation of the *Gāyatrī*, adoration of the Celestials, performance of *Homa* and gifts.

पूर्वजन्मकृतं पापं नरकस्य परिक्षये।
बाधते व्याधिरूपेण तस्य जप्यादिभिः शमः॥५॥

A sin, committed in a previous birth, assails people in the shape of a disease after the termination of the sufferings in a hell.

It is dissipated by recitation etc.

कृच्छ्रञ्च राजयक्ष्मा च प्रमेहो ग्रहणी तथा।
मूत्रकृच्छ्राश्मरीकासा अतिसारभगन्दरौ।।६।।
दुष्टव्रणं गण्डमाला पक्षाघातोऽक्षिनाशनम्।
इत्येवमादयो रोगा महापापोद्भवाः स्मृताः।।७।।

Leprosy, consumption, gonorrhoea, diarrhoea, obstruction in urination, stone, cough, dysentery, fistula, obstinate ulcers, inflammation of the glands, paralysis, loss of eyes, these diseases, says the *Smṛti*, originate from the perpetration of heinous crimes.

जलोदरं यकृत् प्लीहां शूलरोगव्रणानि च।
श्वासाजीर्णज्वरच्छर्दिभ्रममोहगलग्रहाः।।८।।
रक्तार्बुदविसर्पाद्या उपपापोद्भवा गदाः।
दण्डापतानकश्चित्रवपुःकम्पविचर्चिकाः।।९।।
वल्मीकपुण्डरीकाद्यारोगाः पापसमुद्भवाः।
अर्शपाद्य नृणां रोगा अतिपापाद्भवन्ति हि।।१०।।

Dropsy, liver, spleen, colic, ulcer, short-breathing, dyspepsia, fever, cold, forgetfulness, distraction of the senses, *Galagraha* (a kind of disease), bloody tumour, dry spreading itch, are the diseases begotten of minor sins; convulsive fits, appearance of circular figures of various sizes on the body, trembling of the body, itches, elephantiasis, *Pauṇḍarīka* (a kind of leprosy) and other diseases, originate from sins. The diseases of mankind, heard by [the name of] piles, originate from *Atipāpa* (heinous crimes).

अन्ये च बहवो रोगा जायन्त पापसङ्कराः।
उच्यन्ते च निदानानि प्रायश्चित्तानि वै क्रमात्।।११।।

Various other diseases originate from the combination of sins. Their symptoms and penitentiary rites should be spoken of in due order.

महापापेषु सर्वं स्यात् तदर्द्धमुपपातके।
दद्यात् पापेषु षष्ठांशं कल्प्यं व्याधिबलाबलम्।।१२।।

In *Mahāpātakas* (gravest sins), [gifts] must be in full; in minor offences, in half; in other sins, one should give away a sixth, according to the nature of the disease and proportionate to ones power or otherwise.

अथ साधारणं तेषु गोदानादिषु कथ्यते।
गोदाने वत्सयुक्ता गौः सुशीला च पयस्विनी॥१३॥

The general rule for making a gift of kine and other rites, is this :– In the gift of a cow, it should be of a good nature, with a calf and yielding milk.

वृषदाने शुभाऽनड्वान् शुक्लाम्बरसकाञ्चनः।
निवर्त्तनानि भूदाने दश दद्याद्द्विजातये॥१४॥

In the gift of a bull, it should be endued with auspicious marks and decorated with gold and a piece of white cloth. In the gift of earth, one should give away, unto the twice-born, lands of the measurement of ten *Nivarttana*.

दशहस्तेन दण्डेन त्रिंशद्दण्डं निवर्त्तनम्।
दश तान्येव गोचर्म दत्त्वा स्वर्गे महीयते॥१५॥

A *Nivarttana* consists of thirty rods, each rod being ten cubits [in length]. Ten *Nivarttanas* makes one *Gocarma*. By making a gift [of such a piece of land], one lives gloriously in the celestial region.

सुवर्णशतनिष्कन्तु तदर्द्धार्द्धप्रमाणतः।
अश्वदाने मृदु श्लक्ष्णमश्वं सोपस्करं दिशेत्॥१६॥

Where a hundred *Niṣkas* (gold coins) are to be given away, gold, fifty or twenty *Niṣkas* in quantity, [should be given]; in the gift of a horse, one should present a quiet and good-looking animal, bedecked with ornaments.

महिषीं माहिषे दाने दद्यात् स्वर्णायुधान्विताम्।
दद्याद्गजं महादाने सुवर्णफलसंयुतम्॥१७॥

In the gift of a buffalo, one should give away a she-buffalo endued with a golden weapon. And in a great gift, one should give away an elephant with a golden fruit.

लक्षसङ्ख्यार्हणं पुष्पं प्रदद्याद्देवतार्च्चने।
दद्याद्द्विजसहस्राय मिष्ठान्नं द्विजभोजने॥१८॥

In the adoration of a Deity, one should present a hundred thousand excellent flowers. In the matter of feeding the twice-born, one should offer sweet edibles unto a thousand Brāhmaṇas

रुद्रं जपेल्लक्षपुष्पैः पूजयित्वा च त्र्यम्बकम्।
एकादश जपेद्रुदान् दशांशं गुग्गुलैर्वृतैः॥१९॥
हुत्वाभिषेचनं कुर्यान्मन्त्रैर्वरुणदैवतैः।
शान्तिके गणशान्तिश्च ग्रहशान्तिकपूर्वकम्॥२०॥

After adoring the Holder of the Trident (Śiva) with a hundred thousand flowers, one should recite the *Rudra-Mantra*. One should recite the *Rudra-Mantra* eleven times. Having performed the tenth part of a *Homa* with oblations of clarified butter covered with *Guggula*(fragrant gum resin), one should perform *Ābhiṣecanam* (sprinkling with water) with the *Varuṇa-Mantra*. In a *Śānti*-(pacification) rite, one should pacify the goblins after pacifying the planets.

धान्यदाने शुभं धान्यं शारौषष्टिमितं स्मृतम्।
वस्त्रदाने पट्टवस्त्रद्वयं कर्पूरसंयुतम्॥२१॥

In the gift of paddy, as laid down in the *Smṛti*, good paddy of the quantity of a *Khāra* (a measure of grain equal to 16 *Droṇas*) or of six [should be given], and in the gift of cloth, two pieces of silk raiments with camphor [should be given].

दशपञ्चाष्टचतुर उपवेश्य द्विजान् शुभान्।
विधाय वैष्णवीं पूजां सङ्कल्प्य निजकाम्यया॥२२॥
धेनु दद्याद् द्विजातिभ्यो दक्षिणाञ्चापि शक्तितः।
अलङ्कृत्य यथाशक्ति वस्त्रालङ्करणैर्द्विजान्॥२३॥

Having made ten, five, eight, or four, good Brāhmaṇas seated, made up the *Saṅkalpa* (determination) according to ones own desire, performed the adoration of Viṣṇu, one should make presents of kine, according to ones might, unto the twice-born, after having decorated them, proportionate to ones means, with dresses and ornaments.

याचेद्दण्डप्रमाणेन प्रायश्चितं यथोदितम्।
तेषामनुज्ञया कृत्वा प्रायश्चित्तं यथाविधि॥२४॥
पुनस्तान् परिपूर्णार्थानर्च्चयेद्विधिवद्‌द्विजान्।
सन्तुष्टा ब्राह्मणा दध्युरनुज्ञां व्रतकारिणे॥२५॥

One should then solicit from them, the due penance [for a sin] as punishable [by the king]. Then having duly performed the penitential rite with their permission, one should, again, for completing the same, properly adore the twice-born persons. Gratified, the Brāhmaṇas should accord permission unto one who wishes to perform a religious rite.

जपच्छिद्रं तपश्छिद्रं यच्छिद्रं यज्ञकर्मणि।
सर्वं भवति निश्छिद्रं यस्य चेच्छन्ति ब्राह्मणाः॥२६॥

If the Brāhmaṇas desire it, all the faults in the matter of recitation, or in austerity or sacrificial rites disappear.

ब्राह्मणा यानि भाषन्ते मान्यन्ते तानि देवताः।
सर्वदेवमया विप्राः न तद्वचनमन्यथा॥२७॥

The Deities honour what the Brāhmaṇas say. The Brāhmaṇas are at one with all the Deities and their words never prove otherwise.

उपवासो व्रतञ्चैव स्थानं तीर्थफलं तपः।
विप्रैः सम्पादितं सर्वं सम्पन्नं तस्य तत्फलम्॥२८॥

Fasting, religious observance, pilgrimage, religious austerity, if all these are performed by the Vipras, complete becomes the fruit thereof.

सम्पन्नमिति यद्वाक्यं वदन्ति क्षितिदेवताः।
प्रणम्य शिरसा धार्यमग्निष्टोमफलं लभेत्॥२९॥

When the earthly deities (*i.e.*, the Brāhmaṇas) say that it is well-done, one should carry it on his head after saluting them. [Thereby] he reaps the fruit of an *Agniṣṭoma*-rite.

ब्राह्मणा जङ्गमं तीर्थं निर्ज्जलं सार्वकामिकम्।
तेषां वाक्योदकेनैव शुध्यन्ति मलिना जनाः॥३०॥

The Brāhmaṇas are the moving pilgrimages void of water and granting all desires. Persons suffering from the impurity [of sins], are purified by their word-like water.

तेभ्योऽनुज्ञामभिप्राप्य प्रगृह्य च तथाशिषः।
भोजयित्वा द्विजान् शक्त्या भुञ्जीत सह बन्धुभिः॥३१॥

Having obtained their permission and received their blessings, one should, after feeding the twice-born according to ones might, take ones meals along with ones own kinsmen.

॥ इति शातातपीये प्रथमोऽध्यायः॥२॥

Chapter 2

ब्रह्महा नरकस्यान्ते पाण्डुकुष्ठी प्रजायते।
प्रायश्चित्तं प्रकुर्वीत स तत्पातकशान्तये॥१॥

After serving his term in hell, the destroyer of a Brāhmaṇa, is born afflicted with white leprosy. Therefore, for the expiation of that sin, one should perform a penitential rite.

चत्वारः कलशाः कार्याः पञ्चरत्नसमन्विताः।
पञ्चपल्लवसंयुक्ताः सितवस्त्रेण संयुताः॥२॥

Five pitchers should be placed filled with five gems, five leaves and covered with a piece of white cloth.

अश्वस्थानादिमृद्युक्तास्तीर्थोदकसुपूरिताः।
कषायपञ्चकोपेता नानाविधफलान्विताः॥३॥

Earth collected from horse-stable, etc., should be placed into them; they should be filled to the brim with sacred water and contain five bitters and various sorts of fruits.

सर्वौषधिसमायुक्ताः स्थाप्याः प्रतिदिशं द्विजैः।
रौप्यमष्टदलं पद्मं मध्यकुम्भोपरि न्यस्येत्॥४॥

Sarvauṣadhi (sacred medicinal hers) should be placed inside them. And they should be placed on each side by the twice-born. One should then place on the middle pitcher, a lotus of eight petals made of silver.

तस्योपरि न्यसेद्देवं ब्रह्माणञ्च चतुर्मुखम्।
पलार्द्धार्द्धप्रमाणेन सुवर्णेन विनिर्मितम्॥५॥

On it, one should place the figure of the four-faced Deity Brahmā, made of half-a-*Pala* of gold.

अर्च्चेत् पुरुषसूक्तेन त्रिकालं प्रतिवासरम्।
यजमानः शुभैर्गन्धैः पुष्पैर्धूपैर्यथाविधि॥६॥

With scents, flowers, incense, etc., the sacrificer, should duly adore it thrice daily with the *Puruṣasūkta-Mantra*.

पूर्वादिकुम्भेषु ततो ब्राह्मणा ब्रह्मचारिणः।
पठेयुः स्वस्ववेदांस्ते ऋग्वेदप्रभृतीन् शनैः॥७॥

Thereupon the Brāhmaṇas, observing celibacy, should gradually, recite their own Vedas, the *Ṛgveda*, and others, into the pitchers placed in the east and other quarters.

दशांशेन ततो होमो ग्रहशान्तिपुरःसरम्।
मध्यकुम्भे विधातव्यो घृताक्तैस्तिलहेमभिः॥८॥

Thereupon after propitiating the planets, one should perform the tenth part of a *Homa* on the middle pitcher with sesame and gold soaked with clarified butter.

द्वादशाहमिदं कर्म समाप्य द्विजपुंगवः।
तत्र पीठे यजमानमभिषिञ्चेद्यथाविधि॥९॥

Having finished this rite, extending over twelve days, the foremost of the twice-born should sprinkle the sacrificer with water in the altar.

ततो दद्याद्यथाशक्ति गोभूहेमतिलादिकम्।

ब्राह्मणेभ्यस्तथा देवमाचार्याय निवेदयेत्॥१०॥

Thereupon one should, proportionate to his means, present kine, lands, gold, sesame, etc., unto the twice-born. Unto the *Ācārya*, he should give the idol.

आदित्या वसवो रुद्रा विश्वदेवा मरुद्गणाः।
प्रीताः सर्वे व्यपोहन्तु मम पापं सुदारुणम्॥११॥

[He should say:–] "O you Ādityas, Vasus, Rudras, Vaiśvadevas, Maruts, being gratified, do you destroy my most terrible sin.

इत्युदीर्य्य मुहुर्भक्त्या तमाचार्यं क्षमापयेत्।
एवं विधाने विहिते श्वेतकुष्ठी विशुध्यति॥१२॥

Repeatedly reciting this *Mantra* with reverence, he should beg pardon from the *Ācārya*. By observing this regulation, one suffering from white-leprosy, becomes purified.

कुष्ठो गोवधकारी स्यान्नरकान्तेऽस्य निष्कृतिः।
स्थापयेद् घटमेकन्तु पूर्वोक्तद्रव्यसंयुतम्॥१३॥
रक्तचन्दनलिप्ताङ्गं रक्तपुष्पाम्बरान्वितम्।
रत्नकुम्भन्तु तत् कृत्वा स्थापयेद्दक्षिणां दिशम्॥१४॥

The slayer of a cow, after his sufferings in a hell, is born as a leper. His redemption is as follows. He should place a pitcher filled with articles mentioned before. Its body should be pasted with red sandal, filled with red flowers and covered with a red cloth. Having thus made that pitcher red, he should place it in the south.

ताम्रपात्रं न्यसेत् तत्र तिलचूर्णेन पूरितम्।
तस्योपरि न्यसेद्देवं हेमनिष्कमयं यमम्॥१५॥

He should then place on it a copper plate filled with powdered sesame; he should place on it the image of Yama, made with gold of the quantity of a *Niṣka*.

यजेत् पुरुषसूक्तेन पापं मे शाम्यतामिति।

सामपारायणं कुर्यात् कलशे तत्र सामवित्।।१६।।

He should then adore it with the *Puruṣasūkta-Mantra* [praying], "May my sin be dissipated.'' One, well-read in the *Sāmaveda*, should finish the recitation of the *Sāman* near the pitcher.

दशांशं सर्षपैर्हुत्वा पावमान्यभिषेचने।
विहिते धर्मराजानमाचार्याय निवेदयेत्।।१७।।

Having performed the tenth part of the *Homa* with mustard and *Abhiṣecanam* (sprinkling with water) with the *Pāvamānisūkta*, one should present, unto the *Ācārya*, the image of the King of Righteousness.

यमोऽपि महिषमारूढो दण्डपाणिर्भयावहः।
दक्षिणाऽऽशापतिर्देवो मम पापं व्यपोहतु।।१८।।

"May Yama seated on a buffalo, with a dreadful rod in his hand, the presiding Deity of the south, may he remove my sin.''

इत्युच्चार्य विसृज्यैनं मासं सद्भक्तिमाचरेत्।
ब्रह्मगोवधयोरेष प्रायश्चित्तेन निष्कृतिः।।१९।।

Having recited this *Mantra*, one should perform the *Visarjana*-rite.[1] He should then spend a month being filled with reverence and faith. The sin of the destruction of a Brāhmaṇa or a cow is dissipated by this penitential rite.

पितृहा चेतनाहीनो मातृहाऽन्धः प्रजायते।
नरकान्ते प्रकुर्वीत प्रायश्चित्तं यथाविधि।।२०।।

The destroyer of ones own father is born as an inert; and that of mother, as a blind person, after undergoing the pangs of a hell. One should, therefore, duly perform the penitential rite.

प्राजापत्यानि कुर्वीत त्रिंशच्चैव विधानतः।

1. The life of a Deity is invoked in the image at the commencement of the worship; and at the end of it, the said life is said to be thrown into water. *Visarjana* signifies ``to throw off''.

व्रतान्ते कारयेन्नावं सौवर्णपलसम्मिताम्॥२१॥

One should, according to directions, perform thirty *Prājāpatyas*. After the termination of the rite, one should make a boat with gold, in quantity weighing a *Pala.*

कुम्भं रौप्यमयञ्चैव ताम्रपात्राणि पूर्ववत्।
निष्कहेम्ना तु कर्त्तव्यो देवः श्रीवत्सलाञ्छनः॥२२॥

Then placing a pitcher made of silver, one should keep a copper plate on it. Then an image of the Deity (Viṣṇu), bearing the mystic mark of *Śrīvatsa*, should be made of gold of the quantity of a *Niṣka*.

पट्टवस्त्रेण संवेष्ट्य पूजयेत् तां विधानतः।
नावं द्विजाय तां दद्यात् सर्वोपस्करसंयुताम्॥२३॥

Covering it with a silk cloth, one should duly adore it. He should then present, unto a twice born person, the boat containing all the requisites.

वासुदेव जगन्नाथ सर्वभूताश्रयस्थित।
पातकार्णवमग्नं मां तारय प्रणतार्त्तिहृत्॥२४॥

"O Vāsudeva, O lord of the Universe, O you stationed in all creatures, O you the destroyer of the calamity of one who bows unto you, do you rescue me, who am sunk in the ocean of iniquity.''

इत्युदीर्य्य प्रणम्याथ ब्राह्मणाय विसर्जयेत्।
अन्येभ्योऽपि यथाशक्ति विप्रेभ्यो दक्षिणां ददेत्॥२५॥

Having recited this *Mantra* and saluted it, one should present it (*i.e.*, the image) unto a Brāhmaṇa; one should make presents unto other Brāhmaṇas proportionate to ones means.

स्वसृघाती तु बधिरो नरकान्ते प्रजायते।
मूको भ्रातृवधे चैव तस्येयं निष्कृतिः स्मृता॥२६॥

The destroyer of a sister is born as a deaf after the termination of sufferings in a hell. In the destruction of a brother, [one is born] as a dumb. The following is the redemption laid down in the *Smṛti*.

साऽपि पापविशुद्ध्यर्थं चरेच्चान्द्रायणव्रतम्।
व्रतान्ते पुस्तकं दद्यात् सुवर्णफलसंयुतम्।।२७।।

One should, for the expiation of the sin, perform a *Cāndrāyaṇa*-rite. After the termination of this religious observance, one should make gift of a book with a golden fruit.

इमं मन्त्रं समुच्चार्य ब्राह्मणीं तं विसर्जयेत्।
सरस्वति जगन्मातः शब्दब्रह्माधिदेवते।।२८।।

दुष्कर्मकरणात् पापं पाहि मां परमेश्वरि।
बालघाती च पुरुषो मृतवत्सः प्रजायते।।२९।।

Reciting the following *Mantras*, one should throw off the image of the divine wife of Brahmā– "O Sarasvatī, O Mother of the Universe, O presiding Goddess of the words of the Vedas, O great Goddess, rescue me from the sin originating from the iniquitous deeds. A person, slaying a child, is born as one whose children die on birth.

ब्राह्मणोद्वाहनञ्चैव कर्त्तव्यं तेन शुद्धये।
श्रवणं हरिवंशस्य कर्त्तव्यञ्च यथाविधि।।३०।।

For the purification of this sin, one should perform the wedding of a Brāhmaṇa and duly listen to the recitation of [the religious work] *Harivaṁśa*.

महारुद्रजपञ्चैव कारयेच्च यथाविधि।
षडङ्गैकादशै रुद्रै रुद्रः समभिधीयते।।३१।।

One should then duly recite the *Mahārudra*. Eleven Rudras with six *Aṅgas* pass by the name of Rudra.

रुद्रैस्तथेकादशभिर्महारुद्रः प्रकीर्तितः।
एकादशभिरेतैस्तु अतिरुद्रश्च कथ्यते।।३२।।

The aggregate formed by these eleven, is called *Mahārudra*. Similarly this aggregate of eleven is also called *Atirudra*.

जुहुयाच्च दशांशेन दूर्वयायुतसङ्ख्यया।
एकादश स्वर्णनिष्काः प्रदातव्याः सदक्षिणाः॥३३॥

[With this *Mantra*] and ten thousand *Dūrvā*-grass, the tenth part of a *Homa* should be performed. Eleven gold *Niṣkas* should be given away as the sacrificial present.

पलान्येकादश तथा दद्याद्द्विजानुसारतः।
अन्येभ्योऽपि यथाशक्ति द्विज्येभ्यो दक्षिणान्दिशेत्॥३४॥

But these eleven *Palas*, one should present unto a twice-born person according to ones means. One should, also, proportionate to ones might, make presents unto other Brāhmaṇas.

स्नापयेद्दम्पती पश्चान्मन्त्रैर्वरुणदैवतैः।
आचार्याय प्रदेयानि वस्त्रालङ्करणानि च॥३५॥

[The priest] should make the pair bathe afterwards with the *Varuṇa-Mantra*. [The sacrificer] should give unto the *Ācārya* clothes and ornaments.

गोत्रहा पुरुषः कुष्ठी निर्वंशश्चोपजायते।
स च पापविशुद्ध्यर्थं प्राजापत्यशतञ्चरेत्॥३६॥

One, killing a cow, is born as a leper and his family becomes extinct. For the expiation of that sin, one should perform a hundred *Prājāpatya*-penances.

व्रतान्ते मेदिनीं दत्त्वा शृणुयादथ भारतम्।
स्त्रीहन्ता चातिसारौ स्यादश्वत्थान् रोपयेद्दश॥३७॥

After the termination of the rite, one should, after making gifts of lands, listen to the recitation of the *Mahābhāratam*. The slayer of a woman suffers [in another birth] with chronic diarrhoea. He should plant ten *Aśvatthva*-trees.

दद्याच्च शर्कराधेनं भोजयेच्च शतं द्विजान्।
राजहा क्षयरोगी स्यादेषा तस्य च निष्कृतिः॥३८॥

He should then give away a small quantity of sugar, and feed a hundred Brāhmaṇas. The destroyer of a king suffers from consumption. The following is his redemption.

गोभूहिरण्यमिष्टान्नजलवस्त्रप्रदानतः।
घृतधेनुप्रदानेन तिलधेनुप्रदानतः॥३९॥
इत्यादिना क्रमेणैव क्षयरोगः प्रशाम्यति।
रक्तार्बुदी वैश्यहन्ता जायते स च मानवः॥४०॥

By giving away kine, lands, gold, sweet meats, water, clothes, a small quantity of clarified butter and sesame– by making gifts in this order, the disease of consumption is cured. A man, killing a Vaiśya, is born suffering from blood discharges.

प्राजापत्यानि चत्वारि सप्त धान्यानि चोत्सृजेत्।
दण्डापतानकयुतः शूद्रहन्ता भवेन्नरः॥४१॥

Performing four *Prājāpatyas*, one should dedicate paddy [to the quantity of] seven [*Khāri*]. The destroyer of a Śūdra is born as a man suffering from the disease of *Daṇḍāpatānaka*.

प्राजापत्यं सकृच्चैवं दद्याद्धेनुं सदक्षिणाम्
कारुणां च वधे चैव रूक्षभाषः प्रजायते॥४२॥

After performing one *Prājāpatya* one should give away a cow with a money-present. In the destruction of artizans, one is born as being harsh-speeched.

तेन तत्पापशुद्ध्यर्थं दातव्यो वृषभः सितः।
सर्वकार्येष्वसिद्धार्थो गजघाती भवेन्नरः॥४३॥

For the expiation of that sin, a white bull should be given away. A person, slaying an elephant, becomes unsuccessful in all works.

प्रासादं कारयित्वा तु गणेशप्रतिमां न्यस्येत्।
गणनाथस्य मन्त्रन्तु मन्त्रो लक्षमितं जपेत्॥४४॥

Having a palace made, one should place an image of Gaṇeśa, or he should recite the *Gaṇeśa-Mantṛa* a thousand times.

कुलत्थशाकैः पूपैश्च गणशान्तिपुरःसरम्।
उष्ट्रे विनिहते चैव जायते विकृतस्वरः॥४५॥

The gratification of Gaṇa should first be done by the leaves of *Kulathva*-leaves and barley-cakes. By slaying a camel, one is born with a hoarse voice.

स तत्पापविशुद्ध्यर्थं दद्यात् कर्पूरकं पलम्।
अश्वे विनिहते चैव वक्रतुण्डः प्रजायते॥४६॥

For the purification of that sin, one should present camphor to the quantity of a *palam*. By slaying a horse one is born with a crooked face.

शतं पलानि दद्याच्च चन्दनान्यघनुत्तये।
महिषीघातने चैव कृष्णागुल्मः प्रजायते॥४७॥

For the expiation of that sin, one should give away sandal wood, one hundred *palas*, in quantity. By killing a she-buffalo, one is born with *Kṛṣṇagulma* (a chronic enlargement of the spleen).

खरे विनिहते चैव खररोमा प्रजायते।
निष्कत्रयस्य प्रकृतिं सम्प्रदद्याद्धिरणमयीम्॥४८॥

By killing an ass, one is born with ass-like hairs on his body. One should [for the expiation of the sin], present an idol made of gold weighing three *Niṣakas*.

तरक्षो निहते चैव जायते काकरेक्षणः।
दद्याद्रत्नमयीं धेनुं स तत्पातकशान्तये॥४९॥

By killing of *Tarakṣu*-deer, one is born having eyes like those of a crow. For the expiation of that sin, one should give away a cow made of precious stones.

शूकरे निहते चैव दन्तुरो जायते नरः।
स दद्यात्तु विशुद्ध्यर्थं घृतकुम्भं सदक्षिणम्॥५०॥

By killing a boar, a person is born with long and projecting teeth. For the purpose of purification, he should make a gift of a pitcher filled with clarified butter and money.

हरिणे निहते खञ्जः शृगाले तु विपादकः।
अश्वस्तेन प्रदातव्यः सोवर्णपलनिर्मितः॥५१॥

By killing a deer, one is born lame; and a jackal, without foot. By him, a horse made of gold weighing a *Pala*, should be given away.

अजाभिघातने चैव अधिकाङ्गः प्रजायते।
अजा तेन प्रदातव्या विचित्रवस्त्रसंयुता॥५२॥

By killing a goat, one is born with an extra limb. A she-goat covered with a cloth of variegated colours should be given away by him.

उरभ्रे निहते चैव पाण्डुरोगः प्रजायते।
कस्तुरिकापलं दद्याद्ब्राह्मणाय विशुद्धये॥५३॥

By killing a lamb, one is born with jaundice. For purification, he should present unto a Brāhmaṇa one *Pala* of musk.

मार्ज्जारे निहते चैव पीतपाणिः प्रजायते।
पारावतं ससौवर्णं प्रदद्यान्निष्कमात्रकम्॥५४॥

By killing a cat, one is born with a tawny-coloured arm. He should make a present of a pigeon made of gold to the weight of a *Niṣka*.

शुकसारिकयोर्घाते नरः स्खलितवाग्भवेत्।
सच्छास्त्रपुस्तकं दद्यात् स विप्राय सदक्षिणम्॥५५॥

By killing a *Śuka* and a *Sārikā* (a pair of parrots), a man becomes a stammerer in his next birth. He should present unto a Brāhmaṇa a good scriptural work with money.

वकघाती दीर्घनसो दद्याद्गां धवलप्रभाम्।
काकघाती कर्णहीनो दद्याद्गामसितप्रभाम्॥५६॥

The destroyer of a crane is born with a long nose. He should give away a white cow. The destroyer of a crow is born earless. He should give away a black cow.

हिंसायां निष्कृतिरियं ब्राह्मणे समुदाहृता।
तदर्द्धार्द्धप्रमाणेन क्षत्रियादिष्वनुक्रमात्॥५७॥

The expiation for the sin of destruction, now spoken of, is for the Brāhmaṇas. Half of it, in order, should hold good in the case of the Kṣatriyas and other [castes].

।। इति शातातपीये कर्मविपाके हिंसाप्रायश्चित्तविधिर्नाम द्वितीयोऽध्याय:।।२।।

Chapter 3

सुरापः श्यावदन्तः स्यात् प्राजापत्यान्तरं तथा।
शर्करायास्तुलाः सप्त दद्यात् पापविशुद्धये।।१।।

A drinker of spirituous liquor is born with black teeth. After performing a *Prājāpatya*-rite, he should make seven figures with sugar and give them a way for the expiation of his sin.

जपित्वा तु महारुद्रं दशांशं जुहुयात्तिलैः।
ततोऽभिषेकः कर्त्तव्यो मन्त्रैर्वरुणदैवतैः।।२।।

Having recited the *Mahārudra-Mantra*, one should perform the tenth part of a *Homa* with sesame. Then *Abhiṣeka* (sprinkling with water) should be performed with the *Varuṇa-Mantra*.

मद्यपो रक्तपित्ती स्यात् स दद्यात् सर्पिषो घटम्।
मधुनोऽर्द्धघटञ्चैव सहिरण्यं विशुद्धये।।३।।

The drinker of spirituous liquor is born suffering from *Raktapitta* (discharge of blood from the mouth). For purification he should give away a pitcher [either] filled with clarified butter or one-half filled with honey, together with gold.

अभक्ष्यभक्षणे चैव जायते कृमिलोदरः।
यथावत्तेन शुद्ध्यर्थमुपोष्यं भीष्मपञ्चकम्।।४।।

By taking a forbidden food, one is born as a worm in the womb. For purification, one should fast on the *Bhīṣma-Pañcaka*-day.[1]

उदक्या वीक्षितं भुक्त्वा जायते कृमिलोदरः।
गोमूत्रयावकाहारस्त्रिरात्रेणैव शुध्यति।।५।।

By taking food seen by a woman in her courses, one is born

1. Five days from the eleventh to the Fifteenth in the bright-half of the month of Kārtika, sacred to Bhīṣma.

as a worm in the womb. By living on the urine of cow and barley for three nights, one becomes purified.

भुक्त्वा चास्पृश्य संस्पृष्टं जायते कृमिलोदरः।
त्रिरात्रं समुपोष्याथ स तत्पापात् प्रमुच्यते॥६॥

By taking food touched by a person who ought not to be touched, one is born as a worm in the womb. By fasting for three nights he is freed from that sin.

परान्नविघ्नकरणादजीर्णमभिजायते।
लक्षहोमं स कुर्वीत प्रायश्चित्तं यथाविधि॥७॥

By putting obstacles in anothers feeding, one is born with dyspepsia. He should, as a penance, duly perform a hundred thousand *Homas*.

मन्दोराग्निर्भवति सति द्रव्ये कदन्नदः।
प्राजापत्यत्रयं कुर्याद्‌भोजयेच्च शतं द्विजान्॥८॥

He, who partakes of bad food, a good article being available, gets his digestive power impaired. He should perform three *Prājāpatyas* and feed one hundred twice-born persons.

विषदः स्याच्छर्दिरोगो दद्याद्दशपयस्विनीः।
मार्गहा पादरोगी स्यात् सोऽश्वदानं समाचरेत्॥९॥

The administrator of poison becomes subject to cold. He should give away ten milch-kine. He, who obstructs a high road, suffers from the disease of foot. He should make the gift of the horse.

पिशुनो नरकस्यान्ते जायते श्वासकासवान्।
घृतं तेन प्रदातव्यं सहस्रपलसम्मितम्॥१०॥

A wily person, after sufferings in hell, is born with the afflictions of Asthma and Bronchitis. One thousand *Palas* of clarified butter should be given away by him.

धूर्तोऽपस्माररोगी स्यात् स तत्पापविशुद्धये।
ब्रह्मकूर्च्चमयीं धेनुं दद्याद्वाञ्च सदक्षिणाम्॥११॥

A wicked person becomes subject to epilepsy. For the expiation of the sin, he should, after performing *Brahmakūrca*-penance, give away a cow with a money gift.

शूली परोपतापेन जायते तत्प्रमोचने।
सोऽन्नदानं प्रकुर्वीत तथा रुद्रं जपेन्नरः॥१२॥

By giving pain to another, one is born as a sufferer of colic. For the expiation of that sin, he should give away edibles and recite the *Rudra-Mantra*.

दावाग्निदायकश्चैव रक्तातिसारवान् भवेत्।
तेनोदपानं कर्त्तव्यं रोपणीयस्तथा वटः॥१३॥

By putting fire to a forest, one is born as suffering from diarrhoea attended with blood purging. For the expiation of that sin, a fig-tree should be planted by him.

सुरालये जले वाऽपि शकृन्मूत्रं करोति यः।
गुदरोगो भवेत् तस्य पापरूपः सुदारुणः॥१४॥

He, who passes urine even once in a temple or in water, is afflicted with the diseases of the rectum (as piles, fistula, etc.,) diseases as dreadful as the sin itself.

मासं सुरार्च्चनेनैव गोदानद्वितयेन तु।
प्राजापत्येन चैकेन शाम्यन्ति गुदजा रुजः॥१५॥

Diseases of the rectum are cured by the adoration of the deities for a month, gift of a couple of kine and the performance of one *Prājāpatya*-penance.

गर्भपातनजा रोगा यकृत्प्लीहजलोदराः।
तेषां प्रशमनार्थाय प्रायश्चित्तमिदं स्मृतम्॥१६॥

Liver, spleen and dropsy are the diseases which originate from procuring abortions. For their cure the following penitential rite is laid down in the *Smṛti*.

एतेषु दद्याद्विप्राय जलधेनुं विधानतः।
सुवर्णरूप्यताम्राणां पलत्रयसमन्विताम्॥१७॥

In these [diseases] one should present unto a Vipra a *Jaladhenu*, according to the regulation, with three *Palas* of either gold, silver or copper.

प्रतिमाभङ्गकारी च अप्रतिष्ठः प्रजायते।
संवत्सरत्रयं सिञ्चेदश्वत्थं प्रतिवासरम्॥१८॥

He, who breaks an idol, is born without any residence of his own. He should pour water on a *Aśvattha*-tree daily for a year.

उद्वाहयेत् तमश्वत्थं स्वगृह्योक्तविधानतः।
तत्र संस्थापयेद्देवं विघ्नराजं सुपूजितम्॥१९॥

He should then perform the nuptials of the *Aśvatthva*-tree according to the regulations of his own family. Then he should establish the image of the Deity of Impediments (Gaṇeśa) duly adored.

दुष्टवादी खण्डितः स्यात् स वै दद्याद्द्विजातये।
रूप्यं पलद्वयं दुग्धं घटद्वयसमन्वितम्॥२०॥

He, who gives vent to foul words, is born with a broken limb. He should give unto a twice-born person two *Palas* of silver and two pitchers filled with milk.

खल्लोटः परनिन्दावान् धेनु दद्यात् सकाञ्चनाम्।
परोपहासकृत्काणः स गां दद्यात् समौक्तिकाम्॥२१॥

He, who vilifies others, becomes bald-headed [in another birth]. He should make a gift of a cow with gold. He who laughs as others, is born with one ear. He should make a gift of a cow with pearls.

सभायां पक्षपाती च जायते पक्षघातवान्।
निष्कत्रयमितं हेम स दद्यात् सत्यवर्त्तिनाम्॥२२॥

He, who shows partiality in an assembly, is born suffering from paralysis. He should make a gift of gold, three *Niṣkas* in weight, unto one who wends truthful ways.

॥ इति शातातपीये कर्मविपाके प्रकीर्णप्रायश्चित्तं नाम तृतीयोऽध्यायः॥३॥

Chapter 4

कुलघ्नो नरकस्यान्ते जायते विप्रहेमहृत्।
स तु स्वर्णशतं दद्यात् कृत्वा चान्द्रायणत्रयम्।।१।।

The pilferer of a Vipras gold is born, after the sufferings in a hell, as the destroyer of his own family. After performing three *Cāndrāyaṇas*, he should make a gift of a hundred gold coins.

औडुम्बरी ताम्रचौरो नरकान्ते प्रजायते।
प्राजापत्यं स कृत्वात्र ताम्रं पलशतं दिशेत्।।२।।

The pilferer of copper is born, after [serving his term in] hell as suffering from *Audumbara* a kind of leprosy. After performing one *Prājāpatya*, he should make a gift of a hundred *Palas* of copper.

कांस्यहारी च भवति पुण्डरीकसमन्वित:।
कांस्यं पलशतं दद्यादलङ्कृत्य द्विजातये।।३।।

The stealer of belmetal becomes subject to the disease of *Pauṇḍarīka* (a kind of leprosy). Having bedecked a twice-born person with ornaments, he should make a gift, unto him, of a hundred *Palas* of belmetal.

रीतिहृत् पिङ्गलाक्ष: स्यादुपोष्य हरिवासरम्।
रीतिं पलशतं दद्यादलङ्कृत्य द्विजं शुभम्।।४।।

The pilferer of brass is born with tawny-coloured eyes. Fasting on an *Ekādaśī*-day and bedecking a good Brāhmaṇa with ornaments, he should present unto him one hundred *Palas* of brass.

मुक्ताहारी च पुरुषो जायते पिङ्गमूर्द्धज:।
मुक्ताफलशतं दद्यादुपोष्य स विधानत:।।५।।

A person, pilfering pearls, is born with tawny-coloured hairs. Fasting, he should give away a hundred pearls according to proper regulations.

त्रपुहारी च पुरुषो जायते नेत्ररोगवान्।

उपोष्य दिवसं सोऽपि दद्यात् पलशतं त्रपु॥६॥

A person, stealing tin, is born suffering from eye-diseases. Fasting for a day, he should give away one hundred *Palas* of tin.

सीसहारी च पुरुषो जायते शीर्षरोगवान्।
उपोष्य दिवसं दद्यादघृतधेनुं विधानत:॥७॥

A person, pilfering lead, is born as suffering from head-diseases. Fasting for a day, he should give away one *Dhenu* weight of clarified butter according to the proper regulations.

दुग्धाहारी च पुरुषो जायते बहुमूत्रक:।
स दद्यादुग्धधेनुञ्च ब्राह्मणाय यथाविधि:॥८॥

A person, stealing milk, is born as a diabetic patient. He should duly give, unto a Brāhmaṇa, milk one *Dhenu* in weight.

दधिचोर्य्येण पुरुषो जायते मदवान् यत:।
दधिधेनु: प्रदातव्या तेन विप्राय शुद्धये॥९॥

By stealing milk curd a person is born insane. For purification, curd, one *Dhenu* in weight, should be given by him unto a Vipra.

मधुचौरस् तु पुरुषो जायते नेत्ररोगवान्।
स दद्यान्मधुधेनुञ्च समुपोष्य द्विजातये॥१०॥

A stealer of honey is born as being subject to eye-diseases. After fasting, he should give, unto a twice-born person, honey, one *Dhenu* in weight.

इक्षोर्विकारहारी च भवेदुदरगुल्मवान्।
गुडधेनु: प्रदातव्या तेन तद्दोषशान्तये॥११॥

A stealer of sugarcane-preparation (becomes subject) to *Gulma* (chronic enlargement of the liver or spleen). For the expiation of that sin, molasses, one *Dhenu* in weight, should be presented by him.

लौहहारी च पुरुष: कर्बुराङ्ग प्रजायते।
लौहं पलशतं दद्यादुपोष्य स तु वासरम्॥१२॥

A person, stealing iron, is born with spotted limbs. Fasting for a day, he should give away one hundred *Palas* of iron.

तैलचौरस्तु पुरुषो भवेत् कण्ड्वादिपीडितः।
उपोष्य स तु विप्राय दद्यात् तैलघटद्वयम्॥१३॥

A person, stealing oil, suffers from itches, etc. Fasting, he should give, unto a Vipra, two pitchers filled with oil.

आमान्नहरणाच्चैव दन्तहीनः प्रजायते।
स दद्यादश्विनौ हेमनिष्कद्वयविनिर्मितौ॥१४॥

By pilfering uncooked rice, one is born without teeth. He should present images of the twin-Aśvins made of two *Niṣkas* of gold.

पक्वान्नहरणाच्चैव जिह्वारोगः प्रजायते।
गायत्र्याः स जपेल्लक्षं दशांशं जुहुयाद् तिलैः॥१५॥

By pilfering cooked rice, one is born with a disease on the tongue. He should recite the *Gāyatrī* for a hundred thousand times and perform the tenth part of a *Homa* with sesame.

फलहारी च पुरुषो जायते व्रणिताङ्गुलिः।
नानाफलानामयुतं स दद्याच्च द्विजन्मने॥१६॥

A person, stealing fruits, is born with ulcerated fingers. He should give unto a twice-born person ten thousand fruits of sorts.

ताम्बूलहरणेच्चैव श्वेतौष्ठः सम्प्रजायते।
सदक्षिणं प्रदद्याच्च विद्रुमस्य द्वयं वरम्॥१७॥

By pilfering betel-leaves, one is born with white lips. He should give away two most excellent *Vidrumas* (corals) with money presents.

शाकहारी च पुरुषो जायते नीललोचनः।
ब्राह्मणाय प्रदद्याद्वै महानीलमणिद्वयम्॥१८॥

A person, stealing vegetable leaves, is born with black eyes. He should give unto a Brāhmaṇa two most previous sapphires.

कन्दमूलस्य हरणात् ह्रस्वप्राणिः प्रजायते।
देवतायतनं कार्यमुद्यानं तेन शक्तितः।।१९।।

By pilfering trunks or roots, a person is born with a shortened hand. A temple for a Deity or a garden should be made by him according to his might.

सौगन्धिकस्य हरणाद्दुर्गन्धाङ्गः प्रजायते।
स लक्षमेकं पद्मानां जुहुयाज्जातवेदसि।।२०।।

By pilfering scents, one is born with limbs emitting foul smell. He should offer oblations of a hundred thousand lotuses to the Fire.

दारूहारी च पुरुषः खिन्नपाणिः प्रजायते।
स दद्याद्विदुषे शुद्धो काश्मीरजपलद्वयम्।।२१।।

A person, pilfering wood, is born with a palm always perspiring. For purification, he should give, unto a learned person, a *Kusumbha*-flower, two *Palas* in size.

विद्यापुस्तकहारी च किल मूकः प्रजायते।
न्यायेतिहासं दद्याच्च ब्राह्मणाय सदक्षिणम्।।२२।।

The pilferer of learning and books is born dumb. He should give unto, a Brāhmaṇa, works on Nyāya (Logic) and *Itihāsa* (History) with money presents.

वस्त्रहारी भवेत् कुष्ठी सम्प्रदद्यात् प्रजापतिम्।
हेमनिष्कमितञ्चैव वस्त्रयुग्मं द्विजातये।।२३।।

The stealer of a cloth suffers from leprosy. He should give, unto a Brāhmaṇa, the image of Brahmā, made of gold, a *Niṣka* in weight and two pieces of cloth.

ऊर्णाहारी लोमशः स्यात् स दद्यात् कम्बलान्वितम्।
स्वर्णनिष्कमितं हेमवह्निं दद्याद्द्विजातये।।२४।।

The pilferer of wool is born with profuse hairs on his body. He should give, unto a twice-born person an idol of Fire, made of gold, one *Niṣka* in weight, together with a blanket.

पट्टसूत्रस्य हरणान्निर्लोमा जायते नरः।
तेन धेनुः प्रदातव्या विशुद्ध्यर्थं द्विजन्मने॥२५॥

By pilfering silken fibres, a man is born without hairs on his body. For the purposes of purification, a cow should be given by him unto a twice-born person.

औषधीस्यापहरणे सूर्यावर्त्तः प्रजायते।
सूर्यायार्घ्यः प्रदातव्यो मासं देयञ्च काञ्चनम्॥२६॥

By stealing medicinal hers one is born suffering from the disease of *Sūryāvarta*. He should, for a month offer *Arghya* to the sun and give away gold.

रक्तवस्त्रप्रवालादिहारी स्याद्रक्तवातवान्।
सवस्त्रां महिषीं दद्यान्मणिरागसमन्विताम्॥२७॥

The pilferer of crimson-coloured raiment and corals suffers from acute gout. He should give away a she buffalo with a cloth and precious gems.

विप्ररत्नापहारी चाप्यनपत्यः प्रजायते।
तेन कार्यं विशुद्ध्यर्थं महारुद्रजपादिकम्॥२८॥

The pilferer of a Vipras jewels is born son-less. For the purpose of purification the recitation of the *Mahārudra-Mantra* should be done by him.

मृतवत्सोदितः सर्वो विधिरत्र विधीयते।
दशांशहोमः कर्त्तव्यः पलाशेन यथाविधि॥२९॥

Here are laid down all these regulations which, one, whose child dies after birth, should perform. He should duly perform the tenth part of a *Homa* with *Palāśa* twigs.

देवस्वहरणाच्चैव जायते विविधो ज्वरः।
ज्वरो महाज्वरश्चैव रौद्रो वैष्णव एव च॥३०॥

Various fevers originate from the stealth of articles belonging to a deity, such as fever, great fever, *Rudra* fever and *Viṣṇu* fever.

ज्वरे रौद्रं जपेत् कर्णे, महारुद्रं महाज्वरे।
अतिरौद्रं जपेद्रौद्रे वैष्णवे तद्द्वयं जपेत्॥३१॥

One should recite into ears *Rudra-Mantra* in a [simple] fever *Mahārudra* in a high fever, *Atirudra* in a *Rudra* fever, and twice the latter in a *Vaiṣṇava* fever.

नानाविधद्रव्यचौरो जायते ग्रहणीयुतः।
तेनान्नोदकवस्त्राणि हेम देयञ्च शक्तितः॥३२॥

The stealer of various other articles is born suffering from chronic diarrhoea. By him, according to his might, shall be given boiled rice, water, raiments and gold.

॥ इति शातातपीये कर्मविपाके स्तेयप्रायश्चितं नाम चतुर्थोऽध्यायः॥४॥

Chapter 5

मातृगामी भवेद्यस्तु लिङ्गं तस्य विनश्यति।
चाण्डालीगमने चैव हीनकोषः प्रजायते॥१॥

The generative organ of a person disappears who knows his mother. By cohabiting with a Cāṇḍāla woman one is born without testes.

तस्य प्रतिक्रियां कर्तुं कुम्भमुत्तरतो न्यसेत्।
कृष्णावस्त्रसमाच्छन्नं कृष्णमाल्यविभूषितम्॥२॥

For the expiation of that sin, one should place a pitcher in the north covered with a crimson cloth and decorated with crimson-coloured garlands.

तस्योपरि न्यसेद्देवं कांस्यपात्रे धनेश्वरम्।
सुवर्णनिष्कषट्केन निर्मितं नरवाहनम्॥३॥

On it one should place, in a bell metal vessel the image of the god of riches, seated on a man and made of gold to the weight of six *Niṣkas*.

यजेत् पुरुषसूक्तेन धनदं विश्वरूपिणम्।
अथर्ववेदविद् द्विप्रो ह्याथर्वणं समाचरेत्॥४॥

He should adore, with the *Puruṣa-Sūkta Mantra*, the giver of riches having an universal form. A Vipra, conversant with the *Atharvaveda* should recite *Ātharvaṇ*.

सुवर्णपुत्रिकां कृत्वा निष्कविंशतिसंख्यया।
दद्याद्विप्राय संपूज्य निष्पापोऽहमिति ब्रुवन्॥५॥

Having made an idol of gold, twenty *Niṣkas* in weight and adored it, one should dedicate it unto a Vipra saying, "I am freed from my sin.''

धनीनामधिपो देवः शंकरस्य प्रियः सखा।
सौम्याशाऽधिपतिः श्रीमान् मम पापं व्यपोहतु॥६॥

May the beautiful deity, the lord of *Nidhis*, the beloved friend of Śaṅkara, and the presiding deity of the quarter belonging to the moon, destroy my sin.

इमं मन्त्रं समुच्चार्य आचार्याय यथाविधि।
दद्याद् देवं हीनकोषे लिङ्गनाशे विशुद्धये॥७॥

For the purification of the sin encompassing the destruction of the generative organ and the testes, one should recite this *Mantra* and duly give the image unto the *Ācārya*.

गुरुजायाऽभिगमानन्मूत्रकृच्छ्रः प्रजायते।
तेनापि निष्कृतिः कार्या शास्त्रदृष्टेन कर्मणा॥८॥

By violating a preceptors bed one is born suffering from difficult urination. Its expiation shall be effected by rites pointed out by the scriptures.

स्थापयेत् कुम्भमेकन्तु पश्चिमायां शुभे दिने।
नीलवस्त्रसमाच्छन्नं नीलमाल्यविभूषितम्॥९॥

On an auspicious day one should place a pitcher, in the West, covered with a blue cloth and decorated with blue garlands.

तस्योपरि न्यसेद्देवं ताम्रपात्रे प्रचेतसम्।
सुवर्णनिष्कषट्केन निर्मितं यादसाम्पतिम्॥१०॥

On it one should place, in a copper vessel, the image of the deity Varuṇa (the god of water), the lord of aquatic animals, made of gold, six *Niṣkas* in weight.

यजेत् पुरुषसूक्तेन वरुणं विश्वरूपिणम्।

सामविद्ब्राह्मणस्तत्र सामवेदं समाचरेत्॥११॥

With the *Puruṣa-Sūkta Mantra* he should adore Varuṇa of the universal form. A Brāhmaṇa, conversant with the *Sāmaveda*, shall recite *Sāman* there.

सुवर्णपुत्रिकां कृत्वा निष्कविंशतिसंख्यया।

दद्याद्विप्राय सम्पूज्य निष्पापोऽहमिति ब्रुवन्॥१२॥

Having made an idol of gold with twenty *Niṣkas* of gold and adored it, he should give it unto a Vipra saying "I am freed from sin."

यादसामधिपो देवो विश्वेषामपि पावनः।

संसाराब्धौ कर्णधारो वरुणः पावनोऽस्तु मे॥१३॥

May the divine Varuṇa, the lord of aquatic animals, the sanctifier of the universe, the pilot in the ocean of the world, purify me.

इमं मन्त्रं समुच्चार्य आचार्याय यथाविधि।

दद्याद्देवमलंकृत्य मूत्रकृच्छ्रप्रशान्तये॥१४॥

Having daily recited this *Mantra* and decorated the idol, one should present it unto the *Ācārya* for the cure of difficult urination.

स्वसुतागमने चैव रक्तकुष्ठं प्रजायते।

भगिनीगमने चैव पीतकुष्ठं प्रजायते॥१५॥

By knowing ones own daughter, one is born with black leprosy. By knowing ones own sister one is born with yellow leprosy.

तस्य प्रतिक्रियां कर्त्तुं पूर्वतः कलशं न्यसेत्।

पीतवस्त्रसमाच्छन्नं पीतमाल्यविभूषितम्॥१६॥

For averting its action, one should place a pitcher, in the east, covered with a yellow cloth and decorated with yellow garlands.

तस्योपरि न्यसेत् स्वर्णपात्रे देवं सुरेश्वरम्।

सुवर्णनिष्कषट्केन निर्मितं वज्रधारिणम्॥१७॥

Thereon he should place, in a golden vessel the image of the king of the celestials, of the worlds of the thunder-bolt, made of six *Niṣkas* of gold.

यजेत् पुरुषसूक्तेन वासवं विश्वरूपिणम्।
यजुर्वेदं तत्र साम ऋग्वेदञ्च समाचरेत्॥१८॥

He should adore Vāsava, having a universal form, with the *Puruṣa-Sūkta Mantra*. There the *Yajuṣ*, *Sāma* and the *Ṛgveda* shall be recited.

सुवर्णपुत्रिकां कृत्वा सुवर्णदशकेन तु।
दद्याद्विप्राय संपूज्य निष्पापोऽहमिति ब्रुवन्॥१९॥

Having made a golden idol with ten *Niṣkas* and worshipped it, he should present it unto a Vipra saying, "I am freed from the sin."

देवानामधिपो देवो वज्री विष्णुनिकेतनः।
शतयज्ञः सहस्राक्षं पापं मम निकृन्ततु॥२०॥

May the king of the celestials, the wielder of the thunder-bolt, the abode of Viṣṇu, the performer of a hundred sacrifices, and the possessor of a thousand eyes, dissipate my sin.

इमं मन्त्रं समुच्चार्य आचार्याय यथाविधि।
दद्याद्देवं सहस्राक्षं स पापस्यापनुत्तये॥२१॥

Having duly recited this *Mantra*, he should present unto the *Ācārya* the image of the thousand-eyed deity for the expiation of that sin.

भ्रातृभार्याऽभिगमनाद्गलत्कुष्ठं प्रजायते।
स्ववधूगमने चैव कृष्णकुष्ठं प्रजायते॥२२॥

By knowing a brothers wife one is born with an incurable leprosy with fingers and toes falling off. By knowing a sons wife one is born with black leprosy.

तेन कार्यं विशुद्ध्यर्थं प्रागुक्तस्यार्द्धमेव हि।
दशांशहोमः सर्वत्र घृताक्तैः क्रियते तिलैः॥२३॥

By him, for the expiation of the sin, shall be performed a half of the penance mentioned before. A tenth part of the Homa shall be performed, in every case; with sesame, soaked with clarified butter.

यदगम्याभिगमनाज्जायते ध्रुवमण्डलम्।
कृत्वा लौहमयीं धेनुं तिलषष्ठिप्रमाणतः॥२४॥
कार्पासभारसंयुक्तां कांस्यदोहां सवत्सिकाम्।
दद्याद्विप्राय विधिवदिमं मन्त्रमुदीरयेत्।
सुरभिर् वैष्णवी माता मम पापं व्यपोहतु॥२५॥

From cohabiting with women, who should not be known, originates the disease of *Dhruvamaṇḍala* (a kind of leprosy). Having made image of a cow with iron, to the size of sixty sesame, carrying a load of cotton, with bell metal adders and with a calf, one should duly present it unto a Vipra, and recite the *Mantra* "May the mother Surabhi, daughter of Viṣṇu, destroy my sin.'

तपस्विनीसङ्गमने जायते चाश्मरीगदः।
मातुः पापविशुद्ध्यर्थं प्रायश्चित्तं समाचरेत्॥२६॥

From cohabiting with a female ascetic originates the disease of stone in the bladder. One should perform a penitential rite for the expiation of that sin.

दद्याद्विप्राय विदुषे मधुधेनुं यथोदितम्।
तिलद्रोणशतञ्चैव हिरण्येन समन्वितम्॥२७॥

He should give unto a learned Brāhmaṇa, as laid down in the *Śāstras,* one *Dhenu* of honey as well as a hundred *droṇas* of sesame accompanied with gold.

पितृस्वस्त्रभिगमनाद्दक्षिणांशव्रणी भवेत्।
तेनापि निष्कृतिः कार्या अजादानेन शक्तितः॥२८॥

By knowing ones fathers sister one is born with an ulcer on the right half of the body. Expiation shall be performed by him by making gifts of goats according to his might.

मातुलान्यान्तु गमने पृष्ठकुब्जः प्रजायते।
कृष्णाजिनप्रदानेन प्रायश्चित्तं समाचरेत्॥२९॥

By knowing a maternal uncles wife one is born as a haunch-back. By making the gift of a black antelope skin one should perform the penitential rite.

मातृष्वस्त्रभिगमने वामाङ्गे व्रणवान् भवेत्।
तेनापि निष्कृतिः कार्या सम्यग्दानप्रदानतः॥३०॥

By knowing a mothers sister one gets ulcers on the left part of the body. By him redemption shall be effected by making gifts properly.

मृतभार्याऽभिगमने मृतभार्यः प्रजायते।
तत्पातकविशुद्ध्यर्थं द्विजमेकं विवाहयेत्॥३१॥

By knowing a dead wife one is born as one whose wife dies. For the expiation of that sin he should celebrate the nuptials of a Brāhmaṇa.

सगोत्रस्त्रीप्रसङ्गेन जायते च भगन्दरः।
तेनापि निष्कृतिः कार्या महिषीदानयत्नतः॥३२॥

By knowing a woman of his own family one is born with fistula in anus. By him redemption shall be effected by a careful gift of a She-buffalo.

तपस्विनीप्रसङ्गेन प्रमेही जायते नरः।
मासं रुद्रजपः कार्यो दद्याच्छक्त्या च काञ्चनम्॥३३॥

By cohabiting with a female ascetic a person is born suffering from gonorrhoea. He should recite the *Rudra-Mantra* for one month and give away gold according to his might.

दीक्षितस्त्रीप्रसङ्गेन जायते दुष्टरक्तदृक्।
स पातकविशुद्ध्यर्थं प्राजापत्यद्वयं चरेत्॥३४॥

By knowing ones own wife who is initiated, one is born suffering from the vitiation of blood. For the expiation of that sin he should perform *Prājāpatyas*.

स्वजातिजायागमने जायते हृदयव्रणी।
तत्पापस्य विशुद्ध्यर्थं प्राजापत्यद्वयं चरेत्॥३५॥

By knowing the wife of a person belonging to his own caste, one is born suffering from the ulceration of the heart. For the expiation of that sin he should perform two *Prājāpatyas*.

पशुयोनौ च गमने मूत्राघातः प्रजायते।
तिलपात्रद्वयञ्चैव दद्यादात्मविशुद्धये॥३६॥

By cohabiting with a beast, one is born suffering from urinary diseases. For self-purification he should give two plates filled with sesame.

अश्वयोनौ च गमनाद् गुदस्तम्भ प्रजायते।
सहस्रकमलस्नानं मासं कुर्यात् शिवस्य च॥३७॥

By cohabiting with a mare, one is born suffering from constipation of the bowels. For expiation he should bathe Śiva for a month with a thousand lotuses.

एते दोषा नराणां स्युर्नरकान्ते न संशयः।
स्त्रीणामपि भवन्त्येते तत्तत्पुरुषसङ्गमात्॥३८॥

These diseases undoubtedly affect men after the termination of their residence in hells. Likewise they affect women who associate with similar men.

॥ इति श्री शातातपीये कर्मविपाकेऽगम्यागमनप्रायश्चित्तं नाम पञ्चमोऽध्यायः॥५॥

Chapter 6

अश्वसूकरशृङ्गाद्रिद्रुमादिशकटेन च।
भृग्वग्निदारुशस्त्राश्मविषोद्बन्धनजैर्मृताः॥१॥

Those who have been killed by a horse, boar, horns, [by falling down from] a mountain, tree, or an elevated place, by a cart, fire, wood, weapon, stone, poison or hanging.

व्याघ्रौहिगजभूपालचौरवैरिवृकाहताः।
काण्ठशल्यमृता ये च शौचसंस्कारवर्ज्जिताः॥२॥

Those killed by being wounded by a tiger, serpent, elephant, a king, thief, enemy, or a leopard; those killed by a wood or a dart; those for whom no purificatory rites have been performed.

विसूचिकाऽन्नकवलदवतीसारतीं मृता:।
शाकिन्यादिग्रहैर्ग्रस्ता विद्युत्पातहताश्च ये॥३॥

Those killed by cholera, by having rice-balls stuck in the throat, and long standing diarrhoea; those killed by being possessed by *Śākini*[1] and other evil Grahas (planets).

अस्पृश्या अपवित्राश्च पतिता: पुत्रवर्ज्जिता:।
पञ्चत्रिंशत् प्रकारैश्च नाप्नुवन्ति गतिं मृता:॥४॥

Those dead being unworthy of being touched, or suffering from impurity or having no sons– those dead under the following thirty five conditions do not come by a better condition.

पित्राद्या: पिण्डभाज: स्युस्त्रयो लेपभुजस्तथा।
ततो नान्दीमुखा: प्रोक्तस्त्रयोऽप्यश्रुमुखास्त्रय:॥५॥

The three generations upwards from the father are entitled to *Piṇḍas* (the remnants of the food sticking to the hand after offering funeral oblations to the first three ancestors), three upwards that are *Nāndīmukhas* (*i.e.*, to whom a *Śrāddha* is performed on a festive occasion); three upwards that are called *Āsrumukhas*.

द्वादशैते पितृगणास्तर्पिता: सन्ततिप्रदा:।
गतिहीना: सुतादीनां सन्ततिं नाशयन्ति ते॥६॥

Being gratified these twelve orders of *Pitrs* (departed manes) grant children; if they are not placed in proper condition they destroy children.

दश व्याघ्रादिनिहता गर्भं विघ्नन्त्यमी क्रमात्।
द्वादशास्त्रादिनिहता आकर्षन्ति च बालकम्॥७॥

The ten killed by tiger etc., are destructive of conception; the

---

1. A kind of female being attendant on Durgā (supposed to be a demon or fairy).

twelve, killed by weapons etc., destroy the foetus.

विषादिनिहता घ्नन्ति दशसु द्वादशेष्वपि।
वर्षैकबालकं कुर्यादनपत्योऽनपत्यताम्॥८॥

The ten or twelve, killed by poison, etc., destroy a boy one year old. A departed manes, dead without any issue, creates childlessness.

व्याघ्रेण हन्यते यस्तु कुमारीगमनेन च।
विषदश्चैव सर्पेण गजेन नृपदुष्टकृत्॥९॥

He, who cohabits with a maiden, is killed by a tiger; the administrator of poison, by a snake; the mischief-maker of a king, by an elephant.

राज्ञा राजकुमारघ्नश्चौरेण पशुहिंसकः।
वैरिणा मित्रभेदी च वकवृत्तिर्वृकेण तु॥१०॥

The destroyer of a royal prince [is killed by the king]; and the destroyer of an animal, by a thief; he who creates dissensions amongst friends, by an enemy; and one of the conduct of a crane, by a wolf.

गुरुघाती च शय्यायां मत्सरी शौचवर्ज्जितः।
द्रोही संस्काररहितः शुना निक्षेपहारकः॥११॥

The destroyer of a preceptor [dies] on the bed; an envious person, being divorced from purificatory rites; one committing mischief unto other, without any *Saṁskāra* (cremation etc.); and the pilferer of a trust money [is killed] by a dog.

नरो विहन्यतेऽरण्ये शूकरेण च पाशिकः।
क्रिमिभिः कृत्तवासाश्च कृमिणा च निकृन्तनः॥१२॥

One, who kills another by a noose, is killed by a boar in a forest; one making a cloth by killing an insect is killed by an insect.

शृङ्गिणा शंकरद्रोही शकटेन च सूचकः।
भृगुणा मेदिनीचौरा वह्निना यज्ञहानिकृत्॥१३॥

One, who is inimical towards Śaṅkara, [is killed] by a horned animal; and a wicked man by a cart; the stealer of lands, by falling down from an elevated place; and one who obstructs a sacrifice, by fire.

दवेन दक्षिणाचौर शस्त्रेण श्रुतिनिन्दकः।
अश्मना द्विजनिन्दाकृद्विषेण कुमतिप्रदः॥१४॥

The stealer of sacrificial presents [is killed] by forest fire; the vilifier of the *Śruti*, by weapons; the vilifier of the twice-born, by a stone; and one who gives evil tendency, by poison.

उद्बन्धनेन हिंस्रः स्यात् सेतुभेदी जलेन तु।
क्रिमिणा राजदन्तहृदतीसारेण लौहहृत्॥१५॥

He, who commits injury [is killed] by hanging; the breaker of a bridge, by water; the pilferer of the royal rod, by worms; and the stealer of iron, by chronic diarrhoea.

शाकिन्याद्यैश्च म्रियते सदर्पकार्यकारकः।
अनध्यायेऽप्यधीयानो म्रियन्ते विद्युता तथा॥१६॥

He who works with pride, is killed by *Śākinī* and other evil spirits. One studying the Vedas on an interdicted day is killed by a thunder-bolt.

अस्पृश्यस्पर्शसङ्गी च वस्तुमाश्रित्य शास्त्रहृत्।
पतितो मदविक्रेतानपत्यो द्विजवस्त्रहृत्॥१७॥

The pilferer of the sacred books dies touching an article that shall not be touched. The seller of wine dies degraded; and the pilferer of a Brāhmaṇas cloth, childless.

अथ तेषां क्रमेणैव प्रायश्चित्तं विधीयते।
कारयेन्त्रिष्कमात्रन्तु पुरुषं प्रेतरूपिणम्॥१८॥

चतुर्भुजं दण्डहस्तं महिषासनसंस्थितम्।
पिष्टैः कृष्णतिलैः कुर्यात् पिण्डं प्रस्थप्रमाणतः॥१९॥

The penances for all those persons shall in due order be spoken of. One should make with gold, one *Niṣka* in weight, the image of a male being of the form of a *Preta* (the Regent of the dead having four arms, with a rod in hand, seated on a buffalo). He should make a *piṇḍa* (funeral cake) to the size of a *prastha* with flour and black sesame.

मध्वाज्यशर्करायुक्तं स्वर्णकुण्डलसंयुक्तम्।
अकालमूलं कलशं पञ्चपल्लवसंयुतम्॥२०॥
कृष्णवस्त्रसमाच्छन्नं सर्वौषधिसमन्वितम्।
तस्योपरि न्यसेदेवं पात्रं धान्यफलैर्युतम्॥२१॥
सप्तधान्यन्तु सफलं तत्र तत् सफलं न्यसेत्।
कुम्भोपरि च विन्यस्य पूजयेत् प्रेतरूपिणम्॥२२॥

He should place a pitcher filled with honey, clarified butter, and sugar and containing a golden ear-ring, the base of which is not black, containing five leaves, covered with a black cloth and consisting of *Sarbauṣadhi* (lit.- all cure). Thereon he should place a plate filled with paddy and fruits. Then he should place on it seven kinds of paddy with fruits. Having placed the image of the *Preta* on the pitcher he should adore it.

कुर्यात् पुरुषसूक्तेन प्रत्यहं दुग्धतर्पणम्।
षडङ्गञ्च जपेद्रुद्रं कलशे तत्र वेदवित्।२३॥

He should daily offer libations of milk with the *Puruṣa-Sūkta Mantra*, and then one, conversant with Vedas, should recite in the pitcher the *Rudra-Mantra* with six divisions.

यमसूक्तेन कुर्वीत यमपूजादिकं तथा।
गायत्र्याश्चैव कर्त्तव्या जपः स्वात्मविशुद्धये॥२४॥

Similarly, one should celebrate the adoration etc., of Yama with *Yama-Sūkta*. For self-purification of the recitation of the *Gāyatrī* should be performed.

ग्रहशान्तिकपूर्वञ्च दशांशं जुहुयात् तिलैः।
अज्ञातनामगोत्राय प्रेताय सतिलोदकम्॥२५॥
प्रदद्यात् पितृतीर्थेन पिण्डं मन्त्रमुदीरयेत्।

इमं तिलमयं पिण्डं मधुसर्पिःसमन्वितम्॥२६॥

ददामि तस्मै प्रेताय यः पीडां कुरुते मम।

सजलान् कृष्णकलशांस्तिलपात्रसमन्वितान्॥२७॥

द्वादश प्रेतमुद्दिश्य दद्यादेकञ्च विष्णवे।

ततोऽभिषिञ्चदाचार्यो दम्पतीकलसोदकैः॥२८॥

शुचिर्वरायुधधरो मन्त्रैर्वरुणदैवतैः।

यजमानस्ततो दद्यादाचार्याय सदक्षिणाम्॥२९॥

Having propitiated the planets before, he should perform the tenth part of *Homa* with sesame. Then with water sacred to the *Pitṛs* he should offer sesame and water, and *piṇdas* unto the *Preta*, of unknown family and name. Then he should recite the following *Mantra* : "I offer this *piṇdas* consisting of sesame, honey and clarified butter unto that *Preta*, who is troubling me. Then in honour of the *Preta*, he should dedicate unto Viṣṇu twelve black pitchers filled with water and containing a plate of sesame. Then he should sprinkle the *Ācārya* and his wife with the water of the pitcher consecrated with the Varuṇa *Mantra*, "Śucirvarāyudhadhara'' (holder of pure and most excellent weapon). Then the sacrificer shall offer the final present unto the *Ācārya*.

ततो नारायणबलिः कर्त्तव्यः शास्त्रनिश्चयात्।

एष साधारणविधिरगतीनामुदाहृतः॥३०॥

Then offerings should be made unto Nārāyaṇa according to the decisions of the *Śāstra*. This is the general regulation, spoken of for these who die under internal conditions.

विशेषस्तु पुनर्ज्ञेयो व्याघ्रादिनिहतेष्वपि।

व्याघ्रेण निहते प्रेते परकन्यां विवाहयेत्॥३१॥

Special regulations should be known again in cases of persons killed by tigers. If a person is killed by a tiger for him should be performed the nuptials of anothers daughter.

सर्पदंशे नागबलिर्देयः सर्वेषु काञ्चनम्।

चतुर्निष्कमितं हेमगजं दद्याद्गजैर्हते॥३२॥

In case of a snake-bite offerings should be given unto snakes; presents of gold should be made in all cases. One being killed by an elephant one should give away an idol of an elephant made of gold, four *Niṣkas* in weight.

राज्ञा विनिहते दद्यात् पुरुषन्तु हिरणमयम्।
चौरेण निहते धेनुं वैरिणा निहते वृषम्॥३३॥

For one being killed by the king, one should give away a golden figure of a male being; a cow, for being killed by a thief; and a bull, by an enemy.

वृकेण निहते दद्याद्यथाशक्ति च काञ्चनम्।
शय्यामृते प्रदातव्या शय्या तूलीसमन्विता॥३४॥
निष्कमात्रसुवर्णस्य विष्णुना समधिष्ठिता।
शौचहीने मृते चैव द्विनिष्कस्वर्णजं हरिम्॥३५॥

For one being killed by a wolf, one should give away gold according to his might. On a person dying in bed, a bed made of cotton with an image of Viṣṇu made of gold, one *Niṣka* in weight, lying on it, should be given away. For one dying in an impure state, an image of Hari, made of gold, two *Niṣkas* in weight [should be given away].

संस्कारहीने च मृते कुमारञ्च विवाहयेत्।
शुना हते च निक्षेपं स्थापयेन्निजशक्तितः॥३६॥

For one dying without the purificatory rites being performed unto one, the nuptials for a bachelor should performed. A person being killed by a god, one should bury some money, according to his might, under earth.

शूकरेण हते दद्यान्महिषं दक्षिणाऽन्वितम्।
कृमिभिश्च मृते दद्याद्गोधूमान्नं द्विजातये॥३७॥

For a person killed by a boar one should give away a buffalo, accompanied with a money-gift. For one killed by worms one should present food made of wheat unto the twice-born.

श्रृङ्गिणा च हते दद्याद्वृषभं वस्त्रसंयुतम्।
शकटेन मृते दद्यादश्वं सोपस्करान्वितम्।।३८।।

For one killed by a horned animal one should give away a bull covered with a cloth. For one killed by a cart one should give away a properly equipped horse.

भृगुपाते मृते चैव प्रदद्याद्धान्यपर्वतम्।
अग्निना निहते दद्यादुपानहं स्वशक्तितः।।३९।।

For one killed by falling from an elevated place one should give away a *Dhānya Giri*. For one killed by fire one should give away sandals according to his might.

दवेन निहते चैव कर्त्तव्या सदने सभा।
शस्त्रेण निहते दद्यानमहिषीं दक्षिणाऽन्विताम्।।४०।।

For one killed by forest-fire one should call a meeting in his house; and for one killed by a weapon one should give away a she-buffalo accompanied with a money present.

अश्मना निहते दद्यात् सवत्सां गां पयस्विनीम्।
विषेण च मृते दद्यान्मेदिनीं क्षेत्रसंयुताम्।।४१।।

For one killed by stone one should give away a milch-cow with a calf. For one killed by poison one should give lands containing cultivated fields.

उद्बन्धनमृते चापि प्रदद्याद्गां पयस्विनीम्।
मृते जलेन वरुणं हैमं दद्यात्रिनिष्किकम्।।४२।।

For one killed by hanging one should give away a milch-cow; and for one killed by water one should give away the image of Varuṇa made of gold, three *Niṣkas* in weight.

वृक्षं वृक्षहते दद्यात् सौवर्णं स्वर्णसंयुतम्।
अतीसारमृते लक्षं सावित्र्याः संहतो जपेत्।।४३।।

For one killed by [falling down] a tree one should give away a golden tree accompanied with a gold coin. For one killed from chronic diarrhoea, one, being self-restrained, should recite the

Gāyatrī for a hundred thousand times.

शाकिन्यादिमृते चैव जपेद्रुद्रं यथोचितम्।
विद्युत्पातेन निहते विद्यादानं समाचरेत्॥४४॥

For one killed by a Śākinī or any other evil spirit, one should duly recite the *Rudra Mantra*. For one killed by a thunder-bolt one should make gifts of learning.

अस्पर्शे च मृते कार्यं वेदपारायणं तथा।
सच्छास्त्रपुस्तकं दद्याद्वान्तमाश्रित्य संस्थिते॥४५॥

For one dead by touching an article that should not be touched, one should complete the recitation of the Vedas. For one dead while touching a degraded caste one should give away books on sacred literature.

पातित्येन मृते कुर्यात् प्राजापत्यानि षोडश।
मृते चापत्यरहिते कृच्छ्राणां नवतिञ्चरेत्॥४६॥

For one dying in a degraded state one should perform sixteen *Prājāpatyas*. For on dying childless one should perform ninety *Kṛcchras* (distressing penance).

निष्कत्रयमितस्वर्णं दद्यादश्वं हयाहते।
कपिना निहते दद्यात् कपिं कनकनिर्मितम्॥४७॥

For one killed by a horse one should give away a horse made a gold, three *Niṣkas* in weight. For one killed by monkey one should give away a monkey made of gold.

विसूचिकामृते स्वादु भोजयेच्च शतं द्विजाम्।
तिलधेनुः प्रदातव्या कण्ठेऽन्नबले मृते॥४८॥

For one dying of cholera one should treat a century of Brāhmaṇas with sweet edibles. For one killed by fire sticking to the throat one should give away a *Dhenu* of sesame.

केशरोगमृते चापि अष्टौ कृच्छ्रान् समाचरेत्।
एवं कृते विधानेन विदध्यादौर्ध्वदेहिकम्॥४९॥

For one dying of a disease of the hair one should perform

eight *Kṛcchras*. According to this regulation one should perform the funeral rites for them.

ततः प्रेतत्वनिर्मुक्ताः पितरस्तर्पितास्तथा।
दद्युः पुत्रांश्च पौत्राश्च आयुरारोग्यसम्पदः॥५०॥

Thereupon being freed from the condition of a *preta* (dead) the gratified *Pitṛs* (departed manes) grant sons, grand-sons, longevity, health and wealth.

इति शातातपप्रोक्तो विपाकः कर्मणामयम्।
शिष्याय शरभङ्गाय विनयात् परिपृच्छते॥५१॥

Here ends the [account of the] fruits [of various] acts given by *Śātātapa* to his disciple *Śarabhaṅga* accosting him with humility.

॥ इति श्री शातातपीये कर्मविपाकेऽगम्यागमनप्रायश्चित्तं नाम षष्ठोऽध्यायः॥६॥

॥ शातातपस्मृतिः समाप्ता ॥

१२. शङ्खस्मृतिः

12. Śaṅkha Smṛti

Chapter 1

स्वायम्भुवे नमस्कृत्य सृष्टिसंहारकारिणे।

चातुर्वर्ण्यहितार्थाय शङ्खः शास्त्रमथाकरोत्॥१॥

Having made obeisance to the Self-begotten one, the cause of creation and dissolution of the Universe, Śaṅkha, for the good of the four-fold social order, has framed this Code of Laws.

यजनं याजनं दानं तथैवाध्यापनक्रियाम्।

प्रतिग्रहञ्चाध्ययनं विप्रः कर्माणि कारयेत्॥२॥

Celebration of religious sacrifices, officiating as priests at the celebration of religious sacrifices, gift making, teaching, acceptance of gifts, and study are (the acts), which should be done by a Brāhmaṇa.

दानमध्ययनञ्चैव यजनञ्च यथाविधि।

क्षत्रियस्य च वैश्यस्य कर्मेदं परिकीर्त्तितम्॥३॥

Gift-making, study, and due celebration of religious sacrifices are (acts), which should be done by a Kṣatriya or Vaiśya.

क्षत्रियस्य विशेषेण प्रजानां परिपालनम्।

कृषिगोरक्षवाणिज्यं वैश्यस्य परिकीर्त्तितम्॥४॥

Protection of his subjects should be the specific duty of a Kṣatriya; trade, agriculture, and rearing of cattle are the specific duties of a Vaiśya.

शूद्रस्य द्विजशुश्रूषा सर्वशिल्पानि चाप्यथ।

क्षमा सत्यं दमः शौचं सर्वेषामविशेषतः॥५॥

Serving the Brāhmaṇas, and performance of different handicrafts should be the specific duties of a Śūdra. Practice of forbearance, truthfulness, and self-control, and cleanliness of body and spirit are equally obligatory on all, without any distinction of caste.

ब्राह्मणः क्षत्रियाः वैश्यस्त्रयो वर्णा द्विजातयः।
तेषां जन्म द्वितीयन्तु विज्ञेयं मौञ्जिबन्धनम्॥६॥

Brāhmaṇas, Kṣatriyas, and Vaiśyas are the three twice-born castes; their second birth takes place on the occasion of putting on the girdle of sacred rush.

आचार्यस्तु पिता प्रोक्तः सावित्री जननी तथा।
ब्रह्मक्षत्रियविशाञ्चैव मौञ्जिबन्धनजन्मनि॥७॥

In his second birth symbolised by the wearing of the sacred girdle, the preceptor of a Brāhmaṇas, Kṣatriya, or Vaiśya, who imparts the Gāyatrī Mantra, should be regarded as his father, while the Mantra itself should be looked upon as fulfilling the office of his mother.

विप्रा शूद्रसमास्तावद्विज्ञेयास्तु विचक्षणैः।
यावद्वेदे न जायन्ते द्विजा ज्ञेयास्तु तत्परम्॥८॥

Until the commencement of his study of the Vedas, a Brāhmaṇa continues in the status of a Śūdra; he becomes twice-born after that.

॥ इति शङ्खीये धर्मशास्त्रे प्रथमोऽध्यायः॥१॥

Chapter 2

गर्भस्य स्फुटताज्ञाने निषेकः परिकीर्त्तितः।
ततस्तु स्पन्दनात् कार्यं सवनन्तु विचक्षणैः॥१॥

On the full manifestation of the signs of pregnancy, the rite of *Niṣeka* should be performed (unto an *enceinte)* the wise should perform the rite of *Puṁsavanam* (rite for the causation of the birth of a male child unto her, as soon as she would be quick with the child.

आशौचे तु व्यतिक्रान्ते नामकर्म विधीयते।
नामधेयञ्च कर्त्तव्यं वर्णानाञ्च समाक्षरम्॥२॥

On the expiry of the period of birth-uncleanness (of its parents), the rite of nomenclature should be performed unto a babe, and its name should be made to consist of an even number of letters.

मङ्गल्यं ब्राह्मणस्योक्तं क्षत्रियस्य बलान्वितम्।
वैश्यस्य धनसंयुक्तं शूद्रस्य तु जुगुप्सितम् ॥३॥

The name of a Brāhmaṇa child should be (a term) of blissful signification; that of a Kṣatriya child should be a (term) denoting strength and vigour; that of a Vaiśya child should be a term denoting wealth and prosperity, while that of a Śūdra child should be of a lowly import.

शर्मान्तं ब्राह्मणस्योक्तं वर्मान्तं क्षत्रियस्य तु।
धनान्तश्चैव वैश्यस्य दासान्तं वान्तजन्मनः॥४॥

The name of a Brāhmaṇa should be appended with the term *Śavmā* (of divine felicity); that of a Kṣatriya should end with the term *Varmā* (protector); that of a Vaiśya should be appended with the term *Dhana* (wealth), while that of a Śūdra should terminate with term *Dāsa* (servant).

चतुर्थे मासि कर्तव्यमादित्यस्य प्रदर्शनम्।
षष्ठेऽन्नप्राशनं मासि चूडा कार्या यथाकुलम्॥५॥

The rite of exposing the child to the sun, (as well as that of taking it out in the open) should be done in the fourth month of its life while the rite of *Annaprāśanam* should be done in the sixth month and the rite of tonsure, according to the custom prevailing in its father family.

गर्भाष्टमेऽब्दे कर्त्तव्यं ब्राह्मणस्योपनायनम्।
गर्भादेकादशे राज्ञो गर्भात्तु द्वादशे विशः॥६॥

A Brāhmaṇa boy should be invested with the holy thread at the eighth year of his age, inclusive of the period of his inter-uterine life; a Kṣatriya boy should be invested with the holy thread at the eleventh, and a Vaiśya boy, at the twelfth year of his age, reckoned as above described.

षोडशाब्दास्तु विप्रस्य द्विविंशः क्षत्रियस्य तु।
विंशतिः सचतुष्का तु वैश्यस्य परिकीर्त्तिता॥७॥

The time for the rite of delayed investure with the holy thread *(Gauṇa Kāla)* in respect of Brāhmaṇa, Kṣatriya, and Vaiśya boys respectively extends upto the sixteenth, twenty second, and twenty fourth year of their life.

नाभिभाषेत सावित्रीमत ऊर्ध्वं निवर्त्तते॥८॥

विज्ञातव्यास्त्रयोऽप्येते यथाकालमसंस्कृता:।

सावित्रीपतिता व्रात्या: सर्वधर्मबहिष्कृता:॥९॥

Brāhmaṇas, Kṣatriyas, and Vaiśyas, not invested with the holy thread at the proper time, become degraded and divested of the right of performing any religious rite. These unconsecrated ones, shorn of the prerogative of reciting the Gāyatrī Mantra, are dragged down to the level of breakers of vows.

मौञ्जीबन्धो द्विजानान्तु क्रमान्मौञ्जी प्रकीर्त्तिता:।

मार्गवैयाघ्रवास्तानि चर्माणि ब्रह्मचारिणाम्॥१०॥

Members of the three twice-born orders should wear the sacred girdle at the time of being invested with the holy thread. A Brāhmaṇa Brahmacārin should wear a deer-skin; a Kṣatriya, a tiger-skin; and a Vaiśya, a goat's skin; under the circumstance, in the shape of his upper garment.

पर्णपिप्पलबिल्वानां क्रमाद्दण्डा: प्रकीर्त्तिता:।

कर्णकेशललाटेस्तु तुल्या: प्रोक्ता: क्रमेण तु॥११॥

The sacred rods of these three orders should be respectively made of Parṇa, Pippala, and Bilva wood, respectively reaching their hair, ears, and forehead in height.

अवक्रा: सत्वच: सर्वे नाग्निदग्धस्तथैव च।

यज्ञोपवीतं कार्पासक्षौमोर्णानां यथाक्रमम्॥१२॥

The wood should be whole-skinned, unbent, and unburnt. The holy threads of the three (twice-born orders) should be respectively made of cotton, silk, and woolen threads.

आदिमध्यावसानेषु भवच्छब्दोपलक्षितम्।

भैक्षस्य चरणं प्रोक्तं वर्णानामनुपूर्वश:॥१३॥

Brahmacārins of the three twice-born orders should respectively pronounce the term "*Bhavat*" at the begin, middle, and end of their (solicitations) for alms, *as "Bhavat* (you), be pleased to give me alms." "Be pleased, *Bhavat* (you), to give me alms;" and "Be pleased to give me alms, *Bhavat* (you).

॥ इति शङ्खीये धर्मशास्त्रे द्वितीयोऽध्यायः॥२॥

Chapter 3

उपनीय गुरुः शिष्यं वेदमस्मै प्रयच्छति।
भूतकाध्यापको यस्तु उपाध्यायः स उच्यते॥१॥

A preceptor, having invested a pupil with the holy thread, should teach him the Vedas; a preceptor, who gives lessons in the Vedas for money, is called an *Upādhyāya.*

प्रयतः कल्यमुत्थाय स्नाता हुतहुताशनः।
कुर्वीत प्रयतो भक्त्या गुरूणामभिवादनम्॥२॥

A Brahmacārin having quitted his bed early in the morning, and having bathed and performed the *Homa,* should accost, self-controlled, his preceptor.

अनुज्ञातश्च गुरुणा ततोऽध्ययनमाचरेत्।
कृत्वा ब्रह्माञ्जलिं पश्यन् गुरोर्वदनमानतः॥३॥

Then having been commanded by the preceptor, and having cast a look at his face, he should commence the study of the Vedas, with the palms of his hands blended in the manner of a Brahmāñjali.

ब्रह्मावसाने प्रारम्भे प्रणवञ्च प्रकीर्त्तयेत्।
अनध्यायेष्वध्ययनं वर्जयेच्च प्रयत्नतः॥४॥

Both at the commencement and close of his Vedic studies, he should pronounce the *Praṇava* Mantra; the study, of the Vedas should be carefully omitted on days of non-study marked by interdicted lunar phases and astral combinations.

चतुर्द्दशीं पञ्चदशीमष्टमीं राहुसूतकम्।
उल्कापातं महीकम्पमशौचं ग्रामविप्लवम्॥५॥
इन्द्रप्रयाणं सुरतं घनसङ्घातनिस्वनम्।
वाद्यकोलाहलं युद्धमनध्यायं विवर्ज्जयेत्॥६॥

The eighth and fourteenth days of a fortnight, the day of the new or full moon, a solar or lunar eclipse, earth-quakes, meteor-falls, personal uncleanness incidental to the death of a *Sapiṇḍa* or cognate relation, peals of thunder, roaring of rain-clouds, feeling of any amative propensities, conflagrations, village-disturbances, hearing of the sounds of music are the occasions on which the study of the Vedas *is* interdicted.

नाधीयीताभियुक्तोऽपि प्रयत्नान्न च वेगतः।
देवायतनवल्मीकश्मशानशिवसन्निधौ॥७॥

Even having been reprimanded, he should not study the Vedas in a very loud voice, nor near the side of an ant-hill, cremation ground, divine temple, or phallic emblem.

भैक्षचर्यान्तथा कुर्याद्ब्राह्मणेषु यथाविधि।
गुरुणा चाभ्यनुज्ञातः प्राश्नीयात् प्राङ्मुखः शुचिः॥८॥

A Brahmacārin should beg alms of the Brāhmaṇas alone; having been commanded by his preceptor, he, pure in body and mind, should take his meal with his face turned towards the east, on return (from his alms-taking rambles).

हितं प्रियं गुरोः कुर्यादहंकारविवर्ज्जितः॥९॥
उपास्य पश्चिमां सन्ध्यां पूजयित्वा हुताशनम्।
अभिवाद्य गुरुं पश्चाद् गुरोर्वचनकृद्भवेत्॥१०॥

Humble in spirit, and without arrogance, he should do only what is good and beneficial to his preceptor; having performed the evening *Sandhyā* and worshipped the sacred fire, he should make obeisance to his preceptor, and carry out his behests.

गुरोः पूर्वं समुत्तिष्ठेच्छयीत चरमं तथा॥११॥
मधुमांसाञ्जनं श्राद्धं गीतं नृत्यञ्च वर्ज्जयेत्।
हिंसां परापवादं च स्त्रीलीलां च विशेषतः॥१२॥

He should quit his bed before his preceptor rises from his sleep, and lie down after he has slept in the night. He should forego the use of honey, meat-diet, and collyrium, and forswear all music, dancing, *Śrāddhas,* calumny, envy, and female company.

मेखलामजिनं दण्डं धारयेच्च प्रयत्नतः।
अधःशायी भवेन्नित्यं ब्रह्मचारी समाहितः॥१३॥

Observing perfect continence, he should wear his girdle and carry his sacred rod, and lie down, self-controlled, on the bare ground.

एवं व्रतन्तु कुर्वीत वेदस्वीकरणं बुधः।
गुरवे च धनं दत्त्वा स्नायाच्च तदनन्तरम्॥१५॥

The wise should follow these rules while studying the Vedas; having paid honorarium to his preceptor, he should bathe, and finish his studies.

॥ इति शङ्खीये धर्मशास्त्रे तृतीयोऽध्यायः॥३॥

Chapter 4

विन्देत विधिवद्भार्यामसमानार्षगोत्रजाम्।
मातृतः पञ्चमीञ्चापि पितृतस्त्वथ सप्तमीम्॥१॥

(After finishing the study of the Vedas*),* a twice-born one should marry a wife, not of the same *Pravara* (spiritual clanship) or *Gotra* (family) with him, and not in any way related to him within five degrees, on his mother's, or seven degrees, on his father's, side.

ब्राह्मो दैवस्तथैवार्षः प्राजापत्यस्तथासुरः।
गान्धर्वो राक्षसश्चैव पैशाचश्चाष्टमोऽधमः॥२॥

The eight forms of marriage, (recognized by our *Dharma Śāstras,)* are the Brāhma, Daiva, Ārṣa, *Prājāpatya,* Āsura, Gāndharva, Rākṣasa, and Paiśāca.

एते धर्म्यास्तु चत्वारः पूर्वं विप्रे प्रकीर्त्तिताः।
गान्धर्वो राक्षसश्चैव क्षत्रियस्य प्रशस्यते।३॥

Of these, the first four forms of marriage are commendable in respect of Brāhmaṇas; the Gāndharva, and Rākṣasa forms are commendable in respect of Kṣatriyas.

अप्रार्थितः प्रयत्नेन ब्राह्मस्तु परिकीर्त्तितः।
यज्ञेषु ऋत्विजे दैवमादायार्षस्तु गोद्वयम्॥४॥

The form of marriage in which the bride is courtingly given away to the bridegroom, without any solicitation on his part, is called the *Brāhma;* that, in which a girl is given in marriage to a priest officiating at a religious sacrifice (in the shape of a honorarium), is called *Daiva;* while that, in which the bride is given away with the present of a pair of cows, is called *Ārśa.*

प्रार्थिता संप्रदानेन प्राजापत्यः प्रकीर्त्तितः।
आसुरो द्रविणादानाद्गान्धर्वः समयान्मिथः॥५॥

The form of marriage in which the bride is given to one who solicits her hands is called the *Prājāpatyam;* that, in which the bride is purchased or given away for money, is called the *Āsuram;* while that, in which the bride and the bride-groom unite, out of love, is called *Gāndharvam.*

राक्षसो युद्धहरणात् पैशाचः कन्यकाच्छलात्।
तिस्रस्तु भार्या विप्रस्य द्वे भार्ये क्षत्रियस्य तु॥६॥

A marriage by capture is called *Āsuram;* while the one effected through stratagem is called *Paiśācam.*

एकैव भार्या वैश्यस्य तथा शूद्रस्य कीर्त्तिता।
ब्राह्मणी क्षत्रिया वैश्या ब्राह्मणस्य प्रकीर्त्तिता:॥७॥

A Brāhmaṇa can marry three wives, a Kṣatriya can take a couple of wives, while a Vaiśya or Śūdra can marry a single wife. A Brāhmaṇa can marry a Brāhmaṇa, Kṣatriya, or a Vaiśya girl.

क्षत्रिया चैव वैश्या च क्षत्रियस्य विधीयते।
वैश्यैव भार्या वैश्यस्य शूद्रा शूद्रस्य कीर्त्तिता॥८॥

A Kṣatriya should marry a Kṣatriya, or a Vaiśya girl; whereas a Vaiśya or Śūdra should not take a wife other than one of his own caste.

आपद्यपि न कर्त्तव्या शूद्रा भार्या द्विजन्मना।
अस्यां तस्य प्रसूतस्य निष्कृतिर्न विधीयते।९॥

Even in distress, a twice born one should not wed a Śūdra girl, inasmuch as a son begotten by him on her person will never find his salvation.

तपस्वी यज्ञशीलश्च सर्वधर्मभृतां वरः।
ध्रुवं शूद्रत्वमाप्नोति शूद्रश्राद्धे त्रयोदशे।१०॥

Even, he, who is foremost of all virtuous men, and duly celebrates the religious sacrifices and practises penitential austerities, is degraded to the status of a Śūdra by having the thirteen *Śrāddhas* done unto him by (such) a Śūdra son.

नीयते तु सपिण्डत्वं येषां श्राद्धं कुलोद्गतम्।
सर्वे शूद्रत्वमायान्ति यदि स्वर्गजिताश्च ते।११॥

The *Sapiṇḍa* relations whose *Śrāddhas* are performed (by such a Śūdra son) according to the usage of the family, even if they all have conquered (attained to) the region of heaven, are degraded to the status of a Śūdra.

सपिण्डीकरणं कार्यं कुलजस्य तथा ध्रुवम्।
श्राद्धं द्वादशकं कृत्वा श्राद्धे प्राप्ते त्रयोदशे॥१२॥
सपिण्डीकरणं नार्द्धं न च शूद्रस्तथार्हति।
तस्मात् सर्वप्रयत्नेन शूद्रभार्यां विवर्जयेत्॥१३॥

The *Sapiṇḍīkaraṇam Śrāddha* ceremony should be celebrated (by one), after having performed the twelve monthly *Śrāddhas* (of one's deceased relation) in accordance with the usage of one's family; it should not be celebrated on the advent of the thirteenth (unperformed) *Śrāddha,* and a Śūdra is not privileged to do the same. Hence, a twice born one should carefully avoid wedding a Śūdra wife.

पाणिग्राह्यः सवर्णासु गृह्णीयात् क्षत्रिया शरम्।
वैश्या प्रतोदमादद्याद्वेदले तु द्विजन्मनः॥१४॥

A Brāhmaṇa girl shall hold mendicant's cups *(Vaidale)* in her hands, a Kṣatriya girl shall catch hold of an arrow, and a Vaiśya girl shall handle a stick for goading cattle, at the time of wedding.

सा भार्या या वहेदग्निं सा भार्या या पतिव्रता।
सा भार्या या पतिप्राणाः सा भार्या या प्रजावती॥१५॥

She, who bears the sacred fire, is a true wife; she, who is faithful to her lord, is a true wife; she, who is one in spirit with her husband, is a true wife; she, who has borne children, is a true wife.

लालनीया सदा भार्या ताडनीया तथैव च।
लालिता ताडिता चैव स्त्री श्रीर्भवति नान्यथा॥१६॥

A wife should be both caressed and admonished both fondled and checked, a wife becomes the source of beauty and prosperity of the household, and not otherwise.

॥ इति शङ्खीये धर्मशास्त्रे चतुर्थोऽध्याय:॥४॥

Chapter 5

पञ्चसूना गृहस्थस्य चुल्ली पेषण्युपस्कर:।
कण्डनी चोदकुम्भश्च तस्य पापस्य शान्तये॥१॥

There are five places (in the house of a) householder where animal lives are daily destroyed; they are the oven, the broomstick, the grinding stone, the pestle and mortar, and the water pitcher.

पञ्चयज्ञविधानञ्च गृही नित्यं न हापयेत्।
पञ्चयज्ञविधानेन तत्पापं तस्य नश्यति॥२॥

For the expiation of the sin (of this destruction of lives), a householder should daily celebrate the five domestic sacrifices (known as *Pañca yajña),* whereby all his sin would be extinguished.

देवयज्ञो भूतयज्ञ: पितृयज्ञस्तथैव च।
ब्रह्मयज्ञो नृयज्ञश्च पञ्चयज्ञा: प्रकीर्त्तिता:॥३॥

These five religious sacrifices are called *Devayajña, Bhūtayajña, Pitṛyajña,* and *Nṛyajña.*

होमो दैवो बलिर्भौत: पित्र्य: पिण्डक्रिया स्मृत:।
स्वाध्यायो ब्रह्मयज्ञश्च नृयज्ञोऽतिथिपूजनम्॥४॥

A daily performance of *Homa is* called *Deva-Yajña;* a daily offering of oblations is called *Bhūta yajña,* a daily performance of *Śrāddhas* in honour of one's departed manes, as well as offering of libations to them, is called *Pitṛ-yajña,* and practice of hospitality to chance-comers *(Atithis)* at one's house is called *Nṛ-Yajña.*

वानप्रस्थो ब्रह्मचारी यतिश्चैव तथा द्विजः।
गृहस्थस्य प्रसादेन जीवन्त्येते यथाविधि॥५॥

Forest-dwelling hermits *(Vānaprasthas),* Brahmacārins, Yatis, and Brāhmaṇas, all live on the bounties of house-holders.

गृहस्थ एव यजते गृहस्थस्तप्यते तपः।
दाता चैव गृहस्थः स्यात् तस्माच्छ्रेष्ठो गृहाश्रमी॥६॥

It is a householder that celebrates a religious sacrifice, it is he who practises penitential austerities, it is he who makes charities and practises hospitality, hence, foremost is a house-holder of all other religious orders.

यथा भर्त्ता प्रभुः स्त्रीणां वर्णानां ब्राह्मणो यथा।
अतिथिस्तद्वदेवास्य गृहस्थस्य प्रभुः स्मृतः॥७॥

As a husband is the master of his wife, as Brāhmaṇas are the lords of the social orders, so a chance-comer *(Atithi)* is the lord of the house-holder at whose house he arrives.

न व्रतैर्नोपवासेन धर्मेण विविधेन च।
नारी स्वर्गमवाप्नोति प्राप्नोति पतिपूजनात्॥८॥

By worshipping her husband alone, and not so much by dint of fasts, vigils, vows, and penances, etc., a woman can ascend to heaven.

न स्नानेन न होमेन नैवाग्निपारितर्पणात्।
ब्रह्मचारी दिवं याति स याति गुरुपूजनात्॥९॥

By worshipping his preceptor alone, and not so much through the merit of oblations, *Homas,* or fire-worship, that a Brahmacārin can attain to heaven.

नाग्निशुश्रूषया क्षान्त्या स्नानेन विविधेन च।
वानप्रस्थो दिवं याति याति भोजनवर्जनात्॥१०॥

It is by alone abjuring his food, and not so much by dint of forbearance, resignation, and fire-worship, etc. that a *Vānaprastha* (forest-dwelling hermit) can attain to heaven.

न भैक्षैर्न च मौनेन शून्यागाराश्रयेन च।
योगी सिद्धिमवाप्नोति यथा मैथुनवर्जनात्॥१२॥

It is not so much by observing a vow of silence, indigence, or secluded life, as by forswearing sexual intercourse, that *a yogin* can achieve success (work out his own salvation.)

न यज्ञैर्दक्षिणाभिश्च वह्निशुश्रूषया न च।
गृही स्वर्गमवाप्नोति यथा चातिथिपूजनात्॥१२॥

It is not so much by celebrating religious sacrifices, or by worshipping the sacred fire, or by paying honorariums to Brāhmaṇas, as by propitiating *Atithis,* that a house-holder can ascend to heaven.

तस्मात् सर्वप्रयत्नेन गृहस्थोऽतिथिमागतम्।
आहारशयनार्थेन विधिवत् प्रतिपूजयेत्॥१३॥

Hence, a house-holder should duly propitiate an *Atithi,* arrived at his house, by offering him food and a bed.

सायं प्रातश्च जुहुयादग्निहोत्रं यथाविधि।
दर्शञ्च पौर्णमासञ्च जुहुयाच्च तथाविधिः॥१४॥

Morning and evening libations of clarified butter should be cast in the sacred fire; and *Homas* should be duly performed on the day of the new or full moon, as well.

यज्ञैर्वा पशुबन्धैश्च चातुर्मास्यैस्तथैव च।
त्रैवार्षिकाधिकान्नेन[1] पिबेत् सोममतन्द्रितः॥१५॥

In the event of three years' or a year's provision being stored up in his granary, a house-holder should drink lively of the effused juice of *Soma,* either on the occasion of *a Paśubandha, Cāturmāsyam,* or any other religious sacrifice.

इष्टिं वैश्वानरीं कुर्यात्तथा चाल्पधनो द्विजः।
न भिक्षेत धनं शूद्रात् सर्वं दद्यादमभीप्सितम्॥१६॥

A Brāhmaṇa of limited means should celebrate the

---

1. 'त्रैवार्षिकाधिकालस्तु' इत्यपि पाठः।

Vaiśvānarī sacrifices; but under no circumstance should he ask anything of a Śūdra, but give away whatever he wishes to give away.

वृत्तिस्तु न त्यजेद्विद्वानृत्विजं पूर्वमेव तु।
कर्मणा जन्मना शुद्धं विद्यात् पात्रं बलीततम्॥१७॥

An intelligent man should not renounce the means of his livelihood, nor discharge his ancestral priest. An old Brāhmaṇa, pure in birth and consecrated with religious rites, with the skin of his body shriveled and muscles of his limbs loose and flabby, should be regarded as the proper person for the office of a priest.

एतैरेव गुणैर्युक्तं धर्मार्जितधनं तथा।
याजयेत्तु सदा विप्रो ग्राह्यस्तस्मात् प्रतिग्रहः॥१८॥

A Brāhmaṇa should constantly cause him to celebrate religious sacrifices who is possessed of the aforesaid qualifications, and earns an honest living; a Brāhmaṇa is authorized only to receive gifts of such a person.

॥ इति शङ्खीये धर्मशास्त्रे पञ्चमोऽध्यायः॥५॥

Chapter 6

गृहस्थस्तु यदा पश्येद्वलीपलितमात्मनः।
अपत्यस्यैव चापत्यं तदाऽरण्यं समाश्रयेत्॥१॥

A householder, when he finds that his hairs have turned gray and the skin of his body has become loose and wrinkled, and that a son has been born unto his own son, should betake himself to forest.

पुत्रेषु दारान् निक्षिप्य तया वाऽनुगतो वने।
अग्नीनुपचरेन्नित्यं वन्यमाहारमाहरेत्॥२॥

Either having placed his wife in the custody of his sons, or having been accompanied by her to the forest, he (house-holder) should daily propitiate the fire-god and live on produce of the forest.

यदाहारो भवेत् तेन पूजयेत् पितृदेवताः।
तेनैव पूजयेन्नित्यमतिथिं समुपागतम्॥३॥

Those articles of fare, which he would take (during his forest life), he should offer unto his departed manes, and propitiate therewith any chance-comer who may arrive at his hermitage.

ग्रामादाहृत्य चाश्नीयादष्टौ ग्रामान् समाहितः।
स्वाध्यायञ्च सदा कुर्याज्जटाश्च विभृयात्तथा।।४।।

From a village he should procure, self-controlled, eight morsels of food, wear clotted hairs on his head, and daily study the Vedas.

तपसा शोषयेन्नित्यं स्वकञ्चैव कलेवरम्।
आर्द्रवासास्तु हेमन्ते ग्रीष्मे पञ्चतपास्तथा।।५।।

By the practice of *Tapas,* he should cause his body to be more and more lean, every day, stay in wet clothes during the winter, and pass the summer in the practice of the *Pañcatapas* penance (which consists in sitting amidst fires on four sides and with the summer sun burning over the head).

प्रावृष्याकाशशायी स्यान्नक्ताशी च सदा भवेत्।
चतुर्थकालिको वा स्यात् षष्ठकालिक एव वा।।६।।

During the rainy season, he should live unsheltered under the bare expanse of heaven, and take his meals at night, or at the fourth or sixth part of the day.

कृच्छ्रैर्वाऽपि नयेत् कालं ब्रह्मचर्यञ्च पालयेत्।
एवं नीत्वा वने कालं द्विजो ब्रह्माश्रमी भवेत्।।७।।

A self-controlled Brahmacārin, he should live a life of penance and privation in the forest, whereby a twice-born one should become a member of the *Brahmāśrama*.

।। इति शङ्खीये धर्मशास्त्रे षष्ठोऽध्यायः।।६।।

Chapter 7

कृत्वेष्टिं विधिवत् पश्चात् सर्ववेदसदक्षिणम्।
आत्मन्यग्नीन् समारोप्य द्विजो ब्रह्माश्रमी भवेत्।।१।।

Having duly performed a religious sacrifice, and made a honorarium of all his belongings (in the forest), and having installed the sacred fire on his own self (by eating the burnt ashes of the *Homa* fuels,) a twice-born one should enter the order of *Brahmāśramin.*

विधूमे न्यस्तमुसले व्यङ्गारे भुक्तवर्ज्जने।
अतीते पादसम्पाते नित्यं भिक्षां यतिश्चरेत्॥२॥

After the fires had been put on in the ovens (in a village), after the pestles and mortars had been duly laid aside, after the live charcoals had been extinguished in (the houses of villages), and after the villagers had all taken their midday meal, and the village-roads become entirely unfrequented by passers, a *Yati* should stroll out for alms in a village.

न व्यथेत तथालाभे यथालब्धेन वर्त्तयेत्।
न पाचयेत्तथैवान्नं नाश्नीयात् कस्यचिद्गृहे॥३॥

Even having returned in empty hands, he should neither be grieved nor dejected; he should live contended on what he can obtain by begging; he should never allow his rice to be cooked by another, nor take his meal in another man's house.

मृन्मयालाबुपात्राणि यतीनान्तु विनिर्द्दिशेत्।
तेषां सम्मार्जनाच्छुद्धिरद्भिश्चैव प्रकीर्त्तिता॥४॥

Yatis are enjoined to use earthen vessels, or those made of gourd-skin; and it is laid down that their purification consists in simply washing them with water.

कौपीनाच्छादनं वासो बिभृयादसखश्चरन्।
शून्यागारनिकेतः स्याद्यत्र सायंगृहो मुनिः॥५॥

Companionless, he should trudge on his journey, wearing only a girdle-cloth to cover his nudity; he should stay (for the night) wherever he may chance to arrive at the evening, and live in a solitary apartment.

दृष्टिपूतं न्यसेत् पादं वस्त्रपूतं जलं पिबेत्।
सत्यपूतां वदेद्वाक्यं मनःपूतं समाचरेत्॥६॥

He should let fall his foot-steps, purified by sight (*i.e.*, carefully observing that he does not tread on any animate being, drink water purified (filtered) through a piece of cloth, speak words purified with truth, and act what the mind approves of as good.

चन्दनैर्लिप्यतेऽङ्गं वा भस्मचूर्णैर्विगर्हितैः।
कल्याणमप्यकल्याणं तयोरेव न संश्रयेत्॥७॥

Good or bad, whatever may happen in this life, he should be equally indifferent to them all; equally unconcerned if his body is besmeared with sandal paste, or bespattered with clay and ashes.

सर्वभूतहितो मैत्रः समलोष्टाश्मकाञ्चनः।
ध्यानयोगरतो नित्यं भिक्षुर्यायात् परां गतिम्॥८॥

Kind to, and seeking the good of, all creatures, judging gold, stone and brick-bat as of equal value, a *Yati,* absorbed in the contemplation of the Infinite, acquires the highest bliss.

जन्मना यस्तु निर्विण्णो मन्येत च तथैव च।
आधिभिर्व्याधिभिश्चैव तं देवो ब्राह्मणं विदुः॥९॥

Him, who is apathetic, from his birth, to the concerns of life and looks upon this life as a series of mental and physical pain to be borne with the greatest unconcern, the gods know as a Brāhmaṇa.

अशुचित्वं शरीरस्य प्रियस्य च विपर्ययः।
गर्भवासे च वसतिस्तस्मान्मुच्येत नान्यथा॥१०॥

He, who views this body as a reservoir of excrements, and this life, which is started with a residence in the womb, as a crowning, disappointment of all cherished hopes and desires, is alone fit to be liberated.

जगदेतन्निराक्रन्दं न तु सारमनर्थकम्।
भोक्तव्यमिति निर्विण्णो मुच्यते नात्र संशयः॥११॥

The apathetic one, who considers as purposeless and unsubstantial the incidents of this world which are to be some how borne at the best, is undoubtedly liberated from the (chain of necessary existence.)

प्राणायामैर्दहेद्दोषान् धारणाभिश्च किल्विषान्।
प्रत्याहारैरसंसर्गान् ध्यानेनानीश्वरान् गुणान्॥१२॥

The disease germs *(Doṣas)* in the body should be consumed with thc help of *Prāṇāyāma,* sins with the help of the concentration of mind, delusions of the world by witholding the senses from their objects, and the ungodly qualities by dint of meditation.

सव्याहृतिं सप्रणवां गायत्रीं शिरसा सह।
त्रिः पठेदायतप्राणः प्राणायामः स उच्यते॥१३॥

The practice of *Prāṇāyāma* consists in reciting the Gāyatrī *Śiras* Mantra with the mystic Om with inflated lungs (suppressed breath.)

मनसः संयमस्तज्ज्ञैर्द्धारणेति निगद्यते।
संहारश्चेन्द्रियाणाञ्च प्रत्याहारः प्रकीर्त्तितः॥१४॥

The controlling (concentration) of the mind is called *Dhāraṇā* by the knowers of reality, whereas *Pratyāhāra* consists in withdrawing the senses from their objects.

हृदयस्थस्य योगेन देवदेवस्य दर्शनम्।
ध्यानं प्रोक्तं प्रवक्ष्यामि सर्वस्माद्योगतः शुभम्॥१५॥

The act of witnessing the god of gods, ensconsed in one's heart, by means of *Yoga, is* called *Dhyānam* (meditation); all good comes out of this *Yoga.*

हृदिस्था देवताः सर्वा हृदि प्राणाः प्रतिष्ठिताः।
हृदि ज्योतींषि सूर्यश्च हृदि सर्वं प्रतिष्ठितम्॥१६॥

In the heart reside all the gods; all the *Prāṇas* are ensconsed in the heart; all the luminaries (such as the sun, the moon etc.,) reside in the heart; in short every thing has its seat in the heart.

स्वदेहमरणिं कृत्वा प्रणवञ्चोत्तरारणिम्।
ध्याननिर्मथनाभ्यान्तु विष्णुं पश्येद्धृदि स्थितम्॥१७॥

Having made of the body and the *Praṇava,* the two fire churners, and contemplation, the churning, see the all-pervading god situate in the heart.

हृद्यर्कश्चन्द्रमा: सूर्य: सोमो मध्ये हुताशन:।

तेजोमध्ये स्थितं तत्त्वं तत्त्वमध्ये स्थितोऽच्युत:॥१८॥

The sun, the moon, and the fire are ensconsed in the heart. The sun and the moon are on the two sides of the heart, the fire is in their middle. The fundamental principle *(Tattvam)* lies in the fire, and in that principle lies ensconsed the deity that suffers no decay.

अणोरणीयान् महतो महीया

नात्माऽस्य जन्तोर्निहितो गुहायाम्।

तेजोमयं पश्यति वीतशोको

धातु: प्रसादान्महिमानमात्मन:॥१९॥

The griefless one, through the purification of his own soul, beholds the glory of the supreme soul, subtler than the subtlest, and larger than the largest things of the world, burning effulgent in the hearts of all.

वासुदेवस्तमोऽन्धानां प्रत्यक्षो नैव जायते।

अज्ञानपटसंवीतैरिन्द्रियैर्विषयेप्सुभि:॥२०॥

The god Vāsudeva (the all pervading deity) never becomes manifest to those, blind with the delusion of life, since it is the screen of ignorance that veils the senses of those persons.

एष वै पुरुषो विष्णुर्व्यक्ताव्यक्त: सनातन:।

एष धाता विधाता च पुराणो निष्कल: शिव:॥२१॥

This is the eternal, original, god, both manifest and unmanifest; this is Viṣṇu, the sinless, blissful, ordainer of the universe.

वेदाहमेतं पुरुषं महान्त-

मादित्यवर्णं तमस: परस्तात्।

मन्त्रैर्विदित्वा न विभेति मृत्यो-

र्नान्य: पन्था विद्यतेऽयनाय॥२२॥

He dreads not death who knows, with the help of Mantras, this eternal subjectivity situate beyond the confines of *Tamas* (ignorance) and effulgent as the burning sun. There is no other means of salvation.

पृथिव्यापस्तथा तेजोवायुराकाशमेव च।
पञ्चेमानि विजानीयान्महाभूतानि पण्डितः॥२३॥

The principles of earth, water, fire, wind and ether are called the five *Mahābhūtas* (elementals).

चक्षुश्रोत्रे स्पर्शनञ्च रसना घ्राणमेव च।
बुद्धीन्द्रियाणि जानीयात् पञ्चेमानि शरीरके॥२४॥

The eyes, the ears, the skin, the tongue and the nose, these five are called the intellectual (sense) organs of the body.

शब्दो रूपं तथा स्पर्शो रसो गन्धस्तथैव च।
इन्द्रियार्थान् विजानीयात् पञ्चैव विषयान् बुधः॥२५॥

The wise should know sound, colour, touch, flavour, and smell, as the objects of the five above-said sense-organs.

हस्तौ पादावुपस्थश्च जिह्वा पायुस्तथैव च।
कर्मेन्द्रियाणि पञ्चैव नित्यं मति शरीरके॥२६॥

The hands, the legs, the genitals, the tongue, and the anus are the five operative organs of the body.

मनो बुद्धिस्तथैवात्मा व्यक्ताव्यक्तं तथैव च।
इन्द्रियेभ्यः पराणीह चत्वारि प्रवराणि च॥२७॥

The mind, the intellect, the Ego, and the unmanifest Prakṛti, these four, should be regarded as superior and prior (in respect of time) to the above-said organs.

तथाऽऽत्मानं तद्व्यतीतं पुरुषं पञ्चविंशकम्।
तन्तुं ज्ञात्वा विमुच्यन्ते ये जनाः साधुवृत्तयः॥२८॥

The *Puruṣa* or the soul is the twenty-fifth category, and he is beyond all these organs, and *Mahābhūtas,* etc., The virtuous, who know him thus, obtain salvation.

इदन्तु परमं शुद्धमेतदक्षरमुत्तमम्।
अशब्दरसमस्पर्शमरूपं गन्धवर्ज्जितम्।

निर्दुःखमसुखं शुद्धं तद्विष्णोः परमं पदम्॥२९॥

This supreme self of Viṣṇu is holy, eternal, changeless, and beyond the principles of sound, touch, taste, or smell; it knows no pain or pleasure.

विज्ञानसारथिर्यस्तु मनः प्रग्रहबन्धनः।

सोऽध्वनः पारमाप्नोति तद्विष्णोः परमं पदम्॥३०॥

He whose charioteer is true knowledge, and who drives this chariot of the body by taking hold of the reins of mind, alone reaches the goal of his journey, and attains that supreme self of Viṣṇu.

बालाग्रशतशो भागः कल्पितस्तु सहस्त्रधा।

तस्यापि शतशो भागाज्जीवः सूक्ष्म उदाहृतः॥३१॥

If the hundredth part of a point of hair, divided into a hundred parts, is again divided into a thousand parts, the *Ātmā* is subtler than a hundred the part of such a thousandth part.

महतः परमव्यक्तमव्यक्तात् पुरुषः परः।

पुरुषान्न परं किञ्चित् सा काष्ठा सा परा गतिः॥३२॥

एषु सर्वेषु भूतेषु तिष्ठत्यविरलः सदा।

दृश्यते त्वग्र्यया बुद्ध्या सूक्ष्मया सूक्ष्मदर्शिभिः॥३३॥

The unmanifest *Prakṛti is* antecedent to *Mahat* (the principle of intellection), the *Puruṣa* is prior to this unmanifest *Prakṛti.* Beyond *Puruṣa* there is none; he is the last resource, the last category.

॥ इति शङ्खीये धर्मशास्त्रे सप्तमोऽध्यायः॥७॥

Chapter 8

क्रियास्नानं प्रवक्ष्यामि यथावद्विधिपूर्वकम्।

मृद्भिरद्भिश्च कर्त्तव्यं शौचमादौ यथाविधि॥१॥

Now I shall duly describe the mode of ceremonial ablution *(Kriyā Snānam).* First the cleansing of the body should be effected with earth and water.

जले निमग्न उन्मज्ज्य उपस्पृश्य यथाविधि।
तीर्थमावाहनं कुर्यात् तत् प्रवक्ष्याम्यशेषतः॥२॥

Then having dived in and out of the water, and duly performed the rite of *Ācamanam,* he (the bather) should invoke the sacred pools therein, of which I shall presently speak in detail.

प्रपद्ये वरुणं देवमम्भसां पतिमर्चितम्।
याचितं देहि मे तीर्थं सर्वपापापनुत्तये॥३॥

Having invoked the god Varuṇa, the worshipful lord of the oceans, he should address him as follows- "Give me the sacred pool *(Tīrtham),* O god, for the expiation of all sin.

तीर्थमावाहयिष्यामि सर्वाघविनिषूदनम्।
सान्निध्यमस्मिंस्तोये च क्रियतां मदनुग्रहात्॥४॥

I invoke all the sin-absolving *Tīrthas in* this water, do you, out of you graceful compassion towards me, be pleased to locate them herein.

रुद्रात् प्रपद्ये वरदान् सर्वानप्सुसदस्तथा।
सर्वानप्सुसदश्चैव प्रपद्ये प्रयतः स्थितः॥५॥

Then having made obeisance to the god Rudra and all other water-dwelling divinities who grant boons (to their suppliants), he should respectfully say, "I place myself under the protection of the deities of the water.

देवमप्सुसदं वह्निं प्रपद्येऽघनिषूदनम्।
अपः पुण्याः पवित्राश्च प्रपद्ये शरणं तथा॥६॥

Then having supplicated the sin-absolving, effulgent, fire-god, he should say, sacred and holy are the waters. I place myself under their protection."

रुद्रश्चाग्निश्च सर्पश्च वरुणस्त्वाप एव च।
शमयन्त्वाशु मे पापं माञ्च रक्षन्तु सर्वशः॥७॥

May Rudra, Agni, Varuṇa, and the serpent destroy my sin and protect me in every way.

हिरण्यवर्णेति तिसृभिर्ज्जगतीति चतसृभिः।

शन्नोदेवीति च तथा शन्न आपस्तथैव च॥८॥

Thereafter, the three Mantras, running as *Hiraṇya Varṇa,* etc., the four Mantras running as *Jagatī,* etc., and those respectively beginning with *Śanno Devī, Śanna Āpas,* and *Idamāpas Prabahate* etc., should be duly recited.

इदमापः प्रवहते द्यूतञ्च समुदीरयेत्।

एवं सन्मार्ज्जनं कृत्वा छन्द आर्षञ्च देवताः॥९॥

अघमर्षणसूक्तञ्च प्रपठेत् प्रयतः सदा॥१०॥

The *Ṛṣis,* metres, and the deities of these Mantras should be mentioned by name, and thereafter, having performed the *Sanmārjana* rite (ceremonial rubbing), he should recite, in a devout spirit, the *Aghmarṣaṇa (*sin absolving) *Sūktas*.

छन्दोऽनुष्टुप् च तस्यैव ऋषिश्चैवाघमर्षणः।

देवता भाववृत्तञ्च पापक्षये प्रकीर्त्तितः॥११॥

The metre of the Aghamarṣaṇa Sūktam is Anuṣṭubha, its deity is Bhāva Vṛtta, and its Ṛṣi is Aghamarṣaṇa; expiation of one's sin is the purpose for which it should be recited.

ततोऽम्भसि निमग्नः स्यात्त्रिः पठेदघमर्षणम्।

प्रपद्यान्मूर्द्धनि तथा महाव्याहृतिभिर्ज्जलम्॥१२॥

Then having plunged into the water, he (bather) should thrice recite the *Aghamarṣaṇa Sūktam,* and pour water over his head by reciting the *Mahā Vyāhṛti* Mantras.

यथाऽश्वमेधः क्रतुराट् सर्वपापापनोदनः।

तथाऽघमर्षणं सूक्तं सर्वपापप्रणाशनम्॥१३॥

As the horse-sacrifice, the king of all religious sacrifices, tends to extinguish all sin, so the *Aghamarṣaṇa Sūktam is* sin-absolving in its effect.

अनेन विधिना स्नात्वा स्नातवान् धौतवाससा।

परिवर्जितवासास्तु तीर्थनामानि सञ्जपेत्॥१४॥

Having bathed in this manner, a bather should put off wet

clothes and put on clean and dry ones, and mentally recite the names of sacred pools and places.

उदकस्याप्रदानात्तु स्नानशाटीं न पीडयेत्।
अनेन विधिना स्नातस्तीर्थस्य फलमश्नुते॥१५॥

One should not squeeze one's wet clothes after a bath without first offering the dripplings to one's departed manes. He, who bathes in the manner above described, acquires the merit of bathing in a sacred pool.

॥ इति शङ्खीये धर्मशास्त्रे अष्टमोऽध्याय:॥८॥

Chapter 9

अत: परं प्रवक्ष्यामि शुभामाचमनक्रियाम्।
कायं कनिष्ठिकामूले तीर्थमुक्तं करस्य तु॥१॥

Now I shall describe the mode of performing the auspicious rite of *Ācamanam.* The region about the root of the small finger of the hand is called *Kāya Tīrtham.*

अङ्गुष्ठमूले च तथा प्राजापत्यं प्रकीर्त्तितम्।
अङ्गुल्यग्रे स्मृतं दैवं पित्रं तर्ज्जनिमूलकम्॥२॥

The region situate about the root (ball) of the thumb is called the *Prājāpatyam Tīrtham;* the tips of fingers are sacred to the gods, and are, hence, called the *Daiva Tīrthas, while* the region about the root of the *index* finger is called the *Pitṛ Tīrtham.*

प्राजापत्येन तीर्थेन त्रि: प्राश्नीयाज्जलं द्विज:।
द्वि: प्रमृज्य मुखं पश्चादद्भि: खं समुपस्पृशेत्॥३॥

A twice-born one should thrice *drink* water with the region of his hand, known as the *Prājāpatya Tīrtham,* then having twice rinsed his mouth with water he should touch the apertures of his nostrils, ears, *etc., (lit.* the ether of these orifices) with the fingers respectively enjoined to be made use of in these cases.

हृद्गाभि: पूयते विप्र: कण्ठगाभिश्च भूमिप:।
तालुगाभिस्तथा वैश्य: शूद्र: स्पृष्टाभिरन्तत:॥४॥

A Brāhmaṇa is purified by drinking as much water as is

enough to moisten the region of his heart; a Kṣatriya, under the circumstance, should drink a quantity of 'water, enough to trickle down his throat; a Vaiśya, in these cases, should drink enough (water) to moisten his palate; while a Śūdra or a woman should touch his or her teeth and lips with water, while engaged in performing an *Ācamanam*.

अन्तर्जानुः शुचौ देशे प्राङ्मुखः सुसमाहितः।
उदङ्मुखोऽपि प्रयतो दिशश्चानवलोकयन्॥५॥
अद्भिः समुद्धृताभिस्तु हीनाभिः फेनबुद्बुदैः।
वह्निना चाप्यदग्धाभिरङ्गुलीभिरुपस्पृशेत्॥६॥

In a sacred place, self-controlled and with his face turned towards the north, or with his hand placed between his thighs and his face looking towards the east, or without looking at any quarter of the skies, he (the performer) should perform the rite of *Ācamanam* by drinking with the proper fingers, the water which is unboiled and free from froths and bubbles.

तर्जन्यङ्गुष्ठयोगेन स्पृशेन्नेत्रद्वयं ततः।
अङ्गुष्ठानामिकाभ्यान्तु श्रवणौ समुपस्पृशेत्॥७॥

The two eyes should be touched with the thumb and index finger united together; the ears should be touched with the thumb and the ring-finger similarly combined.

कनिष्ठाङ्गुष्ठयोगेन स्पृशेत् स्कन्धद्वयं ततः।
सर्वासामेव योगेन नाभिञ्च हृदयं ततः॥८॥

Then the two shoulders should be successively touched with the thumb and the little finger combined, while the nose and the navel should be touched with all the fingers held together.

संस्पृशेत् तु तथा मूर्द्धा यथा आचमने विधिः॥९॥
त्रिः प्राश्नीयाद् यदम्भस्तु प्रीतास्तेनास्य देवताः।
ब्रह्मा विष्णुश्च रुद्रश्च भवन्तीत्यनुशुश्रुमः॥१०॥

Then the head should be touched with the fingers enjoined to be used (in touching the head) in connection with a rite of *Ācamanam*. We have heard it said that, the three draughts of water drunk by a person (in connection with *Ācamanam)* tend to propitiate the divine trinity of Brahmā, Viṣṇu, and Rudra.

गङ्गा च यमुना चैव प्रीयेते परिमार्ज्जनात्।

नासत्यदस्रौ पीयेते स्पृष्टे नासापुटद्वये॥११॥

The river-goddesses, Gaṅgā and Yamunā are pleased by ones rinsing the mouth with water, while the Aśvins are pleased by one's touching the nostrils, under the circumstance.

स्पृष्टे लोचनयुग्मे तु प्रीयेते शशिभास्करौ।

कर्णयुग्मे तथा स्पृष्टे प्रीयेते अनिलानलौ॥१२॥

The sun and the moon are pleased by one's touching the eyes; and the fire god and the wind god, by touching the ears, in the course of an *Ācamanam*.

स्कन्धयोः स्पर्शनादस्य प्रीयन्ते सर्वदेवताः।

मूर्द्धस्तु स्पर्शनादस्य प्रीतस्तु पुरुषो भवेत्॥१३॥

All the gods are pleased by one's touching the Shoulders, while the *Puruṣa* (self) is pleased by touching the head.

विना यज्ञोपवीतेन तथा मुक्तशिखोऽपि वा।

अप्रक्षालितपादस्तु आचान्तोऽप्यशुचिर्भवेत्॥१४॥

Without the holy thread lying on his shoulder, with out the tuft of hair on his crown being duly tied up in a knot, without having washed his feet before, a person, even if he has performed an *Ācamanam,* should be regarded as impure.

बहिर्जानुरुपस्पृश्य एकहस्तार्पितैर्जलैः।

समलाभिस्तथाद्भिश्च नैव शुद्धिमवाप्नुयात्॥१५॥

Having placed the hands out-side the thighs, or having performed the *Ācamanam* with turbid water, one should not be deemed as pure.

आचम्य च पुरा प्रोक्तं तीर्थसम्मार्ज्जनं ततः।

उपस्पृस्य ततः पश्चान्मन्त्रेणानेन धर्मतः॥१६॥

अन्तश्चरसि भूतेषु गुहायां विश्वतोमुखः।

त्वं यज्ञस्त्वं वषट्कार आपोज्योतीरसोऽमृतम्॥१७॥

Having performed the rites of *Ācamanam,* and *Tīrtha-Sanmārjanam* as above laid down, one should touch the water by reciting the Mantra running *as,* "you pervade the hearts of creatures, you run all through the universe, you are the sacrifice, you are the *Vaṣaṭ,* you are the light, water, nutritious sap, and nectar,"

आचम्य च ततः पश्चादादित्याभिमुखो जलम्।
उदुत्यं जातवेदसं मन्त्रेण प्रक्षिपेत् ततः॥१८॥

Then having performed another *Ācamanam* with his face towards the sun, he should recite the *Udutyam Jātavedasam* etc., Mantra, and offer a libation of water.

एष एव विधिः प्रोक्तः सन्ध्यायाञ्च द्विजातिषु।
पूर्वां सन्ध्यां जपंस्तिष्ठेदासीनः पश्चिमां तथा॥१९॥

This is the rule to be observed by twice-born ones in respect of the performance of the *Sandhyā* rite. The Gāyatrī Mantra should be recited standing during the morning *Sandhyā,* while it should be repeated in a sitting posture during the evening *Sandhyā.*

ततो जपेत् पवित्राणि पवित्रान् वाथ शक्तितः।
ऋषयो दीर्घसन्ध्यत्वाद्दीर्घमायुरवाप्नुयुः॥२०॥

Then the sacred *Mantras* should be recited according to one's might; the *Ṛṣis* used to long perform the *Sandhyās,* hence, they attained longevity.

॥ इति शङ्खीये धर्मशास्त्रे नवमोऽध्यायः॥९॥

Chapter 10

सर्ववेदपवित्राणि सम्प्रवक्ष्याम्यतः परम्।
येषां जपैश्च होमैश्च पूयन्ते मानवाः सदा॥१॥

Now I shall enumerate the most sacred Mantra*s,* called from all the four Vedas; men are purified by reciting these sacred Mantra*s,* or by performing *Homa* and worship therewith.

अघमर्षणं देवव्रतं शुद्धवत्यस्तु यत् सदा।
कुष्माण्ड्यः पावमान्यश्च सर्वसावित्र्य एव च॥२॥

Sin absolving are the *Aghamarṣaṇam Sūktam,* the *Deva Vratam Sūktam,* the *Śudhavati Sūktam,* the *Kuṣmāṇḍī Sūktam,* and the *Pāvamānī Sūktam.*

अभीष्टद्रुपदा चैव स्तोमानि व्याहृतिस्तथा।
भारुण्डानि च सामानि गायत्र्या वै वृतं तथा॥३॥
पुरुषव्रतञ्च भाषञ्च तथा सोमव्रतानि च।
अविज्ञं बार्हस्पत्यञ्च वाक्सूक्तमनृतं तथा॥४॥
शतरुद्रीमथर्वशिरास्त्रिसुपर्णा महीव्रतम्।
गोसूक्तमश्वसूक्तञ्च इन्द्रसूक्तञ्च सामनी॥५॥
त्रीणि पुष्पाङ्गदेहानि रथन्तरञ्चाग्निव्रतं वामदेव्यं व्रतञ्च।
एतानि गीतानि पुनन्ति जन्तून् जातिस्मरत्वं लभते यदीच्छेत्॥६॥

(Similarly,) the Abhiṣṭadrupadā, the Gāyatrī Sirās with the Praṇava Mantra, the Stoma Sūktas, the Seven Vyāhṛtis Bhāruṇḍa Sāmans, the Mantras, composed in the Gāyatrī metre, the Puruṣa Vratam, the Bhāṣa Mantra, the Soma Vratam, the Avijñam, the Bārhaspatyam, the Vāk Sūktam, the Amṛta Mantra, the Śatarudrīya Mantra, the Atharva Śiras Mantra, the Tri Suparṇa, the Mahāvratam, the Go-sūktam, the Aśva Sūktam, the Indra Sūktam, the two Sāmans, the three Puṣpāṅgadikas, the Rathantaram, the Agni Vrata, and the Vāmadevya Mantras are purifying. By chanting these Vedic Mantras, men, are absolved of their sins, and are enabled to recollect the incidents of their former births.

॥ इति शङ्खीये धर्मशास्त्रे दशमोऽध्याय:॥१०॥

Chapter 11

इति वेदपवित्राण्यभिहितानि एभ्य सावित्री विशिष्यते।
नास्त्यघमर्षणात् परमं तज्जलेन व्याहृतिभिः परंहोम:॥१॥

Thus the sacred Mantras from the Vedas have been enumerated; the Sāvitrī Mantra is the holiest of them all; nothing can excel the *Aghamarṣaṇam* in respect of sanctity; the (principal) *Homa* should be performed with water consecrated by reciting the *Aghamarṣaṇam* and the *Vyāhṛtis*.

न सावित्र्याः परं जप्यम्। कुशदृष्यामासीनः कुशोत्तरीयः कुशपाणिः प्राङ्मुखः सूर्याभिमुखो वाक्षमालामादाय देवताध्यायौ तज्जपं कुर्यात्। सुवर्णमणिमुक्तास्फाटिकपद्मपत्रबीजाक्षराणामन्यतमेनाक्षमालां कुर्यात्। ध्यायन् वामहस्तोपरि वा गणयेत्। आदौ देवतामार्षं छन्दश्च स्मरेत्। ततः सप्रणवव्याहृतिकामादावन्ते च शिरसा गायत्रीमावर्त्तयेत्। तथास्याः सविता ऋषिर्विश्वामित्रो गायत्रीछन्दः। प्रणवाद्याभूर्भुवः स्वर्महर्जनस्तपः सत्यमिति व्याहृतयः। आपोज्योतीरसोऽमृतं ब्रह्मभूर्भुवः स्वरोम्॥२॥

The Sāvitrī Mantra is the most sacred of all the Mantra*s* which are used for the purposes of *Japam* (mental repetition). Seated on a cushion of *Kuśa* blades, and bearing a girdle of *Kuśa* (on his left shoulder) flung in the manner of an *Uttarīyam* (upper sheet or garment,) and holding blades of *Kuśa* grass in his hand, with his face turned towards the east or to the sun, a votary, meditating upon the self of the deity, should tell his beads by repeating the Sāvitrī Mantra. The rosary should be strung with beads of gold, gem, or crystal, or with pearls, or with the seeds of lotus or Akṣa, or with lotus petals. Meditating upon the deity, the rosary should be counted with the left-hand. The *Ṛss* and the metre of the *Mantra should* be contemplated at the out-set (before commencing the *Japam)*. Then the Gāyatrī *should be* recited by prefixing the *Vyāhṛtis* and suffixing the *Śiras* Mantra to it. The seven Mantras, such as *Bhūḥ, Bhuvaḥ, Svaḥ, Mahaḥ, Janaḥ, Tapas,* and *Satyam,* with the *Praṇava* Mantra prefixed to each of them are called the *Vyāhṛtis*. The mantra running as *Āpojyotiḥ rasomṛtam Brahma Bhūrbhuvaḥ Svarom* is called the *Śiro* Mantra.

सव्याहृतिका सप्रणवां गायत्रीं शिरसा सह।
ये जपन्ति सदा तेषां न भयं विद्यते क्वचित्॥३॥

With the *Vyāhṛtis* and *Praṇava* prefixed, and, the *Śiro* Mantra affixed, to the Gāyatrī, those who recite it, do not stand in dread of any thing.

दशजप्ता तु सा देवो दिनपापप्रणाशिनी।
शतं जप्ता तथा सा तु सर्वकल्मषनाशिनी।

सहस्रजप्ता तु नृणां पातकेभ्यः समुद्धरेत्॥४॥

That goddess *(*Mantra*)* ten times repeated destroys the sin committed during the day; a hundred times told, she (it) extinguishes all sin, while a thousand times repeated she (it) exonerates one from the effects of sin *(Pātakas)* unknowingly committed.

स्वर्णस्तेयौ कृतघ्नश्च ब्रह्महा गुरुतल्पगः।
सुरापश्च विशुध्येत लक्षजप्तेन सर्वदा॥५॥

A gold-stealer, an ungrateful person, a Brahmanicide, a defiler of his superior's bed *(Gurutalpaga)*, or a drunkard is purified by a hundred thousand times repeating the Gāyatrī.

प्राणायामत्रयं कृत्वा स्नानकाले समाहितः।
अहोरात्रकृतात् पापात् तत्क्षणादेव शुध्यति॥६॥

Having done three *Prāṇāyāmas,* self controlled, while bathing, one is exonerated from the sin committed during that day and night.

सव्याहृतिका सप्रणवाः प्राणायामस्तु षोडशः।
अपि भ्रूणहनं मासात् पुनन्त्यहरहः कृताः॥७॥

Having done sixteen *Prāṇāyāmas,* with the *Vyāhṛti Praṇava* Mantra*s,* one gets rid of the sin of destroying the life of a faetus, or of that committed, each day and night, in the course of a month.

हुता देवी विशेषेण सर्वकामप्रदायिनी।
सर्वपापक्षयकरी वनस्थभक्तवत्सला॥८॥

The (presiding) goddess of the Gāyatrī, propitiated with *Homa* oblations offered unto her by repeating the Gāyatrī Mantra, grants all boons to the offerer; she, kind to her forest-dwelling votaries, causes the expiation of all sin.

शान्तिकामस्तु जुहुयाद्गायत्रीमयुतैः शुचिः।
हर्त्तुकामोऽपमृत्युञ्च घृतेन जुहुयात् तथा॥९॥

Desiring worldly peace and tranquility, one should cast, clean in body and spirit, ten thousand libations of clarified butter in the sacred fire by each time reciting the Gāyatrī; intending to ward off a premature death, one should offer similar libations of clarified butter unto the fire by repeating the same Mantra.

श्रीकामस्तु तथा पद्मैविल्वैः काञ्चनकामतः।

ब्रह्मवर्च्चसकामस्तु जुहुयात् पूर्ववत् तथा॥१०॥

A seeker of personal beauty should perform the *Homa* with lotus flowers, and a seeker of gold with *Bilva* fruits (by repeating) the Gāyatrī Mantra.

घृतयुक्तैस्तिलैर्वह्नौ हुत्वा तु सुसमाहितः।

गायत्र्यायुतहोमात् तु सर्वपापैः प्रमुच्यते॥११॥

One, seeking the beatitude of *Brahma,* should cast self controlled, as before, libations of clarified butter containing sesame seeds, in the fire : by offering ten thousand libations with the repetition of the sacred Gāyatrī, one is exonerated from all sin.

पापात्मा लक्षहोमेण पातकेभ्यः प्रमुच्यते।

ब्रह्मलोकमवाप्नोति प्राप्नुयात् काममीप्सितम्॥१२॥

A sinful soul (Self) acquires its purity by performing such a hundred thousand *Homas,* and attains to the region of *Brahma,* in the full enjoyment of all its wished for objects.

गायत्री चैव जननी गायत्री पापनाशिनी।

गायत्र्यास्तु परं नास्ति दिवि चेह च पावनम्॥१३॥

Gāyatrī is the progentrix of (the universe); Gāyatrī is sin-absolving; nothing more purifying exists than Gāyatrī either in heaven or earth.

हस्तत्राणपदा देवी पततां नरकार्णवे।

तस्मात्तामभ्यसेन्नित्यं ब्राह्मणो नियतः शुचिः॥१४॥

Gāyatrī succours the fallen by their hands from the sea of hell; hence, clean in spirit and body, a Brāhmaṇa should constantly practise (the recitation of the sacred) Gāyatrī.

गायत्रीजाप्यनिरतो हव्यकव्येषु भोजयेत्।

तस्मिन् न तिष्ठते पापमब्बिन्दुरिव भास्करे[1]॥१५॥

A constant practiser of Gāyatrī (Brāhmaṇa reciter) should be feasted on the occasion of *a Daiva or Pitṛ Śrāddha;* sin standeth not in the self of such a Brāhmaṇa, as a water-drop cannot abide in the solar globe.

जपेनैव तु संसिध्येद्ब्राह्मणो नात्र संशयः।
कुर्यादन्यन्न वा कुर्यान्मन्त्रो ब्राह्मण उच्यते॥१६॥

Undoubtedly, a Brāhmaṇa can attain his end (work out his salvation) by simply reciting the Gāyatrī; a Gāyatrī-*reciter,* whether he does any other *Brāhmaṇic* rite or not, should be regarded as a true Brāhmaṇa.

उपांशुः स्याच्छतगुणः साहस्रो मानसः स्मृतः।
नोच्चैर्जप्यं बुधः कुर्यात् सावित्र्यस्तु विशेषतः॥१७॥

A slightly audible repetition of the Gāyatrī Mantra is a hundred times, and a silent mental repetition of the same is a thousand times, more meritorious (than the one commonly made.) The Gāyatrī should never be loudly recited.

सावित्रीजाप्यनिरतः स्वर्गमाप्नोति मानवः।
सावित्रीजाप्यनिरतो मोक्षोपायञ्च विन्दति॥१८॥

A man, who constantly recites the Gāyatrī, goes to heaven, the repetition of the Gāyatrī should be known as the door to the liberation of Self.

तस्मात् सर्वप्रयत्नेन स्नातः प्रयतमानसः।
गायत्रीञ्च जपेद्भक्त्या सर्वपापप्रणाशिनीम्॥१९॥

Hence, having bathed, (a ceremonial bather), self-controlled, should mentally recite the Gāyatrī Mantra, the purifier of all sin, in a devout spirit.

॥ इति शङ्खीये धर्मशास्त्रे एकादशोऽध्यायः॥११॥

---

1. 'पुष्करे' इति पाठान्तरम्।

Chapter 12

स्नातः कृतजपस्तदनु प्राङ्मुखो दिव्येन तीर्थेन देवानुदकेन तर्पयेत्। प्रत्यहं पुरुषसूक्तेनोदकाञ्जलीन् दद्यात् पुष्पाञ्जलीन् भक्त्या। अथ कृतापसव्यो दक्षिणामुखोऽन्तर्जानु पित्र्येण पितृणां श्राद्धप्रकारमुदकं दद्यात्। पित्रे पितामहाय पितामह्यै सप्तमात् पुरुषात् पितृपक्षे यावता नाम जानीयात्। पितृपक्षीयाणां त्रयाणां दत्त्वा मातृपक्षीयाणां गुरूणां सम्बन्धिबान्धवानाञ्च कृत्वा सुहृदां कुर्यात्। भवन्ति चात्रश्लोकाः।

Having bathed, and recited the Gāyatrī a twice-born one, looking towards the east, should propitiate the gods by offering libations of water with (fingers united in the posture known as the) *Daiva Tīrtham,* every day; offerings of flower and water should be made (unto them) by reciting the *Puruṣa Sūktam:* Then, with his face turned towards the south and his hand placed between his thighs, and his holy thread placed on his right shoulder, he should offer libations of water to his departed manes with the *Pitṛ Tīrtham,* and in accordance with the rules of *a Pitṛ Śrāddha.* He should offer three libations of water to each of his father, grand-father, great-grand father, maternal grand-father, maternal, great-grand father, mother, etc. Similarly, libations of water should be offered to each of his maternal grandmothers, *etc.* After that, all the dead relations on his father's or mother's side, whose names he might remember, as well as the souls of his preceptors, brothers-in-law, friends, etc., he should propitiate by offering similar libations of water unto them; the authoritative verses on the subject run as follow :

विना रौप्यसुवर्णेन विना ताम्रतिलेन च।
विना दर्भैश्च मन्त्रैश्च पितृणां नोपतिष्ठते।।१।।

Tarpaṇas done without sesame, *Kuśa* grass, Mantras and copper, silver, or golden libatory vessels, do not become agreeable to the *Pitṛs.*

सौवर्णराजताभ्याञ्च खड्गेनोडुम्बरेण वा।
दत्तमक्षयतां याति पितृणान्तु तिलोदकम्।।२।।

Libations of water, containing sesame seeds and offered unto one's *Pitṛs* with a vessel made of gold copper, or Audumbara wood, or of the thorn of a rhinoceros, last them for all eternity, and bear infinite fruit.

कुर्यादहरहः श्राद्धमन्नाद्येनोदकेन वा।
पयोमूलफलैर्वापि पितॄणां प्रीतिमावहन्॥३।

Every day, *Śrāddhas* should be performed in honour of one's departed manes with fruits, cooked rice, water and milk, whereby they would be pleased.

स्नातस्तु तर्पणं कृत्वा पितॄणान्तु तिलाम्भसा।
पितृयज्ञमवाप्नोति प्रीणन्ति पितरस्तथा॥४॥

He, who, after bathing, offers libations of water containing sesame seeds to his *Pitṛs,* acquires the merit of *Pitṛ yajña;* and they become pleased with him.

॥ इति शङ्खीये धर्मशास्त्रे द्वादशोऽध्यायः॥१२॥

Chapter 13

ब्राह्मणान्न परीक्षेत दैवे कर्मणि धर्मवित्।
पित्र्ये कर्मणि सम्प्राप्ते सूक्तमार्गैः परीक्षणम्॥१॥

Brāhmaṇas should not be tested in connection with the performance of a *Daiva Śrāddha;* they may be examined in respect of their knowledge in Vedic *Sūktas* on the occasion of celebrating *a Pitṛ Śrāddha.*

ब्राह्मणा ये विकर्मणो वैडालव्रतिकाः शठाः।
हीनाङ्गा अतिरिक्ताङ्गा ब्राह्मणाः पङ्क्तिदूषकाः॥२॥

Brāhmaṇas of impious conduct, as well as those who are hypocrites, cherish cruel or killing propensities, cat-fashion, under a calm and benign exterior, or are possessed of a less or excess number of bodily appendages, should be regarded as defilers of the row of Brāhmaṇas (sitting down to a dinner on the occasion of *a Śrāddha ceremony- Paṅktidūṣakas).*

गुरूणां प्रतिकूलाश्च तथाग्न्युत्पातिनश्च ये।

गुरूणां त्यागिनश्चैव ब्राह्मणाः पङ्क्तिदूषकाः॥३॥

Brāhmaṇas, who are hostile to their elders and 'preceptors, or disturb their sacred fire, or desert their parents and preceptors, should be regarded as the defilers of a row of Brāhmaṇas *(Paṅktidūṣakas)*.

अनध्यायेष्वधीयानाः शौचाचारविवर्जिताः।
शूद्रान्नरससम्पुष्टा ब्राह्मणाः पङ्क्तिदूषकाः॥४॥

Brāhmaṇas, who read the Vedas on the interdicted days of study, or are devoid of piety and cleanness, as well as those who fatten upon sustenance supplied by Śūdras, should be regarded as defilers of a row of Brāhmaṇas *(Paṅktidūṣakas)*.

षडङ्गवेदवेत्तारो बह्वृचश्चैव सामगाः।
त्रिणाचिकेतः पञ्चाग्निर्ब्राह्मणाः पङ्क्तिपावनाः॥५॥

Brāhmaṇas, who have studied the Vedas with six; subdivisions, or know a large number of Ṛks or Sāmans (verses), as well as those who worship the five sacred fires, and thrice cast oblations) each day, in the consecrated fire, should be regarded as the sanctifiers of a row of Brāhmaṇas *(Paṅktipāvanās)*.

ब्रह्मदेयानुसन्ताना ब्रह्मदेयाप्रदायकाः।
ब्रह्मदेयापतिर्यश्च ब्राह्मणाः पङ्क्तिपावनाः॥६॥

Brāhmaṇas, issues of Brāhma form of marriage, as well as those who give away or marry such girls in that form of marriage, should be regarded as the sanctifiers of a row of Brāhmaṇas *(Paṅktipāvanās)*.

ऋग्यजुःपारगो यश्च साम्नां यश्चापि पारगः।
अथर्वाङ्गिरोऽध्येता ब्राह्मणाः पङ्क्तिपावनाः॥७॥

Brāhmaṇas, who are well-versed in the *Ṛk, Yajus,* and *Sāma* Vedas, as well as those who have studied the *Atharvan,* should be regarded as the sanctifiers of a row of Brāhmaṇas *(Paṅktipāvanās)*.

नित्यं योगरतो विद्वान् समलोष्टाश्मकाञ्चनः।
ध्यानशीलो यतिर्विद्वान् ब्राह्मणाः पङ्क्तिपावनाः॥८॥

Brāhmaṇas, who constantly practise the Yoga, are erudite,

and given to the contemplation of the God, and regard gold and brick-bats as of equal value, should be regarded as *(Paṅktipāvanas).*

द्वौ दैवे प्राङ्मुखो त्रींश्च पित्र्ये चोदङ्मुखांस्तथा।
भोजयेद्विविधान् विप्रानेकैकमुत यत्र वा॥९॥

Two Brāhmaṇas should be sumptuously fed, with their faces towards the east, on the occasion of the celebration of *a Daiva Śrāddha;* two Brāhmaṇas, with their faces turned towards the north, should be similarly feasted on the occasion of *a Pitṛ Śrāddha* ceremony. A single Brāhmaṇa may be fed on either of these occasions when the means of the celebrator is limited.

भोजयेदथवाप्येकं ब्राह्मणं पङ्क्तिपावनम्।
देशे कृत्वा तु नैवेद्यं पश्चाद्वह्नौ तु तत् क्षिपेत्॥१०॥

A celebrator of extremely limited means would be purified by feeding a single *Paṅktipāvana* Brāhmaṇa. The boiled rice, etc., should be offered in places duly enjoined for the purpose, and their residue should he cast in the fire.

उच्छिष्टसन्निधौ कार्यं पिण्डनिर्वपणं बुधैः।
अभावे च तथा कार्यमग्निकार्यं यथाविधि॥११॥

Oblations should be offered (to the *Pitṛs)* beside the vessel of the unused residue of cooked rice *(Pātrānnam),* in failure whereof they should be duly cast in the fire.

श्राद्धं कृत्वा तु यत्नेन त्वरा क्रोधविवर्जितः।
उष्णमन्नं द्विजातिभ्यः श्रद्धया विनिवेदयेत्॥१२॥

Devoid of hurry or anger, (one) should carefully celebrate the *Śrāddha* ceremony (of one's ancestors), and devoutly offer cooked food to the Brāhmaṇas on the occasions.

भोजयेद्विविधान् विप्रान् गन्धमाल्यानुलेपनैः।
पङ्क्तिविदात्मनो गेहे भोज्यं वा भक्ष्यमेव वा।
अनिवेद्य न भोक्तव्यं पिण्डमूले कथञ्चन॥१३॥

Brāhmaṇas of all orders should be variously feasted and propitiated with presents of perfumes and unguents. A host, on the occasion, should not use any article of fare or luxury, at his house, without first offering it to a Brāhmaṇa.

उग्रगन्धान्यगन्धानि चैत्यवृक्षभवानि च।
पुष्पाणि वर्जनीयानि तथा पर्वतजानि च॥१४॥

Strong-scented or odourless flowers, as well as those which are culled from trees or plants, growing on hills or tomb stones, should not be given.

तोयोद्भुतानि देयानि रक्तान्यपि विशेषतः।
ऊर्णासूत्रं प्रदातव्यं कार्पासमथवा नवम्॥१५॥

Flowers of aquatic plants and of red colour, in special, as well as woolen or new cotton twists should be gifted.

दशा विवर्जयेत् प्राज्ञो यद्यनाहतवस्त्रजाः।
घृतेन दीपो दातव्यस्तिलतैलेन वा पुनः॥१६॥

The threads at the end of a piece of uncut woven cloth should be rejected (for the purpose), and lamps containing clarified butter or sesame oil should be lighted on the occasion).

धूपार्थं गुग्गुलं दद्यात् घृतयुक्तं मधूत्कटम्।
चन्दनञ्च तथा दद्यादिष्टं यत् कुङ्कुमं शुभम्॥१७॥

Sticks made of resin, honey, and clarified butter should be burned, and sandal-paste mixed with *pasted* saffron should be given.

छत्राकं शरशिम्बञ्च पलञ्च सूपकं तथा।
कुष्माण्डालाबुवार्त्ताकुकोविदारांश्च वर्ज्जयेत्॥१८॥

Mushrooms, cooked meat, soup, gourds, bringals, and Kovidāras should be avoided.

पिप्पलीं मरिचञ्चैव तथा वै पिण्डमूलकम्।
कृतञ्च लवणञ्चैव वंशाग्रन्तु विवर्जयेत्॥१९॥

Long pepper, black pepper, round bulbous roots, prepared salt, and lard should not be used on the occasion.

राजमाषान् मसूरांश्च प्रवालकोरदूषकान्।
लोहितान् वृक्षनिर्यासान् श्राद्धकर्मणि वर्जयेत्॥२०॥

Rājamāṣa, lentil seeds, catechu, the pulse known as Koradūṣaka, as well as the red milky exudations of trees should not be used on the occasion of a *Śrāddha* ceremony.

आम्रात-लबली-मूलमूलकान् दधिदाडिमान्।
सकोविदार्यसत्कन्दराजेन मधुना सदा॥२१॥

Horse Apples, Labali fruits, radishes, milk-curd, pomegranates, Kandarājas, honey, sugar, and fried barley powder should be carefully given on the occasion.

शक्तून् शर्करया सार्द्धं दद्याच्छ्राद्धे प्रयत्नतः।
पायसादिभिरुष्णैश्च भोजयित्वा तथा द्विजान्॥२२॥
भक्त्या प्रणम्य आचान्तान् तथा वै दत्तदक्षिणान्।
अभिवाद्य प्रसन्नात्मा अनुव्रज्य विसर्ज्जयेत्॥२३॥

Having sumptuously fed the assembled Brāhmaṇas with warm *Pāyasa* (a kind of sweet porridge, and paid honorariums to them after they have washed their mouth with water, one the celebrator of the *Śrāddha)* should make obeisance to and dismiss, them by following them to a certain distance from one's house.

निमन्त्रितस्तु यः श्राद्धे मैथुनं सेवते द्विजः।
श्राद्धं भुक्त्वा च दत्त्वा च युक्तः स्यान्महतैनसा॥२४॥

A Brāhmaṇa, who having been invited to a *Śrāddha* ceremony, or having dined on the occasion of such a celebration, that day, knows his wife, commits a great sin.

कालशाकं महाशल्कं मांसं वा शकुनस्य च।
खड्गमांसं तथानन्त्यं यमः प्रोवाच धर्मवित्॥२५॥

A Śrāddha ceremony performed by offering oblations of *Kāla Śākas,* bird's flesh, the flesh of a rhinoceros, or a large-scaled fish, bears infinite fruit. This is the opinion of *Yama,* the law-giver.

॥ इति शङ्खीये धर्मशास्त्रे त्रयोदशोऽध्यायः॥१३॥

Chapter 14

यद्दाति गयाक्षेत्रे प्रभासे पुष्करेऽपि च।

प्रयागे नैमिषारण्ये सर्वमानन्त्यमुच्यते॥१॥

A Gift, made at Gayā, Prabhāsa, Puṣkara, or Prayāga, or in the forest of Naimiṣa, bears infinite fruit.

गङ्गायमुनयोस्तीरे तीर्थे वामरकण्टके।

नर्मदायां गयातीरे सर्वमानन्त्यमुच्यते॥२॥

A gift made at any of the following sacred pools or places, *via.,* the banks of the Yamunā, of the Ganges and of the Narmadā, Amarakaṇṭaka and Gayā, bears infinite fruit.

वाराणस्यां कुरुक्षेत्रे भृगुतुङ्गे महालये।

सप्तारण्येऽसिकूपे च यत् तदक्षयमुच्यते॥३॥

Endless is the merit of making a gift at Vārāṇasī, Kurukṣetra, Bhṛgutuṅga, Mahāpatha, Saptāraṇya, or at Asikūpa.

म्लेच्छदेशे तथारात्रौ सन्ध्यायां च विशेषतः।

न श्राद्धमाचरेत् प्राज्ञो म्लेच्छदेशे न च व्रजेत्॥४॥

A wise man should not celebrate a *Śrāddha* ceremony either in a Mleccha country or at dawn, evening or night. He should not visit even Mleccha country.

हस्तिच्छायासूर्यमितचन्द्रर्द्धि राहुदर्शने।

विषुवत्ययने चैव सर्वमानन्त्यमुच्यते॥५॥

Gifts made under the auspicies of *Gaja Chāyā Yoga,* or during a solar or lunar eclipse, as well as those made *on* the last day of *Vaiśākha or Śrāvaṇa, or* when the sun enters the sign of Makara or Karka, bear infinite fruit.

प्रौष्ठपद्यामतीतायां मघायुक्तां त्रयोदशीम्।

प्राप्य श्राद्धन्तु कर्त्तव्यं मधुना पायसेन च॥६॥

The wise should perform *Śrāddhas* on the day of the tenth phase of the moon's wane after the day of the full moon in the month of *Bhādra* with oblations of honey and *Pāyasa.*

प्रजां पुष्टिं तथा स्वर्गमारोग्यञ्च धनं तथा।
नृणां प्राप्य सदा प्रीतिं प्रयच्छन्ति पितामहाः॥७॥

The *Pitṛs,* propitiated with the celebration of *Śrāddha* ceremonies, grant joy, opulence, progeny, and residence in heaven to their performers.

॥ इति शङ्खीये धर्मशास्त्रे चतुर्दशोऽध्यायः॥१४॥

Chapter 15

जनने मरणे चैव सपिण्डानां द्विजोत्तमाः।
त्र्यहाच्छुद्धिमवाप्नोति योऽग्निवेशसमन्वितः॥१॥

O You, the foremost of the twice-born ones, Brāhmaṇas, who practise *Yoga* and worship the consecrated fire, should be clean after the day of the birth or death of any of their *Sapiṇḍa* relations.

सपिण्डता तु पुरुषे सप्तमे विनिवर्त्तते।
जनने मरणे विप्रो दशाहेन विशुध्यति॥२॥

The *Sapiṇḍa* relationship endures up to the seventh degree of consanguinity. A Brāhmaṇa becomes unclean for ten days on the birth or death of *a Sapiṇḍa* relation.

क्षत्रियो द्वादशाहेन वैश्यः पक्षेण शुध्यति।
मांसेन तु तथा शूद्रः शुद्धिमाप्नोति नान्तरा॥३॥

A Kṣatriya becomes clean after twelve days, a Vaiśya becomes clean after a fortnight, and a Śūdra becomes clean after a month (under the circumstances). None of these will be clean before the appointed time.

रात्रिभिर्मासतुल्याभिर्गर्भस्रावे विशुद्ध्यति।
अजातदन्तवाले तु सद्यः शौचं विधीयते॥४॥

On an abortion of pregnancy taking place in the family, (the *Sapiṇḍa* relations of the father) would remain unclean for a number of days equal to that of the months of gestation, while in connection with the death of a child, dead before cutting its teeth, the uncleanness ceases on the day of its death.

अहोरात्रात्तथा शुद्धिर्बाले त्वकृतचूडके।

तथैवानुपनीते तु त्र्यहाच्छुध्यन्ति मानवा:।।५।।

The uncleanness lasts for a whole day and night on the death of a child, dead before the rite of tonsure being done unto him, while it continues for three days in respect of the death of one, dead without being invested with the holy thread.

मृतानां कन्यकानान्तु तथैव शूद्रजन्मन:।

अनूढभार्य: शूद्रस्तु षोडशाद्वत्सरात् परम्।।६।।

मृत्युं समवगच्छेत्तु मासं तस्यापि बान्धवा:।

शुद्धिं समवगच्छन्ति नात्र कार्या विचारणा।।७।।

The *Sapiṇḍa* relations of a girl's (father) would remain unclean for three days from the date of her death, while the period of uncleanness in respect of the death of an unmarried Śūdra youth of sixteen years would last for a month. His *Sapiṇḍa* relations would remain unclean for a month. There should be no disputing this fact.

पितृवेश्मनि कन्या या रज: पश्यन्त्यसंस्कृता।

तस्यां मृतायां नाशौचं कदाचिदपि शाम्यति।।८।।

Uncleanness, incidental to the death of an unmarried girl who dies after menstruating in her father's house, does never abate.

हीनवर्णाद् यदा नारी प्रमादात् प्रसवं व्रजेत्।

प्रसवे मरणे तज्जमशौचं नोपशाम्यति।।९।।

The period of uncleanness, incidental to the birth or death of a child begot by a man of an inferior caste on a woman of a superior one, shall never abate as far as its mother is concerned.

समानं खल्वशौचन्तु प्रथमे तु समापयेत्।

असमानं द्वितीयेन धर्मराजवचो यथा।।१०।।

Of two concurrent and uniform uncleanness, the prior one will extinguish the latter. Of two concurrent but disuniform ones, the former will be extinguished, after the term of the later. This is opinion of the lord of virtue (Yama).

देशान्तरगतः श्रुत्वा सत्त्वानां मरणोद्भवौ।
यच्छेषं दशरात्रस्य तावदेवाशुचिर्भवेत्॥११॥

On hearing of the birth or death of one's relation in a distant country, one would remain unclean for the unexpired portion of the period of ten days, after the hearing.

अतीते दशरात्रे तु तावदेव शुचिर्भवेत्।
तथा संवत्सरेऽतीते स्नान एव विशुध्यति॥१२॥

Having heard such a news after the expiry of ten days from the date of occurrence, one would remain unclean for that day only, while having heard it after a year, one would be pure again by a simple ablution.

अनीरसेषु पुत्रेषु भार्यास्वन्यगतासु च।
परपूर्वासु च स्त्रीषु त्र्यहाच्छुद्धिरिहेष्यते॥१३॥

A man would remain unclean for three days only on the death of a son though not of his own loins, or on that of a wife living with another, or previously married by him.

मातामहे व्यतीते तु चाचार्ये च तथा मृते।
गृहे मृतासु दत्तासु कन्यासु च त्र्यहं तथा॥१४॥

A man would remain unclean for three days on the death of his preceptor, maternal grand-father, or of a married daughter in his own house.

विनष्टे राजनि तथा जाते दौहित्रके गृहे।
आचार्यपत्नीपुत्रेषु दिवसेन च मातुले॥१५॥

A man would remain unclean for a single day on the death of the king of his country, on the birth of a son of his daughter, and on the death of his maternal uncle, or of a son or wife of his preceptor.

मातुले पक्षिणीं रात्रिं शिष्यर्त्विग्बान्धवेषु च।
सब्रह्मचारिणि तथा अनूचाने तथा मृते॥१६॥

On the death of one's maternal uncle, one would be unclean

for an entire day and night, while the period of uncleanness in respect of the death of one's priest, disciple, or of a fellow student of the Vedas, is one day only.

एकरात्रं त्रिरात्रं वा षड्रात्रं मासमेव च।
शूद्राः सपिण्डवर्णानामशौचं क्रमतः स्मृतम्॥१७॥

A Brāhmaṇa would remain unclean for one day, three days, six days and ten days respectively on the birth or death of Brāhmaṇa, Kṣatriya, Vaiśya or Śūdra *Sapiṇḍa* relation of his.

सपिण्डे क्षत्रिये शुद्धिः षड्रात्रं ब्राह्मणस्य तु।
वर्णानां परिशिष्टानां द्वादशाहं विनिर्दिशेत्॥१८॥

A Brāhmaṇa would remain unclean for six days on the birth or death of his Kṣatriya *Sapiṇḍa;* the period of uncleanness in respect of the remaining castes being twelve days only.

सपिण्डे ब्राह्मणे वर्णाः सर्व एवाविशेषतः।
दशरात्रेण शुध्येयुरित्याह भगवान् यमः॥१९॥

Members of all castes would remain unclean for ten days on the death of a Brāhmaṇa *Sapiṇḍa* relation. This is the ordinance of Yama.

भृग्वग्निपतनाम्भोभिर्मृतानामात्मघातिनाम्।
पतितानामशौचञ्च शस्त्रविद्युद्धताश्च ये॥२०॥

No uncleanness exists in respect of a violent death by falling from the brow of a hill, or by hanging, drowning, burning, lightning, or sword-cut, etc., as well as in connection with the death of a suicide or degraded person.

यती व्रती ब्रह्मचारी सूपकारश्च दीक्षितः।
नाशौचभाजः कथिता राजाज्ञाकारिणश्च ये॥२१॥

A Yati, a king, a Brahmacārin, a confectioner, as well as those who are initiated, or are in the king's employ, are never disqualified by a birth or death uncleanness.

यस्तु भुङ्क्ते पराशौचे वर्णी सोऽप्यशुचिर्भवेत्।
अमुष्य शुचौ शुद्धिश्च तस्याप्युक्ता मनीषिभिः॥२२॥

A Brahmacārin partaking of the food prepared by a person

affected with a birth or death uncleanness, will be unclean; he would be pure after the lapse of the period of uncleanness of the owner of such food. This is the opinion of the wise.

पराशौचे नरो भुक्त्वा कृमियोनौ प्रजायते।

भुक्त्वान्नं म्रियते यस्य तस्य जातौ प्रजायते।।२३।।

Those, who partake of the boiled rice of an unclean person, are re-born as insects; a man gets the same caste as the man, whose boiled rice he partakes of, before dying.

दानं प्रतिग्रहो होमः स्वाध्यायः पितृकर्म च।

प्रेतपिण्डक्रियावर्ज्जमशौचं विनिवर्त्तते।।२४।।

All religious acts to be performed in honour of one's departed manes, save giving and receiving gifts, offering oblations to *Pretas,* casting libations in the sacrificial fire, and studying the Vedas, are interdicted during a period of uncleanness.

।। इति शङ्खीये धर्मशास्त्रे पञ्चदशोऽध्यायः।।१५।।

Chapter 16

मृन्मयं भाजनं सर्वं पुनःपाकेन शुध्यति।

मलैर्मूत्रैः पुरीषैर्वा ष्ठीवनैः पूयशोणितैः।।१।।

संस्पृष्टं नैव शुध्येत पुनः पाकेन मृन्मयम्।

एतैरेव यदि स्पृष्टं ताम्रसौवर्णराजतम्।।२।।

All earthen vessels, defiled by impure things other than bodily excrements, are purified by again burning them in fire; under the latter condition they should be rejected and thrown away.

शुध्यत्यावर्त्तितं पश्चादन्यथा केवलाम्भसा।

अम्लोदकेन ताम्रस्य सोमस्य त्रपुषस्तथा।।३।।

Vessels made of copper, silver, or gold, and defiled by the touch of bodily excrements should be purified by melting and recasting them; defiled by the touch of any other impure thing they should be purified by washing them with water.

क्षारेण शुद्धिः कांसस्य लोहस्यापि विनिर्दिशेत्।

मुक्तामणिप्रबालानां शुद्धिः प्रक्षालनेन तु॥४॥

Articles made of copper, lead, or brass should be purified by rubbing them with any acid substance; articles made of iron or bell-metal should be purified by rubbing them with any alkaline substance, while those made of pearls or corals should be purified by simply washing them with water.

अजानाञ्चैव भाण्डानां सर्वयाश्ममयस्य च।

शाकमूलफलानाञ्च विदलानां तथैव च॥५॥

Articles made of stone or conch shells, as well as potherbs, vegetables and pulses should be purified by simply washing them with water.

मार्ज्जनाद्यज्ञपात्राणां पाणिना यज्ञकर्मणि।

उष्णाम्भसा तथा शुद्धिः सकेशानां विनिर्दिशेत्॥६॥

Sacrificial vessels, during the celebration of a religious sacrifice, should be purified by rubbing them with the palms of the hand, while those articles, defiled by the contact of hair, should be purified by washing them with warm water.

शय्यानापणानान्तु सूर्यस्य किरणैस्तथा।

शुद्धिस्तु प्रोक्षणाद्यज्ञे करकेन्धनयोस्तथा॥७॥

Cushions, beddings, and market-sheds, anywise polluted by impure contacts, are purified by an exposure to the sun; sacrificial vessels are purified by sprinkling water over them.

मार्जानाद्वेश्मनां शुद्धिः क्षितेः शोधस्तु तत्क्षणात्।

सम्मार्ज्जनेन तोयेन वाससां शुद्धिरिष्यते॥८॥

A room is purified by washing it with water, the ground is instantaneously purified by washing it with water, clothes are purified by washing them with water.

बहूनां प्रोक्षणाच्छुद्धिर्धान्यादीनां विनिर्दिशेत्।

प्रोक्षणात् संहतानाञ्च काष्ठानाञ्चैव तत्क्षणात्॥९॥

A large quantity of paddy, kept in a room or vessel, is purified by sprinkling it over with water; articles made of pieces of wood fastened together are purified by rubbing them with water.

सिद्धार्थकानां कम्पेन श्रृङ्गदन्तमयस्य च।
गोवालैः फलपात्राणामस्थ्नां श्रृङ्गवतां तथा।।१०।।
निर्यासानां गुडानाञ्च लवणानां तथैव च।
कुसुम्भकुसुमानाञ्च ऊर्णाकार्पासयोस्तथा।।११।।

White mustard seeds should be purified by winnowing them with a winnow; articles made of horns or tusks of animals should be purified by rubbing them with cow-hair. The venerable Yama has enjoined that articles made of leaves, shells of fruits, or of horns, as well as milky exudations of trees, salts, treacle, Kusumbha fruits, wool, and cotton should be purified by sprinkling water over them.

प्रोक्षणात् कथिता शुद्धिरित्याह भगवान् यमः।
भूमिष्ठमुदकं शुद्धं तथा शुचि शिलागतम्।।१२।।
वर्णगन्धरसैर्दुष्टैर्वर्जितानां तथा भवेत्।
शुद्धं नदीगतं तोयं सर्वदैव सुखाकरम्।।१३।।

Water defiled by any impure contact should be purified by pouring it over the earth, or by keeping it in a stone vessel; water that is devoid of any offensive taste, odours, or colour is pure; the water of a running brook or river is always pure and wholesome.

शुद्धं प्रसारितं पण्यं शुद्धाश्चाश्वादयो मुखे।
मुखवर्ज्जन्तु गौः शुद्धा मार्ज्जारश्चाश्रमे शुचिः।।१४।।

Articles of trade or merchandise spread out for show, the mouths of such animals as horses, etc., all the limbs of cows except their mouths, and domesticated cats should be regarded as always pure.

शय्या भार्या शिशुर्वस्त्रमुपवीतं कमण्डलुः।
आत्मनः कथितं शुद्धं न तच्छुद्धं परस्य च।।१५।।

The bed, wife, child, sacred thread, wearing cloth and the *Kamaṇḍalu* vessel of ones' own are always pure as far as one's own self is concerned; belonging to others one should consider them as impure.

नारीणाञ्चैव चात्मानां शकुनानां शुनां मुखम्।
रात्रौ प्रसरणे वृक्षे मृगयायां सदा शुचिः॥१६॥

The face of one's own wife is pure during the night, pure is the mouth of a bird perched on a tree, the mouth of a dog is pure during a hunting excursion, the mouth of a calf is pure during an act of milching.

शुद्धा भर्त्तुश्चतुर्थेऽह्नि स्नाता नारी रजस्वला।
दैवे कर्मणि पित्र्ये च पञ्चमेऽहनि शुध्यति॥१७॥

A woman becomes pure by ablution on the fourth day of her menses; for the purposes of a *Daiva* or *Pitrya Śrāddha* she becomes pure on the fifth day.

रथ्याकर्दमतोयेन ष्ठीवनाद्येन वाप्यथ।
नाभेरूर्ध्वं नरः स्पृष्टः सद्यः स्नानेन शुध्यति॥१८॥

A man polluted by the touch of spittal or muddy water of the road, above his navel, should regain his purity by instantaneously bathing.

कृत्वा मूत्रपुरीषञ्च लेपगन्धापहं तथा।
उद्धृतेनाभ्यसा स्नानं मृदा चैव समाचरेत्॥१९॥

After urination or defecation, one should rub the impure orifices of the organs concerned with earth, enough to remove the bad smell, and then wash them with water, previously lifted for the purpose.

मेहने मृत्तिकाः सप्त लिङ्गे द्वे च प्रकीर्त्तिते।
एकस्मिन् विंशतिर्हस्ते द्वयोर्दैयाश्चतुर्दश॥२०॥

After micturition, one should twice rub the external orifice of one's urethra, and seven times the palms of his hands, with earth, and then wash them with water; after defecation a person should twenty-one times rub the palm of his left hand, and fourteen times the palms of his both hands, with earth, and then wash them with water.

तिस्रस्तु मृत्तिका देयाः कृत्वा तु नखशोधनम्।
तिस्रस्तु पायदोर्ज्ञेयाः शौचकामस्य सर्वदा॥२१॥

After cleansing the nails, the hands should be thrice rubbed with clay; wishing personal cleanness one should always wash one's feet with clay and water.

शौचमेतद्गृहस्थानां द्विगुणं ब्रह्मचारिणम्।
द्विगुणञ्च वनस्थानां यतीनां द्विगुणं तथा॥२२॥
मृत्तिका च विनिर्द्दिष्टा त्रिपर्वं पूर्यते यया॥२३॥

These rules of cleanness will hold good in cases of householders; Brahmacārins should doubly perform those acts of personal purification which are enjoined to be done by householders; forest-dwelling hermits should do thrice as much as those done by Brahmacārins, and Yatis should do twice as much as the *Vānaprasthas* in these respects. Acts of personal cleansing should be done with a quantity of earth, enough to fill the three phalanges of fingers.

॥ इति शङ्खीये धर्मशास्त्रे षोडशोऽध्यायः॥१६॥

Chapter 17

नित्यं त्रिषणवस्नायी कृत्वा पर्णकुटी वने।
अधःशायी जटाधारी पर्णमूलफलाशनः॥१॥
ग्रामं विशेत भिक्षार्थं स्वकर्म परिकीर्त्तयन्।
एवं कालं समास्थाय वर्षे च द्वादशे गते॥२॥

Bathing at morning, noon and evening, each day, living, in a thatched cottage of dry leaves, and, on roots and bulbs of the forest, wearing large clotted hairs, and lying down on bare ground in the night, he (a gold-stealer, etc.,) should enter a village for alms, proclaiming his guilt to all and sundry. For twelve years he should live this life of penance.

रुक्मस्तेयी सुरापायी ब्रह्महा गुरुतल्पगः।
व्रतेनैकेन शुध्यन्ति महापातकिनश्च ये॥३॥

A gold-stealer, a drunkard, a Brahmanicide, or a defiler of

this elder's or preceptor's bed, or a person guilty of any of the *Mahāpātakas,* is purified by practising the above-said penance.

यागस्थं क्षत्रियं हत्वा वैश्यं हत्वा तु याजकम्।
एतदेव व्रतं कुर्यादाश्रमं विनिदूषकः।।४।।

The same penance should be practised for expiating the sin of killing a Kṣatriya engaged in celebrating a religious sacrifice, or a Vaiśya performer of religious sacrifices, or for the purpose of extinguishing the sin of defiling a hermitage.

कूटसाक्ष्यं तथैवोक्त्वा निक्षेपञ्च प्रहृत्य च।
एतदेव व्रतं कुर्याच्छक्त्या च शरणागतम्।।५।।

This expiatory penance should be practised after having given false evidence, or after having killed a person taken under protection, or after having misappropriated a trust property.

आहिताग्निः स्त्रियं हत्वा मित्रं हत्वा तथैव च।
हत्वा गर्भमविज्ञातमेतदेव व्रतं चरेत्।।६।।

A custodian of the sacred fire, after having unwillingly killed a friend or a woman, or after having unknowingly effected an abortion of pregnancy, should practise this (above said) expiatory penance.

व्रतस्थञ्च द्विजं हत्वा पार्थिवञ्चाकृताश्रमम्।
एतदेवं व्रतं कुर्याद्द्विगुणञ्च विशुद्धये।।७।।

For the expiation of his sin, this penance should be doubly practised by a man, who has killed a Brāhmaṇa during the observance of a vow, or a Kṣatriya, who has not settled down in life as a house-holder.

क्षत्रियस्य तु पादोनं तदर्द्धं वैश्यघातने।
अर्द्धमेव सदा कुर्यात् स्त्रीवधे पुरुषस्तथा।।८।।

After having killed a Kṣatriya, false to his proper duties in life, a three quarter part of the same penance should be practised for expiation; after having killed a similar Vaiśya or a woman, only a half of the penance should be practised.

पादन्तु शूद्रहत्यायामुदक्यागमने तथा।

गोवधे च तथा कुर्यात् परदारगतस्तथा॥९॥

After having killed a Śūdra, or after having known a woman during her menses, a quarter part of the same penance should be practised for expiation; (similarly,) a quarter part of the same penance should be practised for extinguishing the sin of killing a cow, or of knowing another man's wife.

पशून् हत्वा तथा ग्राम्यान् मासं कुर्याद्विचक्षणः।

आरण्यानां वधे चैव तदर्द्धन्तु विधीयते॥१०॥

For a month, a wise man should continuously practise this penance after having killed any village (domesticated) animal; the term of the penance is a fortnight only in respect of killing a wild fowl or beast.

हत्वा द्विजं तथा सर्पं जलेशयविलेशयौ।

सप्तरात्रं तथा कुर्याद्व्रतन्तु ब्राह्मणस्तथा॥११॥

A Brāhmaṇa, having killed a serpent, or a hole-dwelling or an aquatic animal, should practise the same penance for a term of seven days.

अनस्थ्नान्तु शतं हत्वा सास्थ्नां दशशतं तथा।

ब्रह्महत्याव्रतं कुर्यात् पूर्णं संवत्सरं तथा॥१२॥

Having killed a hundred invertebrate animals, or a thousand vertebrate ones, one should practise, for a year, the penance enjoined to be practised for the expiation of the sin of Brāhmanicide.

यस्य यस्य च वर्णस्य वृत्तिच्छेदं समाचरेत्।

तस्य तस्य वधे प्रोक्तं प्रायश्चितं समाचरेत्॥१३॥

Having destroyed the means of livelihood of a member of any particular caste, the same expiatory penance should be practised as has been laid down for atoning the sin of killing him.

अपहृत्य तु वर्णानां भुवमेव प्रमादतः।

प्रायश्चित्तमथ प्रोक्तं ब्राह्मणानुमतं चरेत्॥१४॥

Having unknowingly encroached upon the land of a

Brāhmaṇa, Kṣatriya, Vaiśya, or of a Śūdra, one should practise an expiatory penance with the permission of Brāhmaṇas.

गोऽजाश्वस्यापहरणे सीसानां रजतस्य च।
जलापहरणे चैव कुर्यात् संवत्सरं व्रतम्॥१५॥

Having stolen a cow, goat, or horse, or water, lead or silver, one should continuously practise the above said penance for a year.

तिलानां धान्यवस्त्राणां शस्त्राणामाभिषस्य च।
संवत्सरार्द्धं कुर्वीत व्रतमेतत् समाहितः॥१६॥

Having stolen sesame seeds, paddy, cloths, arms, or raw meat, one should practise, self-controlled, the above-said penance for a half year.

तृणकाष्ठे च तक्राणां रसानामपहारकः।
मासमेकं व्रतं कुर्याद्दन्तानां सर्पिषां तथा॥१७॥

Having stolen hays, faggots, whey, milk, tusks of elephants, or clarified butter, one should practise the above-said penance for a month.

लावणानां गुडानाञ्च मूलानां कुसुमस्य च।
मासार्द्धस्तु व्रतं कुर्यादेतदेव समाहितः॥१८॥

Having stolen salt, treacle, edible roots or flowers, or articles made of them, one should practise, self-controlled, the above said penance for a fortnights.

लोहानां वेदलानाञ्च सूत्राणां चर्मणां तथा।
एकरात्रं व्रतं कुर्यात्तद्वदेव समाहितः॥१९॥

Having stolen iron, pulses, cotton twists, or hydes, one should practise the above-said penance for an entire night.

भुक्त्वा पलाण्डुं लशुनं मद्यञ्च कवकानि च।
नारं मलं तथा मांसं विड्वराहं खरं तथा॥२०॥
गौधैरकुञ्जरोष्ट्रञ्च सर्वं पञ्चनखं तथा।
क्रव्यादं कुक्कुटं ग्राम्यं कुर्यात् संवत्सरं व्रतम्॥२१॥

Having eaten an onion, garlic, or mushroom, or the flesh of a camel, elephant, ass, lizard (Godhikā), domesticated hog, or cock, or of any of the five nailed animals (such as dog etc.), or having taken wine, or human excrements, one should practise the above-said penance for a whole year.

भक्ष्याः पञ्चनखस्त्वेते गोधाकच्छपशल्वकाः।
सङ्गश्च शशकश्चैव तान् हत्वा तु चरेद्व्रतम्।।२२।।

Golden coloured *godhās,* tortoises, procupines, hares, although they belong to the group of five nailed creatures, are animals whose flesh may be eaten; but having killed any of these animals, one should practise the above-said penance.

हंसं मद्गुरकं काकं काकोलं खञ्जरीटकम्।
मत्स्यादांश्च तथा मत्स्यान् बलाकाशुकसारिकाः।।२३।।
चक्रवाकं प्लवं कोकं मण्डुकं भुजगं तथा।
मासमेतद्व्रतं कुर्यान्नात्र कार्या विचारणा।।२४।।

Having killed a swan, crow, king-fisher, heron, parrot, crane, *Madguraka* owl, *Khañjirata,* diver, or any such bird, or a frog or snake, one should practise the above-said penance, for a month, without the least hesitation.

राजीवान् सिंहतुण्डांश्च शकुलांश्च तथैव च।
पाठीनरोहितौ भक्ष्यौ मत्स्येषु परिकीर्त्तितौ।।२५।।

Having killed a crane, or a *Śakula or Siṁhatuṇḍa,* fish, one should practise the above said penance. Of fishes the species known as *Pāthīna* and *Rohita* are edible.

जलेचरांश्च जलजान् मुखपादान् सुविष्किरान्।
रक्तपादान् जालपादान् सप्ताहं व्रतमाचरेत्।।२६।।

Having killed such aquatic birds as *Jalapāda* (webbfooted crane), *Raktapāda, Suviskiras,* etc., one should practise the above said penance for a week.

तित्तिरिञ्च मयूरञ्च लावकञ्च कपिञ्जरम्।
वाद्ध्रीणसं वर्त्तकञ्च भक्ष्यानाह यमः सदा।।२७।।

Pheasants, peacocks, Lāvakas, Kapiñjaras, Vartakas, and Bārdhrīṇasas are birds, whose flesh, according to the holy Yama, may be always eaten.

भुक्त्वा चैवोभयदन्तं तथैकशफदंष्ट्रिणः।
तथा भुक्त्वा तु मासं वै मासार्द्धं व्रतमाचरेत्॥२८॥

Having eaten the flesh of a two tusked animal, one should practise the above-said penance for a month; having eaten that of a one-tusked animal, or of an animal with unbifurcated hoops, one should practise the above-said penance for a fortnight.

स्वयं मृतं वृथामासं माहिषं वाजमेव च।
गोश्च क्षीरं विवत्साया महिष्याश्च तथा पयः॥२९॥
सन्धिन्यमेध्यं भक्षित्वा पक्षन्तु व्रतमाचरेत्।
क्षीराणि यान्यभक्ष्याणि तद्विकाराशने बुधः॥३०॥

Having eaten the flesh of an animal that has died a natural death, or that of one not killed in a religious sacrifice, or the flesh of a horse or buffalo, or having taken the milk of a cow or she buffalo whose calf is dead, or that has been in heat or impregnated, one should practise the above-said penance for a fort night.

सप्तरात्रं व्रतं कुर्याद् यदेतत् परिकीर्त्तितम्।
लोहितान् वृक्षनिर्यासान् व्रणानां प्रभवांस्तथा॥३१॥

Having taken the milk of a forbidden female animal, or an article of confectionary made thereof, or the milky exudation of any red plant which is supposed to produce ulcers, one should practise the above-said penance for seven days.

केवलानि तथान्नानि तथा पर्युषितञ्च यत्।
गुडपाकं तथा भुक्त्वा त्रिरात्रन्तु व्रती भवेत्॥३२॥

Having eaten stale boiled rice, or that which has been cooked over night, as well as articles cooked with treacle, one should practise the penance for three days.

दधिभक्तञ्च शुक्तेषु यच्चान्यद्दारुसम्भवम्।
गुडयुक्तं भक्षयित्वा तक्रं निन्द्यमिति श्रुतिः॥३३॥

यवगोधूमजं सत्त्वं विकाराः पयसाश्च ये।
राजवाहश्च कुल्यश्च भैक्ष्यं पर्युषितं भवेत्॥३४॥
सजीवपक्वमांसञ्च सर्वं यत्नेन वर्जयेत्।
संवत्सरं व्रतं कुर्यात् प्राश्यैतान् ज्ञानतस्तथा॥३५॥

All acid fluids except milk, curd, sweet saps of trees, bad whey prepared with the addition of treacle, cakes made of wheat or barley, certain preparations of milk, *Kulyas, Raja vāhas,* all stale articles other than those obtained as alms, as well as the meat of an animal roasted alive, should be always avoided; having knowingly consumed any of these articles one should practise the penance for a year.

शूद्रान्नं ब्राह्मणो भुक्त्वा तथा रङ्गावतारिणः।
बद्धस्य चैव चोरस्यावीरायाः स्त्रियस्तथा॥३६॥
कर्मकारम्य वेनस्य क्लीबस्य पतितस्य च।
रुक्मकारस्य तक्ष्णाश्च तथा वार्द्धुषिकस्य च॥३७॥
कदर्यस्य नृशंसस्य वेश्यायाः कितवस्य च।
गणान्नं भूमिपालान्नमन्नञ्चैव श्वजीविनः॥३८॥
मौनकान्नं सूतिकान्नं भुक्त्वा मासं व्रतं चरेत्।
शूद्रस्य सततं भुक्त्वा षणमासान् व्रतमाचरेत्॥३९॥

Having eaten the boiled rice cooked by a Śūdra, or by a professional actor, or by a thief in prison, or by a woman without any guardian, or by a black-smith, or by a *Vena* (a sect of Śūdras), *Kira* (a sect of Śūdras), goldsmith, carpenter, or courtesan, or by a miserly, cruel or degraded person, or by a mercenary soldier, farmer of revenue, or wine seller, or by a person affected by a birth uncleanness, a Brāhmaṇa should practise the above-said penance for a month. Having continuously partaken of the boiled rice cooked by a Śūdra, a Brāhmaṇa should practise the above-said penance for six months.

वैश्यस्य च तथा स्त्रीणां मासमेकं व्रतं चरेत्।
क्षत्रियस्य तथा भुक्त्वा द्वौ मासौ च व्रतं चरेत्॥॥४०॥

Having eaten the boiled rice cooked by a Vaiśya, or by a

female stranger, one should practise the penance for three months; similarly having eaten that cooked by a Kṣatriya, one should practise the penance for two months.

ब्राह्मणस्य तथा भुक्त्वा मासमेकं समाचरेत्।
अपः सुराभाजनस्थाः पीत्वा पक्षं व्रती भवेत्।।४१।।

Having partaken of the unused residue of a Brāhmaṇas meal, one should practise the penance for a month; having taken water kept in a wine-basin, one should practise the penance for a fortnight.

शूद्राच्छिष्टाशने सामं पक्षमेकं तथा दिशः।
क्षत्रियस्य तु सप्ताहं ब्राह्मणस्य तथा दिनम्।।४२।।

Having partaken of the unused residue of the meal of a Śūdra, Vaiśya, Kṣatriya, or Brāhmaṇas, one should respectively practise the penance for a month, fortnight, weak, and day.

अथ श्राद्धाशने विद्वान् मासमेकं व्रती भवेत्।
परिवित्तिः परिवेत्ता यया च परिविद्यते।।४३।।
व्रतं संवत्सरं कुर्याद्दातृयाजकपञ्चमाः।
शुनोच्छिष्टं तथा भुक्त्वा मासमेकं व्रती भवेत्।।४४।।

An erudite person, having partaken of a meal, slightingly offered, should practise the penance for a month; he, who marries before the marriage of his elder brother, the girl thus married, the person who gives her away in marriage, and the priest who officiates at the ceremony, should practise, each of them, the penance for a year. Similarly, having partaken of food previously eaten by a dog, one should practise the penance for a month.

दूषितं केशकीटैश्च मूषिकानुकुलेन च।
मक्षिकामशकेनापि त्रिरात्रन्तु व्रती भवेत्।।४५।।

Having partaken of food polluted by the touch of a mouse or mongoose, or infested with flies, mosquitoes, or hairs, one should practise the penance for three days.

वृथाकृशरसंयावपायमापूपशष्कुलीः।
भुक्त्वा त्रिरात्रं कुर्वीत व्रतमेतत् समाहितः।।४६।।

Having eaten cakes (and the articles of confectionary known as) *Śuṣkuli, Sañyavs; Pāyasa* or *Kṛśarā* (a preparation of rice, meat, pulse, and butter), not offered to the gods, one should practise the penance for three days.

नील्या चैव क्षतो विप्रः शुना दुष्टस्तथैव च।
त्रिरात्रन्तु व्रतं कुर्यात् पुंश्चलीदशनक्षतः॥४७॥

A Brāhmaṇa, wounded with an Indigo twig, or bitten by a dog, or suffering from a wound caused by the bite of an unchaste woman, should practise the penance for three days.

पादप्रतापनं बह्नौ क्षिप्ता बह्नौ तथाप्यधः।
कुशैः प्रमृज्य पादौ च दिनमेकं व्रतं चरेत्॥४८॥

Having heated the soles of his feet over fire, or having cast anything impure therein, or having rubbed the soles of his feet with the blades of *Kuśa* grass, a Brāhmaṇa should practise the penance for a day.

क्षत्रियस्तु रणे हत्वा पृष्ठं प्राणपरायणम्।
संवत्सरव्रतं कुर्याच्छित्वा पिप्पलपादपम्॥४९॥

A Kṣatriya, who having killed an enemy in battle, timorously flies from the field, afraid of his own life, should continuously practise the above-said expiatory penance for an entire year; similarly, having felled down an Aśvattha tree, one should practise the same penance for a year.

दिवा च मैथुनं कृत्वा स्नात्वा दुष्टजले तथा।
नग्नां परस्त्रियं दृष्ट्वा दिनमेकं व्रती भवेत्॥५०॥

Having visited his wife during the day, or bathed in foul water, or seen the nudity of another man's wife, a, man should practise the penance for a day.

क्षिप्ताग्नावशुचि द्रव्यं तद्वदम्भसि मानवः।
मासमेकं व्रतं कुर्यादपक्रुध्य तथा गुरुम्॥५१॥

Having cast any foul substance in fire or water, or used angry words to one's preceptor, one should practise the penance for a month.

तथा विशेषजं पीत्वा पानीयं ब्राह्मणस्तथा।
त्रिरात्रन्तु व्रतं कुर्याद्वामहस्तेन वा पुनः॥५२॥

Having drunk water without closely observing it, or with his left hand, a Brāhmaṇas should practise the penance for three days.

एकपङ्क्त्युपविष्टेषु विषमं यः प्रयच्छति।
स च तावदसौ पक्षं प्रकुर्याद् ब्राह्मणो व्रतम्॥५३॥

He, who unequally serves viands to Brāhmaṇas seated in the same row at a dinner, should practise, for a fortnight, the penance laid down for expiating the sin of a Brahmanicide.

धारयित्वा तुलाञ्चैव विषमं वनिजस्तथा।
सुरालवणपात्रेषु भुक्त्वा क्षीरं व्रतं चरेत्॥५४॥
विक्रीय पाणिना मद्यं तिलानि च तथाचरेत्॥५५॥

A merchant, having used false weights in trade, and a person, having kept milk in a wine-pot or in a salt-pot, or having sold sesame with his hands, should practise the above-said penance for expiation.

हुङ्कारं ब्राह्मणस्योक्त्वा हुङ्कारञ्च गरीयसः।
दिनमेकं व्रतं कुर्यात् प्रयतः सुसमाहितः॥५६॥

Having angrily roared unto a Brāhmaṇas or a preceptor, one should practise, self-controlled, for a day, the above-said penance.

प्रेतस्य प्रेतकार्याणि कृत्वा वै धनहारकः।
वर्णानां यद्व्रतं प्रोक्तं तद्व्रतं प्रयतश्चरेत्॥५७॥

He, who offers funeral oblations to a deceased person, inherit the property, left by him. Having inherited (the property) he should practise the form of penance, enjoined as proper for the caste he belongs to, on the occasion.

कृत्वा पापं न गूहेत गुह्यमानं हि वर्द्धते।
कृत्वा पापं बुधः कुर्यात् पर्षदानुमतं व्रतम्॥५८॥

Hide not you guilt after its commission, inasmuch as hiding increases its heinousness; having committed a sin, a wise man should undertake the proper expiatory penance.

स्थित्वा च श्वापदाकीर्णे बहुव्याधमृगे वने।
न ब्राह्मणो व्रतं कुर्यात् प्राणबाधभयात् सदा।।५९।।

A Brāhmaṇas, living in a forest abounding in savage and furious, beasts, or in hunters, or at a place where life is manifestly insecure, should not practise any penance.

संतो हि जीवतो जीवं सर्वपापमपोहति।
व्रतैः कृच्छ्रैस्तथा दानैरित्याह भगवान् यमः।।६०।।

Continuing in life, an individual may get rid of all kinds of sin by practising penances and charities. This is what is said by the lord Yama.

शरीरं धर्मसर्वस्वं रक्षणीयं प्रयत्नतः।
शरीराच्च्यवते धर्मः पर्वतात् सलिलं यथा।।६१।।

A (healthy) body is the source of all pieties; hence, the body should be preserved (in health) with the utmost care. Virtues well up from a healthy body, as fountains spring up from beneath a hill side.

आलोक्य सर्वशास्त्राणि समेत्य ब्राह्मणैः सह।
प्रायश्चित्तं द्विजो दद्यात् स्वेच्छया न कदाचन।।६२।।

Brāhmaṇas, having pondered over the injunctions of all the Ethical Codes, and in unanimity with other. Brāhmaṇas, should lay down the form of expiation in a given case, and never do so out of his own accord, and without consultation.

।। इति शङ्खीये धर्मशास्त्रे सप्तदशोऽध्यायः।।१७।।

Chapter 18

त्र्यहं त्रिषवणस्नाने प्रकुर्यादघमर्षणम्।
निमज्ज्य नक्तं सरिति न भुञ्जीत दिनत्रयम्॥१॥

Every day, one should thrice bathe and practise the *Aghamarṣaṇam Vratam* ablution in a river in the night, and forbear eating three meals.

वीरासनं सदा तिष्ठेद्गाश्च दद्यात् पयस्विनीम्।
अघमर्षणमित्येतत् कृतं सर्वाघनाशनम्॥२॥

One should always sit in tie posture known as the *Virāsanam,* and make gifts of milch cows. This is what constitutes the *Aghamarṣaṇam,* the expiation for all sin.

त्र्यहं सायं त्र्यहं प्रातस्त्र्यहमद्यादयाचितम्।
परं त्र्यहञ्च नाश्नीयात् प्राजापत्यं चरन् व्रतम्॥३॥

For the first three days of its observance, a vowist should eat his meal at morning; at evening during the second, three days; and eat what is obtained by begging during the next three days, and! fast for the last three days of the penance. This, is what constitutes the *Prājāpatyam Vratam.*

त्र्यहमुष्णं पिबेदापस्त्र्यहमुष्णं घृतं पिबेत्।
त्र्यहमुष्णं पयः पीत्वा वायुभक्षी दिनत्रयम्॥४॥

For the first three days, a vowist should take nothing but warm water; during the next three days he should take warm clarified butter, and warm water during the next three days; and fast for the last three days of the penance. This is what constitutes a *Tapta Kṛcchra Vratam.*

तप्तकृच्छ्रं विजानीयादेतदुक्तं सदा व्रतम्।
द्वादशेनोपवासेन पराकः परिकीर्त्तितः॥५॥
विधिनोदकसिद्धानि समश्नीयात् प्रयत्नतः।
शक्तून् हि सोदकान् मांसं कृच्छ्रवारुणमुच्यते॥६॥

A Parāka Vrata consists in fasting for twelve successive days; *Vāruṇa Kṛcchra Vratam* consists in, living upon, solution of fried barley powder, for a month, according to regulation.

बिल्वैरामलकैर्वापि कपित्थैरथवा शुभै:।
मासेन लोकेऽतिकृच्छ्रं कथ्यते द्विजसत्तमै:।।७।।

The foremost of the Brāhmaṇa call one's continuous living on *Bilva, Āmalaka* and *Kapittha fruits,* for a month, an *Ātikṛcchra Vratam.*

गोमूत्रं गोमयं क्षीरं दधि सर्पि: कुशोदकम्।
एकरात्रोपवासन्तु कृच्छ्रं सान्तपनं स्मृतम्।।८।।
व्रतैस्तु त्र्यहमभ्यस्तैर्महासान्तपनं स्मृतम्।

A *Kṛcchra Sāntapanam Vratam* consists in living on a compound of cow-dung, cow urine, cow milk cow-butter, curdled cow milk, and the washings of *Kuśa* blades on the first day of its observance, and in fasting on the day following; these austerities, thrice practised, constitutes *a Mahā Sāntapanam Vratam.*

पादद्वयं तथा त्यक्त्वा सक्तूनां परिवामनात्।
उपवासान्तराभ्यासात् तुलापुरुष उच्यते।।९।।
गोपुरीषाशनो भूत्वा मासं नित्यं समाहित:।
व्रतन्तु वार्द्धिकं कुर्यात् सर्वपापापनुत्तये।।१०।।

A Tulāpuruṣa Vratam consists in eating fried barley-powder and fasting, on alternate days, for a month; a Vārdhika Vratam, which destroys all sins, consists in living on cow-dung, each day, for a month.

ग्रासं चन्द्रकलावृद्ध्या प्राश्नीयाद्वर्द्धयन् सदा।
ह्रासमयंस्तु कलाहानौ व्रतं चान्द्रायणं स्मृतम्।।११।।

A Cāndarāyaṇam Vratam consists in one's gradually increasing and decreasing the number of morsels of food with the successive increase or waning of the lunar phases.

मन्त्रं विद्वान् जपेद्भक्त्या जुहुयाच्चैव शक्तित:।
अयं विधिस्तु विज्ञेय: सुधीभिर्विमलात्मभि:।
पापात्मनस्तु पापेभ्यो नात्र कार्या विचारणा।।१२।।

Persons, conversant with the Mantras, should mentally recite them and perform *Homas,* with their recitations, according to their capacity. This is the means of absolution laid down for sinners by the pure-hearted and the virtuous.

शङ्खप्रोक्तमिदं शास्त्रं योऽधीते प्रयत: सुधी:।
सर्वपापविनिर्मुक्त: स्वर्गलोके महीयते॥१३॥

The intelligent, who carefully peruse this *Śāstram* framed by the holy *Śaṅkha,* are exonerated from all sin, and are glorified in heaven.

॥ इति शङ्खीये धर्मशास्त्रेऽष्टादशोऽध्याय:॥१८॥

॥ शङ्खस्मृति: समाप्ता ॥

१३. लिखितस्मृतिः

13. Likhita Smṛti

इष्टापूर्त्तौ तु कर्त्तव्यो ब्राह्मणेन प्रयत्नतः।
इष्टेन लभते स्वर्गं पूर्त्ते मोक्षमवाप्नुयात्॥१॥

Sacrifice or other religious rites and the digging of tanks, etc., shall be performed with care by a Brāhmaṇa. By *Iṣṭa* (religious rite) one attains to the celestial region, and by *Pūrtta* (digging of tanks, etc.,) one attains to emancipation.

एकाहमपि कर्त्तव्यं भूमिष्ठमुदकं शुभम्।
कुलानि तारयेत् सप्त यत्र गौर्वितृषा भवेत्॥२॥

[Such a tank at least be excavated] that sacred water may lie on earth at least for a day; that, (*i.e.*, a tank) in which the thirst of a cow is satisfied, rescues seven generations.

भूमिदानेन ये लोका गोदानेन च कीर्त्तिताः।
तल्लोकान् प्राप्नुयान्मर्त्यः पादपानां प्ररोपणे॥३॥

By planting trees a mortal attains to those regions which are described [as being attainable] by the gift of lands or kine.

वापीकूपतडागानि देवतायतनानि च।
पतितान्युद्धरेद्यस्तु स पूर्त्तफलमश्नुते॥४॥

He, who re-excavates and restores dilapidated wells, tanks, lakes, and temples, reaps the fruits of *Pūrtta* acts.

अग्निहोत्रं तपः सत्यं वेदानाञ्चैव पालनम्।
आतिथ्यं वैश्वदेवञ्च इष्टमित्यभिधीयते॥५।

Adoration of the sacred Fire, ascetic austerity, truthfulness, the protection of the Vedas, hospitality and the worship of the Vaiśvadevas are spoken of as *Iṣṭa*.

इष्टापूर्ते द्विजातीनां सामान्यो धर्म उच्यते।
अधिकारी भवेच्छूद्रः पूर्ते धर्मे न वैदिके॥६॥

The [three] twice-born castes have equal rights in both *Iṣṭa* and *Pūrtta* works. A Śūdra is entitled to [perform] *Pūrtta* [works] but not Vedic rites.

यावदस्थि मनुष्यस्य गङ्गातोयेषु तिष्ठति।
तावद्वर्षसहस्राणि स्वर्गलोके महीयते।७।।

As long as the bone of a man exists in the Ganges water for so many thousands of year he lives gloriously in the celestials region.

देवतानां पितृणाञ्च जले दद्याज्जलाञ्जलिम्।
असंस्कृतमृतानाञ्च स्थले दद्याज्जलाञ्जलिम्।।८।।

One should offer libations of water in water unto the celestials and the Pitṛs. For those dead without going through the purificatory rites one should offer libations of water on land.

एकादशाहे प्रेतस्य यस्य चोत्सृज्यते वृषः।
मुच्यते प्रेतलोकात्तु पितृलोकं स गच्छति।।९।।

The deceased, for whom a bull is let loose on the eleventh day, is released from the region of the dead, and goes to that of the *Pitṛs*.

एष्टव्या बहवः पुत्राः यद्यप्येको गयां व्रजेत्।
यजेत वाऽश्वमेधेन नीलं वा वृषमुत्सृजेत्।।१०।।

Many sons should be sought for, because one of them at least may happen to go to Gayā, or celebrate a horse-sacrifice, or dedicate a *Nīla* bull.

वाराणस्यां प्रविष्टस्तु कदाचिन्निष्क्रमेद्यदि।
हसन्ति तस्य भूतानि अन्योऽन्यं करताडनैः।।११।।

If one, after entering Varanasi, leaves that place on any occasion and goes elsewhere, the *Bhūtas* (spirits) laugh, striking their palms, amongst themselves.

गयाशिरे तु यत्किञ्चिन्नाम्ना पिण्डन्तु निर्वपेत्।
नरकस्थो दिवं याति स्वर्गस्था मोक्षमाप्नुयात्।।१२।।

The person naming whom one offers a *piṇḍa* at *Gayaśiras*, goes to the celestial region, if stationed in a hell; and attains to emancipation, if residing in the celestial region.

आत्मनो वा परस्यापि गयाक्षेत्रे यतस्ततः।

यन्नाम्ना पातयेत् पिण्डं तं नयेद्ब्रह्म शाश्वतम्॥१३॥

One takes him, whether he be his own relative or an outsider, to the eternal region of Brahman, by naming whom he offers a *piṇḍa* at any palce in the sacred shrine of Gayā.

लाहितो यस्तु वर्णेन शङ्खवर्णखुरस्तथा।

लाङ्गुलशिरसोश्चैव स वै नीलवृषः स्मृतः॥१४॥

That which has a crimson colour, white hoops, tail and head, is called in the *Smṛti*, a *Nīla* bull.

नवश्राद्धं त्रिपक्षे च द्वादशस्वेव मासिकम्।

षण्मासो चाब्दिकञ्चैव श्राद्धान्येतानि षोडश॥१५॥

The first, twelve monthly, two six monthly and the annual, ones, these are the sixteen *Śrāddhas*.

यस्यैतानि न कुर्वीत एकोद्दिष्टानि षोडश।

पिशाचत्वं स्थिरं तस्य दत्तेः श्राद्धशतैरपि॥१६॥

The *Piśācahood* of the person, for whom these sixteen *Ekoddiṣṭa Śrāddhas* are not performed, remains fixed even if a hundred [annual] *Śrāddhas* are offered.

सपिण्डीकरणादूर्ध्वं प्रतिसंवत्सरं द्विजः।

मातापित्रोः पृथक्कुर्यादेकोद्दिष्टं मृतेऽहनि॥१७॥

After the performance of the *Sapiṇḍīkaraṇa Śrāddha* a twice-born person should perform, every year, the *Ekoddiṣṭas* on days of their death, separately for his lather and mother.

वर्षे वर्षे तु कर्त्तव्यं मातापित्रास्तु सन्ततम्।

अदैवं भोजयेच्छ्राद्धं पिण्डमेकं तु निर्वपेत्॥१८॥

Every year, for the gratification of ones father and mother, one should perform a *daiva* (rite for the deities) and offer one *piṇḍa* only.

संक्रान्तावुपरागे च पर्वण्यपि महालये।
निर्वाप्यास्तु त्रयः पिण्डा एकतस्तु क्षयेऽहनि॥१९॥

On the last day of a month, on the two eclipses, on a *Parva*, and on *Mahālaya* three *piṇḍas* should be offered, and one on the day of death.

एकोद्दिष्टं परित्यज्य पार्वणं कुरुते द्विजः।
अकृतं तद्विजानीयात् स नाम पितृघातकः॥२०॥

If a twice-born person performs the *Pārvaṇa Śrāddha* neglecting the *Ekoddiṣṭa,* know that as fruitless; and he is known as the destroyer of his father.

अमावास्यां क्षयो यस्य पितृपक्षेऽथवा यदि।
सपिण्डीकरणादूर्ध्वं तस्योक्तः पार्वणो विधिः॥२१॥

After the performance of the *Sapiṇḍakaraṇa,* [the annual *Śrāddha*] should be celebrated according to the regulation of the *Pārvaṇa* for him who dies on an *Amāvasyā* day in the *Pitṛ* fortnight (the dark half of Bhādrapada).

त्रिदण्डग्रहणादेव प्रेतत्वं नैव जायते।
अहन्येकादशे प्राप्ते पार्वणन्तु विधीयते॥२२॥

[He who dies] after holding the triple staff, does not come by the condition of a *preta* (deceased), on the eleventh day of his death a [*Śrāddha*] should be performed according to the *Pārvaṇa* regulations.

यस्य संवत्सरादर्वाक् सपिण्डीकरणं स्मृतम्।
प्रत्यहं तन्मोदकुम्भं दद्यात् संवत्सरं द्विजः॥२३॥

A twice-born person should offer daily a pitcher filled with water for him for whom a *Sapiṇḍakaraṇ* subsequent to the annual [*Śrāddha*] is laid down in the *Smṛti*.

पत्या चैकेन कर्त्तव्यं सपिण्डीकरणं स्त्रियाः।
पितामह्याऽपि तत्तस्मिन् सत्येवन्तु क्षयेऽहनि॥२४॥
तस्यां सत्यां प्रकर्त्तव्यं तस्याः श्वश्वेति निश्चितम्॥२५॥

On the day of her death, with one [*piṇḍa*] a *Sapiṇḍakaraṇa,* for a woman should be performed by her husband. It should be mixed with that for the paternal grandmother. The later living, it should be mixed with that for her mother-in-law, or grand-mother-in-law. This is the fixed rule.

विवाहे चैव निर्वृत्ते चतुर्थेऽहनि रात्रिषु।
एकत्वं सा गता भर्त्तुः पिण्डे गोत्रे च सूतके॥२६॥

After the termination of the nuptial rite, and on the night of the fourth day, a woman becomes one with her husband, in a *piṇḍa*, *gotra* (family), and impurity consequent upon births and deaths therein.

स्वगोत्राद्भ्रश्यते नारी उद्वाहात् सप्तमे पदे।
भर्त्तृगोत्रेण कर्त्तव्यं दान् पिण्डोदकक्रिया॥२७॥

At the seventh *pada* (foot-step)[1] after marriage a woman becomes divorced from his own family. Gifts, and the offering of *piṇḍas* and water should be done [according to the regulation of] her husbands *gotra* (family).

द्विमातुः पिण्डदानन्तु पिण्डे पिण्डे द्विनामतः।
षण्णां देयास्त्रयः पिण्डा एवं दाता न मुह्यति॥२८॥

By taking the name of the two in every *piṇḍa* it should be offered for the two mothers. Three *piṇḍas* should be offered for the six. The giver, by doing so, does not become stupefied.

अथ चेन्मन्त्रविद्युक्त शारीरैः पङ्क्तिदूषणैः।
अदोषं तत् यमः प्राह पङ्क्तिपावन एव सः॥२९॥

Even if he be a Brāhmaṇa, conversant with *Mantras*, and affected by physical sins as well as those affecting a row (diners), still Yama calls him sinless; and such a person is the sanctifier of the row.

अग्नीकरणशेषन्तु पितृपात्रे प्रदापयेत्।
प्रतिपाद्य पितॄणाञ्च न दद्याद्वैस्वदैविके॥३०॥

1. The seven steps at a marriage (the bride and bridegroom walk together seven steps after which the marriage becomes irrevocable).

The residue of the oblation offered to the Fire, one should place in a *Pitṛ* vessel and distribute amongst the *Pitṛs*; he should never put it in a vessel for the Vaiśvadevas.

अनग्निको यदा विप्रः श्राद्धं करोति पार्वणम्।
तत्र मातामहानाञ्च कर्त्तव्यमभयं सदा॥३१॥

If a Vipra, who does maintain the Sacred Fire, performs a *Pārvaṇa Śrāddha*, he should always perform fearlessly that for his ancestors in the maternal line.

अपुत्रा ये मृताः केचित् पुरुषा वा स्त्रियोऽपि वा।
तेभ्य एव प्रदातव्यमेकोद्दिष्टं न पार्वणम्॥३२॥

Ekoddiṣṭa and not a *Pārvaṇa Śrāddha* should be offered unto them, men or women who die sonless.

यस्मिन् राशिगते सूर्ये विपत्तिः स्याद्द्विजन्मनः।
तस्मिन्नहनि कर्त्तव्यं दानं पिण्डोदकक्रियाः॥३३॥

On the self same *Tithi* on which a twice-born person dies, gifts and the offering of funeral cakes and water should be made unto him.

वर्षवृद्ध्यभिषेकादि कर्त्तव्यमधिकेन तु।
अधिमासे तु पूर्वं स्याच्छ्राद्धं संवत्सरादपि॥३४॥

Birthday ceremony and *Abhiṣeka* (consecration by sprinkling water) should never be done in the redundant month. But the *Śrāddha*, preceding the annual one, may take place in the redundant month.

स एव हेयोद्दिष्टस्य येन केन तु कर्मणा।
अभिधानान्तरं कार्यं तत्रैवाहःकृतं भवेत्॥३५॥

That month is considered interdicted for every rite. In the other (*i.e.*, pure) part of the month and in the same *Tithi* any rite may be performed.

शालाऽग्नौ पचते अन्नं लौकिकेनापि नित्यशः।
यस्मिन्नेव पचेदन्नं तस्मिन् होमो विधीयते॥३६॥

One may daily cook rice with the fire, kept in the house, or with an ordinary one. It is laid down that *Homa* should be performed in that fire with which rice is cooked.

वैदिके लौकिके वाऽपि नित्यं हुत्वा ह्यतन्द्रितः।
वैदिके स्वर्गमाप्नोति लौकिके हन्ति किल्विषम्।। ३७।।

One should zealously offer oblations every day to the *Vaidika* and *Laukika*(ordinary) fire. By [offering oblations] to the *Vaidika* one attains to the celestial region, and those to the *Laukika* dissipate sins.

अग्नौ व्याहृतिभिः पूर्वं हुत्वा मन्त्रैस्तु शाकलैः।
संविभागन्तु भूतेभ्यस्ततोऽश्नीयादनग्निमान्।।३८।।

He, who does not preserve the sacred fire, should offer oblations to the Fire reciting the *Śakala Mantra* preceded by *Vyāhṛti*, and then, distributing food amongst the *Bhūtas* (evil spirits), should himself take meals.

उच्छेषणन्तु नोत्तिष्ठेद्यावद्विप्रविसर्ज्जनम्।
ततो गृहबलिं कुर्यादिति धर्मो व्यवस्थितः।।३९।।

He should not touch the food so long the Brāhmaṇa are not dismissed. He should then perform *Gṛhavali*. This is the established religious ritual.

दर्भाः कृष्णाजिनं मन्त्रा ब्राह्मणश्च विशेषतः।
नैते निर्माल्यतां यान्ति याक्तव्यास्ते पुनः पुनः।।४०।।

Darbhās (grass), black antelope skins, *Mantras* and Brāhmaṇas, in particular, never become desecrated, so they may be employed repreatedly.

पानमाचमनं कुर्यात् कुशपाणिः सदा द्विजः।
भुक्त्वा नोच्छिष्टतां याति एष एव विधिः सदाः।।४१।।
पान आचमने चैव तर्पणे दैविके सदा।
कुशहस्तो न दुष्येत यथा पाणिस्तथा कुशः।।४२।।

A twice-born person should always, with a *Kuśā* in his hand, drink water and rinse his mouth. It is not considered as sullied as the residue of his meals. This is always the regulation. A *Kuśā* is as unsulliable as the hand.

वामपाणौ कुशान् कृत्वा दक्षिणेन उपस्पृशेत्।
विनाचमन्ति ये मूढा रुधिरेणाचमन्ति ते॥४३॥

The blades of *Kuśā* grass should be caught hold of with the left hand, and the mouth should be rinsed with the right. The ignorant, who do not retain *Kuśās* in their left hands on the occasion, are supposed to rinse their mouths with blood.

नीवीमध्येषु ये दर्भाः ब्रह्मसूत्रेषु ये कृताः।
पवित्रांस्तान् विजानीयाद्यथा कायस्तथा कुशः॥४४॥

Kuśā blades fastened with the waist-knot of a wearing cloth, or with the strings of a holy thread should be always regarded as unsullied, in as much as they are as pure as the body itself.

पिण्डे कृतास्तु ये दर्भाः यैः कृतं पितृतर्पणम्।
मूत्रोच्छिष्टपुरीषञ्च तेषां त्यागो विधीयते॥४५॥

Kuśā blades in touch with the *Piṇḍas* dedicated to ones departed manes, or with any kind of excreted matter, as well as those used in offering libations of water to *Pitṛs*, should be rejected as unclean.

दैवपूर्वन्तु यच्छ्राद्धमदैवं चापि यद् भवेत्।
ब्रह्मचारी भवेत् तत्र कुर्याच्छ्राद्धन्तु पैतृकम्॥४६॥

One should practise *Brahmacaryam* (absolute continence) on the occasion of celebrating a *Pārvaṇa* or *Ekoddiṣṭa Śrāddha*, as well as in connection with celebrating the one which is undertaken with the sole object of propitiating ones departed manes.

मातुः श्राद्धन्तु पूर्वं स्यात् पितृणां तदनन्तरम्।
ततो मातामहानाञ्च वृद्धौ श्राद्धत्रयं स्मृतम्॥४७॥

Oblations should be first given to ones departed manes on the mothers side, then to those on the fathers side, and thereaftef to those on the maternal grand-fathers side,[1] in connection with the celebration of a *Vṛddhi Śrāddha* (offerings made to ones departed manes on prosperous occasions such, as the birth of a son, etc.)

क्रतुर्दक्षो वसुः सभ्यः कालकामौ धुरिलोचनौ।
पुरूरवामाद्रवाश्च विश्वे देवाः प्रकीर्त्तिताः॥४८॥

Kratu and Dakṣa, Vasu and Satya, Kāla and Kāma, Dhuri and Locana and Purūravā and Mādravas, are, in couples, styled as Vaiśvadevas.

आगच्छन्तु महाभागा विश्वेदेवा महाबलाः।
ये यत्र विहिताः श्राद्धे सावधाना भवन्तु ते॥४९॥

May the mighty Vaiśvadevas, of illustrious fate, come and grant us the boon in respect of the celebration of those *Śrāddhas* of which they have been respectively ordained to act as the presiding deities.

इष्टिश्राद्धे क्रतुर्दक्षो वसुः सभ्यश्च वैदिके।
कालः कामोऽग्निकार्येषु अम्बरे धुरिलोचनौ।
पुरूरवा माद्रवाश्च पार्वणेषु नियोजयेत्॥५०॥

Kratu and *Dakṣa* are the Vaiśvadevas, who should be invoked to preside over an *Iṣṭa Śrāddha* ceremony. (A *Śrāddha* celebrated for the fruition of any earthly desire). *Vasu* and *Satya* are the Vaiśvadevas, who should be invoked in connection with a *Deva Śrāddha (Śrāddha* celebrated in honour of the gods). *Kāla* and *Kāma* are the Vaiśvadevas, who should be addressed on the occasion of an *Agni Kārya* (oblation to the Fire god), *Dhuri* and *Locana* in respect of *Ambara, Kārya* and *Purūravā* and *Mādravas* in connection with a *Pārvaṇa Śrāddha* (the general ceremony of offering oblations to all the manes on days of *Pārvaṇa* such as, the new moon, etc.)

यस्यास्तु न वेदभ्राता न विज्ञायेत वा पिता।

---

1. A *Sāma Vedī* Brāhmaṇa need not make any offering to manes on his mothers side (*Mātṛpakṣa*) in connection with a *Vṛddhi Śrāddha*. This is the regulation:– Tr.

नोपयच्छेत तां प्राज्ञः पुत्रिकाकर्मशङ्कया॥५१॥

A wise man should not wed a girl without an uterine (or step-brother) of her own and whose fathers name is not known, apprehending lest she might have been previously given away as a *Putrikā*.

अभ्रातृकां प्रदास्यामि तुभ्यं कन्यामलङ्कृताम्।
अस्यां यो जायते पुत्रः स मे पुत्रो भविष्यति॥५२॥

"I give this daughter, who has got no uterine brother of her own, duly bedecked with ornaments, to you. The male child begotten on her person shall be a son of mine.'' The girl, who is thus given away, is called a *Putrikā*.

मातुः प्रथमतः पिण्डं निर्वपेत् पुत्रिकासुतः।
द्वितीयन्तु पितुस्तस्यास्तृतीयं तत्पितुः पितुः॥५३॥

The son begotten on a *Putrikā* daughter should first offer oblations to his mother, then to his mothers father, and the to his fathers father.

मृणमयेषु च पात्रेषु श्राद्धे यो भोजयेत् पितॄन्।
अन्नदाता पुरोधाश्च भोक्ता च नरकं व्रजेत्॥५४॥

He, who feeds (offers oblations to) his departed manes in earthen vessels on the occasion of a *Śrāddha*, is consigned to hell in the company of the invited Brāhmaṇas and the priest officiating at the ceremony.

अलाभे मृन्मयं दद्यादनुज्ञातस्तु तैर्द्विजैः।
घृतेन प्रोक्षणं कुर्यान् मृदः पात्रं पवित्रकम्॥५५॥

Earthen vessels may be substituted for other kinds of utensils, on the occasion, with the permission of the congregated Brāhmaṇas, provided they be first smeared with clarified butter. Such earthen vessels are not impure.

श्राद्धं कृत्वा परश्राद्धे यस्तु भुञ्जीत विह्वलः।
पतन्ति पितरस्तस्य लुप्तपिण्डोदकक्रिया:॥५६॥

The departed manes of a person, who himself, having

performed a *Śrāddha*, dines, that day, out of greed, in connection with anothers *Śrāddha*-ceremony, stand deprived of oblations and libations of water, and come by a worse condition in the nether regions.

श्राद्धं दत्त्वा च भुक्त्वा च अध्वानं योऽधिगच्छति।
भवन्ति पितरस्तस्य तन्मासं पांसुभोजनाः॥५७॥

The departed manes of a person, who himself having performed a *Śrāddha,* or having dined in connection with one done by another, travels, that day, more than a distance of one *Krośa* (two miles), eat dust for a whole month reckoned from that date.

पुनर्भोजनमध्वानं भारध्ययनमैथुनम्।
दानं प्रतिग्रहं होमं श्राद्धं कृत्वाष्ट वर्ज्जयेत्॥५८॥

Having performed a *Śrāddha* ceremony, one should refrain from doing the following eight things, viz., eating a second time that day, travelling, carrying a weight, reading, sexual intercourse, giving or taking of any gift and performance of a *Homa*.

अध्वगामी भवेदश्वः पुनर्भोक्ता च वायसः।
कर्मकृज्जायते दासः स्त्रीगमने च शूकरः॥५९॥

By travelling (under the circumstance) one is born as a horse in ones next birth; by eating a second meal, a crow; by doing any work, a slave; by knowing a wife, a hog.

दशकृत्यः पिबेदापः सावित्र्या चाभिमन्त्रिताः।
ततः सन्ध्यामुपासीत शुध्येत तदनन्तरम्॥६०॥

One should first drink a little water consecrated by ten times reciting the *Sāvitrī Mantra*, and after that attend to ones daily *Sandhyā* rite. By so doing one is absolved from all sins incidental to doing forbidden acts [under the auspices of a *Śrāddha* ceremony].

आर्द्रवासास्तु यत् कुर्याद्बहिर्जानु च यत्कृतम्।

सर्वं तन्निष्फलं कुर्याज्जपहोमप्रतिग्रहम्॥६१॥

An act of *Japa, Homa*, or gift-taking not performed by one in wet-clothes, or without covering ones knees, proves abortive (in respect of its religious merit).

चान्द्रायणं नवश्राद्धे पराको मासिके तथा।
पक्षत्रये तु कृच्छ्रं स्यात् षण्मासे कृच्छ्रमेव च॥६२॥
ऊनाब्दिके त्रिरात्रं स्यादेकाहः पुनराब्दिके।
शावे मासन्तु मुक्त्वा वा पादकृच्छ्रं विधीयते॥६३॥

A rite of *Cāndrāyaṇa* penance should be practised before celebrating an *Ādya Śrāddha;* a *Parāka Vrata*, in connection with a monthly *Śrāddha;* a *Tapta Kṛcchra Vrata* in connection with the one which is practised at the close of every third week (*Tripakṣa)* or of a complete month, or of the first six months of a year; a three nights fast, in connection with the one to be performed on the completion of the second-half of the year (*Ūnābda*); and one nights (one day and night) fast, in connection with the celebration of a *Sapiṇḍīkaraṇa* ceremony (A *Śrāddha* ceremony, celebrated on the completion of a year from the date of the death of a deceased person, or earlier, if happens to be performed in connection with any special act such as, the marriage or *Upanayana* of any of his sons or daughters, etc., and which is supposed to liberate his spirit from the mansions of the *Pretas)*. Uncleanness incidental to an act of helping in the cremation of a dead body is removed by practising a *Pāda Kṛcchra* (quarter part of a *Kṛcchra Vrata*) penance for a month from the date of the cremation.

सर्पविप्रहतानाञ्च शृङ्गिदंष्ट्रिसरीसृपैः।
आत्मनस्त्यागिनाञ्चैव श्राद्धमेषां न कारयेत्॥६४॥

A rite of *Śrāddha* should not be performed unto the spirit of a suicide, nor of one, either dead through the curse of a Brāhmaṇa, or killed by a snake, lizard, or a fanged or horned animal.

गोभिर्हतं तथोद्बद्धं ब्राह्मणेन तु घातितम्।

तं स्पृशन्ति च ये विप्रा गोऽजाश्वाश्च भवन्ति ते॥६५॥

By touching the corpse of a person killed by a cow, or a Brāhmaṇa, or dead from the effects of voluntary strangulation, a Brāhmaṇa is reborn as a cow, or a horse. The contact of such a dead body is interdicted.

अग्निदाता तथा चान्ये पाशच्छेदकराश्च ये।
तप्तकृच्छ्रेण शुध्यन्ति मनुराह प्रजापतिः॥६६॥

The cutter of a noose or of a chord of binding strings as well as the one guilty of incendiarism, should expiate his guilt by practising a *Tapta Kṛcchra* penance. This is ordained by the patriarch Manu.

त्र्यहमुष्णं पिवेदापस्त्यहमुष्णं पयः पिबेत्।
त्र्यहमुष्णं घृतं पीत्वा वायुभक्षो दिनत्रयम्॥६७॥

The performance of a *Tapta Kṛcchra Vrata* consists in living on a little warm water alone for the first three days; on a little warm milk alone for the second three days; on a little warm clarified butter alone for the third three days; and on air alone for the last or fourth three days of the entire term of the penance.

गोभूहिरण्यहरणे स्त्रीणां क्षेत्रगृहस्य च।
यमुद्दिश्य त्यजेत् प्राणांस्तमाहुर्ब्रह्मघातकम्॥६८॥

The man, in remembrance of (whose guilt), one, who has been robbed of a wife, field, house, cow, land, or gold, suffers self-immolation, should be regarded as a Brāhmaṇa*ghātin* (Brahmanicide).

उद्यताः सह धावन्ते यद्येको धर्मघातकः।
सर्वे ते शुद्धिमृच्छन्ति स पक्को ब्रह्मघातकः॥६९॥

There is atonement for the guilt of an abettor or accomplice of a ravisher of female chastity. The ravisher alone should be regarded as Brāhmaṇa*ghātin*.

पतितान्नं यदा भुङ्क्ते भुङ्क्ते चाण्डालवेश्मनि।
स मासार्द्धं चरेद्वारि मासं कामकृतेन तु॥७०॥

By unwilling partaking of boiled rice (lit. any kind of food) in a *Cāṇḍālas* house, as well as of that prepared by a fallen or degraded person, one should live on water alone for a fortnight. The term of the penance should be extended to a month in cases where the delinquency has been knowingly committed.

योगेन पतितेनैव स्पर्शे स्नानं विधीयते।
तेनैवोच्छिष्टसंस्पृष्ट प्राजापत्यं समाचरेत्।।७१।।

The touch of a fallen *yogin* should be expiated by an ablution; that of the residue of the meals of the degraded by the performance of a *Prājāpatya Vratam*.

ब्रह्महा च सुरापायी स्तेयो च गुरुतल्पगः।
महान्ति पातकान्याहुस्तत्संसर्गी च पञ्चमः।।७२।।

Killing of a Brāhmaṇa, wine-drinking, theft of gold to the weight of more than eighty Rattis, and defiling ones preceptors bed[1] are the four cardinal sins, the fifth being the one born of the company of such a sinful person.

स्नेहाद्वा यदि वा लोभाद्भयादज्ञानतोऽपि वा।
कुर्वन्त्यनुग्रहं ये तु तत्पापं तेषु गच्छति।।७३।।

By helping a sinner falling under any of the five preceding categories in matters of expiation, either out of affection, greed, fear, or ignorance, one commits the same sin as the sinner seeking such expiation.

उच्छिष्टोच्छिष्टसंस्पृष्टो ब्राह्मणस्तु कदाचन।
तत्क्षणात् कुरुते स्नानमाचमेन शुचिर्भवेत्।।७४।।

A Brāhmaṇa happening to touch before washing his mouth after eating another similarly circumstanced as himself, should bathe that moment and rinse his mouth with water, whereby he would be clean again.

कुब्जवामनषण्डेषु गद्गदेषु जडेषु च।

1. *Guru-talpaga*-means the defiler of a preceptors bed; but the scholiast interpretes the term as signifying an act of knowing ones step mother. – Tr.

जात्यन्धे बधिरे मूके न दोषः परिवेदने॥७५॥

A man commits no sin by marrying before his elder brothers marriage where the later is either a hunchback, dwarf, eunuch, or idiot, or is deaf, dumb born-blind, or of indistinct speech.

क्लीबे देशान्तरस्थे पतिते व्रजितेऽपि वा।
योगशास्त्राभियुक्ते च न दोषः परिवेदने॥७६॥

On ones elder brother happening to loose his virility, or to have resorted to the practice of *Yoga*, or to a life of asceticism, or to be degraded in life on account of a sojourn to a country a residence wherein is considered degrading (*i.e.*, supposed to degrade a man in society), one is at liberty to marry even before the marriage of such an elder brother.

पूरणे कूपवापीनां वृक्षच्छेदनपातने।
विक्रीणीत गजञ्चाश्वं गोवधं तस्य निर्दिशेत्॥७७॥

A penitential rite, similar to that laid down in connection with an act of cow-killing, should be practised by one who sells horses or elephants for money, or mischievously fills up a tank or well, or fells or cuts down a tree.

पादेऽङ्गरोमवपनं द्विपादे श्मश्रु केवलम्।
तृतीये तु शिखावर्जं चतुर्थे तु शिखावपः॥७८॥

All the hairs of the body should be shaved in cases where a penance to the extent of a *Pāda* (quarter) measure would be found to be enjoined. In two *Pādas* or half penance, the penitent should shave his moustaches only; all the hairs of the head excepting the tuft on the crown, in three legged (*Tripāda*) or three quarter penances; and the hair of the entire head in full or four-footed ones.

चाण्डालोदकसंस्पर्शे स्नानं येन विधीयते।
तेनैवोच्छिष्टसंस्पृष्टः प्राजापत्यं समाचरेत्॥७९॥

An act of ablution is the expiation for touching boiled rice prepared by a *Cāṇḍāla;* a *Prājāpatya Vrata*, for touching the remnants of his meal.

चाण्डालघटभाण्डस्थं यत्तोयं पिवते द्विजः।
तत्क्षणात् क्षिपते यस्तु प्राजापत्यं समाचरेत्॥८०॥

A *Prājāpatya Vrata* is the penance for a Brāhmaṇa unwillingly drinking water out of a *Cāṇḍālas* cup or water vessel and vomiting or belching out the same immediately after drinking.

यदि नोत्क्षिप्यते तोयं शरीरे तस्य जीर्यति।
प्राजापत्यं न दातव्यं कृच्छ्रं सान्तपनं चरेत्॥८१॥

A *Kṛcchra Sāntāpana* instead of a *Prājāpatya Vrata* would be the expiatory penance in his case if the water is not ejected out of and retained and digested in the stomach.

चरेत् सान्तपनं विप्रः प्राजापत्यन्तु क्षत्रियः।
तदर्द्धन्तु चरेद्वैश्यः पादं शूद्रे तु दापयेत्॥८२॥

A Brāhmaṇa should practise a *Kṛcchra Sāntāpana Vrata*; a Kṣatriya, a *Prājāpatya Vrata*; a Vaiśya, a half *Prājāpatya* and a Śūdra, a quarter part of the last named penance.

रजस्वला यदा स्पृष्टा शुना शूकरवायसैः।
उपोष्य रजनीमेकां पञ्चगव्येन शुध्यति॥८३॥

A woman in her periods, happening to be touched by a dog, hog or crow, should observe a single nights fast and regain her cleanness by taking *Pañcagavyam*.[1]

अज्ञानतः स्नानमात्रमानाभेस्तु विशेषतः।
अत ऊर्ध्वं त्रिरात्रं स्यान्मदिरास्पर्शने मतम्॥८४॥

A man by unintentionally touching a woman in her menses somewhere below her navel should instantaneously bathe. A three nights fast is the expiation in cases where the contact is intentional and at a part of the body above her umbilicus.

बालश्चैव दशाहे तु पञ्चत्वं यदि गच्छति।

---

1. Cow-dung, cow's urine, cow milk, milk-curd and *ghṛta*.

सद्य एव विशुध्येत नाशौचं नोदकक्रिया॥८५॥

The *Sapiṇḍas* of a male child, dead within ten days of its birth, are not affected by uncleanness incidental to the death; and no libations of water should be offered to its spirit in such a case.

शावसूतक उत्पन्ने सूतकन्तु यदा भवेत्।
शावेन शुध्यते सूतिर्न सूतिः शावशोधिनी॥८६॥

A birth-uncleanness (uncleanness due to the birth of a child in the family) occurring within the term of one due to a death (in the same family) should terminate with the latter. But a death-uncleanness, occurring within the term of a birth-uncleanness, does not abate with its extinction. Death-uncleanness is stronger than birth-uncleanness.

षष्ठेन शुद्ध्येतैकाहं पञ्चमे त्र्यहमेव तु।
चतुर्थे सप्तरात्रं स्यात् त्रिपुरुषे दशमेऽहनि॥८७॥

Agnates related to a deceased person within sixth degree of consanguinity are unclean for one day, within the fifth degree of consanguinity, for seven days; and within the third degree of consanguinity for ten days only.[1]

मरणारब्धमाशौचं संयोगो यस्य नाग्निभिः।
आ दाहात्तस्य विज्ञेयं यस्य वैतानिको विधिः॥८८॥

The period of uncleanness due to the death of a deceased Brāhmaṇa without the consecrated fire (*Nirāgni*) should be counted from after the hour of his death, while that in respect of a *Sāgnika* Brāhmaṇa (with the consecrated fire) should be counted from after the cremation of his dead body.

आममांसं घृतं क्षौद्रं स्नेहाश्च फलसम्भवाः।
अन्त्यभाण्डस्थिता ह्येते निष्क्रान्ताः शुचयः स्मृताः॥८९॥

Raw meat, clarified butter, honey and oils expressed out of the seeds of fruits (such as almond oil, etc.), kept in the vessel of another unclean person, become clean as soon as they are taken

---

1. Not followed by the Bengal School.– *Tr.*

out of it.

मार्ज्जनीरजसासक्ते स्नानवस्त्रघटोदके।
नवाम्भसि तथा चैव हन्ति पुण्यं दिवाकृतम्॥९०॥

The dust, raised by the ends of a broomstick and happening to defile the bathing or drinking water of a person kept in a vessel, or touching his bathing apparel, tends to destroy his religious merit on the moment of such contact or defilement.

दिवा कपित्थच्छायायां रात्रौ दधिषु सक्तुषु ।
धात्रीफलेषु सर्वत्र अलक्ष्मीर्वसते सदा॥९१॥

Ill luck (*alakṣmī*) resides in the shade of a *Kapittha* tree during the day, in the mixture of milk-curd and barley powder during the night, and constantly in the kernels of Āmalaka fruit.

यत्र यत्र च सङ्कीर्णमात्मानं मन्यते द्विजः।
तत्र तत्र तिलैर्होमं गायत्र्यष्टशतं जपेत्॥९२॥

One should perform three *Homas* and a hundred times recite the Gāyatrī Mantra in connection with each act he thinks to be of evil augury.

॥ इति लिखित-स्मृतिः ॥

१४. व्यासस्मृतिः

14. Vyāsa Smṛti

Chapter 1

वाराणस्यां सुखासीनं वेदव्यासं तपोनिधिम्।

पप्रच्छुर्मुनयोऽभ्येत्य धर्मान् वर्णव्यवस्थितान्।।१।।

The holy sages (Munis) approached that repository of penitential sanctity, Veda Vyāsa, who was blissfully seated in his hermitage at Vārāṇasī and asked him questions regarding the duties of the members of different social orders (*Varṇas*).

स पृष्टः स्मृतिमान्स्मृत्वा स्मृतिं वेदार्थगर्भिताम्।

उवाचाथ प्रसन्नात्मा मुनयः श्रूयतामिति।।२।।

He of excellent memory having been thus interrogated by (other holy sages) recollected the Smṛtis as propounded in the Vedas and complacently said, hear, O Munis!

यत्र यत्र स्वभावेन कृष्णसारो मृगः सदा।

चरते तत्र वेदोक्तो धर्मो भवितुमर्हति।।३।।

Religious rites inculcated in the Vedas should be practised in countries where black antelopes are found to roam about in nature.

श्रुतिस्मृतिपुराणानां विरोधो यत्र दृश्यते।

तत्र श्रौतं प्रमाणन्तु तयोर्द्वैधे स्मृतिर्वरा।।४।।

In matters of discrepancy between the Śrutis, Smṛtis, and Purāṇas, the former should be held as decisive, whereas the Smṛtis should have preference in all topics where there would be a difference of opinion between them and the Purāṇas.

ब्राह्मणक्षत्रियविशस्त्रयो वर्णा द्विजातयः।

श्रुतिस्मृतिपुराणोक्तधर्मयोग्यास्तु नेतरे।।५।।

The term "twice-born" denotes the Brāhmaṇas, Kṣatriyas and Vaiśyas. Only these three orders are entitled to practise religious rites propounded in the Śrutis, Smṛtis and Purāṇas in exclusion of all other castes.

शूद्रो वर्णश्चतुर्थोऽपि वर्णत्वाद्धर्ममर्हति।
वेदमन्त्रस्वधास्वाहावषट्कारादिभिर्विना।।६।।

The fourth order is the Śūdra, hence the Śūdras; are entitled to practise religious rites, but they are not privileged to recite any Vedic Mantra, nor to pronounce the terms Svāhā, Svadhā and Vaṣaṭ.

विप्रवद्विप्रविन्नासु क्षत्रविन्नासु क्षत्रवत्।
जातकर्माणि कुर्वीत ततः शूद्रासु शूद्रवत्।।७।।

The daughter of a Brāhmaṇa, duly wedded to a Brāhmaṇa, is called a *Vipravinna*. All religious rites and ceremonies such as, postnatal rites, etc., should be done unto the male child of a *Vipravinna* according to the regulations laid down in respect of a Brāhmaṇa; those unto the male child of a Brāhmaṇa by a Kṣatriya wife (Kṣatra-vinna) should be done in the manner of a Kṣatriya; while those unto the son of a Brāhmaṇa by his lawfully married Śūdra wife in the manner of a Śūdra.

वैश्यासु विप्रक्षत्राभ्यां ततः शूद्रासु शूद्रवत्।
अधमादुत्तमायान्तु जातः शूद्राधमः स्मृतः।।८।।

All religious rites should be done unto a male child begot by a Brāhmaṇa or a Kṣatriya on his married Vaiśya wife in the manner of a Vaiśya, while those unto the son of a Śūdra mother, under the circumstance should be done in the manner of a Śūdra. A son begot by a man of inferior caste on a woman of superior caste is worse than a Śūdra.

ब्राह्मण्यां शूद्रजनितश्चाण्डालो धर्मवर्जितः।
कुमारीसम्भवस्त्वेकः सगोत्रायां द्वितीयकः।।९।।

A son begot by a Śūdra on a Brāhmaṇa girl should be considered as a Cāṇḍāla. Such a son is debarred from practising any religious rite. There are three kinds of Cāṇḍālas. To the first kind or order belong the sons begotten on unmarried girls. To the second order belong the sons begot by persons on wives belonging to their own Gotras.

ब्राह्मण्यां शूद्रजनितश्चाण्डालस्त्रिविध: स्मृत:।
वर्द्धकी नापितो गोप आशाय: कुम्भकारक:।।१०।।
वणिक्किरातकायस्थमालाकारकुटुम्बिन:।
वरटो मेदचाण्डालोदासश्वपचकोलका:।।११।।
एतेऽन्त्यजा: समाख्याता ये चान्ये च गवाशना:।
एषां सम्भाषणात् स्नानं दर्शनादर्कवीक्षणम्।।१२।।

To the third kind belong the sons begotten by Śūdra fathers on mothers who are Brāhmaṇas. Vardhakis (carpenters), Nāpitas (barbers), Gopas (milkmen), Āśāpas, Kumbhakāras (potters), Vaṇik (traders), Kāyasthas (Userers), Mālākāras (flower-men), Varaṭas, Medas, Cāṇḍālas, Dāsas, Śvapacas, Kolas and beefeaters belong to the lowest castes of men. Even a conversation with a person of any of these castes should be expiated by an ablution and a sight of the sun.

गर्भाधानं पुंसवनं सीमन्तो जातकर्म च।
नामक्रियानिष्क्रमणेऽन्नाशनं-वपन-क्रिया।।१३।।
कर्णवेधो व्रतादेशो वेदारम्भक्रियाविधि:।
केशान्त:स्नानमुद्वाहो विवाहाग्निपरिग्रह:।।१४।।
त्रेताऽग्निसंग्रहश्चेति संस्कारा: षोडश स्मृता:।
नवैता: कर्णवेधान्ता मन्त्रवर्जं क्रिया: स्त्रिया:।।१५।।

The rites of *Garbhādhānam* (religious rites performed for the conception of one's wife), *Puṁsavanam* (religious rites performed for the causation of the birth of a male child), *Simantonnayanam* (described below), *Jātakarma* (postnatal rites), *Nāmakaraṇam* (rite of first nomenclature), *Niṣkramaṇam* (formal taking out of the child in the open), *Annaprāśanam* (ceremony of first feeding the child with boiled rice), *Vapanam* (ceremony of tonsure), *Karṇavedha* (ceremony of perforating the child's ear-lobes), *Vratādeśa* (the ceremony of investure with the holy thread), *Vedārambha* (ceremonial commencement of the study of the Vedas), *Keśāntam* (ceremony of cutting the child's hair),

Snānam (ceremonial ablution), *Vivāhāgni-parigraha* (the ceremony of lighting up the nuptial fire which is kept burning ever afterwards), *Tretāgni-saṁgraha* (the ceremony of kindling the three different kinds of fire known as *Dakṣiṇāgniḥ*, *Gārhapatyāgriḥ* and *Āhavanīyāgniḥ* which are kept burning till the death of the lighter), are the sixteen purificatory rites ordained to be performed in the case of a Brāhmaṇa in the scriptures.[1]

विवाहो मन्त्रतस्तस्या: शूद्रस्यामन्त्रतो दश।
गर्भाधानं प्रथमतस्तृतीये मासि पुंसव:।।१६।।
सीमन्तश्चाष्टमे मासि जाते जातक्रिया भवेत्।
एकादशेऽह्नि नामार्कस्येक्षा मासि चतुर्थके।।१७।।

The recitation of any Mantra by a woman is prohibited in the ten ceremonies commencing with the Jātakarma and ending with the *Karṇavedha*; but she is privileged to recite Mantras in connection with the celebration of her marriage ceremony. These ten rites should be done unto the Śūdras without any Mantras whatsoever. The rite of *Garbhādhānam* should be done unto one's wife on the first appearance of her menses; the rite of *Puṁsavanam* in the third month of her first pregnancy and the rite of *Simantonnayanam* (the ceremony of the parting of the hair), during the eighth month of gestation. The rite of *Jātakarma* should be done unto a child on the sixth day of its birth; the rite of *Nāmakaraṇam*, on the eleventh day and the rite of *Niṣkramaṇam* in the fourth month of its birth.

षष्ठे मास्यन्नमश्नीयाच्चूडाकर्म कुलोचितम्।
कृतचूडे च बाले हि कर्णवेधो विधीयते।।१८।।

The rite of *Annaprāśanam* should be done unto it in the eleventh month and the ceremony of tonsure according to the custom of its father's family (but before it completes the third year of its age). After the ceremony of tonsure that of *Karṇavedha* should be done unto a child.

---

1. The number is reduced to ten in the case of a Brāhmaṇa who is not a custodian of the sacred fire. Tr.

विप्रो गर्भाष्टमे वर्षे क्षत्र एकादशे तथा।
द्वादशे वैश्यजातिस्तु व्रतोपनयनमर्हति॥१९॥

The son of a Brāhmaṇa should be invested with the holy thread at the eighth year of his age reckoned from the period of his inter-uterine life. Similarly, the investure with the holy thread in the case of a Kṣatriya or Vaiśya child should be made at the eleventh and twelfth year respectively.

तस्या प्राप्तव्रतस्यायं कालः स्याद्द्विगुणाधिकः।
वेदव्रतच्युतो व्रात्यः स व्रात्यः स्तोममर्हति॥२०॥

Sons of Brāhmaṇas, Kṣatriyas and Vaiśyas not invested with the holy thread after having respectively attained the ages of fifteen years and two months twenty-one years and two months and twenty-three years and two months, become deprived of the right of investure and studying the Vedas. They are called *Vrātyas*. Such children should expiate their guilt by performing a *Vratyastoma* sacrifice.

द्वे जन्मनी द्विजातीनां मातुः स्यात् प्रथमं तयोः।
द्वितीयं छन्दसां मातुर्ग्रहणाद्विधिवद्गुरोः॥२१॥

Brāhmaṇas, Kṣatriyas and Vaiśyas are called the twice-born. Their first births take place when they are delivered of their mother's womb; their second when they duly accept the Gāyatrī Mantra from their preceptors.

एवं द्विजातिमापन्नो विमुक्तो वान्यदोषतः।
श्रुतिस्मृतिपुराणानां भवेदध्ययनक्षमः॥२२॥

Thus made twice-born and free from all other faults, they become entitled to study the Vedas, *Smṛtis* and *Purāṇas*.

उपनीतो गुरुकुले वसेन्नित्यं समाहितः।
विभृयाद्दण्डकौपीनोपवीताजिनमेखलाः॥२३॥

Having been duly invested with the holy thread, they should reside in the houses of their preceptors, observing perfect celibacy, wearing the girdle girdle-cloth, holy thread and using the staff and deer-skin.

पुण्येऽह्नि गुर्वनुज्ञातः कृतमन्त्राहुतिक्रियः।
स्मृत्वोङ्कारञ्च गायत्रीमाभेद्वेदमादितः॥२४॥

On an auspicious day and having obtained the permission of their preceptors, they should cast oblations into the sacred fire and commence the study of the Vedas by reciting the *Oṁkāra* and the Gāyatrī.

शौचाचारविचारार्थं धर्मशास्त्रमपि द्विजः।
पठेत गुरुतः सम्यक् कर्म तद्दिष्टमाचरेत्॥२५॥

A twice-born (pupil) should study the *Dharma Śāstras* under the guidance of his preceptor for learning the rules of decorum and cleanliness (both mental and physical) and do whatever is beneficial to his master.

ततोऽभिवाद्य स्थविरान् गुरुञ्चैव समाश्रयेत्।
स्वाध्यायार्थं तदायत्तं सर्वदा हितमाचरेत्॥२६॥

Then having made obeisance to the elders, he should sit beside his preceptor, constantly exert his best for the furtherance of his studies and do nothing else than what is beneficial to him (preceptor).

नापक्षिप्तोऽपि भाषेत न व्रजेत् ताडितोऽपि वा।
विद्वेषमथ पैशुन्यं हिंसनञ्चार्कवीक्षणम्॥२७॥

Even having been reprimanded by his preceptor, he should not make any reply in retort, nor go away even when driven away by the former.

तौर्यत्रिकानृतोन्मादपरिवादानलङ्क्रियाम्।
अञ्जनोद्वर्त्तनादर्शस्रग्विलेपनयोषितः॥२९॥
वृथाटनमसन्तोषं ब्रह्मचारी विवर्ज्जयेत्।
ईषच्चलितमध्याह्नेऽनुज्ञातो गुरुणा स्वयम्॥३०॥

Living a life of perfect celibacy, he should renounce all hatred, envy, malice, idle glances at the sun, singing, dancing, intoxication (lit: insanity), calumny, personal decorations, application of collyrium along the eyelids, contemplation of himself in the mirror, smearing they body with scented unguents, use of sandal pastes or garlands of flowers idle strolls and discontent.

अलोलुपश्चरेद्भैक्षं वृत्तिषूत्तमवृत्तिषु।
सद्योभिक्षाऽन्नमादाय वित्तवत्तदुपस्पृशेत्॥३०॥

A little after midday and with the permission of his preceptor, he should ungreedily ask for alms of men of good conduct and regulated habits (*Niyama*) and having obtained the alms, he should instantly retire therefrom, considering the articles of gift as riches.

कृतमाध्याह्निकोऽश्नीयादनुज्ञातो यथाविधि।
नाद्यादेकान्नमुच्छिष्टं भुक्त्वा चाचामितामियात्॥३१॥

Having performed the midday rites, he should take his meal with the permission of his preceptor. He should not take only cooked rice, nor that which is the residue of another's meal. At the close of his meal he should rinse his mouth with water.

न्यान्याद्भिक्षितमादद्यादापन्नो द्रविणादिकम्।
अनिन्द्यामन्त्रितः श्राद्धे पैत्रेऽद्याद्गुरुचोदितः॥३२॥

Even while in distress; the acceptance of any wealth excepting the alms is prohibited. He may dine in connection with a *Pitṛ Śrāddha* if thereto invited by a person without any disqualification and if his preceptor approves it.

एकान्नमप्यविरोधे व्रतानां प्रथमाश्रमी।
भुक्त्वा गुरुमुपासीत कृत्वा सन्धुक्षणादिकम्॥३३॥
समिधोऽग्नावादधीत ततः परिचरेद्गुरुम्।
शयीत गुर्वनुज्ञातः प्रह्वश्च प्रथमं गुरोः॥३४॥
एवमन्वहमभ्यासी ब्रह्मचारी व्रतं चरेत्।
हितोपवादः प्रियवाक् सम्यग्गुर्वर्थसाधकः॥३५॥

A single meal, which is not incompatible with the spirit of *Brahmacaryam* is what is enjoined to be taken by him (the student), every day. Having partaken of it, he should wait upon his preceptor. Then having cast twigs of sacred trees (*Samid*) into the sacrificial fire, he should attend to his preceptor's comforts.

In the night and with the permission of his teacher, he should lie down in a recumbent posture, after the former, had been comfortably laid in bed.

नित्यमाराधयेदेनमासमाप्तेः श्रुतिग्रहात्।
अनेन विधिनाऽधीतवेदमन्त्रो द्विजो नयेत्॥३६॥

A *Brahmacārin* should thus daily practise his vow until the completion of his study of the Vedas; he should devote himself to the good of his master, be sweet of speech and devout in spirit.

शापानुग्रहसामर्थ्यमृषीणाञ्च सलोकताम्।
पयोऽमृताभ्यां मधुभिः साज्यैः प्रीणन्ति देवताः॥३७॥

The twice-born one, who studies the Vedas in this manner, becomes capable of (effectively) cursing or granting boon to other persons and lives in the same region with the Ṛsis, after death

तस्मादहरहर्वेदमनध्यायमृते पठेत्।
यदङ्गं तदनध्याये गुरोर्वचनमाचरेत्॥३८॥

Milk, wine, honey and clarified butter are the articles which the gods are fond of. He should constantly study the Vedas except on the interdicted days. On such days their other collateral subjects should be studied with the preceptors permission.

व्यतिक्रमादसंपूर्णमनहङ्कृतिराचरेत्।
परत्रेह च तद्ब्रह्म अनधीतमपि द्विजम्॥३९॥

An infringement of the preceptors order makes all studies of the Vedas abortive. Hence, one should study them in a submissive spirit. Even a little study of the Vedas stands their twice-born reader in good stead both in this world and the next.

यस्तूपनयनादेतदामृत्योर्व्रतमाचरेत्।
स नैष्ठिको ब्रह्मचारी ब्रह्मसायुज्यमाप्नुयात्।
उपकुर्वाणको यस्तु द्विजः षड्विंशवार्षिकः॥४०॥

The ritualistic (*Naiṣṭhika*) *Brahmacārin*, who practises this vow from his *Upanayana* (investure with the holy thread) till death, attains to Brahma.

केशान्तकर्मणा तत्र यथोक्तचरितव्रतः।
समाप्य वेदान् वेदौ वा वेदं वा प्रसभं द्विजः।
स्नायीत गुर्वनुज्ञातः प्रदत्तोदितदक्षिणः॥४१॥

The twice-born one, who practises this vow for thirty-six years, is called a *Upakurvaṇaka*. At the close of this *Vrata*, the vowist should shave his head. Thus having finished the study of all the Vedas or of any part thereof, he (the student) should give honorarium to his preceptor (*Dakṣiṇā*) after having obtained his permission thereto and bathe thereafter.

॥ इति श्रीवेदव्यासीये धर्मशास्त्रे प्रथमोऽध्यायः॥१॥

Chapter 2

एवं स्नातकतां प्राप्तो द्वितीयाश्रमकाङ्क्षया।
प्रतीक्षेत विवाहार्थमनिन्द्यान्वयसंभवाम्॥१॥

At the close of such Vedic studies and having performed the rite of *Avabhṛtha* ablution (lit.-ceremony of ablution at the completion of a principal sacrifice) a twice-born one, wishing to be a house-holder, should seek the hands of a girl of unimpeachable birth and family.

अरोगो दुष्टवंशोत्थामशुल्कदानदूषिताम्।
सवर्णामसमानार्षाममातृपितृगोत्रजाम्॥२॥
अनन्यपूर्विकां लध्वीं शुभलक्षणसंयुताम्।
धृताधोवसनां गौरीं विख्यातदशपूरुषाम्॥३॥
ख्यातनाम्नः पुत्रवतः सदाचारवतः सतः।
दातुमिच्छोरर्दुहितरं प्राप्य धर्मेण चोद्वहेत्॥४॥

The daughter of an erudite father of good conduct and having sons of his own loins and born of a family free from all blemishes or any contagious or hereditary disease, and not plighted for money to any other bridegroom before, and not of the same *Pravara* and *Gotra* with him, nor related to him as a *Sapiṇḍa* in his father's or mother's side and belonging to his own *varṇa* and social order, slender, of auspicious signs; clad in silken garments and not above eight years of age[1] and whose paternal ancestors to the tenth degree in the ascending line were all men of renown; should be solemnly wedded by a (twice-born) according to religious rites, if proffered in marriage.

ब्राह्मोद्वाहविधानेन तदभावेऽपरो विधिः।
दातव्यैषा सदृक्षाय वयोविद्याऽन्वयादिभिः॥५॥

A daughter should be given in marriage to a (twice-born) one, befitting her family in respect of learning, birth, etc., and suited to her in years, according to the rites of a Brāhman marriage or according to any other regulation where the former would not avail.

पितृवत् पितृभ्रातृषु पितृव्यज्ञातिमातृषु।
पूर्वाभावे परो दद्यात् सर्वाभावे स्वयं व्रजेत्॥६॥

Her father, grand-father, brother, uncle, cognates and mother are successively entitled to give away a girl in marriage. In the absence of a father, a grandfather will formally give her away and so on, in the order of enumeration. The bride can herself give her away in the absence of any of these relations.

यदि सा दातृवैकल्याद्रजः पश्येत् कुमारिका।
भ्रूणहत्याश्च यावत्यः पतितः स्यात् तदप्रदः॥७॥

The sin incidental to (an act of) procuring abortion (lit: destruction of the foetus) is committed, if through the negligence of her giver a girl menstruates before her marriage. He, who does not give away a daughter in marriage before she attains her puberty becomes degraded.

तुभ्यं दात्याम्यहमिति ग्रहीष्यामीति यस्तयोः।
कृत्वा समयमन्योन्यं भजते न स दण्डभाक्॥८॥

Both the giver and the taker of a girl (in marriage) stand exonerated from all penalties if the latter gives her away saying, "I give this girl to you," and the latter accepts the gift by saying, "I take her (as my wife)."

1. Several Commentators interpret the term as denoting "fair-coloured."

त्यजन्नदुष्टां दण्ड्यः स्याद्दूषयंश्चाप्यदूषिताम्॥९॥

A man by desserting a blameless girl or defiling an innocent one, makes himself liable to punishment.

ऊढायां हि सवर्णायामन्यां वा काममुद्वहेत्।

तस्यामुत्पादितः पुत्रो न सवर्णात् प्रहीयते॥१०॥

(A twice born) one can take a wife who is not of his own caste (Varṇa), even after marrying one of his own order (Varṇa). The son begotten on the wife of one's own caste, does not stand as an *Asavarṇa* (of a differcnt caste) son to one under the circumstance.

उद्वहेत् क्षत्रियां विप्रो वैश्याञ्च क्षत्रियो विशाम्।

न तु शूद्रां द्विजः कश्चिन्नाधमः पूर्ववर्णजाम्।

A Brāhmaṇa can marry a Kṣatriya or Vaiśya girl; a Kṣatriya can take a Vaiśya wife and a Vaiśya can wed a Śūdra's daughter. But the member of an inferior caste can not wed a girl of superior caste.

नानावर्णासु भार्यासु सवर्णा सहचारिणी।

धर्माधर्मेषु धर्मिष्ठा ज्येष्ठा तस्य स्वजातिषु॥१२॥

Amongst wives of different castes, she, who is of the same caste with her lord, should be his companion in matters of piety and religion. Of several wives all belonging to the same caste as their lord, she, who has the greatest attachment to piety, should have preference as regards companionship in the celebration of religious rites, etc.

पाटितोऽयं द्विजाः पूर्वमेकदेहः स्वयम्भुवा।

पतयोऽर्द्धेन चार्द्धेन पत्नयोऽभूवन्निति श्रुतिः॥१३॥

The god Brahmā cleft his body in two, of yore. Out of one part sprang the husbands and out of the other the wives. This is what the Śruti relates.

यावन्न विन्दते जायां तावदर्द्धो भवेत् पुमान्।

नार्द्धं प्रजायते सर्वं प्रजायेतेत्यपि श्रुतिः॥१४॥

A man, so long he does not take a wife, is but (a) half

(incomplete) being. A half (thing) can not beget. A whole (thing) only can beget. This is the dictum of the Śruti.

गुर्वी सा भूस्त्रिवर्गस्य वोढुं नान्येन शक्यते।
यतस्ततोऽन्वहं भूत्वा स्ववशो बिभृयाच्च ताम्॥१५॥

A wife is weightier than the world with its virtues, wealth and enjoyment, since with the help of no other auxiliary than a wife can he bear its burden. Hence, one should marry and by constant practice of self-control duly maintain her.

कृतदारोऽग्निपत्नीभ्यां कृतवेश्मा गृहं वसेत्।
स्वकृत्यं वित्तमासाद्य वैतानाग्निं न हापयेत्॥१६॥

Having married, a man should live with his wife and the sacred fire in his own house, not neglecting his duties and the Vaitānika (sacrificial) fire with the advent of opulence.

स्मार्तं वैवाहिके वह्नौ श्रौतं वैतानिकाग्निषु।
कर्म कुर्यात् प्रतिदिनं विधिवत् प्रीतिपूर्वत:॥१७॥

Each day he should cheerfully perform the *Smārta* rites with the help of the nuptial fire and those inculcated in the *Śrutis* with that of the sacrificial one.

सम्यग्धर्मार्थकामेषु दम्पतिभ्यामहर्निशम्।
एकचित्ततया भाव्यं समानव्रतवृत्तित:॥१८॥

Day and night, the wedded couple should be one in spirit in respect of all matters of piety, gain and desire (enjoyment). They should be one in vows and practices.

न पृथग्विद्यते स्त्रीणां त्रिवर्गविधिसाधनम्।
भावतो ह्यतिदेशाद्वा इति शास्त्रविधि: पर:॥१९॥

A woman has no separate existence from her lord in matters of piety, gain and desire. The Śāstras have enjoined this dependency of love.

पत्यू: पूर्वं समुत्थाय देहशुद्धिं विधाय च।
उत्थाप्य शयनाद्यानि कृत्वा वेश्मविशोधनम्॥२०॥

A wife should quit her bed before her lord, cleanse (wash) her person, fold up the beds and make her house clean and tidy.

मार्जनैर्लेपनैः प्राप्य साग्निशालं स्वमङ्गणम्।
शोधयेदग्निकार्याणि स्निग्धान्युष्णेन वारिणा॥२१॥

Then having entered the chamber of *Homa* (sacrificial fire) she should (first) wash and plaster its floor and then the yard of her house and after that, wash with warm water the vessels of oils, clarified butter, etc., which are used in connection with Agnikāryas and keep them in their proper places.

प्रोक्षणैरिति तान्येव यथास्थानं प्रकल्पयेत्।
द्वन्द्वपात्राणि सर्वाणि न कदाचिद्वियोजयेत्॥२२॥
शोधयित्वा तु पात्राणि पूरयित्वा तु धारयेत्।
महानसस्य पात्राणि बहिः प्रक्षाल्य सर्वथा॥२३॥

Utensils or implements, which are used in couples (such as the pestle and mortar, etc.) should never be separated. The vessels (of rice etc.) should be cleansed and refilled with their respective contents and the kitchen-utensils should be taken out, cleansed and replaced in their proper positions.

मृद्भिश्च शोधयेच्चुल्लीं तत्राग्निं विन्यसेत्ततः।
स्मृत्वा नियोगपात्राणि रसांश्च द्रविणानि च॥२४॥

The oven should be repaired and replastered with earth and clay and the fire should be lighted therein. Thus having performed her morning (house-hold) duties and pondered over the dishes of different flavours (to be prepared, that day) and allotment of work to different workers and the daily expenditure of the household, she should make obeisance to her elders and superiors.

कृतपूर्वाह्णकार्या च स्वगुरूनभिवादयेत्।
ताभ्यां भर्तृपितृभ्यां वा भ्रातृमातुलबान्धवैः॥२५॥

Then she should decorate her person with the ornaments given to her by her father-in-law, husband, father, mother, maternal uncle, or relations.

वस्त्रालंकाररत्नानि प्रदत्तान्येव धारयेत्।
मनोवाक्कर्मभिः शुद्धा पतिदेशानुवर्तिनी॥२६॥

छायेवानुगता स्वच्छा सखीव हितकर्मसु।
दासीवादिष्टकार्येषु भार्या भर्तुः सदा भवेत्।।२७।।

Pure in her thought, speech and action and obedient to the dictates of her lord, she should follow him (in life) like his own shadow, seek his good like a trusted friend and minister to his desires like a servant.

ततोऽन्नसाधनं कृत्वा पतये विनिवेद्य तत्।
वैश्वदेवकृतैरन्नैर्भोजनीयाश्च भोजयेत्।।२८।।

Then having finished cooking, she should report of it to her husband saying, "the rice is cooked." The husband having made offerings therewith to the Vaiśvadevas, she should first feed the children and then serve out the morning meal to her lord.

पतिश्चैवाभ्यनुज्ञातः शिष्टमन्वाद्यमात्मना।
भुक्त्वा नयेदहःशेषमायव्ययविचिन्तया।।२९।।

Then, with the permission of her lord, she would partake of the residue of the boiled rice and cooked dishes (described above) and spend the closing portion of the day in contemplation of the family earnings and expenditure.

पुनः सायं पुनः प्रातर्गृहशुद्धिं विधाय च।
कृतान्नसाधना साध्वी सुभृशं भोजयेत् पतिम्।।३०।।

Having again attended to the cleansings of the house, etc., at evening, she should cook the night meals (of the household) and provide her husband with a sumptuous repast.

नातितृप्त्या स्वयं भुक्त्वा गृहनीतिं विधाय च।
आस्तीर्य साधु शयनं ततः परिचरेत् पतिम्।।३१।।

Then the cheerful lamps should be lighted and she, having spread out a comfortable bed, attend to massage the body of her lord.

सुप्ते पतौ तदभ्याशे स्वपेत्तद्गतमानसा।
अनग्ना चाप्रमत्ता च निष्कामा च जितेन्द्रिया।।३२।।

After her husband had slept, she should lie down by her side, not entirely bereft of clothes, with her mind fully centered in his self, cautious, non-desiring, and with her passions held under a healthy control.

नोच्चैर्वदेन्न परुषं न बहून् पत्युरप्रियम्।
न केनचित् विवदेच्च अप्रलापविलापिनी॥३३॥

She should not speak too loudly, nor harshly or unpleasantly to her lord, avoiding all quarrels, lamentations and perfidies.

न चातिव्ययशीला स्यान्न धर्मार्थविरोधिनी।
प्रमादोन्मादरोषैर्षावञ्चनञ्चाभिमानिताम्॥३४॥
पैशुन्यहिंसाविद्वेषमदाहंकारधूर्तता:।
नास्तिक्यं साहसं स्तेयं दम्भान् साध्वी विवर्ज्जयेत्॥३५॥

She should not be prodigal in her purse, nor hostile to the spirit of piety or gain. Carelessness, fickleness of mind, anger, envy, deception, vanity, rivalry, mischievousness, cruelty, inordinate pride, cunningness, atheism, daringness, discontent and dissimulation are the fifteen vices which a chaste wife should always try to renounce.

एवं परिचरन्ती सा पतिं परमदैवतम्।
यश: शमिह यात्येवं परत्र च सलोकताम्॥३६॥

A chaste wife, who thus worships her lord, acquires fame and blessings in this life and lives in the same region with him, after death.

योषितो नित्यकर्मोक्तं नैमित्तिकमथोच्यते।
रजोदर्शनतो दोषात् सर्वमेव परित्यजेत्॥३७॥

I have described the daily or general duties of wives, now hear me discourse on their specific ones. A wife, on the appearance of her flow, should renounce all those duties, as she becomes unclean. Bashfully she should reside in a lonely chamber, avoiding the eyes of her friends and relations.

सर्वैरलक्षिता शीघ्रं लज्जितान्तर्गृहे वसेत्।
एकाम्बरावृता दीना स्नानालंकारवर्ज्जिता॥३८॥
मौनिन्यधोमुखी चक्षु:पाणिपद्भिरचञ्चला।

अश्नीयात् केवलं भक्तं नक्तं मृन्मयभाजने॥३९॥

Clad in a single sheet of cloth and forsaking ornaments and ablution, she should sit silent with her eyes cast downward. Avoiding all listless movements of her eyes and extremities, she should take boiled rice at night alone during her periods.

स्वपेद्भूमावप्रमत्ता क्षपेदेवमहस्त्रयम्।
स्नायीत च त्रिरात्रान्ते सचैलमुदिते रवौ॥४०॥

Having passed three nights in such a staid condition of mind, she should wash her clothes and bathe, on the morning of the fourth day.

विलोक्य भर्तृवदनं शुद्धा भवति धर्मतः।
कृतशौचा पुनः कर्म पूर्ववच्च समाचरेत्॥४१॥

Then having seen the face of her husband she would be clean again, whereupon she should resume her usual household duties as before.

रजोदर्शनतो या स्यूरात्रयः षोडशर्त्तवः।
ततः पुंबीजमक्लिष्टं शुद्धे क्षेत्रे प्ररोहति॥४२॥

The sixteen (successive) nights from the first appearance of the flow in women are called the Menstrual period. Healthy male seeds (sperms) cast into healthy fields (female reproductive organs) during this period are found to sprout lead to conception).

चतस्रश्चादिमा रात्रीः पर्ववच्च विवर्ज्जयेत्।
गच्छेद्युग्मासु रात्रीषु पौष्णपित्रर्क्षराक्षसान्॥४३॥

The first four nights of the period should be avoided as Parva days, as well as those marked by the asterisms called Revatī, Pitrakṣa and Rākṣasa. Fecundation should take place on each even night during the menstrual period alone.

प्रच्छादितादित्यपथे पुमान् गच्छेत् सुयोषितः।
क्षौमालंकृदवाप्नोति पुत्रं पूजितलक्षणम्॥४४॥

A man, clad in a silk garment and duly bedecked with ornaments, should visit his wife on (any of these even) nights, whereby he would get a son bearing all auspicious signs on his person.

ऋतुकालेऽभिगम्यैवं ब्रह्मचर्ये व्यवस्थित:।
गच्छन्नपि यथाकामं न दुष्ट: स्यादन्यकृत्॥४५॥

Even the vow of a Brahmacārin, who visits his wife during her menstrual period, is not vitiated by so doing. Even he, who does not know any other woman, commits no sin by going unto his own wife during her menstrual period according to the natural inclinations of his mind.

भ्रूणहत्यामवाप्नोति ऋतौ भार्यापराङ्गुख:।
सा त्ववाप्यान्यतो गर्भं त्याज्या भवति पापिनी॥४६॥

A husband not visiting his wife during her menstrual period is guilty of foeticide. The infidel wife, who gets herself impregnated by another man is fit to be abandoned by her lord.

महापातकदुष्टा च पतिगर्भविनाशिनी।
सद्वृतचारिणीं पत्नीं त्यक्त्वा पतति धर्मत:॥४७॥

A wife, procuring abortion of her pregnancy caused by her husband, is guilty of a *Mahāpātakam*. A husband, by unjustly desserting his own innocent wife, becomes a spiritual out-caste.

महापातकदुष्टोऽपि नाप्रतीक्ष्यस्तया पति:।
अशुद्धे क्षयमादूरं स्थितायामनु चिन्तया॥४८॥

A chaste wife should not renounce her lord, even if he be guilty of a *Mahāpātakam*, praying that his sin might be extinguished in no distant time.

व्यभिचारेण दुष्टानां पतीनां दर्शनादृते:।
धिक्कृतायामवाच्यायामन्यत्र वासयेत् पति:॥४९॥
पुनस्तामार्तवस्नातां पूर्ववद्व्यवहारयेत्।
धूर्ताञ्च धर्मकामघ्नीमपुत्रां दीर्घरोगिणीम्॥५०॥
सुदुष्टां व्यसनासक्तामहितामधिवासयेत्।
अधिविन्नामपि विभु: स्त्रीणान्तु समतामियात्॥५१॥
विवर्णा दीनवदना देहसंस्कारवर्ज्जिता।

पतिव्रता निराहारा शोच्यते प्रोषिते पतौ॥५२॥
मृतं भर्तारमादाय ब्राह्मणी वह्निमाविशेत्।
जीवन्ती चेत्त्यक्तकेशा तपसा शोधयेद्वपु:॥५३॥

A husband should not look at the face of his faithless wife. He should banish her in a distant country after a good censuring. A faithless wife may be again entrusted with the wifely duties by her lord after her next menstrual ablution (at the close of her next monthly flow) after the act of infidelity and treat her as his own wife as before. A husband may forsake and banish in any distant country, any of the following wives, *viz.*, those who are deceitful, faithless (lit : forsaking virtue or religion) hostile to her husband's desires, invalid (suffering from an incurable or long-standing disease), wicked, addicted to wine, gambling, or hunting excursions, or inimical to his interests. A husband should count a superseded wife (*adhivinnā*) still as a wife of his own after he has married a second time. A good wife should renounce all pleasures as long as her husband would be absent in a distant country. The widow of a Brāhmaṇa should either immolate herself in fire with the corpse of her deceased husband or observe a vow of lifelong Brahmacaryam. (Continence) from that date, shaving the hair of her head and foregoing all articles of luxury.

सर्वावस्थासु नारीणां न युक्त: स्यादरक्षणम्।
तदेवानुक्रमात् कार्यं पितृभर्तृसुतादिभि:॥५४॥
जाता: सुरक्षिता या ये पुत्रपौत्रप्रपौत्रका:।
ये यजन्ति पितॄन् यज्ञैर्मोक्षप्राप्तिमहोदयै:॥५५॥
मृतानामग्निहोत्रेण दाहयेद् विधिपूर्वकम्।
दाहयेदविलम्बेन भार्या चात्र व्रजेत् सा॥५६॥

Under no circumstance women should be kept unprotected. Fathers, husbands and sons should take them under their guardianship in succession. The dead bodies of deceased and well born wives, who leave behind them sons, grandsons and great grandsons, etc., should be duly cremated. They (wives) attain to the same region with their husbands, who had performed Pitṛ

Yajñas in their lives and are hence entitled to spiritual emancipation, after death.

॥ इति श्रीवेदव्यासीये धर्मशास्त्रे द्वितीयोऽध्याय:॥२॥

Chapter 3

नित्यं नैमित्तिकं काम्यमिति कर्म त्रिधा मतम्।

त्रिविधं तच्च वक्ष्यामि गृहस्थस्यावधार्यताम्॥१॥

The acts of a house-holder may be classified as *Nitya*, *Naimittika* and *Kāmya*. Now hear me describe each of these kinds in detail.

यामिन्या: पश्चिमे यामे त्यक्तनिद्रो हरिं स्मरेत्।

आलोक्य मङ्गलद्रव्यं कर्मावश्यकमाचरेत्॥२॥

A householder should quit his bed at the close of the last quarter of the night, meditating upon the self of gods Hari. Then having seen auspicious articles, he should commence the necessary works of his daily life.

कृतशौचो निषेव्याग्नीन्दन्तान् प्रक्षाल्य वारिणा।

स्नात्वोपास्य द्विज: सन्ध्यां देवादींश्चैव तर्पयेत्॥३॥

Then having eased and washed himself, he should bask in the glare of fire. After that, he should cleanse his teeth with water, bathe, perform his rite of *Sandhyā* worship and after libations of water to the gods and *Pitṛs* in succession (as regulated).

वेदवेदाङ्गशास्त्राणि इतिहासानि चाभ्यसेत्।

अध्यापयेच्च सच्छिष्यान् सद्विप्रांश्च द्विजोत्तम:॥४॥

Then the best of Brāhmaṇas should study the Vedas, histories

---

1. A *Kāmyam karma* is an act whose performance is imperatively obligatory on all persons and a non-performance whereof detracts one's religious merits, though its performance does not make any addition to it.

A *Naimittikam karma* is an act whose performance is not imperatively obligatory, nor its non-performance detracts from or performance adds to, one's religious merit. It is a specific act enjoined to be performed on a special occasion.

A *Kāmyam karma* is an act which is performed for the fruition of any definite object, such as a residence in heaven, or the birth of a male child etc.

(*Itihāsas*) and the kindred branches of knowledge (*Vedāṅgas*), give instruction to his own pupils and feed the good Brāhmaṇas.

अलब्धं प्रापयेल्लब्धा क्षणमात्रे समापयेत्।
समर्थो हि समर्थेन नाविज्ञातः क्वचिद्वसेत्॥५॥

Acquire that which has not been already acquired and having obtained it distribute it as soon as possible. Equals should not sit with equals without first reporting their own presence or arrival.

सरित्सरसि वापीषु गर्तप्रस्रवणादिषु।
स्नायीत यावदुद्धृत्य पञ्च पिण्डानि वारिणा॥६॥

In tanks, lakes, wells and fountains, etc., belonging to others, one should bathe duly after having first taken five handfuls of clay (*Pañca-Piṇḍa*) therefrom.

तीर्थाभावेऽप्यशक्त्यो वा स्नायात् तोयैः समाहृतैः।
गृहाङ्गणगतस्तत्र यावदम्बरपीडनम्॥७॥

In cases where *Tīrthas* would be unavailable, or in those wherein ablution would not be practicable, one should bathe in the court-yard of a house with water enough to wet and be rinsed out of, his cloth.

स्नानमब्दैवतैः कुर्यात् पावनैश्चापि मार्जनम्।
मन्त्रैः प्राणांस्त्रिराचम्य सौरैश्चार्कं विलोकयेत्॥८॥

The rite of ablution should be performed by reciting the *Āpohiṣṭhā* Mantra; the rite of purification (*Mārjanam*) should be done by reading the one beginning with *Drupadādiva Mumuñcāna*. After the bath, the bather should thrice practise *Prāṇāyāma* and look at the sun by reciting the Sūryopasthāpana Mantra.

तिष्ठन् स्थित्वा तु गायत्रीं ततः स्वाध्यायमारभेत्।
ऋचाञ्च यजुषां साम्नामथर्वाङ्गिरसामपि॥९॥
इतिहासपुराणानां वेदोपनिषदां द्विजः।
शक्त्या सम्यक् पठेन्नित्यमल्पमप्यासमापनात्॥१०॥

Then having recited the Gāyatrī, the twice-born ones should commence the study of the Vedas. Having studied portion of the

Sāman, *Yajus* and *Atharvan*, they should commence reading the *Itihāsas*, *Purāṇas*, and Upaniṣads, either entirely or in parts, if a complete perusal is not feasible. This should be done every day.

स यज्ञदानतपसामखिलं फलमाप्नुयात्।
तस्मादहरर्वेदं द्विजोऽधीयीत वाग्यतः॥११॥

A twice-born one, through the merit of such studies, acquires all the virtues which can be acquired by celebrating religious sacrifices, by making gifts and practising penitential austerities. Hence, he should read the Vedas, every day, without indulging in any idle talk.

धर्मशास्त्रेतिहासादि सर्वेषां शक्तितः पठेत्।
कृतस्वाध्यायः प्रथमं तर्पयेच्चाथ देवताः॥१२॥

The Dharma *Śāstras, Itihāsas* and *Purāṇas* should be read, if possible, in their entireties and at the end of such studies a twice-born one should first offer libations of water to the gods.

जान्वा च दक्षिणं दर्भैः प्रागग्रैः सयवैस्तिलैः।
एकैकाञ्जलिदानेन प्रकृतिस्थोपवीतकः॥१३॥

The rite of *Tarpaṇam* (offering libation) should be performed as follows : – He (performer of the rite) should sit with his face looking eastward and his right knee flexed and placed on the ground. (Thus seated) he should catch hold of his holy thread in the usual posture and a *Kuśā* blade with the first phalanx of his right thumb and offer a single libation of water containing barley corn to the Gods by reciting the *Devā, Yakṣā*, etc., Mantra– (May the gods, *Yakṣas*, etc., be pleased, etc.).

समजानुद्वयो ब्रह्मसूत्रहार उदङ्मुखः।
तिर्यग्दर्भश्च वामाग्रैर्यवैस्तिलविमिश्रितैः॥१४॥

Then he should sit with his knees flexed and placed on the ground and his face turned towards the north, catching hold of his holy thread in the posture of a necklace and offer two libations of water containing barley and sesame unto each spirit of men with the end of a *Kuśā* blade held at the root of his little finger. The libations should be cast towards the north.

अम्भोभिरुत्तरक्षिप्तैः कनिष्ठामूलनिर्गतैः।
द्वाभ्यां द्वाभ्यामञ्जलिभ्यां मनुष्यांस्तर्पयेत्ततः॥१५॥
दक्षिणाऽभिमुखः सव्यं जान्वा च द्विगुणैः कुशैः।
तिलैर्जलैश्च देशिन्या मूलदर्भाद्विनिःसृतैः॥१६॥
दक्षिणां सोपवीतः स्यात् क्रमेणाञ्जलिभिस्त्रिभिः।
सन्तर्पयेद्दिव्यपितृंस्तत्परांश्च पितृन् स्वकान्॥१७॥

Then seated with his left knee flexed and his holy thread placed on his right shoulder, he, looking eastward, should offer three libations of water, containing sesame only, unto his father, grandfather and great grandfather, as well as unto his departed maternal grandfather, maternal great grandfather, maternal great great grandfather and so on, unto the spirits of his paternal grand-mother and paternal great grand-mother, with the end of a *Kuśā* blade, double the ordinary length, held at the root of his right index finger.

मातृमातामहांस्तद्वत्त्रीनेवं हि त्रिभिस्त्रिभिः।
मातामहाश्च येऽप्यन्ये गोत्रिणो दाहवर्जिताः॥१८॥

The spirits of deceased persons belonging to the family of one's maternal grandfather or to one's own Gotra and whose corpses had not been duly cremated, should be separately propitiated with the offering of a single oblation, each.

तानेकाञ्जलिदानेन तर्पयेच्च पृथक् पृथक्।
असंस्कृतप्रमीता ये प्रेतसंस्कारवर्ज्जिताः॥१९॥

The water squeezed out of the wearing cloth of a performer of Tarpaṇam should be offered as libations unto the spirits of those deceased in his family, who had died without the rite of Annaprāśanam having been done unto them, or whose dead bodies had not been cremated.

वस्त्रनिष्पीडनाम्भोभिस्तेषामाप्यायनं भवेत्।
अतर्पितेषु पितृषु वस्त्रं निष्पीडयेच्च यः॥२०॥

The departed manes of him, who thus squeezes water drops out of his wearing cloth and offers them as libation (as above described) without first having offered libations of water unto them, despair of obtaining any water at all, with the gods and Ṛṣis, such as Sanaka etc.

निराशाः पितरस्तस्य भवन्ति सूरमानुषैः।
पयोदर्भस्वधाकारगोत्रनामतिलैर्भवेत्॥२१॥

A rite of *Tarpaṇam* done with water containing *Kuśā* blades and sesame, and by reciting their Gotras and names with the term *Svadhā* (obeisance) appended thereto, becomes gratifying to the Pitṛs. One done without any of these factors proves abortive.

सुदत्तं तत् पुनस्तेषामेकेनापि वृथा विना।
अन्यचित्तेन यद्दत्तं यद्दत्तं विधिवर्ज्जितम्॥२२॥

A rite of *Tarpaṇam* done by a person while thinking of other things, or not according to the regulations of the *Śāstras* or without being seated on a proper cushion, proves as blood to his departed manes.

अनासनस्थितेनापि तज्जलं रुधिरायते।
एवं सन्तर्पिताः कामैस्तर्पकांस्तर्पयन्ति च॥२३॥

The Pitṛs propitiated with a *Tarpaṇam* duly performed as above regulated, grants all wished for things to its performer.

ब्रह्मविष्णुशिवादित्यमित्रावरुणनामभिः।
पूजयेल्लक्षितैर्मन्त्रैर्जलमन्त्रोक्तदेवताः॥२४॥

The deities mentioned in the *Jalamantra* should be worshipped by reciting the Mantras in which the names of Brahmā. Viṣṇu, Śiva, Āditya, Mitra and Varuṇa, occur.

उपस्थाय रवेः काष्ठां पूजयित्वा च देवताः।
ब्रह्माग्नीन्द्रौषधीजीवविष्णुनामहतांहसाम्॥२५॥
अपां यत्तेति सत्कायं नमस्कारैः अनामभिः।
कृत्वा मुखं समालभ्य स्नानमेवं समाचरेत्॥२६॥

Having performed the rite of *Sūryopasthāpanam* with his face turned towards the east, a twice-born one should purify the water by invoking the names of Brahmā, Agni, Indra, Ausadhi, Jīva and Viṣṇu. In connection with this rite he should recite the Mantra,

Yat, etc., with the term *Namas* appended to it, by addressing the name of each of these (divinities). After that, he should rinse his mouth and bathe.

ततः प्रविश्य भवनमावसथ्ये हुताशने।
पाकयज्ञांश्च चतुरो विदध्याद्विधिवद्द्विजः॥२७॥
अनाहितावसथ्याग्निरादायान्नं घृतप्लुतम्।
शाकलेन विधानेन जुहुयाल्लौकिकेऽनले॥२८॥

Then having entered his house, a twice-born one should perform the four *Pāka-Yajñas* (simple domestic sacrifices) with the help of the *Āvasathya* fire (the sacred fire kept in the house). He, whose Āvasathya fire has not been lighted at all, should perform the Homa by casting oblations of boiled rice soaked in clarified butter in the *Laukika* fire, according the regulations of the *Śākala* (a school of the Ṛgveda) school.

व्यस्ताभिर्व्याहृतीभिश्च समस्ताभिस्ततः परम्।
षड्भिर्देवकृतस्येति मन्त्रवद्भिर्यथाक्रमम्॥२९॥

The oblations should be cast in the sacred fire by severally and combinedly reciting the *Vyāhṛtis* and the six Mantras running as *Deva Kṛtasya* etc.

प्राजापत्यं स्विष्टकृतं हुत्वैवं द्वादशाहुतीः।
ओङ्कारपूर्वः स्वाहान्तस्त्यागः स्विष्टविधानतः॥३०॥

After that, the *Prājāpatya Sviṣṭakṛt Homa* should be performed by offering twelve oblations unto the fire, prefixing *Om* and appending *Svāhā* to the Mantra according to the *Sviṣṭa* regulation.

भुवि दर्भान् समास्तीर्य बलिकर्म समारभेत्।
विश्वेभ्यो देवेभ्य इति सर्वेभ्यो भूतेभ्य एव च॥३१॥
भूतानां पतये चेति नमस्कारेण शास्त्रवित्।
दद्याद्बलित्रयञ्चाग्रे पितृभ्यश्च स्वधा नमः॥३२॥

The oblations should be offered on *Kuśā* blades spread out on the ground and the one, well-versed in the *Śāstras*, should first offer three oblations by prefixing *Om* and appending *Namas* to the Mantra as follows :– Om, to Viṣvadevas (*Namas*) obeisance; *Om*, to all the beings (*Bhūtas*) *Namas* (obeisance); *Om*, to the lord of all the beings (*Būtānām Patayae*) *Namas* (obeisance); and after that, *Om*, to *Pitṛs* (obeisance) *Namas*.

पात्रनिर्णेजनं वारि वायव्यां दिशि निक्षिपेत्।
उद्धृत्य षोडशग्रासमात्रमन्नं घृतोक्षितम्॥३३॥
इदमन्नं मनुष्येभ्यो हन्तेत्युक्त्वा समुत्सृजेत्।
गोत्रनामस्वधाकारैः पितृभ्यश्चापि शक्तितः॥३४॥
षड्भ्योऽन्नमन्वहं दद्यात् पितृयज्ञविधानतः।
वेदादीनां पठेत् किञ्चिदल्पं ब्रह्ममथाप्तये॥३५॥

The washings of the vessels should be cast in the North-West and sixteen morsels of boiled rice soaked in clarified butter should be offered, by saying, "these (morsels of) boiled rice to men" (*Idam Annam Manuṣyebhyaḥ Hanta*). A twice-born one should offer six oblations of boiled rice to his six departed manes (father, grandfather, great-grand father, maternal grandfather, maternal great grandfather and maternal great grandfather) by mentioning the name and *Gotra* of each and by appending the term *Svadhā* to each of these Mantra*s*, according to ones might and the regulations of the Pitṛ Yajña. A few texts of the Vedas should be recited on the occasion for the completion of the Brahma-Yajña.

ततोऽन्यदन्नमादाय निर्गत्य भवनाद्बहिः।
काकेभ्यः स्वपचेभ्यश्च प्रक्षिपेद्ग्रासमेव च॥३६॥

Then having taken a quantity of boiled rice in his hand, he should walk out of his room and offer morsels of it to crows and Svapacas (Cāṇḍālas, lit., dog-feeders).

उपविश्य गृहद्वारि तिष्ठेद्यावन्मूहूर्त्तकम्।
अप्रमुक्तोऽतिथिं लिप्सर्भावशुद्धः प्रतीक्षकः॥३७॥
आगतं दूरतः शान्तं भोक्तुकाममकिञ्चनम्।
दृष्ट्वा संमुखमभ्येत्य सत्कृत्य प्रश्नयार्च्चनैः॥३८॥

Then in a pure spirit and for a period of forty-eight minutes

(*Muhūrta*), the house-holder should calmly wait at his gate for any chance-comer (*Atithi*) and having found any hungry, sober *Atithi* coming from a distance, he should reverentially accost and welcome him to his house.

पादधावनसम्मानाभ्यञ्जनादिभिरर्च्चित:।
त्रिदिवं प्रापयेत् सद्यो यज्ञस्याभ्यधिकोऽतिथि:॥३९॥

He should give him water for washing his feet and show him every mark of respect. An *Atithi*, duly honoured, is greater than a *Yajña* (sacrifice), inasmuch as he makes his host entitled to the merit of heaven on the very day of his arrival.

कालागतोऽतिथिर्दृष्टवेदपारो गृहागत:।
द्वावेतौ पूजितौ स्वर्गं नयतोऽधस्त्वपूजितौ॥४०॥

An *Atithi* and a Brāhmaṇa well-versed in the Vedas, happening to arrive at one's house during the celebration of the *Vaiśvadevas* sacrifice, should be duly honoured. Propitiated with hospitality both of them lead their host to heaven; dishonoured they lead him to hell.

विवाह्य स्नातकक्ष्माभृदाचार्यसुहृदृत्विज:।
अर्घ्या भवन्ति धर्मेण प्रतिवर्णं गृहागता:॥४१॥

A marriage relation, a *Snātaka*, a king, an *Ācārya*, a friend and a *Ṛtvik*, even happening to call at one's house, each year, should be religiously respected.

गृहागताय सत्कृत्य श्रोत्रियाय यथाविधि।
भक्त्योपकल्पयेदेकं महाभागं विसर्ज्जयेत्॥४२॥

One should honour a Śrotriya arrived at one's house and dismiss him with the gift of a cow.

विसर्ज्जयेदनुव्रज्य सुतृप्तश्रोत्रियातिथीन्।
मित्रमातुलसम्बन्धिबान्धवान् समुपागतान्॥४३॥
भोजयेद्गृहिणो भिक्षां सत्कृतां भिक्षुकोऽर्हति।
स्वाद्वन्नमश्नन्नस्वादु ददद्गच्छत्यधोगतिम्॥४४॥

One should bid farewell to an *Atithi*, or to a Śrotriya guest, by following him a little beyond the compound of one's own house.

One should feed one's friends, maternal uncles, agnates and marriage-relations arrived at one's house. A *Yati* is privileged to accept alms from a house-holder proffered with respect.

गर्भिण्यातुरभृत्येषु बालवृद्धातुरादिषु।

बुभुक्षितेषु भुञ्जानो गृहस्थोऽश्नाति किल्विषम्।।४५।।

The man, who partakes of good food himself, comes by a worse fate by giving bad food to another. A house-holder eats sin by eating before the infants, old men, sick folks and pregnant women in his house are relieved of their hunger.

नाद्यादगृध्येन्नपाकाद्यं कदाचिदनिमन्त्रितः।

निमन्त्रितोऽपि निन्द्येन्न प्रत्याख्यानं द्विजोऽर्हति।।४६।।

Without being invited one should not eat, nor desire to eat, any cooked food at another's house. A twice-born one is at liberty to reject an invitation by a man of questionable repute.

शूद्राभिशस्तवार्द्धुष्यवाग्दुष्टक्रूरतस्कराः।

क्रुद्धापविद्धबद्धोग्रवधबन्धनजीविनः।।४७।।

शैलूषशोण्डिकोन्नद्धोन्मत्तव्रात्यव्रतच्युता।

नग्ननास्तिकनिर्लज्जपिशुनव्यसनान्विताः।।४८।।

कदर्यस्त्रीजितानार्यपरवादकृता नराः।

अनीशाः कीर्तिमन्तोऽपि राजदेवस्वहारकाः।।४९।।

शयनासनसंसर्गवृत्तकर्मादिदूषिताः।

अश्रद्दधाताः पतिता भ्रष्टाचारादयश्च ये।।५०।।

अभोज्यान्नाः स्युरन्नादो यस्य यः स्यात्स तत्समः।

नापितान्वयमित्रार्द्धसीरिणो दासगोपकाः।।५१।

Boiled rice (cooked food) belonging to a Śūdra, to a calumniated person, to an usurer, to one of false speech, to a cruel man, to a thief, to one of an irascible temperament, to one abandoned by one's parents, to a slave, to the haughty, to a butcher or hunter, to an actor, to a wine-seller, to an arrogant, insane, *Vrātya*, or shameless person, to a breaker of vows, to an atheist, to a miser, to one who goes a naked, to one in danger, to a non-Āryan, to a woman, to a calumniator, to a renowned though dependent person, to a stealer of king's revenue or divine chattels, to one defiled through evil company, conduct, food, or bed, to an irreverent man, to a degraded person, or to a man of despicable conduct, is unfit to be partaken of. He, who partakes of such a man's boiled rice, becomes equally degraded with him.

शूद्राणामप्यमीषान्तु भुक्त्वाऽन्नं नैव दुष्यति।
धर्मेणान्योन्यभोज्यान्ना द्विजास्तु विदितान्वया:॥५२॥

Boiled rice belonging to a Nāpita (barber), Kulamitra, Ardhaśiri (ploughman), Dāsa or Gopālaka, (though these men are all Śūdras), may be eaten without the fear of committing any sin. Twice born ones of known families can safely partake of one another's boiled rice.

स्ववृत्त्योपार्जितं मेध्यमाकरस्थममाक्षिकम्।
अश्वलीढमगोघ्रातमस्पृष्टं शूद्रवायसै:॥५३॥

Boiled rice procured with one's own earnings, or kept in a vessel which is not defiled by the touch of wine, nor licked by a dog, nor smelled by a cow, nor touched by a crow or a Śūdra, is always pure.

अनुच्छिष्टमसन्दुष्टमपर्युषितमेव च।
अम्लानबाह्यमन्नाद्यमाद्यं नित्यं सुसंस्कृतम्॥५४॥

Such boiled rice, as well as that which has not been previously partaken of, nor stale or prepared over night, nor taken out of the kitchen and is nicely cooked, should be eaten, every day.

कृशरापूपसंयावपायसं शष्कुलीति च।
नाश्नीयाद्ब्राह्मणो मांसमनियुक्त: कथञ्चन॥५५॥

The several preparations of (rice, pulse, barley and wheat, etc.) known as *Kṛśarā, Sanyāva, Apūpa* and *Pāyasa*, are edible and a Brāhmaṇa while not officiating as a priest at any religious sacrifice, should not take meat or animal food.

क्रतौ श्राद्धे नियुक्तो वा अनश्नन् पतति द्विज:।
मृगयोपार्जितं मांसमभ्यर्च्य पितृदेवता:॥५६॥

क्षत्रियो द्वादशोनं तत् क्रीत्वा वैश्योऽपि धर्मतः।
द्विजो जग्ध्वा वृथामांसमभ्यर्च्य पितृदेवता:॥५७॥

A Brāhmaṇa, engaged in the celebration of a religious sacrifice, becomes degraded by not taking meat. A Kṣatriya should eat the cooked flesh of a quarry after having propitiated therewith the gods and his departed manes. A Vaiśya can take meat, lawfully obtained for money, after having worshipped therewith his departed manes.

निरयेष्वक्षयं वासमाप्नोत्याचन्द्रतारकम्।
सर्वान् कामान् समासाद्य फलमश्वमखस्य च॥५८॥

A twice-born one, by eating the cooked flesh of an animal wantonly slaughtered (not killed in any sacrifice), sufferers the pangs of hell for eternal time, or as long as the sun and stars would shine in heaven. A Brāhmaṇa, by abjuring meat, acquires the merit of a horse-sacrifice, all his desires are fructified and he becomes an emancipated self even though he be a house-holder.

मुनिसाम्यमवाप्नोति गृहस्थोऽपि द्विजोत्तमः।
द्विजभोज्यानि गव्यानि महिषाणि पयांसि च॥५९॥
निर्दशासन्धिसम्बन्धि वत्सवन्ति पयांसि च।
पलाण्डूश्वेतवृन्ताकरक्तमूलकमेव च॥६०॥

A twice-born one can drink the milk of a cow or she-buffalo; but that milk should be seasonably milched after the tenth day of her parturition, her calf continuing in a healthy state. The milk of a cow or she-buffalo in heat or in pregnancy should be rejected as unwholesome.

गृञ्जनारुणवृक्षासृग् जन्तुगर्भफलानि च।
अकालकुसुमादीनि द्विजो जग्ध्वैन्दवं चरेत्॥६१॥

A twice-born one, who has eaten an onion, white bringel, red radish, red garlic or turnip, Jantugarbha fruit or any unseasonable flower or taken the milky juice of an Aruṇa tree, should practise a *Cāndrāyaṇa Vrata*.

वाग्दूषितमविज्ञातमन्यपीडितकार्यपि।
दूतेभ्योऽन्नमदत्त्वा च तदन्नं गृहिणो दहेत्॥६२॥

Boiled rice (food) which has come from an unknown source or has been defiled by speech (ordered to be set apart for another) or has been acquired by giving pain to anyone and out of which morsels have not been proffered to any creature, burns down a house-holder as fire if he partakes of it.

हैमराजतकाश्येषु पात्रेष्वद्यात् सदा गृही।
तदभावे साधुगन्धलोध्रद्रुमलतासु च॥६३॥
पलाशपद्मपत्रेषु गृहस्थो भोक्तुमर्हति।
ब्रह्मचारी यतिश्चैव श्रेयो: यद्भोक्तुमर्हति॥६४॥

A house-holder should always take his food in golden or silver vessels, or in golden or silver vessels, or in those made of bell-metal, substituting the fragrant leaves of the Palāśa, Lodhra, or Padma for them in cases where they would be unavailable. A *yati* or a Brahmacārin should use the kind of utensil which he thinks proper for his cult.

अभ्युक्ष्यान्नं नमस्कारैर्भुवि दद्याद्बलित्रयम्।
भूपतये भुव: पतये भूतानां पतये तथा॥६५॥

Having sprinkled of water over the boiled rice (served out to him), a twice-born one should cast three small oblations thereout on the ground, saying, "to the lord of *Bhu* obeisance (*Namas*), to the lord of *Bhuva* obeisance (*Namas*) and to the lord of beings (*Bhūtānām pataye Namas*) obeisance.

अप: प्राश्य तत: पश्चात् पञ्चप्राणाहुतिक्रमात्।
स्वाहाकारेण जुहुयाच्छेषमद्याद्यथासुखम्॥६६॥

Then having moistened his mouth with a handful of water he should do *Homa* unto the five vital airs, appending the term *Svāhā* to the name of each of them and thereafter partake of the boiled rice, as desirable.

अनन्यचित्तो भुञ्जीत वाग्यतोऽन्नमकुत्सयन्।
आतृप्तेरन्नमश्नीयादक्षुण्णं पात्रमुत्सृजेत्॥६७॥

Silently and without any other thought in his mind or anywise condemning it, he should partake of the boiled rice until the satisfaction of hunger. After that, he should sprinkle water over the plate and leave it.

उच्छिष्टमन्नमुद्धृत्य ग्रासमेकं भुवि क्षिपेत्।
आचान्तः साधुसङ्गेन सद्विद्यापठनेन च॥६८॥
वृत्तवृद्धकथाभिश्च शेषाहमतिवाहयेत्।

He should take a morsel out of the residue of boiled rice and cast it on the ground. Then having washed his mouth, he should pass the rest of the day in good company with topics of ancient lore and in the study of *Itihāsas* and good literature.

सायं सन्ध्यामुपासीत हुत्वाऽग्निं भृत्यसंयुतः॥६९॥
अपोशानक्रियापूर्वमश्नीयादन्वहं द्विजः।
सायमप्यतिथिः पूज्यो होमकालागतोऽनिशम्॥७०॥
श्रद्धया शक्तितो नित्यं श्रुतं हन्यादपूजितः।

On the approach of evening, he should attend to his *Sandhyā* worship and cast oblations in the sacred fire Every day, a twice-born one should eat in the company of his servants and dependants. An *Atithi* arrived at the time of his evening *Homa* should be honoured by a house-holder to the best of his ability, inasmuch as a dishonoured *Atithi* robs the piety of the household.

नातितृप्त उपस्पृश्य प्रक्षाल्य चरणौ शुचिः॥७१॥
अप्रत्यगुत्तरशिराः शयीत शयने शुभे।
शक्तिमानुदिते काले स्नानं सन्ध्यां न हापयेत्॥७२॥

He should not overload his stomach with food and having washed his mouth and feet at the close of his evening meal, a house-holder should lie down in a comfortable bed with his head not turned towards the North or the West. Unless badly jeopardised in health or otherwise incapable, a twice-born one should never neglect the timely performance of his *Homa* and *Sandhyā* rites.

ब्राह्मे मुहूर्ते चोत्थाय चिन्तयेद्धितमात्मनः।
शक्तिमान् मतिमान् नित्यं वृत्तमेतत् समाचरेत्॥७३॥

Quitting his bed within forty eight minutes of the sun-rise, he should ponder over his own earthly interests. A capable and healthy man should thus act every day in his life.

॥ इति श्रीवेदव्यासीये धर्मशास्त्रे तृतीयोऽध्यायः॥३॥

Chapter 4

इति व्यासकृतं शास्त्रं धर्मसारसमुच्चयम्।
आश्रमे यानि पुण्यानि मोक्षधर्माश्रितानि च॥१॥

This Scriptural Code framed by the holy Vyāsa is but a compendium of all kinds of pieties. All virtues and pieties (enjoined to be performed) by the four orders are intimately connected with the liberation of self.

गृहाश्रमात् परो धर्मो नास्ति नास्ति पुनः पुनः।
सर्वतीर्थफलं तस्य यथोक्तं यस्तु पालयेत्॥२॥

Verily, verily (the holy Vyāsa) has repeatedly said unto men that, a household is the best hermitage in the world. He, who faithfully discharges the duties of a house-holder, acquires the merit of visiting all the holy shrines.

गुरुभक्तो भृत्यपोषी दयावाननसूयकः।
नित्यजापी च होमी च सत्यवादी जितेन्द्रियः॥३॥
स्वदारे यस्य सन्तोषः परदारनिवर्त्तनम्।
अपवादोऽपि नो यस्य तस्य तीर्थफलं गृहे॥४॥

The house-holder, who reveres his elders and preceptors, supports his servants, is kind, unenvious, truthful and self-controlled, daily performs his *Homa* and *Japa* (divine contemplation and mental recitation of a Mantra), is faithful to his own wife without coveting that of another and gives no handle to obloquy, acquires the merit of a pilgrimage, without stirring out of his own house.

परदारान् परद्रव्यं हरते यो दिने दिने।
सर्वतीर्थाभिषेकेण पापं तस्य न नश्यति॥५॥

Ablutions in all the holy pools cannot absolve the sin of him, who daily steals or covets, other men's wives and riches.

गृहेषु सवनीयेषु सर्वतीर्थफलं ततः।
अन्नदस्य त्रयो भागाः कर्त्ता भागेन लिप्यते॥६॥

A true and dutiful house-holder bathing in his own yard acquires the merit of all holy ablutions. Three quarters of piety belong to a house-holder as the giver of food, the remaining quarter attaches itself to him as the master of the household.

प्रतिश्रयं पादशौचं ब्राह्मणानाञ्च तर्पणम्।
न पापं संस्पृशेत्तस्य बलिभिक्षां ददाति यः॥७॥

Sin can never approach the threshold of a house wherein the master hospitably accommodates the Brāhmaṇas, washes the dust off their feet, gratifies them with food, makes offerings to Vaiśvadevas and doles out alms to the indigent.

पादोदकं पादधृतं दीपमन्नं प्रतिश्रयम्।
यो ददाति ब्राह्मणेभ्यो नोपसर्पति तं यमः॥८॥

The god of death (Yama) can never touch the man, who gives to the Brāhmaṇas water for washing their feet, shoes, food and hermitages to live in and welcomes them home by waiving lighted lamps before them.

विप्रपादोदकक्लिन्ना यावत्तिष्ठति मेदिनी।
तावत् पुष्करपात्रेषु पिबन्ति पितरोऽमृतम्॥९॥

The departed manes of a person drink nectar out of cups of lotus leaves so long as the washings of the feet of Brāhmaṇas stand moistening the earth of his court-yard.

यत् फलं कपिलादाने कार्तिक्यां ज्येष्ठपुष्करे।
तत् फलं ऋषयः श्रेष्ठा विप्राणां पादशौचने॥१०॥

O you foremost of the Ṛsis the merit, which is acquired by making gifts of Kapilā cows on the day of the full moon in Kārtika, is likewise acquired by washing the feet of Brāhmaṇas.

स्वागतेनाग्नय: प्रीता आसनेन शतक्रतु:।
पितर: पादशौचेन अन्नाद्येन प्रजापति:॥११॥

The fire god can be gratified by welcoming the Brāhmaṇas; Indra, by offering seats unto them; *Pitṛs* by washing their feet and the (god) Prajāpati, by giving food unto them.

मातापित्रो: परं तीर्थं गङ्गा गावो विशेषत:।
ब्राह्मणात् परमं तीर्थं न भूतं न भविष्यति॥१२॥

One's own parents are shrines of excellent sanctity, no doubt, though kine and the Ganges are holier; but the Brāhmaṇas are the holiest of the holies on earth a holier thing than they is not, nor ever will be.

इन्द्रियाणि वशीकृत्य गृह एव वसेन्नर:।
तत्र तस्य कुरुक्षेत्रं नैमिषं पुष्कराणि च॥१३॥
गङ्गाद्वारञ्च केदारं सन्निहत्य तथैव च।
एतानि सर्वतीर्थानि कृत्वा पापै: प्रमुच्यते॥१४॥

All the holy pools and shrines such as, Kurukṣetra, Naimiśa, Puṣkara, Gaṅgādvāra and Kedāra voluntarily visit the householder in his own house, who has subdued all his senses and desires. He is absolved of all sin.

वर्णानामाश्रमाणाञ्च चातुर्वर्णस्य भो द्विजा:।
दानधर्मं प्रवक्ष्यामि यथा व्यासेन भाषितम्॥१५॥

O you Brāhmaṇas, now I shall relate to you the virtue of charity or gift-making as it should be practised by the members of the four social orders and as it was narrated by the holy Vyāsa of yore.

यद्ददाति विशिष्टेभ्यो यच्चाश्नाति दिने दिने।
तच्च वित्तमहं मन्ये शेषं कस्याभिरक्षति॥१६॥

That wealth alone, which a man spends in gifts to the good Brāhmaṇas or in gratification of his own desires, is the only true wealth, the rest is but trust.

यद्ददाति यदश्नाति तदेव धनिनो धनम्।
अन्ये मृतस्य क्रीडन्ति दारैरपि धनैरपि॥१७॥

The riches of the rich are what they enjoy and endow. Others play with the widows and riches of those who neither enjoy nor endow, after their death.

किं धनेन करिष्यन्ति देहिनोऽपि गतायुषः।
यद्वर्द्धयितुमिच्छन्तस्तच्छरीरमशाश्वतम्॥१८॥

What does his wealth avid the soul of a man, after death, (since) transient is the very body which he tries to nourish with the aid there of?

अशाश्वतानि गात्राणि विभवो नैव शाश्वतः।
नित्यं सन्निहितो मृत्युः कर्त्तव्यो धर्मसंग्रहः॥१९॥

Transient is wealth, transient are the limbs of one's body. The only reality is that death is fast approaching. Acquire pieties, every day.

यदि नाम न धर्माय न कामाय न कीर्त्तये।
यत् परित्यज्य गन्तव्यं तद्धनं किं न दीयते॥२०॥

Why not give away your riches in charity which you shall have to leave behind, after death, if you have not already spent them in acts of piety, enjoyment or fame?

जीवन्ति जीविते यस्य विप्रा मित्राणि बान्धवाः।
जीवितं सफलं तस्य आत्मार्थे को न जीवति॥२१॥

Truly realised is the end of his life on whose life depends the livelihood of his friends, relations and Brāhmaṇas. Who does not live for his own ends in this world?

पशवोऽपि हि जीवन्ति केवलात्मोदरम्भराः।
किं कायेन सुगुप्तेन बलिना चिरजीविना॥२२॥

Even the beasts live and pamper their own bellies. Of what use is the strength, health and longevity of him who does not do any act of public good?

ग्रासादर्द्धमपि ग्रासमर्थिभ्यः किं न दीयते।

इच्छाऽनुरूपो विभवः कदा कस्य भविष्यति॥२३॥

If you have but a morsel of food, why don't you give half of it to the poor? Will anybody ever get his wished for riches in this life?

अदाता पुरुषस्त्यागी धनं सन्त्यज्य गच्छति।
दातारं कृपणं मन्ये मृतोऽप्यर्थं न मुञ्चति॥२४॥

Verily do I consider a miser to be a man of great renunciation, inasmuch as he leaves behind him all his hoarded riches, after death. A charitable man is the veritable miser living, since he would be benefited by his wealth (spent in charities) in the next world.

प्राणनाशस्तु कर्त्तव्यो यः कृतार्थो न सो मृतः।
अकृतार्थस्तु यो मृत्युं प्राप्तः खरसमो हि सः॥२५॥

One day we shall have to quit this life. He dies not who has realised the end of his life (by making charities). A miser, dead, is like an ass, who only carries other men's ingots on his back.

अनाहूतेषु यद्दत्तं यच्च दत्तमयाचितम्।
भविष्यति युगस्यान्तस्तस्यान्तो न भविष्यति॥२६॥

Even space and time will die one day, but the merit of a spontaneous and voluntary gift (lit. Made without the asking or to a person come without any call) will never suffer any death.

मृतवत्सा यथा गौश्च कृष्णा लोभेन दुह्यते।
परस्परस्य दानानि लोकयात्रा न धर्मतः॥२७॥

A reciprocity of gifts may be a social function, but is no virtue. It does not bear any religious merit, like the milk of a black cow (whose calf is dead), milched out of greed and proffered to the gods, etc..

अदृष्टे चाशुभे दानं भोक्ता चैव न दृश्यते।
पुनरागमनं नास्ति तत्र दानमनन्तकम्॥२८॥

Verily the enjoyers (beneficiaries) of a charitable endowment, contingent on the happening of a future calamity, are not actually seen. But since eternal is the merit of a gift, the maker of a gift never reverts to the plain of human existence.

मातापितृषु यद्द्याद्भ्रातृषु श्वशुरेषु च।

जायापत्येषु यद्द्यात् सोऽनन्तः स्वर्गसंक्रमः॥२९॥

By making gifts to one's parents, brothers, father-in-law, mother-in-law, wife or children, one is entitled to an eternal residence in heaven.

पितुः शतगुणं दानं सहस्रं मातुरुच्यते।

भगिन्यां शतसाहस्रं सोदरे दत्तमक्षयम्॥३०॥

A gift made to one's father is hundred times more meritorious than the one made to an outsider, those made to one's mother and sister being respectively ten times greater than the latter. A gift made to one's brother bears eternal fruit.

अहन्यहनि दातव्यं ब्राह्मणेषु मुनीश्वराः।

आगमिष्यति यत्पात्रं तत्पात्रं तारयिष्यति॥३१॥

O you lords of Munis! Every day gifts should be made to the Brāhmaṇas. Any one coming and asking for gifts (charities) should be succoured.

किञ्चिद्वेदमयं पात्रं किंचित् पात्रं तपोमयम्।

पात्राणामुत्तमं पात्रं शूद्रान्नं यस्य नोदरे॥३२॥

Several recipients of gifts (receivers of charities) may be persons well-versed in the Vedas, or practisers of penitential austerities. But the best of such takers are those who have never partaken of a Śūdra's boiled rice.

यस्य चैव गृहे मूर्खो दूरे चापि गुणान्वितः।

गुणान्विताय दातव्यं नास्ति मूर्खे व्यतिक्रमः॥३३॥

A gift should be made to an erudiate person living at a distance in preference to an illiterate one living close by one's house. Nothing can be humiliating (insulting) to an illiterate Brāhmaṇa.

देवद्रव्यविनाशेन ब्रह्मस्वहरणेन च।

कुलान्यकुलता यान्ति ब्राह्मणातिक्रमेण च॥३४॥

The status of well-birth is extinguished by one's stealing an article consecrated to divine use, or belonging to a Brāhmaṇa and by insulting a Brāhmaṇa as well.

ब्राह्मणातिक्रमो नास्ति विप्रे वेदविवर्जिते।
ज्वलन्तमग्निमुत्सृज्य न हि भस्मनि हूयते।।३५।।

By not making any gift to a Brāhmaṇa, ignorant of the Vedas, one does not commit the sin of insulting a Brāhmaṇa. Oblations are cast in the sacred fire and not in its ashes.

सन्निकृष्टमधीयानं ब्राह्मणं यो व्यतिक्रमेत्।
भोजने चैव दाने च हन्यात्त्रिपुरुषं कुलम्।।३६।।

He, who causes a Brāhmaṇa, who has been studying the Vedas in the vicinity, to be superseded in a matter of feeding or gift-taking, destroys his three fold relations.

यथा काष्ठमयो हस्ती यथा चर्ममयो मृगः।
यश्च विप्रोऽनधीयानस्त्रयस्ते नामधारकाः।।३७।।

A Brāhmaṇa, who has not studied the Vedas, does, like a wooden elephant or a leather-deer, but bear the name of the genus he belongs to.

ग्रामस्थानं यथा शून्यं यथा कूपश्च निर्जलः।
यश्च विप्रोऽनधीयानस्त्रयस्ते नामधारकाः।।३८।।

Like a desserted hamlet, like a waterless well, a Brāhmaṇa, who has not read the Vedas, is a Brāhmaṇa only in name.

ब्राह्मणेषु च यद्दत्तं यच्च वैश्वानरे हुतम्।
तद्धनं धनमाख्यातं धनं शेषं निरर्थकम्।।३९।।

An article given to a Brāhmaṇa (well versed in the Vedas) or cast in the sacred fire by way of ablution, constitutes the true wealth (possession) of a person, the rest is but insignificant.

सममब्राह्मणे दानं द्विगुणं ब्राह्मणब्रुवे।
सहस्रगुणमाचार्ये ह्यनन्तं वेदपारगे।।४०।।

A gift made to a *Bruva* Brāhmaṇa is doubly meritorious than the one made to a *Sama* Brāhmaṇa. A gift made to an *Ācārya* is a thousand times more meritorious than the latter, while the one made to a Brāhmaṇa well versed in Vedas bears immortal fruit.

ब्रह्मबीजसमुत्पन्नो मन्त्रसंस्कारवर्ज्जितः।
जातिमात्रोपजीवी च स भवेद्ब्राह्मणः समः॥४१॥

One, born of the seeds of a Brāhmaṇa but not purified with any of the purificatory rites or Mantras and making use of his caste as a means of livelihood, is called a Sama Brāhmaṇa.

गर्भाधानादिभिर्मन्त्रैर्वेदोपनयनेन च।
नाध्यापयति नाधीते स भवेद्ब्राह्मणब्रुवः॥४२॥

A Brāhmaṇa, unto whom all the purificatory rites of *Garbhādhānam*, etc., have been performed, but who has neither read nor taught any part of the Vedas, is called a *Bruva* Brāhmaṇa.

अग्निहोत्री तपस्वी च वेदमध्यापयेच्च यः।
सकल्पं सरहस्यञ्च तमाचार्यं प्रचक्षते॥४३॥

A Brāhmaṇa, who practises penitential austerities and performs the rite of Homa, every day and teaches the Vedas with their *Kalpas* and *Rahasyas*, is called an *Ācārya*.

इष्टिभिः पशुबन्धैश्च चातुर्मास्यैस्तथैव च।
अग्निष्टोमादिभिर्यज्ञैर्येन चेष्टं स इष्टवान्॥४४॥
मीमांसते च यो वेदान् षड्भिरङ्गैः सविस्तरैः।
इतिहासपुराणानि स भवेद् वेदपारगः॥४५॥

A Brāhmaṇa, who duly celebrates the *Paśubandha Cāturmāsya, Agniṣṭoma* and other Vedic sacrifices, propounds the true import of the Vedic texts with the six allied branches of study in cases of doubt or discrepancy and regularly studies the *Itihāsas* and *Purāṇas*, should be alone regarded as well versed in the Vedas (Veda*pāragaḥ*).

ब्राह्मणो येन जीवन्ति नान्यो वर्णः कथञ्चन।
ईदृक्पथमुपस्थाय कोऽन्यस्तं त्यक्तुमुत्सहेत्॥४६॥

Members of no other castes live such a glorious life as the

Brāhmaṇas do. Who is that, who having trodden such a glorious path, will relinquish it?

ब्राह्मणः स भवेच्चैव देवानामपि दैवतम्।
प्रत्यक्षञ्चैव लोकस्य ब्रह्मतेजो हि कारणम्॥४७॥

Brāhmaṇas constitute the divinity of the gods. They are the stuff which the energy of Brahma is made of and form the apparent cause of the creation and continuity of the worlds.

ब्राह्मणस्य मुखं क्षेत्रं निष्कर्करमकण्टकम्।
वापयेत् तत्र बीजानि सा कृषिः सार्वकामिकी॥४८॥

In the field-like mouth of a Brāhmaṇa, which is free from all gravels and thorns (of falsehood and harsh words) should be sown the seeds of sacrificial Mantras. The cultivator who does this (gets all religious rites and sacrifices performed by Brāhmaṇas) witnesses the fruition of all his desires.

सुक्षेत्रे वापयेद्बीजं सुपात्रे दापयेद्धनम्।
सुक्षेत्रे च सुपात्रे च क्षिप्तं नैव हि दुष्यति॥४९॥

In good fields the seeds must be sown; in good recipients the gifts should be stored. Whatever is cast in a good field or recipient can not suffer any deterioration.

विद्याविनयसम्पन्ने ब्राह्मणे गृहमागते।
क्रीडन्त्योषधयः सर्वा यास्यामः परमां गतिम्॥५०॥

The cereals (food-grains in one's store) begin to dance with pleasure on the arrival of a modest and erudite Brāhmaṇa at one's house, saying, "we shall come by a better fate."

नष्टशौचे व्रतभ्रष्टे विप्रे वेदविवर्जिते।
दीयमानं रुदत्यन्नं भयाद्वै दुष्कृतं कृतम्॥५१॥

Grains of rice given to an unholy Brāhmaṇa, who has broken his vows and neglected the study of the Vedas, begin to cry in dismay, saying, "what evils have we committed to be punished with such a degradation.

प्रीतिपूर्णमुखं विप्रं सुभुक्तमपि भोजयेत्।
न च मूर्खं निराहारं षड्रात्रमुपवासिनम्॥५२॥

A Brāhmaṇa well versed in the Vedas should be repeatedly repasted even after satiety, whereas an illiterate one, fasting even for six consecutive nights, should not be helped with food.

यानि यस्य पवित्राणि कुक्षौ तिष्ठन्ति भो द्विजाः।
तानि तस्य नियोज्यानि न शरीराणि देहिनाम्।।५३।।
यस्य देहे सदाश्नन्ति हव्यानि त्रिदिवौकसः।
कव्यानि चैव पितरः किम्भूतमधिकं ततः।।५४।।

Holy things, whose likes are in the stomach of a Brāhmaṇa, should be alone given to him. Who are the more worthy recipients of gifts than the Brāhmaṇas in whose body the gods partake of their *Havyas* (libations of clarified butter proffered to the gods) and the *Pitṛs*, their *Kavyas* (oblations)? Beings are not their bodies and hence organisms cannot be revered as holy.

यद् भुङ्क्ते वेदविद्विप्रः स्वकर्मनिरतः शुचिः।
दातुः फलमसङ्ख्यातं प्रतिजन्म तदक्षयम्।।५५।।

The article of gift eaten or taken by dutiful, pure-hearted, (Brāhmaṇa) reader of the Vedas, bears immortal merit, which does not suffer any diminution through one's successive rebirths.

हस्त्यश्वरथयानानि केचिदिच्छन्ति पण्डिताः।
अहं नेच्छामि मुनयः कस्यैताः शस्यसम्पदः।।५६।।

Several scholars desire for gifts of horses and elephants, others discard them, saying, "to whom does this wealth belong and who is the real master of grains or riches.

वेदलाङ्गलकृष्टेषु द्विजक्षेत्रेषु सत्सु च।
यत् पुरा पातितं बीजं तस्यैताः शस्यसम्पदः।।५७।।

The seeds (of knowledge), previously sown in the fields of Brāhmaṇas duly ploughed with the plough of the Vedas, have sprouted as the only true corn in life.

शत्रुषु जायते शूरः सहस्रेषु च पण्डितः।
वक्ता शतसहस्रेषु दाता भवति वा न वा।।५८।।

Of a hundred, one is born a hero; of a thousand, a wise man

and of a hundred thousand, an orator. I doubt whether a man of true charities will ever take his birth or not.

न रणे विजयाच्छूरोऽध्ययनान्न च पण्डितः।
न वक्ता वाक्पटुत्वेन न दाता चार्थदानतः॥५९॥

A conquest does not make a hero, nor studies a wise man. Eloquence does not make an orator, nor gifts a charitable man.

इन्द्रियाणां जये शूरो धर्मं चरति पण्डितः।
हितप्रियोक्तिभिर्वक्ता दाता सम्मानदानतः॥६०॥

He, who has conquered his senses, is the real hero, He, who practises virtues is really wise. A speaker is he, who discusses pleasant and beneficial topics, and he, who gives with reverence, is the maker of true gifts.

यद्येकपङ्क्त्यां विषमं ददाति स्नेहाद्भयाद्वा यदि वार्थ हेतोः।
वेदेषु दृष्टं ऋषिभिश्च गीतं तद्ब्रह्महत्यां मुनयो वदन्ति॥६१॥

One by making gifts if varied values to Brāhmaṇas all seated in the same row, either out of affection, fright or greed, commits the sin of Brahmanicide. It is so related in the Vedas and the *Ṛsis* sing of it as such.

उसरे वापितं बीजं भिन्नभाण्डेषु गोदुहम्।
हुतं भस्मनि हव्यञ्च मूर्खे दानमशाश्वतम्॥६२॥

Gifts made unto an illiterate (Brāhmaṇa) like seeds sown in a sandy soil or clarified butter kept in a pot of ashes or libations poured over burnt out cinders, prove abortive (fail to bear any merit).

मृतसूतकपुष्टाङ्गो द्विजं शूद्रान्नभोजने।
अहमेवं न जानामि कां योनिं स गमिष्यति॥६३॥

In what kind of womb will the twice-born one (Brāhmaṇa), who lives on boiled rice of those, who are unclean with the uncleanness due to any death or birth in their families or partakes of that prepared by a Śūdra, take his birth (in his next incarnation)? Verily I can not say that.

शूद्रान्नेनोदरस्थेन यदि कश्चिन्म्रियेत यः।

स भवेत् शूकरो नूनं तस्य वा जायते कुलम्॥६४॥

He, who dies with a Śūdra's boiled rice in his stomach, is sure to be reborn as a hog and all his progeny will belong to the same genus, after death.

गृध्रो द्वादश जन्मानि सप्तजन्मानि शूकरः।

श्वानश्च सप्तजन्मानि इत्येवं मनुरब्रवीत्॥६५॥

He will be born as a vulture in his twelve successive rebirths; as a hog, in seven and as a dog, in seven. This is what Manu has opined on the subject.

अमृतं ब्राह्मणान्नेन दारिद्र्यं क्षत्रियस्य च।

वैश्यान्नेन तु शूद्रान्नं शूद्रान्नान्नरकं व्रजेत्॥६६॥

He, who dies with the boiled rice of a Brāhmaṇa in his stomach, acquires nectar, after death. Dieing with that of a Kṣatriya in his stomach, he is punished with indigence in his next birth; with that of a Vaiśya in his stomach, he is consigned to the vile necessity of eating a Śūdra's boiled rice again and with that of a Śūdra boiled rice in his stomach, he is consigned to the torments of hell, in his next life.

यश्च भुङ्क्तेऽथ शूद्रान्नं मासमेकं निरन्तरम्।

इह जन्मनि शूद्रत्वं मृतः श्वा चैव जायते॥६७॥

The Brāhmaṇa, who partakes of a Śūdra's boiled rice continuously for a month, becomes degraded to the status of Śūdra, in this life and will be born as a dog in the next.

यस्य शूद्रा पचेन्नित्यं शूद्रां च गृहमेधिनी।

वर्जितः पितृदेवैस्तु रौरवं याति स द्विजः॥६८॥

The gods and the Pitṛs desert the Brāhmaṇa, who takes a Śūdra wife or partakes of boiled rice cooked by her and he is consigned to the pangs of Raurava hell, after death.

भाण्डसङ्करसङ्कीर्णाः नानासङ्करसङ्कराः।

योनिसङ्करसङ्कीर्णा निरयं यान्ति मानवाः॥६९॥

The Brāhmaṇa, who cooks his food in vessels defiled by the touch of men of vile castes or do those acts which are calculated to degrade a twice-born one in his social status, or promiscuously go unto women of forbidden castes, is sure to be consigned to hell, after death.

पङ्क्तिभेदी वृथापाकी नित्यं ब्राह्मणनिन्दकः।

आदेशी वेदविक्रेता पञ्चैते ब्रह्मघातकाः॥७०॥

Cooking of boiled rice for the gratification of one's own hunger without dedicating it to the use of Brāhmaṇas, *Atithis* and the god presiding over a row of Brāhmaṇa at a dinner, constant vilification of Brāhmaṇas and selling the Vedas for money (mercenary teaching of the Vedas) are the five acts which rank equally with an act of Brahmanicide in respect of sin.

इदं व्यासकृतं नित्यमध्येतव्यं प्रयत्नतः।

एतदुक्ताचारवतः पतनं नैव विद्यते॥७१॥

Every day, this Śāstras, framed by Vyāsa, should be carefully studied and those, who follow the regulations herein-laid down, suffer no fall in life.

॥ इति श्रीवेदव्यासीये धर्मशास्त्रे चतुर्थोऽध्यायः॥४॥

१५. गौतमस्मृतिः

15. Gautama Smṛti

Chapter 1

वेदो धर्ममूलं तद्विदाञ्च स्मृतिशीले दृष्टो धर्मव्यतिक्रमः। साहसञ्च महतां न तु दृष्टोऽर्थो वरदौर्बल्यात्, तुल्यबलविरोधे विकल्पः॥

The Vedas, and the ethical rules, observed by those, well-versed in them (Vedas), are the source of virtue (morals). Even great men are (sometimes) found to transgress the moral laws and to act improperly. Through an innate weakness of the heart, the great sometimes lose sight of the true end of life. In a conflict between two equally authoritative opinions on a particular subject, one of them must be followed.

उपनयनं ब्राह्मणस्याष्टमे नवमे, पञ्चमे वा काम्यं, गर्भादिः सङ्ख्या वर्षाणां, तद्द्वितीयं जन्म। तद्यस्मात् स आचार्यो वेदानुवचनाच्च। एकादशद्वादशयोः क्षत्रियवैश्ययोः। आषोडशाद्ब्राह्मणस्य पतिता सावित्री, द्वाविंशते राजन्यस्य द्व्यधिका या वैश्यस्य। मौञ्जीज्यामौर्वीसौत्र्यो मेखलाः क्रमेण कृष्णरूरूबस्ताजिनानि वासांसि, शाणक्षौमचीरकुतपाः, सर्वेषां कार्पासञ्चाविकृतम्। काषायमप्येके। वार्क्षं ब्राह्मणस्य, माञ्जिष्ठहारिद्रे इतरयोः।

A Brāhmaṇa child should be invested with the holy thread (either) at the fifth, eighth, or ninth year of his life. The computation should be made inclusive of the period of his inter-uterine life. This rite of investure is a second birth. Hence, he, who invests him with the thread, is his preceptor, inasmuch as it is he who teaches him the Vedas. Sons of Kṣatriyas, and of Vaiśyas should be respectively invested with the holy thread at the age of eleven and twelve. A Brāhmaṇa child, not invested with the thread before he is sixteen, becomes degraded. Sons of Kṣatriyas and of Vaiśyas, not respectively invested with the holy thread before their twenty-second and twenty-fourth year, are likewise degraded. Girdles *(Muñjis)* made of *Kuśa* blades, of bow-strings, and of cotton twists should be respectively used by

Brāhmaṇas, Kṣatriyas and Vaiśyas during the ceremony of investiture; and they should respectively wear, at the time, goat-skins, or skins of antelope, or of Ruru (dear), and cloths made of hemp twists, or silk cloths, and those known as *Cira Kutapas* (cotton home-spuns). Cloths made of cotton-twists may be used by members of all twice-born castes on the occasion. Certain authorities aver that Brāhmaṇas should wear cloths made of twists of trees; Kṣatriyas should wear cloths dyed with *Mañjiṣṭhā;* and Vaiśyas, those tinged with turmeric, on the occasion.

वैल्वपलाशौ ब्राह्मणस्य दण्डावश्वत्थपैलवौ शेषे, यज्ञियो वा सर्वेषामपीडिता यूपचक्राः सवल्कला (सशल्कला) मूर्द्धललाटनासाग्रप्रमाणाः। मुण्डजटिलशिखाजटाश्च। द्रव्यहस्त उच्छिष्टोऽनिधायाचमेद्। द्रव्यशुद्धिः परिमार्ज्जनप्रदाहतक्षणनिर्णेजनानि तैजसमार्त्तिकदारवतान्तवानां, तैजसवदुपलमणिशंखशुक्तीनां, दारुवदस्थिभूम्योरावपनञ्च, भूमेश्चैलवद्रज्जुविदलचर्मणामुत्सर्गो वात्यन्तोपहतानाम्। प्राङ्मुख उदङ्मुखो वा शौचमारभेत्। शुचौ देशे आसीनो दक्षिणं बाहुं जान्वन्तरा कृत्वा यज्ञोपवीत्या मणिबन्धनात् पाणौ प्रक्षाल्य वाग्यतो हृदयस्पृशस्त्रिश्चतुर्वाऽप आचामेत्। द्विः प्रमृज्यात् पादौ, चाभ्युक्षेत् खानि चोपस्पृशेच्छीर्षण्यानि मूर्द्धनि च दद्यात्। सुप्ता भुक्त्वा क्षुत्वा च पुनः दन्तश्लिष्टेषु दन्तवदन्यत्र जिह्वाभिमर्षणात्। प्राक्च्युतेरित्येके। च्युते स्वास्त्रावविद्विद्यान्निगिरन्नेव तच्छुचिः। न मुख्या विप्रुष उच्छिष्टं कुर्वन्ति ताश्चेदङ्गे निपतन्ति। लेपगन्धापकर्षणे शौचममेध्यस्य। तदद्भिः पूर्वं मृदा। च मूत्रपुरीषरेतोविस्त्रंसनाभ्यवहारसंयोगेषु च यत्र चाम्नाया विदध्यात्।

पाणिना सव्यमुपसंगृह्याङ्गुष्ठमधीहि भो इत्यामन्त्रयेत् गुरुः। तत्र चक्षुर्मनःप्राणोपस्पर्शनं दर्भैः प्राणायामास्त्रयः पञ्चदशमात्राः। प्राक्कूलेष्वासनञ्च ॐपूर्वा व्याहृतयः पञ्चसप्तान्ताः। गुरोः पादोपसंग्रहणं प्रातर्ब्रह्मानुवचने चाद्यन्तयोरनुज्ञात उपविशेत्। प्राङ्मुखो दक्षिणतः शिष्य उदङ्मुखो वा सावित्रीञ्चानुवचनमादितो ब्रह्मण आदाने ॐकारस्याऽन्यत्रापि। अन्तरागमने पुनरुपसदने श्वनकुलसर्पमण्डूकमार्ज्जाराणां त्र्यहमुपवासो विप्रवासश्च; प्राणायामा घृतप्राशनञ्चेतरेषाम्। श्मशानाध्ययने चैवम्।

Rods made of *Bilva* and *Palāśa* wood should be used by Brāhmaṇas; those made of *Aśvattha* and *Pilu* wood should be respectively used by Kṣatriyas and Vaiśyas, in connection with investiture ceremonies; or rods made of the wood of any sacrificial tree may be used by members of all the (twice-born) castes, on the occasion. The rods should be made of whole-skinned wood, and be of sufficient lengths to respectively reach the crowns, foreheads, and tips of noses of Brāhmaṇa, Kṣatriya and Vaiśya infants, during the celebration of the ceremony.

A Brāhmaṇa child should shave his entire head, a Kṣatriya child should wear braided hairs, and a Vaiśya child should wear a tuft of hair on the crown of his head (on the occasion of investiture with the holy thread.)

Having touched an unused residue of another's meal with an article of (fare) in one's hand, one should perform an *Ācamana,* without placing that article on the ground, whereby it would be pure again. Earthen or metallic vessels, as well as articles made of wood, or of cotton twists, anywise defiled by an impure contact, should be again purified by respectively rubbing, burning, cutting, and washing them with water. The purification of gems, as well as of articles made of conch-shells or mothers of pearls, should be made, as laid down in respect of metallic pots or vessels. Earthen vessels or articles made of bones should be re-purified in the manner of wooden ones. A plot of ground should be re-purified by ploughing it. Hydes, pulses, and ropes of threads should be re-purified in the manner of clothes. Articles, which are extremely polluted, should be rejected and thrown away.

All acts of purification should be commenced by looking towards the north or to the east. Seated in a pure place, with his right hand placed between his thighs, and catching hold of his holy thread, a worker of purification should wash his hands from his elbows, downward; and observing perfect silence, he should three or four times, perform the rite of *Ācamana* with water, enough to tricle down into the region of his heart. Then having twice rubbed or washed his feet with water, he should touch his eyes, and the apertures of his mouth, ears, and nostrils (lit. orfices of the sense-organs situated in the superclavicular region) with water, or place wet hands over them. He should rinse his mouth with water *(Ācamana)* as above laid down, after having sneezed or risen from a sleep or a meal. Any thing pricked or tucked into between the teeth, which cannot be touched with the tip of the tongue, should be regarded as pricked or tucked into between the teeth. According to certain authorities, a thing tucked between the teeth, should be considered as such until it falls off. When fallen off, it should be spitted out like saliva, and the mouth would be thereby purified. Drops of one's own spittals, falling on one's own body, do not make it impure. One's body, cleansed of the deposit of an impure substance, and free from a bad smell, should be regarded as pure. After urination or defecation, one should cleanse the external orfices of the organs concerned with earth and water, as laid down by the regulation.

A preceptor, taking hold of the small finger of his pupil's left hand, should address him as, "O you, read." Then a pupil should touch his eyes, ears, and the regions of his life and intellect with a blade of *Kuśa* grass, fifteen times repeat the *Mantra (*by placing his hand over) each of these localities, and thrice practise *Prāṇāyāma.* Sitting on a cushion of *Kuśa* grass previously spread out, he should recite five or seven *Vyāhṛtis* preceded by the *Praṇava,* each morning, both at the commencement and close of his Vedic study. He should formally make obeisance to his preceptor; and seated on his right, with his face turned towards the north or to the east, he should recite the *Gāyatrī;* and the *Praṇava Mantrah (Oṁ),* after the recitation of the *Gāyatrī.* On a dog, ichneumon, snake, frog or a cat happening to pass between him and his preceptor, at the time of reading the Vedas, a disciple shall fast, and live apart from his preceptor, for three days. He should practise *Prāṇāyāma,* and live on clarified butter, on any other animal happening to pass between them. This rule should be observed after having read the Vedas at a cremation ground.

॥ इति गौतमीये धर्मशास्त्रे प्रथमोऽध्यायः॥१॥

Chapter 2

प्रागुपनयनात् कामचारवादभक्षोऽहुतो ब्रह्मचारी यथोपपादमूत्रपुरीषो भवति; नास्याचमनकल्पो विद्यतेऽन्यत्रोपमार्ज्जनप्रधावनावीक्षणेभ्यो न तदुपस्पर्शनादशौचं न त्वेवैनमग्निहवनबलिहरणयोर्नियुञ्ज्यान्न ब्रह्माभिव्याहारेदन्यत्र स्वधानिनयनात्। उपनयनादिनियम:। उक्तं ब्रह्मचर्यमग्नीन्धनभैक्षचरणे सत्यवचनमपामुपस्पर्शनम्। एके गोदानादि। बहि: सन्ध्यार्थञ्चातिष्ठेत् पूर्वमासीतोत्तरां सज्योतिष्याज्योतिषो दर्शनाद्वाग्यतो नादित्यमीक्षेत, वर्जयेन्मधुमांसगंधमाल्यादि वा स्वप्नाञ्जनाभ्यञ्जनयानोपानच्छत्रकामक्रोधलोभमोहवाद्यवादनस्नानदन्तधावनहर्षनृत्यगीतपरिवादभयानि।

गुरुदर्शने कर्णप्रावृतावसक्थिकापाश्रयणपादप्रसारणानि निष्ठीवितहसितविजृंभितास्फोटनानि स्त्रीप्रेक्षणालम्भने मैथुनशङ्कायां द्यूतं हीनवर्णसेवामदत्तादानं हिंसाम् आचार्यतत्पुत्रस्त्रीदीक्षितनामानि शुष्कां वाचं मद्यं नित्यं ब्राह्मण:। अध:शय्याशायी पूर्वोत्थायी जघन्यसंवेशी वागुदरकर्मसंयत:। नामगोत्रे गुरो: समानतो निर्दिशेत्। अर्चिते श्रेयसि चैवम्। शय्यासनस्थानानि विहाय प्रतिश्रवणमभिक्रमणं वचनादृष्टेनाध:स्थानासनस्तिर्यग्वा तत्सेवायाम्। गुरुदर्शने चोत्तिष्ठेत, गच्छन्तमनुव्रजेत्, कर्म विज्ञाप्याख्यायाहूताध्यायी युक्त: प्रियहितयोस्तद्भार्यापुत्रेषु चैवम्। नोच्छिष्टाशनस्नपनप्रसाधनपादप्रक्षालनोन्मर्दनोपसंग्रहणानि। विप्रोष्योपसंग्रहणं गुरुभार्याणां तत्पुत्रस्य च नैके युवतीनाम्।

Acts, conversations, and eatings, unsanctified by regulations, and committed and made by one, before one's investiture with the holy thread, do not produce any demerit, inasmuch as one is not entitled to practise *Brahmacārya,* or to cast oblations in the sacred fire, before that. A person, before being invested with the holy thread, does not stand under the obligation of following the rules of purification, after attending to the calls of nature. His bodily purification consists in simply washing or sprinkling his body with water, in contradistinction to the practice of *Ācamana*. He suffers no defilement by the touch of any impure substance. He should not be employed in performing a *Homa,* or in offering oblations to the gods. He is precluded from reciting any Vedic *Mantra* except on the occasion of *a Śrāddha* ceremony, celebrated in honour of his departed manes.

All regulations and injunctions of the *Śāstras* should be followed by a person from after the ceremony of his investiture with the holy thread, and since then, he should duly attend to the study of the Vedas and to the kindling of the sacred fire, practise truthfulness, and perform the rites of *Ācamana.* According to certain authorities, he may make gifts of cows since that time.

One should perform the daily *Sandhyās* out-side one's own room. The rite of morning *Sandhyā* should be performed standing; while that of evening *Sandhyā* should be performed, in perfect silence, till the appearance of the stars and planets in the heavens. One should not look at the sun; and a *Brahmacārin* should forego the use of honey, (cooked) meat, scents, garlands of flowers, shoes, umbrellas, vehicles of all kinds, and unguents.

He should renounce all fright, anger, greed, ignorance, music, calumny, sexual intercourse, lust, gambling, thievish or killing propensities, and the service of the mean. He should not clean his teeth, or prick his ear-holes, or stretch or screw up his legs, or sit with his chin supporting on his hand, or laugh or yawn, or contort his limbs, or twist his body, in the presence of his preceptor. He should not address the sons or wife of his preceptor by their names, and avoid using any harsh language. (A disciple) should lie down in a lower bed than that of his preceptor's, and sleep after he has slept, leaving his bed before he rises. He should curb his tongue, appetite and arms. The name of a preceptor should be always mentioned with respect. One should thus behave to all of one's elders and superiors. He should avoid (sitting on) the same bed, or seat with his preceptor, or at a place where his preceptor sits. Serving a preceptor consists in hearing his behests from a lower seat, and in meekly and faithfully carrying them out. A disciple should stand up (rise from his seat) at the sight of his preceptor, and follow him whenever he goes out. Interrogated by his preceptor, he should give true and correct answers to his queries, sit down to study whenever he may be pleased to direct him in that behalf, and do nothing but what is pleasant and beneficial to him (preceptor). Likewise he should behave to his preceptor's sons and wife. He should not eat the unused residue of the meals of his preceptor's sons and wife, nor should he press their legs, nor catch hold of them (during an act of obeisance), nor help them in bathing or decorating their persons.

According to certain authorities, a preceptor's wife happening to be young, a disciple should not touch her feet during an act of obeisance; but returning from a sojourn in a distant country, he may be allowed to catch hold of her feet.

व्यवहारप्राप्तेन सार्ववर्णिकं भैक्षचरणमभिशस्तं पतितवर्ज्जम्। आदिमध्यान्तेषु भवच्छब्द: प्रयोज्या वर्णानुपूर्वेण। आचार्यज्ञाति-गुरुस्वेच्छालाभेऽन्यत्र। तेषां पूर्वं परिहरन् निवेद्य गुरुवेऽनुज्ञातो भुञ्जीत। असंनिधौ तद्भार्यापुत्रसब्रह्मचारिसद्भ्य:। वाग्यतस्तृप्यन्नलोलुप्यमान: सन्निधायोदकं स्पृशेत्। शिष्यशिष्टिरवधेनाशक्तौ रज्जुवेणुविदलाभ्यां तनुभ्याम्, अन्येन घ्नन् राज्ञा शास्य:। द्वादशवर्षाण्येकैकवेदे ब्रह्मचर्यं चरेत् प्रतिद्वादशवर्षेषु वा ग्रहणान्तं वा। विद्यान्ते गुरुरर्थे निमन्त्र्य: तत: कृतानुज्ञातस्य वा ज्ञानम्। आचार्य: श्रेष्ठो गुरूणां मातेत्येके मातेत्येके।

A Vedic student is at liberty to beg alms of all and of all castes, except those who are degraded or of bad repute. While soliciting alms, Brāhmaṇa, Kṣatriya, and Vaiśya (students) should pronounce the term "Bhavat" (you) respectively at the commencement, middle, and end of their solicitations. One should neither beg alms of one's own preceptor, nor of one's cognates, or of members of one's preceptor's family. In the event of failing to secure alms from any other person, alms may be asked of the afore-mentioned persons in the inverse order of enumeration. All articles; obtained by begging, should be made over to the preceptor. After that, with the permission of his preceptor, first had and obtained, he (disciple) should sit down to his meal. In the event of the preceptor being absent from his home, articles of fare, obtained by begging, should be made over to his wife or son, or to a senior fellow-student. Silently he should eat his meal till the appetite is fully satisfied. He should rise up from his dinner just as he has taken his fill, without casting any greedy look on the food left unconsumed.

A preceptor should admonish his disciple without beating him, or inflicting any kind of corporeal punishment on him. In cases of emergency he may be chastised with a cut piece of rope, or with a bamboo twig without leaves. A king should punish a preceptor for chastising his pupil in any other way. Each Veda should be studied, for twelve years, or until it is thoroughly mastered and understood; and a pupil should live a life of perfect *Brahmacārya* during each such period of twelve years. At the close of his studies, he should pay a honorarium to his preceptor and take an ablution with the permission of the latter. A teacher is the foremost of all preceptors or superiors; according to others a mother is the highest of them all.

इति गौतमीये धर्मशास्त्रे द्वितीयोऽध्याय:।।२।।

Chapter 3

तस्याश्रमविकल्पमेके ब्रुवते ब्रह्मचारी गृहस्थो भिक्षुर्वैखानसं इति तेषां गृहस्थो योनिरप्रजनत्वादितरेषाम्। तथोक्तं ब्रह्मचारिण आचार्याधीनत्वमात्रं गुरो: कर्मशेषेण जपेत्। गुर्वभावे तदपत्यवृत्तिस्तदभावे वृद्धे सब्रह्मचारिण्यग्नौ वा। एवंवृत्तो ब्रह्मलोकमेवाप्नोति जितेन्द्रिय:। उत्तरेषाञ्चैतदविरोधी। अनिचयो भिक्षुरूर्ध्वरेता ध्रुवशीला वर्षासु भिक्षार्थी ग्राममियात्। जघन्यमनिवृत्तं चरेत्। निवृत्ताशीर्वाक्चक्षु:कर्मसंयत:। कौपीनाच्छादनार्थं वासो बिभृयात् प्रहीणमेके निर्णेजनाविप्रयुक्तम्। ओषधीवनस्पतीनामंगमुपाददीत। न द्वितीयामपहर्त्तुं रात्रिं ग्रामे वसेत्। मुण्ड:शिखी वा वर्ज्जयेज्जीववधसमीभूतेषु हिंसानुग्रहयोरनारंभो वैखानसो वने मूलफलाशी तप:शील:श्रावणकेनाग्निमाधायाग्राम्यभोजी देवपितृमनुष्यभूतर्षिपूजक: सर्वातिथि: प्रतिसिद्धवर्ज्जं भैक्षमप्यपयुञ्जीत न फालकृष्टमधितिष्ठेद्, ग्रामञ्च न प्रविशेज्जटिलश्चीराजिनवासा नातिशयं भुञ्जीत। एकाश्रमं त्वाचार्या: प्रत्यक्षविधानाद्गार्हस्थस्य गार्हस्थस्य।।

Certain authorities aver that a (disciple), after the close of his Vedic studies, is free to choose and adopt any of the four orders of *Brahmacārin, Gṛhastha* (Householder), *Bhikṣu* Mendicant friar), and *Vaikhānasa* (forest dwelling hermits). These orders are but the offspring of that of house-holders; inasmuch as they preclude the possibility of progeny. Of all these orders *(Āśramas)* that of *Brahmacārin* entails the perpetual surveillance to one's preceptor. Having served the preceptor, he should recite the sacred *Mantras*. In the absence of the preceptor, the same honour should be given to his son, and in the absence of the latter a senior disciple of the preceptor should be duly served. In the absence of all these he should attend to the sacred fire duly consecrated by his preceptor before his death. He, who lives such a life, self-controlled, goes to the region of Brahma (after death). The order of house-holder is neither hostile to, nor incompatible with, the three aforesaid orders. *A Bhikṣu,* who does not store up any thing for the morrow, lives a life of perfect continence, and is a man of steady habits and temperament, should go into villages for alms during the rainy season. He may obtain alms from all except the fallen and the depraved. Without giving blessings to any body, and restraining his tongue, sight and bearing, he should put on the girdle cloth only to cover his nudity. The same girdle cloth, even if it becomes extremely dirty, should neither be cleansed nor washed. He should live on fruits of trees and grains of cereals, and avoid staying two consecutive nights in a village, for alms. Either he should completely shavc the hair of his head, or wear a tuft of hair on its crown. Equally indifferent to all creatures, he should refrain from destroying any life; or from showing any special kindness to any being.

A Vaikhānasa (forest-dwelling hermit) should live on fruits and edible roots of the forest; practising penitential austerities, he should kindle up the sacred fire in the month of *Śravana.* He should forego all artificial preparations of food used in villages or made by man. Firmly devoted to the propitiation of the gods, of the *Pitṛs,* and of the celestial sages, he is free to accept the hospitality of all, except the fallen and the depraved. He may live by begging under certain circumstances. He should abjure all articles of fare containing any thing reared by ploughing, and refrain from entering any village whatsoever. He should wear clotted hairs and be claid in rags or skin, observing temperance in eating. Certain Acāryayas hold the order of householders

(*Gṛhastha*) to be the best of all, since its benefits are witnessed, every day, (in this life).

इति गौतमीये धर्मशास्त्रं तृतीयोऽध्याय:॥३॥

Chapter 4

गृहस्थ: सदृशीं भार्यां विन्देतानन्यपूर्वां यवीयसीम्। असमानप्रवरैर्विवाह ऊर्ध्वं सप्तमात् पितृबन्धुभ्य वीजिनश्च मातृबन्धुभ्य: पञ्चमात्। ब्राह्मो विद्याचारित्रबन्धुशीलसम्पन्नाय दद्यादाच्छाद्यालंकृताम्।

A house-holder should marry a wife of his own caste, younger in his years, and not previously wedded to another. A marriage should take place between parties not belonging to the same *Pravara* (spiritual clanship) Persons not related to each other within five degrees of consanguinity on their mother's side, or within seven degrees on their father's, or not standing to each other in the relationship of a father's *Bandhu,* may be joined in wed-lock. [The form Of marriage] in which a girl, bedecked with ornaments and clad in excellent clothes, is given away in marriage to an erudite man of good conduct and respectable connections, is called the Brāhma form of marriage.

संयोगमन्त्र: प्राजापत्ये सहधर्म्मं चरतामिति। आर्षे गोमिथुनं कन्यावते दद्यात्। अन्तर्वेद्यृत्विजे दानं देव:। अलङ्कृत्येच्छन्त्या स्वयं संयोगो गान्धर्व:। वित्तेनानतिस्त्रीमतामासुर:। प्रसह्यादनाद्राक्षस:। असंविज्ञानोपसंगमनात्पैशाच:। चत्वारो धर्म्या: प्रथमाना: षडित्येके। अनुलोमानन्तरैकान्तरद्व्यन्तरासु जाता: सवर्णाम्बष्ठोग्रनिषाददौष्यन्तपारशवा:। प्रतिलोमासु सुतमागधायोगवृक्षत्तृवैदेहकचण्डाला:। ब्राह्मण्यजीजनत् पुत्रान् वर्णेभ्य आनुपुर्व्याद् ब्राह्मणसुतमागधचण्डालान् तेभ्य एव क्षत्रिया मूर्द्धावसिक्तक्षत्रियधीवरपुल्कसान्, तेभ्य एव वैश्या भृज्यकण्ठकमाहिष्यवैश्यवैदेहान तेभ्य एव पारशवयवनकरणशूद्रान् शूद्रेत्येके। वर्णान्तरगमनमुत्कर्षाभ्यां सप्तमेन पञ्चमेन चाचार्या:। सृष्ट्यन्तरजातानाञ्च प्रतिलोमास्तु धर्महीना:। शूद्रायाञ्च असमानायाञ्च शूद्रात् पतितवृत्तिरन्त्य: पापिष्ठ:। पुनन्ति साधव: पुत्रास्त्रिपौरुषानार्षाद्दश: दैवाद्दशैव, प्राजापत्याद्दश, पूर्वान् दश परानात्मानञ्च ब्राह्मीपुत्रा: ब्राह्मीपुत्रा:।

The form in which the bride and the bridegroom are united together with the injunction that, "both of, you lead the life of viture, united in holy wedlock" is called the *Prājāpatyam.*

In the *Ārśam* form of marriage a cow and a bullock are gifted to the bridegroom. The *Daivam* form of marriage consists in giving away a girl in marriage, on the sacrificial platform, to a priest officiating at a religious sacrifice. The form in which a youth, and a maiden bedecked with ornaments, are joined in wedlock, out of love, is called the *Gāndharvam.* The form of marriage in which a bride is purchased for money, is called the *Āsuram.* The form in which the marriage is effected by kidnapping the bride is called the *Rākṣasam.* A marriage, which takes place owing to the bride being ravished by the bridegroom during her sleep, is called the *Paiśācam.* The first four forms of marriage are based on virtue, while certain authorities hold the first six forms to be so.

Sons, issues of marriages celebrated between parties of the same caste (Brāhmaṇas), between Brāhmaṇas and Kṣatriya girls, and between Brāhmaṇa and Vaiśya girls, are respectively called Savarṇas, Amvaṣṭas, Ugras, Niaśādas, Dauṣmantas and Pāraśavas. Similarly sons begot by men, on women, of the same castes, or of castes second and third in succession in the in-verse order of enumeration, are respectively (called Sutas, Magadhas, Ayogavas, Kṣatras, Vaidehas, and *Cāṇḍālas.* According to others, sons begotten on Brāhmaṇa women by Brāhmaṇas, Kṣatriyas, Vaiśyas and Śūdras, are respectively called Brāhmaṇas, Sutas, Magadhas, and *Cāṇḍālas.* Similarly, sons begot on Kṣatriya women by Brāhmaṇas, Kṣatriyas, Vaiśyas and Śūdras, are called Murdhāvasiktas, Kṣatriyas, Dhivaras, and Pukkasas. Likewise, sons begotten on the person of a Vaiśya woman by a Brāhmaṇa, Kṣatriya, Vaiśya, or Śūdra, are respectively called Bhrijjakanthas, Māhiṣyas, Vaiśyas and Vaidehas. In the same manner, sons begotten on a Śūdra woman by a Brāhmaṇas, Kṣatriya, Vaiśya or a Śūdra are respectively designated as Paraśavas, Yavanas, Karana, and Śūdras. Sons begot by fathers belonging to a superior caste on mothers belong to a caste immediately, and next to immediately, inferior to theirs (fathers) in the order of enumeration, respectively retain their racial superiority up to the seventh and fifth generations, while sons begot by fathers belonging to an inferior caste on mothers belonging to one immediately superior, or to one next to that in superiority to, that of theirs (fathers') in the inverse order of enumeration, retain their degraded status up to the fifth and seventh generations respectively. Sons begot by men of inferior castes on women of superior castes in the inverse order of enumeration are disqualified from performing any religious rites such as *Śrāddhas,* etc.) Sons, who are the issues of inter-marriages among Śūdras of different castes, become degraded and extremely depraved. Issues of *Ārṣa* forms of marriage sanctify their ancestors up to the third degree; those of *Daiva* and *Prājāpatya* forms purify their anscestors up to the tenth degree, while those of Brāhma forms sanctify the spirits of their cognates up to the third degree both in the ascending and descending line.

इति गौतमीये धर्मशास्त्रे चतुर्थोऽध्यायः॥४॥

Chapter 5

ऋतावुपेयात् सर्वत्र वा प्रतिषिद्धवर्ज्जम्। देवपितृमनुष्यभूतर्षिपूजको नित्यस्वाध्यायः। पितृभ्यश्चोदकदानं यथोत्साहमन्यद्कार्यादिरग्निर्दायादिर्वा। तस्मिन् गृह्याणि देवपितृमनुष्यज्ञाः स्वाध्यायश्च। बलिकर्माग्नावग्निर्धन्वन्तरिर्विश्वेदेवाः प्रजापतिः सृष्टिकृदितिहोमः। दिग्देवताभ्यश्च यथास्वं द्वारे मरुद्भ्यो गृहदेवताभ्यो प्रविश्य ब्रह्मणे मध्ये अद्भ्य उदकुम्भ आकाशायेत्यन्तरिक्षे नक्तञ्चरेभ्यश्च सायम्। स्वस्तिवाच्यभिक्षादानप्रश्नपूर्वन्तु ददातिषु चैवं धर्मेषु समद्विगुणसाहस्रानन्त्यानि फलान्यब्राह्मणब्राह्मणश्रोत्रियवेदपारगेभ्यः। गुर्वर्थनिवेशौषधार्थवृत्तिक्षीणयक्ष्यमाणाध्ययनाध्वसंयोगवैश्वजितेषु द्रव्यसंविभागो बहिर्वेदिभिक्षमाणेषु कृतान्नमितरेषु। प्रतिश्रुत्याप्यधर्मसंयुक्ताय न दद्यात्। क्रुद्धहृष्टभीतार्त्तलुब्धबालस्थविरमूढमत्तोन्मत्तवाक्यान्यनृता न्यपातकानि। भोजयेत् पूर्वमतिथिकुमारव्याधितगर्भिणीसुवासिनीस्थविरान् जघन्यांश्च। आचार्यपितृसखीनान्तु निवेद्य वचनक्रियाः ऋत्विगाचार्यश्वशुरपितृव्यमातुलानामुपस्थाने

मधुपर्क: संवत्सरे पुन: पूजिता यज्ञविवाहयोरर्वाक् राज्ञश्च श्रोणियस्य। अश्रोत्रियस्यासनोदके श्रोत्रियस्य तु पाद्यमर्घ्यमन्नविशेषांश्च प्रकारयेन्नित्यं वा संस्कारविशिष्टं मध्यतोऽन्नदानमवैद्यसाधुवृत्ते विपरीते तु तृणोदकभूमि: स्वागतमन्तत: पूज्यानत्याशश्च शय्यासनावसथानुव्रज्योपासनानि संदृक्श्रेयसो: समान्यल्पशोऽपि हीने असमानग्रामोऽतिथिरेक-रात्रिकाऽधिवृक्षसूर्योपस्थायी कुशलानामयारोग्याणामनुप्रश्नोत्यं शूद्रस्याब्राह्मणस्यानतिथिरब्राह्मणो यज्ञे संवृतश्चेत् भोजनन्तु क्षत्रियस्योर्ध्वं ब्राह्मणेभ्योऽन्यान् भृत्यै: सहानृशंसार्थमानृशंसार्थम्।

During the menstrual period (from the fourth to the fifteenth day after the appearance of the flow), each month, one should visit one's wife, on any day except those interdicted (by the regulations). Each day, the Vedas should be studied and offerings should he made unto the gods, *Pitṛs,* men, animals and *Ṛ-is.* One should offer libations of water to one's departed manes, attend to the duties of every day life, and devise means of earning money with the utmost energy (one is capable of putting forth). Studying the Vedas, and offering oblations to the gods and to one's departed manes, and practising hospitalities *(Manuṣya yajña)* are acts which are included within one's household duties. Burnt offerings should be offered in the sacred, fire and unto the fire-god, Dhanvantari (celestial surgeon), Viśvedevas, Prajāpati and the creator. Offerings should be made unto the presiding deities of the different quarters of the heaven in angles of a (sacrificial chamber) respectively sacred to each of them. Offerings should be made unto the *Maruts* and house-hold gods at the door of a room; those unto Brahmā should be offered after entering it; those unto the water-god should be offered in a pitcher, full of water; those unto the deities of the firmament should be offered by reciting the *Mantra-* "Oṁ obeisance to firmament," while those in honour of the spirits that roam about in the night, should be offered at the advent if even tide, each day. Blessings and alms should be given after being requested to that end, or gifts should be made for any religious purpose. Gifts made to a non-Brāhmaṇa, to a Brāhmaṇa, to a *Śrotriya,* and to one well-versed in Vedas, respectively bear ordinary, double, and a thousand times (as much) merit, (as an ordinary one), and infinite fruit. Gifts (charities) should be distributed to pupils begging alms for their preceptors, to the sick soliciting medicines, to the indigent, to persons intending to celebrate any religious sacrifice, to students, to journey men in straitened circumstances, and to those engaged in celebrating *Viśvajit* sacrifices. To others asking for alms on the border of a religious platform, should be given cooked rice. Even having promised him, a gift should not be made to an impious or wicked person. An untruth spoken by an angry, elated, frightened, agonised or a greedy person, as well as by an infant, old man, or an idiot, or by an intoxicated or insane person, constitutes no sin.(A house-holder) should first feed, in his house, the infants, old men, pregnant women, sick-folks and married girls residing in his house *(Suvāsini),* as well as those who cannot be pursuaded to take their meals a little after and all chance comers (arrived at his house). All matters (of business) should be submitted to the deliberations of one's preceptor and father's friends, and one should act according to, and abide by, their decision on the subject. One should worship with offerings of *Madhuparkas* one's *Ṛtviks,* preceptors, father-in-law, and uncles, as well as a king or *a Śrotriya* happening to come to one's house within a year, or within that time after the celebration of a marriage or sacrificial ceremony. A seat and water (for washing his feet) should be given to a *non-Śrotriya* Brāhmaṇa calling at one's house, while *Arghyam* and water for washing his feet and some kinds of food should be given to a *Śrotriya* calling at one's house. Cooked rice should be given to all good men, other than professional physicians, arrived at one's house, while to men of reverse stamp should be offered grass cushions, water and seats. In the absence of all these, one should offer a hearty welcome to all persons calling at one's house. The elders and superiors should be always respected. One's equals or superiors (happening to call at one's house) should be always served with beds, seats, sleeping rooms, and unfailing attention, and one should bid them adieu by following them up to a little distance from one's house.

Even those courtesies and hospitalities should be shown, to a small extent, to one's inferiors, or to small men calling at one's house. A resident of a distant village, not having any appointed place of abode in one's own village, should be treated, for a single night, with the honours of an *Atithi* (chance-comer). A sun worshipper should pass the night under a tree without sharing one's hospitality as an *Atithi.* Peace, health, prosperity and freedom from disease should be respectively enquired into, in respect of Brāhmaṇas, Kṣatriyas, Vaiśyas and Śūdras. A Śūdra, or a degraded Brāhmaṇa can never entertain an *Atithi. A* degraded Brāhmaṇa invited on the occasion 'of a sacrificial ceremoney should be served with meals 'after a Kṣatriya. Members of all castes other than Brāhmaṇas should be complacently fed in the company of one's (Brāhmaṇas) servants.

इति गौतमीये धर्मशास्त्रे पञ्चमोऽध्यायः॥५॥

Chapter 6

पादोपसंग्रहणं गुरुसमवायेऽन्वहम्। अभिगम्य तु विप्रोष्य मातृपितृतद्बन्धूनां पूर्वजानां विद्यागुरूणां तत्तद्गुरूणाञ्च सन्निपाते परस्य। नाम प्रोच्याहमयमित्यभिवादोऽज्ञसमवाये स्त्रीपुंयोगेऽभिवादतोऽनियमेके नाविप्रोष्य स्त्रीणाममातृपितृव्यभार्याभगिनीनां नोपसंग्रहणं भ्रातृभार्याणां श्वश्र्वाश्च। ऋत्विक्छ्वशुरपितृव्यमातुलानान्तु यवीयसां प्रत्युत्तानमनभिवाद्यान्तथान्यः पूर्वः पौरोऽशीतिकारयः शूद्रोऽप्यपत्यसमेनावरोऽप्यार्यः शूद्रेण नाम चास्य वर्जयेत्। राज्ञश्चाजपः प्रेष्यो भो भवन्निति वयस्यः समानेऽहनि जातो दशवर्षबृद्धः पौरः पञ्चभिः कलाधरः श्रोत्रियश्चारणस्त्रिभिः राजन्यो वैश्वकर्मविद्याहीनो दीक्षितस्य प्राक् क्रयात्। वित्तबन्धुकर्मजातिविद्यावयांसि मान्यानि परबलीयांसि श्रुतस्य सर्वेभ्यो गरीयस्तन्मूलत्वाद्धर्मस्य श्रुतेश्च। चक्रिदशमीस्थाणुग्राह्य-वधूस्नातकराजभ्यः पथो दानं राज्ञी तु श्रोत्रियाय श्रोत्रियाय।

One should catch hold of one's preceptor's feet, every day, when first meeting him. Having returned from a distant country, a man should first fall at the feet of one considered most revered among his parents, maternal or paternal relations, elders, and preceptors happening to be present together in a company. One should make obeisance by mentioning one's name as "I am so and so." No kind of formal courtesy or obeisance need be observed or made in an assembly of fools, or among husbands and wives. Except on the occasion of starting on a distant journey, one should not catch hold of the feet of any of one's female relations except those of one's mother, aunt (father's elder brother's wife) and elder sister. One shall never make obeisance to one's mother-in-law to the wife of one's elder brother by catching hold of her feet. One should rise up' from one's seat, at the presence of a priest, father-in-law, uncle, or of a maternal uncle, younger to one's own self in years, and not make obeisance to any of them. One should not make obeisance to one's elders in years (other than Brāhmaṇas, although living in the same house or village with one's self. A Brāhmaṇa should treat a Śūdra, even of full eighty years, as his own child, but a member of a superior caste, although younger in years than a Śūdra, should be bowed down by the latter.

A Śūdra shall not address a member of any superior caste by name, nor any body should be allowed to address the king by his name. Servants, who should not be called by their names, ought to be addressed as " O you, O you." Similarly, *a Śrotriya* born on the same day with an addressor, *a Cāraṇa* residing in the same house with him and his senior by ten years, a *Kalābhara* older than him by five years, a Vaiśya official, three years older than his self, an illiterate Kṣatriya and an initiated disciple should be addressed as "O you, O you," and not by their names. Wealth, connections (rich friends), office, birth, deeds, knowledge and age are the factors which primarily add to the respectability of a person. Each of these preceding factors is higher than the one immediately following it in the order of enumeration. But knowledge is the highest of them all, in as much as it is the source of health and virtues. One should give way to a wheelman, to an old man, to a bride, to a *Snātaka* to a king, and to one of tender years who should he protected.

इति गौतमीये धर्मशास्त्रे षष्ठोऽध्याय:॥६॥

Chapter 7

आपत्कल्पो ब्राह्मणस्याब्राह्मणाद्विद्योपयोगोऽनुगमनं शुश्रूषासमाते-ब्राह्मणो गुरुर्यजनाध्यापनप्रतिग्रहाः सर्वेषां पूर्वः पूर्वो गुरुस्तदलाभे क्षत्रवृत्तिस्तदलाभे वैश्यवृत्तिः। तस्यापण्यं गन्धरसकृतान्नतिलशाणक्षौमाजिनानि रक्तनिर्णिक्ते वाससी क्षीरञ्च सविकारं मूलफलपुष्पौषधमधुमांसतृणोदकापथ्यानि पशवश्च हिंसासंयोगे पुरुषवशा कुमारीहेतवश्च नित्यं भूमिब्रीहियवाजाव्यश्वर्षभधेन्वनडुहश्चैके। विनिमयस्तु रसानां रसैः पशूनां च न लवणाकृतान्नयोस्तिलानाञ्च समेनामेन तु पक्कस्य सम्प्रत्यर्थे सर्वधातुवृत्तिरशक्तावशूद्रेण तदप्येके प्राणसंशये तद्वर्णसङ्करोऽभक्ष्यनीयमस्तु। प्राणसंशये ब्राह्मणोऽपि शस्त्रमाददीत राजन्यो वैश्यकर्म वैश्यकर्म।

In times of distress a Brāhmaṇa may learn an art or a science from a non-Brāhmaṇa teacher, and he should serve and follow his preceptor until the close of his study. Among the Brahmanic offices of celebrating religious sacrifices, teaching, and receiving gifts, each preceding function is more meritorious than the one immediately following it in the order of enumeration. Failing to, secure any of these offices, a Brāhmaṇa is authorized to live by the profession of a Kṣatriya (military profession, in failure whereof he is at liberty to adopt the profession of a Vaiśya (trade, agriculture, and cattle rearing). A Brāhmaṇa even if he lives by trade etc., *as* a Vaiśya, shall refrain from selling perfumes, sweet vegetable saps, articles of confectionary, sesame, hemp-twists, silk cloths, skins, dyed, or bleached cloths, milk or its modifications, edible roots, fruit, flowers, medicines, honey, hay, flesh, water, or any unwholesome article of fare for money. Animals such as goats, cows, etc., should not be sold to a butcher, or to one who may be reasonably apprehended to kill them. Men, girls, arms and weapons, land, paddy, barley, she-goats, and lamb, etc., should never be sold. According to certain authorities bullocks, kine, castrated bulls, are not marketable commodities. One kind of vegetable sap may be sold in exchange of another kind. Similarly, animals should be exchanged for one another, and salt, confection and sesame must be exchanged for similar substances of equal weight. Cooked articles may be exchanged for raw ones, and if possible a Brāhmaṇa may deal in all kinds of metals. Members of all castes, except Śūdras, failing to earn a livelihood by their respective professions, may live by trade. Several, authorities hold the latter view. Even while making this interchange of caste-professions, a Brāhmaṇa should refrain from eating any article forbidden to be taken by offspring of intermarriages among those castes. In cases where life is jeopardised a Brāhmaṇa is authorised to bear arms, and a Kṣatriya to live by trade.

इति गौतमीये धर्मशास्त्रे सप्तमोऽध्याय:॥७॥

Chapter 8

द्वौ लोके धृतव्रतो राजा ब्राह्मणश्च बहुश्रुतस्तयोश्चतुर्विधस्य मनुष्यजातस्वान्त:संज्ञानां चलनपतनसर्पणानामायत्तं जीवनं प्रसूतिरक्षणमसङ्करो धर्म:। स एष बहुश्रुतो भवति लोकवेदवेदाङ्गविद्वाकोवाक्येतिहास-पुराण-कुशलस्तदपेक्षस्तद्वृत्तिश्चत्वारिंशता संस्कारै: संस्कृतस्त्रिषु कर्म्मस्वभिरत: षट्सु वासामयाचारिकेष्वभिविनीत: षड्भि: परिहार्यो राज्ञा वध्यश्चावध्यश्चादण्ड्यबहिष्कार्यश्चापरिवाद्यश्चापरिहार्यश्चेति।

गर्भाधानपुंसवनसीमन्तोन्नयनजातकर्मनामकरणान्नप्राशने चौलोपनयनं चत्वारि वेदव्रतानि स्नानं सहधर्मचारिणीसंयोग: पञ्चानां यज्ञानामनुष्ठानं देवपितृमनुष्यभूत ब्रह्मणामेतेषाञ्चाष्टकापार्वणश्राद्धश्रावण्याग्रहायणीचैत्राश्वयुजीति सप्तपाकयज्ञसंस्था अग्न्याधेयमग्निहोत्रदर्शपौर्णमासावग्रहणं चातुर्मास्यनिरूढ-पशुबन्धसौत्रामणीति सप्तहविर्यज्ञसंस्था अग्निष्टोमोऽत्यग्निष्टोम उक्थ: षोडशी वाजपेयाऽतिरात्रोऽप्तोर्याम इति सप्त सोमसंस्था इत्येते चत्वारिंशत् संस्कारा:। अथाष्टावात्मगुणा: दयासर्वभूतेषु क्षातिरनसूया। शौचमनायासो मङ्गलमकार्पण्यमस्पृहेति। यस्यैते न चत्वारिंशत् संस्कारा न चाष्टावात्मगुणा न स ब्रह्मण: सायुज्यं सालोक्यञ्च गच्छति। यस्य तु खलु संस्काराणामेकदेशोऽप्यष्टावात्मगुणा अथ स ब्रह्मण: सायुज्यं सालोक्यञ्च गच्छति गच्छति।

There are two persons in this world whose lives: a-re perpetual vows. The one is the king the other is a Brāhmaṇa. Of these one having the higher knowledge is the greater. The inner (racial) instincts of the four orders of society are perishable (changeable). The (racial) lives of men of all the four orders are subject to change, aberrations, and hybridisation. Virtue consists in preserving the purity of one's native stock. He alone is called a man of varied profound) knowledge *(Vahn Śruta)* who is conversant with the Vedas, *Vedāṅgas* (subdivisions of the Vedas*)*, history, *Purāṇas,* literature, and laws of human nature, constantly tries to imitate (realise) the teachings of the Vedas in his life, is consecrated with the forty forms of consecratory rites, is devoted to the performance of (three kinds of) acts, humble to persons suffering from the six kinds of distempers, and has conquered the six senses. Such a person, even if he has committed any delinquency, should not be punished, condemned, or banished by his king from his native country. The forty consecratory rites are *Garbhādhānam, Puṁsavanam, Sīmantonnayanam, Jātakarma, Nāmakaraṇam, Annaprāśānam, Cūḍākaraṇam, Brahmacaryam* with a view to study the four Vedas, ceremonial ablutions, marriage, celebration of religious sacrifices in honor of the deities and one's departed manes, the daily practice of hospitalities to men and beasts, celebration of *Śrāddha* ceremonies under the auspicies of the full moon in the months of *Śrāvana, Agrahāyaṇa, Caitra,* and *Aśvina,* as well as of those known as *Ashtakas,* rite of depositing fuels on the sacred fire, *Agnihotram, Darśa Pūrṇamāsa* (a religious sacrifice celebrated on days of the full and new moon, each month), *Cāturmāsyam* (a religious vow observed for four months from the month of *Śrāvaṇa* to that of *Agrahāyaṇa* and closed with the celebration of a religious sacrifice, *Nirudha Puśubandha,* (a kind of Vedic sacrifice), and of *Sautrāmaṇī, Agniṣṭoma, Uktha, Ṣoḍasī, Vājapeya, Atirātram* and *Āptoryāma* these seven *forms* of *Soma yajña*. The eight forms of spiritual virtues are kindness towards all creatures, forbearance, non-hostility, cleanness (of spirit), annihilation of the desire of hurting any body, doing good to all, absence of niggardliness, and apathy. Persons not consecrated with the above-said forty consecratory rites, or not possessing these eight spiritual virtues, can never attain to the region of Brahma, or hold communion with him; on the contrary, those, consecrated with most of these forty consecratory rites and possessing a major portion of these spiritual virtues, are enabled to hold communion with Brahma, and to live in the same region with that Supreme Being.

इति गौतमीये धर्मशास्त्रे अष्टमोऽध्यायः॥८॥

Chapter 9

स विधिपूर्वं स्नात्वा भार्यामभिगम्य यतोक्तान् गृहस्थधर्मान् प्रयुञ्जान इमानि व्रतान्यनुकर्षेत् स्नातको नित्यं शुचिः सुगन्धः स्नानशीलः सति विभवे न जीर्णमलवद्वासाः स्यान्न रक्तमुल्वणमन्यधृतं वा वासो विभृयान्न स्त्रगुपानहौ निर्णिक्तमशक्तौ न रूढश्मश्रुरकस्मान्नाग्निमपश्च युगपद्धारयेन्नाञ्जलिना पिवेन्न तिष्ठन्नुद्धृतेनोदकेनाचामेन्न शूद्राशुच्येकपाण्यावर्जितेन न वाय्वग्निं विप्रादित्यापो देवता गाश्च प्रतिपश्यन् वा मूत्रपुरीषामेध्यान्युदस्येन्नैव देवताः प्रति पादौ प्रसारयेन्न पर्णलोष्ठाश्मभिर्मूत्रपुरीषापाकर्षणं कुर्यात्। न भस्मकेशनखतुषकपालामेध्यान्यधितिष्ठेन्न म्लेच्छाशुच्यधार्मिकैः सह सम्भाषेत संभाष्य पुण्यकृतो मनसा ध्यायेत्। ब्राह्मणेन वा सह संभाषेत। अधेनुं धेनुभव्येति ब्रूयादभद्रं भद्रमिति कपालं भगालमिति मणिधनुरितीन्द्रधनुः। गां धयन्ती परस्मै नाचक्षीत न चैनां वारयेन्न मिथुनीभूत्वा शौचं प्रति विलम्बेत्। न च तस्मिन् शयने स्वाध्यायमधीयीत न चापररात्रमधीत्य पुनः प्रतिसंविशेन्नाकल्पां नारीमभिरमयेन्न रजस्वलां न चैनां श्लिष्येन्न कन्यामग्निमुखोपधमनविगृह्यवादबहिर्गन्धमाल्यधारणपापीयसावलेखनभार्यासह-भोजनञ्जनावेक्षणकुद्वारप्रवेशनपादधावनामन्दिग्धस्थभोजन नदीबाहुतरणवृक्षविष-मारोहणावरोहणप्राणव्यवस्थानानि च वर्जयेन्न सन्दिग्धां नावमधिरोहेत। सर्वत एवात्मानं गोपायेन्न प्रावृत्य शिरोऽहनि पर्यटेत् प्रावृत्य तु रात्रौ मूत्रोच्चारे च न भूमावनन्तर्द्धाय नाराचावसथान्न भस्मकरीषकृष्टच्छायापथिकाम्येषु उभे मूत्रपुरीषे दिवा कुर्यादुदङ्मुख सन्ध्ययोश्च रात्रौ तु दक्षिणामुखः पालाशवासनं पादुके दन्तधावनमिति वर्जयेत्। सोपानत्कश्चाशनासनशयनाभिवादननमस्कारान् वर्ज्जयेत्। न पूर्वाह्णमध्यन्दिनापराह्णानफलान् कुर्याद्वा यथाशक्तिधर्मार्थकामेभ्यस्तेषु च

धर्मोत्तरः स्यान्न नग्नां परयोषितमीक्षेत न पदासनमाकर्षेन्न शिश्नादरपाणिपादवाक्क्षुश्चापलानि कुर्याच्छेदनभेदनविलेखनविमर्दनास्फोटनानि नाकस्मात् कुर्यान्नोपरिवत्सतन्त्रीं गच्छेन्न कुलस्कलः स्यान्न यज्ञमवृतो गच्छेद्दर्शनाय तु कामं न भक्ष्यानुत्सङ्गे भक्षयेन्न रात्रौ प्रेष्याहृतमूद्धृतस्नेहविलेपनपिण्याकमथितप्रभृतीनि चातुर्वीर्याणि नाश्नीयात्। सायं प्रातस्त्वन्नमभिपूजितमनिन्दन् भुञ्जीत न कदाचिद्रात्रौ नग्नः स्वपेत् स्नायाद्वा। यद्यात्मवन्तो वृद्धाः सम्यग्विनीता दम्भलोभमोहवियुक्ता वेदविद आचक्षते तत् समाचरेत्। योगक्षेमार्थमीश्वरमधिगच्छेत्। नान्यमन्यत्र देवगुरुधार्मिकेभ्यः प्रभूतैधोदकयवसकुशमाल्योपनिष्क्रमणमार्यजनभूयिष्ठमनलसमृद्धं धार्मिकाधिष्ठितं निकेतनमावसितुं यतेत। प्रशस्तमङ्गल्यदेवतायतनचतुष्पथादीन् प्रदक्षिणमावर्त्तेत। मनसा वा तत्समग्रमाचारमनुपालयेदापत्कल्पः। सत्यधर्मा आर्यवृत्तः शिष्टाध्यापकशौचशिष्टः श्रुतिनिरतः स्यान्नित्यमहिंसो मृदुः दृढकारी दमदानशील एवमाचारो मातापितरौ पूर्वापरान् सम्बन्धान् दुरितेभ्यो मोक्षयिष्यन् स्नातकः शश्वद्ब्रह्मलोकान्न च्यवते न च्यवते।

Having completed his study of the Vedas, a Brāhmaṇa should duly perform a ceremonial ablution, and marry. After that, he should discharge the duties of a householder, according to the injunctions of the *Śāstras,* and undertake the observance of the following rules of conduct (*Vratas)*

He should duly bathe, each day, (according to scriptural ordinances), and nourish a clean soul in a clean body. He should use excellent perfumes, and take an ablution (in a river if possible, each day. He should forego wearing an old or dirty, or an unclean and dyed cloth, or one previously worn by another, if his means admits of such a conduct. He should not put any shoes or rosary, incapable of being re-purified, and must not grow a beard except under circumstances enjoined in the scriptures. He should not simultaneously catch hold of a water-pot and a fire (lighted substance) with his both hands, nor drink water with the united palms of his hands. Standing he should not rinse his month with water previously collected for the purpose. He should not perform a rite of *Ācamanam* with water anywise defiled by the touch of a Śūdra or of any impure substance, nor with that poured out by catching hold of the water-vessel with one hand. He should not urinate or evacuate the contents of his bowels, or caste any other impure organic matter looking towards the sun, or facing the wind, or looking at a cow Brāhmaṇa, or a divine image. He should not stretch his legs towards the image of any deity, nor draw out his feces or urine with a stone. He should avoid sitting on husks, ashes, hairs, and bits of broken bones. He should not hold any conversation with a Mleccha, or with a pariah, and must not forget to mentally recite the names of saintly persons, or to talk to a Brāhmaṇa immediately after, in the event of being forced to enter into such a conversation.

A person having no kine of his own should be addressed as *Dhenuhhavya* (fortunate with cows), and an ungentle person *(Abhadra)* should be accosted as "Gentleman" Skeletal bones *(Kapālas)* should be called Bhagālas (skulls), and a rainbow *(Indradhanu)* should be called a *Mani Dhanu (lit* : a Gem-bow). Seeing a calf stealthily sucking the milk of its mother, one should not report the fact to her owner, nor a man should make the least delay in washing his person after a coitus, or read the Vedas while sitting or lying down in that defiled bed.

Having left his bed and studied before the break of dawn, a person should not lie down again, nor a man should sexually know a woman in her menses, nor one unbedecked with ornaments, one should not even embrace a girl who has not attained her puberty, nor a woman in her menses. A fire should not be kindled by blowing with the mouth, nor one should use obscene words, nor stir abroad garlanded, or smeared with sandal paste. One should not cast even a look at a wicked person, nor sit down to a meal in the company of one's wife.

A wife should not be seen even while performing her toilette, nor a house (room) should be entered by a private door *(lit* : filthy passage) One should not cause his feet to be washed by another, nor eat his meal at a place of questionable safety. Swiming across a river, climbing trees or inaccessible heights, and doing things which are ordinarily supposed to imperil life, should be always condemned. One should avoid getting into a risky boat, and do one's utmost to protect one's self. One should not go out covering one's head in the day, nor uncovering it in the night. Easing one's self at an uncovered and unscreened place, or close to one's house, or over ashes or dry cow-dung, or on the road, or in the shade, is always condemnable. At morning or evening, as well as during the day, one should ease one's self by looking towards the north, and towards the south during the night. Sandals, tooth-brushes, and seats, made of Palāśa wood, should never be used.

One should not eat, sit down, lie down, welcome, or bow down (to a superior), with one's shoes on. The morning, noon, and evening should be respectively made fruitful by pursuing matters of piety, wealth, and enjoyment. Piety, wealth and enjoyment are the sources of virtue. The nudity of another man's wife should never be observed, nor seats and cushions should be dragged on with the legs. All udity of the eyes, genitals bands, and legs, and overloading of the stomach should be foresworn. Biting of nails or weeds) digging into the ground with toes, rubbing and twisting the limbs of 'the body (are acts) which should never be done. One should not leap over the tether of a bound cow or bullock, nor do any thing that brings disgrace on his family.

One should not attend the celebration of a religious sacrifice without first being elected (as a priest) to that end; but one, may so attend as a mere on-looker. Eating by taking morsels-of food, kept in the folds of the tugged up hem of one's wearing cloth, is bad. Pressed by one's female slave, one should not take, in the night, the combination of the articles of fare known as *Caturvīryayam*.. Morning and evening, a person should eat his meal without anywise condemning the food served out to him, Bathing, or sleeping without clothes, in the night, should be condemned as unwholesome. One should act, as persons of venerable age, who are the knowers of their Selves and perusers of the Vedas and are likewise devoid of greed, pride and delusion, would advise one to act (on definite occasions.) For the attainment of bliss through *Yoga,* an, individual should resort to his lord *(Īśvara)* and not to any other being. A spiritual preceptor, a tutelary deity, and pious men in general are called *Īśvaras*. One should rear one's dwelling house in a country where water., *Kuśa* grass and garlands of flowers are obtained, and which is inhabited by a large number of *Āryas,* and Brāhmaṇas, custodians of the consecrated fire. One should circumambulate spacious and holy divine temples, or devoutly walk along its quadrangles. I These rules of conduct should be faithfully followed and observed by all till death., It is imperatively obligatory oṇ a to be cleanly in their habits, truthful in spirit and conduct, gentle in their speech and discourse, open and straight forward in their dealings, and faithful to the teachings of the Vedas. Those, who are charitable, loving in their hearts, amiable in dispośition, firm in the discharge of their duties, and have subdued their senses, succour the souls of their parents, together with those of seven generations of their relations both in the ascending and descending lines. *Snātakas,* who are perpetual vowists and constant practisers of austerities, suffer no fall from the region of Brahma.

इति गौतमीये धर्मशास्त्रे नवमोऽध्याय:॥९॥

Chapter 10

द्विजातीनाध्ययनमिज्या दानम्। ब्राह्मणस्याधिका: प्रवचनयाजनप्रतिग्रहा: पूर्वेषु नियमस्त्वाचार्यज्ञातिप्रियगुरुधनविद्याविनिमयेषु ब्रह्मण: सम्प्रदानमन्यत्र यथोक्तात् कृषिवाणिज्ये चास्वयंकृते कुसीदञ्च। राज्ञोऽधिकं रक्षणं सर्वभूतानां न्याय्यदण्डत्वं विभृयाद् ब्राह्मणान् श्रोत्रियान् निरुत्साहांश्चाब्राह्मणानकरांश्चोपकुर्वाणाश्च योगश्च विजये भये विशेषेण चर्या च रथधनुर्भ्यां संग्रामे संस्थानमनिवृत्तिश्च न दोषो हिंसायामाहवेऽन्यत्र व्यश्वसारथ्यायुधकृताञ्जलिप्रकीर्णकेशपराङ्मुखोपविष्टस्थलवृक्षारूढदूतगोब्राह्मणवादिभ्य: क्षत्रियश्चेदन्यस्तमुपजीवेत् तद्वृत्ति: स्यात् जेता लभेत सांग्रामिकवित्तं वाहनन्तु राज्ञ उद्धारश्चापृथग्जयेऽन्यत् तु यथार्हं भाजयेद्राजा राज्ञे बलिदानं कर्षकैर्दशममष्टमं षष्ठं वा पशुहिरण्ययोरप्यके पञ्चाशद्भागात् विंशतिभाग:

शुल्कः पण्ये मूलफलपुष्पौषधमधुमांसतृणेन्धनानां षष्ठं तद्रक्षणधर्म्मित्वात् तेषु ते नित्ययुक्तः स्यादधिकेन वृत्तिः शिल्पिनो मासिमास्येकैकं कर्म कुर्युरेतेनात्मोपजीविनो व्याख्याताः। नीचक्रीयन्तश्च भक्त तेभ्योऽपि दद्यात्। पण्यं वणिग्भिरर्थापचये न देयं प्रनष्टमस्वामिकमधिगम्य राज्ञे प्रब्रूयुः विख्याप्य संवत्सरं राज्ञो रक्ष्यमूर्द्धमधिगन्तुश्चतुर्थं राज्ञः शेषः स्वामी ऋक्थक्रय-संविभागपरिग्रहाधिगमेषु ब्राह्मणस्याधिकं लब्धं क्षत्रियस्य विजितं निर्विष्टं वैश्यशूद्रयोर्निध्यधिगमो राजधनं न ब्राह्मणस्याभिरूपस्याब्राह्मणा व्याख्यातः षष्ठं लभेतेत्येके चौरहृतमुपजित्य यथास्थानं गमयेत्। कोशाद्वा दद्यात्। रक्ष्यं बालधनमाव्यवहारप्रापणात् समावृत्तेर्वा।

वैश्यस्याधिकं कृषिवणिक्पाशुपाल्यकुसीदम्। शूद्रश्चतुर्थो वर्ण एकजातिस्तस्यापि सत्यमक्रोधः शौचमाचमनार्थे पाणिपादप्रक्षालनमेवेके श्राद्धकर्म भृत्यमरणं स्वदारवृत्तिः परिचर्या चोत्तरेषां तेभ्यो वृत्तिं लिप्सेत जीर्णान्युपानच्छत्रवासः कूर्चान्युच्छिष्टाशनं शिल्पवृत्तिश्च। यञ्चायाश्रितो भर्त्तव्यस्तेन क्षीणोऽपि तेन चोत्तरस्तदर्थोऽस्य निचयः, स्यादनुज्ञातोऽस्य नमस्कारो मन्त्रः पाकयज्ञैः स्वयं यजेतेत्येके। सर्वे चोत्तरोत्तरं परिचरेयुः। आर्य्यानार्ययोर्व्यतिक्षेपे कर्मणः साम्यं साम्यम्।

Every twice-born one is entitled to prosecute the study of the Vedas, to celebrate Vedic sacrifices, and to practise charities. Of these, teaching, celebrations of religious sacrifices, and acceptance of gifts are functions which specifically from the right of a Brāhmaṇa. A duly initiated preceptor, cognates, and friends of a Brāhmaṇa, as well as his relations, older in his years, may teach him the Vedas in consideration of fees. Brāhmaṇas, failing to earn a living by any of the above said means, may live by taking to agriculture, trade, or money-lending. A king has several special duties of his own in addition to those described as obligatory on people in general. They are (1) Protection of all, (2) Just punishment of the wicked according to the provisions of scriptural laws, (3) supporting Brāhmaṇas who are *Śrotriyas,* or do not exert themselves for any worldly gain, or are devoid of all means of earning, or are in a state of pupelage, intending to settle down as householders at the close of their Study *(Upakurvāṇa)*

(4) constant readiness and exertion for the conquest of foreign territories, (5) adoption of extreme caution during times of distress, (6) and the leading of his soldiers in battle from his war-chariot with a bow and arrow in his hands, without setting his back upon his foes. Destruction of life in war is not culpable, but a king by killing an antagonist, whose horse or charioteer has been shot dead, or whose arms and weapons have been broken or damaged, or a Brāhmaṇa, or a messenger sitting or lying down maimed at the root of a tree, or a person taken captive in war, or sitting with his hairs disheveled, commits sin. A Kṣatriya, serving under a foreign king should be allowed to do all things that can be legitimately done by his king. A victor has the sole right to booties obtained in wax. Animals of conveyance and (surplus) treasures seized in war should go to the king. A king should distribute treasures (booties) other than these among his subordinates. A subject is bound to pay revenue to his king. Cultivators should pay a tenth, eighth, or a sixth part of their produce to the king as revenue. Several authorities aver that a fiftieth part of the profit on animals and gold should be paid to the king. Generally a twentieth part of the profits of trade, and a six part of that made on fruit, honey, flowers, medicines, or bulbs should go to the coffer of a king, inasmuch as a king ensures the safe possession of all these articles.

The surplus of the revenue, after defraying all the charges of a good and efficient government, should be appropriated by a king for his personal expenses. Artisans of different guilds should serve the king with their skilled labour, each month, turn and turn about, all the year round. Free workers or craftsmen, even including potters and boatmen, should thus serve their sovereign. They will be entitled to get their food only from the royal store during their term of service. Tradesmen would not pay the king's taxes in the event of their goods being sold in the market at rates lesser than their cost price, On obtaining an unclaimed good, or an article whose owner's name is not known, one should immediately inform the king of the matter; and the king shall cause a proclaimation to be made within his territory, stating the description of the article thus obtained, and asking for proofs of its ownership. It shall be lawful for a king to keep such an article in his custody for a year. Failing to ascertain its real owner within that time, the king shall cause a fourth part of the value of the article to be paid over to the person who had first found it out, making over the balance to the public treasury.

All coparceners are equally entitled to a property obtained by right of inheritance, or acquired by that of sale, purchase, or gift. Only Brāhmaṇas are entitled to (unclaimed) estates originally acquired by way of a gift; Kṣatriyas are solely entitled to (unclaimed) properties acquired by conquest; Vaiśyas are solely entitled to unclaimed properties acquired by trade, while Śūdras are solely entitled to those acquired by service.

A king shall have no right to an underground treasure found by a Brāhmaṇa; whereas the procedure to be adapted in respect of non-Brāhmaṇa finders have been set forth above. According to certain authorities a non-Brāhmaṇa is entitled to a sixth part of an underground treasure found and unearthed by him.

In a case of the ft, a king shall cause the stolen article to be recovered from the thief and make it over to its rightful owner. A king shall protect the estate of an infant till he attains the age of discretion.

Vaiśyas are authorised to ply on a trade or agriculture, and to rear cattle and carry on money lending, in addition to the four duties of prosecuting (Vedic) studies, celebrating religious sacrifices, and making gifts. The fourth order of society is Śūdra, and Śūdras are all of one caste. Even Śūdras should practise forbearance, toleration, and truthfulness, and wash their hands and feet for the purposes of Ācamanam. A Śūdra is competent to celebrate the Śrāddha ceremonies in honour of his departed manes. A Śūdra shall support his own servants, and devote himself to the services of any of the three superior social orders. A Śūdra shall take his salary from his master. He shall put on the old and cast off clothes of his master, wear his old shoes, use his old umbrellas, and partake of the unused residue of his meals.

Otherwise a Śūdra may earn his livelihood by doing any kind of handicraft. The person, whom a Śūdra might serve as his master, is bound to support him in his old age, even if he becomes incapable of doing further service. Likewise, a Śūdra is bound to support his master in his old age, or if fallen on evil days. His master shall have a right to his estate, and he will be competent to order him to accept other men's service. "*Namas*" (obeisance) is the only *Mantra* which a Śūdra is competent to utter. According to several authorities; a Śūdra is competent to do the *Pākayajña.* Members of an inferior social order should respectively serve members of superior social orders. In the absence of any distinctive function or profession, *Āryas* and *Anāryas* are equal in status (caste).

इति गौतमीये धर्मशास्त्रे दशमोऽध्याय:॥१०॥

Chapter 11

राजा सर्वस्येष्टे ब्राह्मणवर्ज्जं, साधुकारी स्यात् साधुवादी त्रय्यामान्वीक्षिक्याञ्चाभिविनीत: शुचिर्जितेन्द्रियो गुणवत्सहायोऽपायसम्पन्न: सम: प्रजासु स्याद्धितञ्चासां कुर्वीत। तमुपर्यासीनमधस्था उपासीरन्नन्ये ब्राह्मणेभ्यस्तेऽप्येनं मन्येरन्। वर्णानामाश्रमांश्च न्यायतोऽभिरक्षेच्चलतश्चैनान् स्वधर्म्मे स्थापयेद्धर्मस्थो ह्यंशभाग्भवतीति विज्ञायते। ब्राह्मणञ्च पुरो दधीत विद्याभिजनवाग्रूपवय:शीलसम्पन्नं न्यायव्रतं तपस्विनं, तत्प्रसूत: कर्माणि कुर्वीत। ब्रह्मप्रसूतं हि क्षत्रमृध्यते न व्यथत इति च विज्ञायते।

यानि च दैवोत्पातचिन्तका: प्रब्रूयुस्तान्याश्रयेत्, तदधीनमपि ह्येके योगक्षेमं प्रतिजानते। शान्तिपुण्याहस्वस्त्ययनायुष्यमङ्गलसंयुक्तन्याभ्युदयिकानि विद्वेषिणां सम्बलनमभिचारद्विषद्व्याधिसंयुक्तानि च शालाग्नौ कुर्याद्यथोक्तमृत्विजोऽल्पानि। तस्य व्यवहारो वेदो धर्मशास्त्राण्यङ्गान्युपवेदा: पुराणं देशजातिकुलधर्माश्चाम्नायैरविरुद्धा: प्रयाण:। कृषिवणिक्-पाशुपाल्यकुसीदकारव: स्वे स्वे वर्गे। तेभ्यो यथाधिकारमर्थान् प्रत्यवहृत्य धर्मव्यवस्थान्यायाविगमे तर्कोऽभ्युपायस्तेनाभ्यूह्य यथास्थानं गमयेद्विप्रतिपत्तौ त्रयीविद्यावृद्धेभ्य: प्रत्यवहृत्य निष्ठां गमयेदथाहास्य नि:श्रेयसं भवति। ब्रह्म क्षत्रेण सम्प्रवृत्तं देवपितृमनुष्यान् धारयतीति विज्ञायते।

दण्डो दमनादित्याहुस्तेनादान्तान् दमयेद्वर्णाश्चाश्रमाश्च स्वकर्मनिष्ठा: प्रेत्य कर्म्मफलमनुभूय तत: शेषेण विशिष्टदेशजातिकुल-रूपायु:श्रुतवृत्तवित्तसुखमेधसो जन्म प्रतिपद्यन्ते विद्याञ्च। विपरीता नश्यन्ति तानाचार्योपदेशो दण्डश्च पालयते, तस्माद्राजाचार्यावनिद्यावनिन्द्यौ।

A king is the sovereign lord of all except the Brāhmaṇas should always do good to his subjects and speak in a sweet and majestic voice. He should be well versed in the Vedas and science of reasoning. Pure, self controlled, full of resources and equipped with the willing service of efficient men, he should deal even handed justice to his subjects, and do what preeminently conduces to their good Members of all the three social orders except Brāhmaṇas should make obeisance to a king, seated on a higher seat (than the rest of his courtiers), and even Brāhmaṇas should show him every mark of deference. A king shall lawfully protect the members of the four social orders in the due discharge of their proper duties-, and walking by the path of virtue he shall make others- conform to that path, and cause them to perform their respective duties in life. A king is supposed to take a share in, the virtues of his subjects. A just, erudite; eloquent, well born, handsome, elderly Brāhmaṇa of unimpeachable character, who has, practised penitential, austerities, should be appointed as the royal priest, and a king should do all (religious) acts according to his advice. The energy of the Kṣatriyas (military vigour) backed by the energy of the Brāhmaṇas (knowledge and wisdom) leads to success and suffers no defeat. The words of men, who have the gift of reading and foretelling dreadful natural phenomena, should be listened to with the greatest readiness. Several authorities aver that the safety and prosperity of a king solely depends upon these people (readers of unnatural phenomena). The royal Ṛtviks shall undertake the performance of those mystic rites, in the sacred fire chamber, that are calculated to bring peace, health, prosperity and a long life to their sovereign, and such like acts of bliss, or to kill or Jeopardise the health of his adversaries.

A king shall adjudicate the contentions of his subjects.

Injunctions found in the Vedas, Vedāṅgas, Purāṇas, and customs of a country or family, and racial usages, not incompatible with those injunctions, are the factors which should determine the decision of a royal tribunal in these cases. Customs obtaining among traders, rearers of cattle, money lenders and artisans, should be respectively taken into consideration in adjudicating the contentions of these people. A king should learn all about these usages from the members of those respective guilds, and award what is found due to each in conformity with the principles of equity and good conscience. In cases of doubt, the opinions of erudite Brāhmaṇas, well versed in the Vedas, should be consulted, and the judgment should be given according to their decision. By so doing a king shall come by good and bliss in this life. It is manifestly true that the energy of the Kṣatriyas backed by that of the Brahmaṇas forms the main stay of the regions of the celestials, Pitṛs and men. The creation (primary object) of punishment is for checking the miscreants and wrong-doers. Members of the four social orders, true to their respective duties in life, after having enjoyed the unenjoyed residue of the fruit of their works, are reborn as long-lived, intelligent, erudite, virtuous individuals in families of special sanctity. Those, who are false to their duties in life, are destroyed. Punishing the wrong doers, and rewarding the virtuous have been laid down by the wise, hence kings and wise men are never condemnable.

इति गौतमीये धर्मशास्त्रे एकादशोऽध्यायः॥११॥

Chapter 12

शूद्रो द्विजातीनभिसन्ध्यायाभिऽहत्य च वाग्दण्डपारुष्याभ्यामङ्गं मोच्यो येनोपहन्यादार्यस्त्र्यभिगमने लिङ्गोद्धारः। स्वहरणञ्च गोप्ता चेद्वधोऽधिकोऽथाहास्य। वेदमुपश्रृण्वतस्त्रपुजतुभ्यां श्रोत्रप्रतिपूरणमुदाहरणे जिह्वाच्छेदः धारणे शरीरभेद आसनशयनव्राक्पथिषु समप्रेप्सुर्दण्ड्यः शतम्। क्षत्रियो ब्राह्मणाक्रोशे दण्डपारुष्ये द्विगुणम्। अध्यर्द्धं वैश्यः। ब्राह्मणस्तु क्षत्रिये पञ्चाशत् तदर्धं, वैश्ये न शूद्रे किञ्चित् ब्राह्मणराजन्यवत् क्षत्रियवैश्यावष्टापाद्यं। स्तेयकिल्विषं शूद्रस्य द्विगुणोत्तराणोत्तरेषां प्रतिवर्णं विदुषोऽतिक्रमे

दण्डभूयस्त्वम्। फलहरितधान्यशाकादाने पञ्चकृष्णलमल्पे। पशुपीडिते स्वामिदोष:, पालसंयुक्ते तु तस्मिन् पथि क्षेत्रेऽनावृते पालक्षेत्रिकयो:। पञ्चमाषा गवि षडुष्ट्रखरेऽश्वमहिष्योर्दशाजाविषु द्वौ द्वौ सर्वविनाशे शतं, शिष्टाकरणे प्रतिषिद्धसेवायाञ्च, नित्यं चेलपिण्डादूर्ध्वं स्वहरणञ्च। गोऽग्न्यर्थे तृणमेधान् वीरुद्वनस्पतीनाञ्च पुष्पाणि स्ववदाददीत फलानि चापरिवृतानाम्। कुसीदवृद्धिर्धर्म्या विंशति:, पञ्चमाषकी मासं नातिसांवत्सरीभेके, चिरस्थाने द्वैगुण्यं प्रयोग्य। मुक्ताधिर्न वर्द्धते दित्मतोऽवरूद्धस्य च। चक्रकालवृद्धि: कारिताकायिकाशिखाधिभोगाश्च कुसीदं। पशूपजलोमक्षेत्रशत-वाह्येषुभातिपञ्चगुणम्। जड़ापोगण्डधनं दशवर्षभुक्तं परै: सन्निधौ भोतुरश्रोत्रियप्रव्रजितराजन्यधर्मपुरुषै:। पशुभूमिस्त्रीणामनतिभोग ऋक्थभाजि ऋणं प्रतिकुर्य्यु: प्रातिभाव्यवणिक्शुल्कमद्यद्युतदण्डान् पुत्रानध्याभवेयु-र्निष्वन्नादियाचितावक्तीताधेया नष्टा: सर्व्वा न निन्दिता न पुरूषापराधेन। स्तेन: प्रकीर्षकेशो मुषली राजानमिवात् कर्मचक्षाण: पूतो वधमोक्षाभ्यामघ्नेन्नेनस्वी रा। न शारीरो ब्राह्मणदण्ड: कर्मवियोगविख्यापनविवासनाङ्ककरणान्यप्रवृत्ती प्रायश्चित्ती स चौरसम: सचिवो मतिपूर्व्वे प्रतिगृहीताप्यधर्मसंयुक्ते। पुरुषशक्त्यपराधानुवन्धविज्ञानाद्दण्डनियोगोऽनुज्ञानं वा वेदवित् समवायवचनाद वेदवित्समवायवचनात्।

A king shall cause that limb of a Śūdra to be cut off with which he might have assaulted or offended a Brāhmaṇa. A Śūdra, detected in the act of sexually knowing a Brāhmaṇa woman, or guilty of that offence, should be punished by cutting off his genitals. A Śūdra who has robbed a Brāhmaṇa, or keeps any article belonging to a Brāhmaṇa concealed after having stoolen it, may be punished with death. A king shall cause molten lead or shellac to be poured into the ear-holes of a Śūdra who has willfully heard a recitation of the Vedas. Similarly, the punishment for his reciting the Vedas is the cleaving of his tongue. A fine of a hundred *Paṇas* should be realised from a Śūdra striving to be equal to a Brāhmaṇa in a bed or seat, or treating a Brāhmaṇa on the road as an equal. Similarly, a fine of equal value should be realised from a Kṣatriya who might have badly treated a Brāhmaṇa, whereas the fine should be doubled in cases of actual assault. For the offence of rudely treating a Brāhmaṇa, a Vaiśya should be punished with a fine of two hundred and fifty *Paṇas.*(On the other hand) for the offence of rudely handling a Kṣatriya, a Brāhmaṇa should be made to a pay a money penalty of fifty *Paṇas,* while his punishment for rudely be having with a Vaiśya would be a fine of half as much amount. No Brāhmaṇa should be punished for roughly handling a Śūdra. As a Brāhmaṇa is punished for doing any offensive treatment to a Kṣatriya, so a Kṣatriya is punished for offensively behaving with a Śūdra. The offence of gold theft should be successively regarded as doubly more heinous in respect of Vaiśya, Kṣatriya and Brāhmaṇas stealers than that committed by a Śūdra. Members of all castes should be equally punished for the offence of abusing Brāhmaṇas. A fine of five *Krsnala* is the punishment for taking a small quantity of turmeric, paddy, or potherbs without the knowledge of its rightful owner. A master is liable for the mischief done by an animal owned by him, or the keeper of such an animal shall be held responsible in the event of its being lent to him for keeping. In the event of any mischief being done by a stray cattle on the road or in an unfenced field, the owner of the animal or of the field should be successively held responsible for it. An owner of a cow or a bullock shall be liable to pay a fine of five *Māṣas,* that of a camel six *Māṣas,* and of an ass five *Māṣas* for any mischief done by any of these animals. An owner of a horse or of a she-buffalo shall be liable to pay a fine of ten *Māṣas* for any mischief done by it, the penalty to be paid by an owner of a goat or a lamb, under the circumstances, being two *Māṣas* only. A fine of a hundred *Māṣas* should be paid by the owner of a stray animal for its destroying the whole crop of a field; money-penalty of the same amount should be paid by a man for his omission in doing the right act, or for his commission of a wrong one. Moreover, all the money, except that found necessary for defraying the expenses of his food and clothing, should be confiscated. Hay for cattle, fuels for fire, flowers from plants and creepers, even though belonging to others, may be collected by one as one's own. Similarly, one may collect fruits from trees growing in an unfenced orchard not one's own.

Interest on money (lent) should not exceed a twentieth part thereof. According to certain authorities, interest may be charged at the rate of five *Māṣas* per month in the event of the term of the loan being more than a year. Interest on money lent for a long period should double the amount of principal. Interest must not be charged from after a mortgaged property has been redeemed by paying off the principal, or in the event of the person of a mortgagor, intending to redeem the mortgaged property, being seized by the creditor (mortgagee) Compound interest *(Cakra Vṛddhi)* on money lent may be allowed under certain circumstances. Personal services by a mortgagor, or enjoyment of the mesne profits of a mortgaged property may be counted as payment of interest. Interests on animals, precious stones, wool, fields, etc., should not be charged at more than five times the ordinary rate. A person holding an uninterrupted and continuous possession of a property in the face of its owner, other than an infant or an idiot, shall acquire a proprietary right therein. But such a continuous possession of a property owned by a *Śrotriya,* king or an itinerant *Brahmacārin,* or by a person of renowned virtues would not give rise to any title thereto in favour of the possessor. Any thing short of an absolute possession of animals, land and slave girls would not create a right thereto in favour of the person holding possession thereof.

The heirs of a person are bound to pay off his debts. But a son is not bound to discharge a debt incurred by his deceased father in his life-time for standing as a surety for another, or due by him to a wine-shop or a gambling saloon, or to his king as an unpaid tax on a trade. No unblameable person is bound to make good any food stuff, treasure, etc., held in trust by him, in the event of their being accidentally destroyed. But he is bound to make good the loss if they are destroyed through his wilful negligence.

A stealer of gold, weighing about eight *Ratis,* shall surrender himself to the king with a club in his hand, confessing his guilt in dishevelled hairs. He shall be exonerated of his crime, if he dies or not, after having been assaulted by the king with that club. A king commits sin by not striking the culprits hard in these cases. All forms of Brāhmaṇas are above corporeal punishment. A Brāhmaṇa, found guilty of an offence, should be deprived of his privileges, and his king shall cause his guilt to be proclaimed in the country, and banish him there from by branding his body with sticks of hot iron. A king, by punishing a Brāhmaṇa in any other form, shall be liable to atone for his sin.

An abettor of theft, as well as the person who receives any stolen article with a guilty knowledge, should be regarded as equally punishable as a thief. Punishments should be inflicted in consideration of the heinousness of a crime and of the bodily strength of a criminal, or otherwise according to the dictates of persons, well-versed in the Vedas.

इति गौतमीये धर्मशास्त्रे द्वादशोऽध्याय:॥१२॥

Chapter 13

विप्रतिपत्तौ साक्षिणि मिथ्यासत्यव्यवस्था बहव: स्युरनिन्दिता: स्वकर्म्मसु प्रात्ययिका राज्ञाश्च निष्प्रीत्यनभितायाश्चान्यतरस्मिन्नपि शूद्रा। ब्राह्मणस्त्वब्राह्मणवचनादनुरोध्योऽनिबन्धाश्चेन्नासमवेता: पृष्टो: प्रब्रूयुरवचने च दोषिण: स्यु: स्वर्ग: सत्यवचने विपर्यते नरक:। अनिबन्धेरपि वक्तव्यं पीडाकृते निबन्ध: प्रमत्तोक्ते च साक्षिसभ्यराजकर्त्तृषु दोषो धर्मतन्त्रपीडायाम्। शपथेनैके सत्यकर्मणा तद्देवराजब्राह्मणसंसदि स्यादब्राह्मणानां क्षुद्रपश्चैनृते साक्षीं दश हन्ति, गोऽश्वपुरुषभूमिषु दशगुणोत्तरान् सर्व वा भूमौ हरणे नरको, भूमिवदप्सु, मैथुनसंयोगे च पशुवन्मधुसर्पिषो: गोवद्वस्त्रहिरण्यधान्यब्रह्मसु, यानेष्वश्ववन्मिथ्यावचने। याप्यो दण्ड्यश्च साक्षी, नानृतवचने दोषो जीवनञ्चेत्तदधीनं न तु पापीयसो जीवनं राजा प्राड्विवाको ब्राह्मणो वा शास्त्रवित्, प्राड्विवाको मध्यो भवेत्। संवत्सरं प्रतीक्षेत प्रतिभायां धेन्वनडुहस्त्रीप्रजनसंयुक्तेषु शीघ्रमात्ययिके च। सर्वधर्मेभ्यो गरीय: प्राड्विवाके सत्यवचनं सत्यवचनम्।

In cases of litigation, a king shall ascertain what is true and what is false from the witnesses. Even honest Śūdras, devoid of all feelings of envy and partiality, and whom the king may safely trust, may be cited as witnesses. A greater preference should be attached to the statement of a Brāhmaṇa than that of a non Brāhmaṇa (witness). Witnesses, not formally adduced to give testimony, are not bound to appear at the court, but such witnesses, (accidentally) present in the court, if interrogated by the king, must speak truth, in as much as truth-speaking leads to heaven, and a lie is the key to hell-door. Even non-subpoened witnesses may give testimony in cases where (summoned) witnesses have fallen ill. An intoxicated person may cite witnesses to speak in his behalf. The king, the members of a tribunal, and even witnesses present therein acquire demerit through any violation of moral laws (in the course of a legal proceeding). Non-Brāhmaṇa witnesses shall give testimony either on oath or on solemn affirmation. Their evidences should be taken in the assembly of the king and the Brāhmaṇas, or before an imaged deity. Ten generations of a witness, giving false evidence on account of (for the acquisition of) a small animal, go to hell. False testimony, given on account of a cow, horse, or a man, leads ten, thousand, ten thousand and a hundred thousand generations of the speaker to hell. By speaking falsehood for the ownership of a land one commits the same sin as is committed by killing all the animals.

Falsehood spoken for (safe-guarding) the right of water produces a sin which is similar to that spoken of for the sake of a proprietary right in land. Falsehood, spoken in connection with an act of sexual intercourse, equally soils the soul of the speaker as the two above. Falsehood, spoken on account of honey and melted butter, is equally venal as that spoken on account of a domestic animal. Falsehood, spoken for the sake of a cloth, paddy, or the Vedas, is equally defiling as that spoken for the sake of a cow. Falsehood, spoken for the sake of a carriage or conveyance, is equally culpable as that spoken for the sake of a horse. A king shall punish a perjuring witness either with a fine or corporeal punishment. A falsehood, spoken for saving the life of a good man (falsely accused of an offence), constitutes no sin; but such a lie for the sake of saving the life of a wicked person should never be told. A king or his judges shall adjudicate legal proceedings. In proceedings concerning wives, kine, disputes of pregnancy, recognisances should be taken for a year, and the trial should go on after that time. Matters, of which a delayed adjudication may result in loss or damage, should be peremptorily adjudicated. Truth spoken before the president of a royal tribunal *(Prādviveka)* forms the highest virtue.

इति गौतमीये धर्मशास्त्रे त्रयोदशोऽध्यायः॥१३॥

Chapter 14

शावमाशौचं दशरात्रमृत्विग्दीक्षितब्रह्मचारिणां सपिण्डानामेकादशरात्रं, क्षत्रियस्य द्वादशरात्रं, वैश्यस्यार्द्धमासमेकं मासं शूद्रस्य। तच्चेदन्तःपुनरापतेत् तच्छेषेण शुध्येरन्, रात्रिशेषे द्वाभ्यां, प्रभाते तिसृभिर्गोब्राह्मणहतानामन्वक्षं राजक्रोधाच्च। युद्धप्रायोनाशकशस्त्राग्निविषोदकोद्बन्धनप्रपतनैश्चेच्छतां पिण्डनिवृत्तिः सप्तमे पञ्चमे वा जननेऽप्येवं मातापित्रोस्तन्मातुर्वागर्भमाससमा रात्रिः स्रंसने गर्भस्य, त्र्यहं वा श्रुत्वा चोर्ध्वं दशम्याः पक्षिणी असपिण्डयोनिसम्बन्धे सहाध्यायिनि च सब्रह्मचारिण्येकाहं श्रोत्रिये चोपसम्पन्ने प्रेतोपस्पर्शने। दशरात्रमशौचमभिसन्धाय चेदुक्तं वैश्यशूद्रयोरार्त्तवीर्वा पूर्वयोश्च। त्र्यहं वाचार्यतत्पुत्रस्त्रीयाज्यशिष्येषु चैवमवरश्चेद्वर्णः पूर्वं वर्णमुपस्पृशेत् पूर्वो वावरं तत्र शावोक्तमाशौचं। पतितचण्डालसूतिकोदक्याशवस्पृष्टितत्स्पृष्ट्युपस्पर्शने सचैलोदकोपस्पर्शनाच्छुध्येच्छवानुगमे च। शुनश्च यदुपहन्यादित्येके उदकदानं सपिण्डे कृतचूडस्य तत्स्त्रीणाञ्चानतिभाग एकेऽप्रदत्तानाम्। अधःशय्यासनिनो ब्रह्मचारिणः सर्वे न मार्जयेरन्न मासं भक्षयेयुराप्रदानात्। प्रथमतृतीयपञ्चमसप्तमनवमेषूदकक्रिया वाससाञ्चत्यागः अन्त्ये त्वन्त्यानां दन्तजन्मादि मातापितृभ्यां तूष्णीं माता बालदेशान्तरितप्रव्रजितासपिण्डानां सद्यःशोचम्। राज्ञाञ्च कार्यविरोधात्। ब्राह्मणस्य च स्वाध्यायानिवृत्त्यर्थं स्वाध्यायानिवृत्त्यर्थम्।

The period of death-uncleanness in respect of the initiated, *Ṛtviks* and *Brahmacārins,* lasts for ten nights, that in respect of the cognates of a deceased relation is for eleven nights, Kṣatriyas remain unclean for twelve nights, Vaiśyas remain unclean for fifteen days, and Śūdras remain unclean for a month under the circumstance. A death uncleanness occurring within the term of a previous and existing one terminates with the latter. A new death-uncleanness, occurring in the small hours of the night on which a previous one would abate, lasts for another two days, while occurring on the morning of that date it lasts for three days more. The period of uncleanness incidental to the death of a person killed by a cow or a Brāhmaṇa lasts for three nights only. No death uncleanness should be observed in connection with the death of a suicide, dead by poison, hanging or drowning, or of a person dead from observing a religious fast *(Prāyopaveṣanam),* or of one killed by fire or an arrow, or in a battle, or in appeasement of a royal wrath.

The tie of *Sapiṇḍaship* terminates either in the fifth or seventh degree of consanguinity, and rules laid down in connection with death uncleanness shall hold good of birth uncleanness as well. The period of uncleanness incidental to the occurrence of a miscarriage of pregnancy in one's family lasts for as many number of days as that of the month at which the miscarriage has taken place, the observance of which is binding only on the parents. A death or birth uncleanness, heard of after the tenth day of its occurrence, should be observed by the hearer) for another three days. *Asapiṇḍa* relations of a dead person remain unclean for two days after his death, while a disciple, on the death of his preceptor, remains unclean for a day and night: Similarly, the period of uncleanness to be observed in connection with the death of a *Śrotriya* is one day only. Such an uncleanness incidental to touching or carrying a dead body is one day. Śūdras and Vaiśyas remain unclean for ten days by voluntarily partaking of the boiled rice of a person labouring under a death or birth uncleanness; while Brāhmaṇas and Kṣatriyas, in distress, who have partaken of the cooked rice of one defiled by a birth, or death, uncleanness, should likewise remain unclean for ten days. A man remains unclean for three days on the death of a spiritual preceptor, or of a wife or son of a spiritual preceptor, or of a *Yajamāna* or of a disciple. A member of a superior caste touching the dead body of a member of an inferior caste, and *vice versa,* should observe a period of uncleanness laid down in respect of the member of the caste of the deceased. Having touched a *Cāṇḍāla,* parturient woman, or a woman in her menses, or a dead body, or a person defiled by the touch of any of these persons, one should regain one's purification by bathing with one's clothes on. Likewise, a man, having followed a corpse to a cremation ground, should recover his personal purity by bathing with all his clothes on. Certain authorities hold that having touched cooked food eaten by a dog *(lit :* unused residue of a dog's meal) one should regain one's purity by acting as above described.

इति गौतमीये धर्मशास्त्रीय चतुर्द्दशोऽध्याय:॥१४॥

Chapter 15

अथ श्राद्धममावस्यायां पितृभ्यो दद्यात्। पञ्चमीप्रभृति चापरपक्षस्य यथाश्राद्धं सर्वस्मिन् वा द्रव्यदेशब्राह्मणसन्निधाने वा कालनियम:, शक्तित: प्रकर्षेद्गुणसंस्कारविधिरन्नस्य। नवावरान् भोजयेदरूजो यथोत्साहं वा ब्राह्मणान् श्रोत्रियान् वाग्रूपवय:शीलसम्पन्नान्। युवेभ्यो दानं प्रथममेके पितृवन्न च तेन मित्रकर्म कुर्यात्। पुत्राभावे सपिण्डा मातृसपिण्डा: शिष्याश्च दद्युस्तदभावे ऋत्विगाचार्य्यौ। तिलमाषव्रीहियवोदकदानैर्मासं पितर: प्रीणन्ति, मत्स्यहरिणरुरुशशकूर्मवराहमेषमांसै: संवत्सराणि, गव्यपय:पायसैर्द्वादश-वर्षाणि, वार्ध्रीणसेन मांसेन कालशाकच्छागलौहखड्गमांसैर्मधुमिश्रैश्चानन्त्यम्। न भोजयेत् स्तेनक्लीवपतितनास्तिक-तद्वृत्तिवीरहाग्रेदिधिषूपतिषुपति-स्त्रीग्रामयाजकाजपालोत्सृष्टाग्निमद्यपकुचरकूटसाक्षिप्रातिहारिकानुपपत्तिर्यस्य च। कुण्डाशी सोमविक्रयगारदाहीगरदावकीर्णिगणप्रेष्यागम्यागामिहिंस्रपरिवित्ति-परिवेत्तृपर्याहितपर्याधातृत्यक्तात्मदुर्बला: कुनखिश्यावदन्त: श्वित्रिपौनर्भव-कितवाजप्रेष्यप्रातिरूपिकशूद्रापतिनिराकृतिकिलासी कुसीदी वणिक् शिल्पोपजीविज्यावादित्रतालनृत्यगीतशीलान् पित्रा चाकामेन विभक्तान्। शिष्यांश्चैके सगोत्रांश्च भोजयेदूर्ध्वं त्रिभ्यो गुणवन्तम्। सद्य:श्राद्धी

शूद्रातल्पगस्तत्पुरीषे मासं नयति पितृंस्तस्मात् तदहर्ब्रह्मचारी स्यात्। श्वपचचाण्डालपतितावेक्षणे दुष्टं तस्मात् परिश्रुते दद्यात् तिलैर्वा किरेत् पङ्क्तिपावनो वा शमयेत्। पङ्क्तिपावनाः षडङ्गाज्ज्येष्ठसामिकस्तिणाचिकेत-स्त्रिमधुस्त्रिसुपर्णः पञ्चाग्निः स्नानको मन्त्रब्राह्मणवित् धर्मज्ञो ब्रह्मदेयानुसन्धान इति हविःषु चैव दुर्बलादीन् श्राद्ध एवैके श्राद्ध एवैके।

Now I shall discourse on the mode of celebrating *Śrāddha* ceremonies. Gifts should be made on the day of the new moon for the peace of the soul of one's deceased father; similar gifts may be likewise made on the fifth days of lunar months. *Śrāddhas* should be performed on the receipt of articles enjoined to be used in the *Śrāddha* ceremonies, and on the advent of Brāhmaṇas, fit to be employed for the purpose at a place or country, where such performances are held as highly meritorious. The cooking and quality of the rice (to be used in connection with *a Śrāddha* ceremony) should be made as good as one's means would admit of. Nine or any odd number of *Śrotriya* Brāhmaṇas of unimpeachable character, and full of health, vigour, and personal beauty, and possessing eloquence and learning, should be feasted on the occasion of *a Śrāddha* ceremony. Certain authorities aver that young Brāhmaṇas should be feasted instead, and the performer of the ceremony should look upon each of them as his own father, and refrain from making friends or friendly ribaldry with them. In the absence of a son, one's *Sapiṇḍas,* disciples, or *Sapiṇḍas* on the mother's side, shall be competent to celebrate one's *Śrāddha* ceremony.

In the absence of disciples, one's priest (Ṛtvik) and spiritual preceptor shall be competent to perform one's *Śrāddha.* An offering, consisting of sesame, *Masha* pulse, barley, *Vṛhi* grain, and water, offered unto one's departed manes, gratifies their cravings (for *Piṇḍas)* for a month. *A Śrāddha* ceremony celebrated with the offerings of venison, or mutton, or with the flesh of a hare, R*uru* dear, rhinoceros, or boar, in honour of one's departed manes, fills them with satisfaction for a year. *A Śrāddha* performed with the offerings of cow-milk, and sweet porridge

(Pāyasa) fills them (with satisfaction) for a year. Offerings, consisting of the flesh of a large or black goat, or of that of a rhinoceros or *Kālasāka,* smeared with honey, and made unto one's departed manes, fill them with satisfaction for a period of twelve years. Thieves, eunuchs, degraded persons, atheists, *Virahās*[1] *Didhiśupatis*[2] *Agredidhiśupatis*[3] and men who act in the capacity of priests to women only, worshippers of village deities, goat-keepers, drunkards, gluttons, wicked or depraved individuals, professional false witnesses and warders should not be fed on the occasion of *a Śrāddha* ceremony. Similarly, persons who partake of the boiled rice prepared by *Kuṇḍas,*[4] sellers of *Soma* Juice, incendiaries, poisoners, *Avakirnis,*[5] keepers of concubines, persons who have willfully known interdicted women, cruel men, individuals who have married before the marriage of their elder brothers, and such elder brothers, storers of grain, persons abandoned by their own people, parasites, individuals suffering from bad nails, psoriasis, purrigo and kindred cutaneous affections, professional sureties, usurers, trades-men, artisans, archers, and professional dancers, singers and musicians should not be fed in connection with celebrations of *Śrāddha* ceremonies. Individuals whom their fathers have reluctantly separated from the family commensality should not be likewise fed on the occasion of a *Śrāddha* ceremony. Several authorities aver that one's cognates and disciples should not be fed in connection with the celebration of one's *Śrāddha* ceremony.

A performer of *a Śrāddha* ceremony should cause to be fed

---

1. Virahās. Persons who have neglected their domestic fires.
2. Didhiśupatis. Persons who have carnal intercourse with their brothers' widow without any religious injunctions.–*Tr.*
3. Husbands of married women whose elder sisters are still unmarried.
   जेष्ठायां यद्यनूड़ायां कन्यायामुह्यतेऽनुजा।
   सा चाग्रेदिधिषुर्ज्ञेया पूर्वांच दिविषु मता।।
4. A son born in adultery while the married husband of his mother is living.
5. Religious students who have commited acts of incontinence.–*Tr.*

that day (date of the celebration of the *Śrāddha)* Brāhmaṇas, possessed of more than three qualifications. A *Śrāddha* ceremony performed by a person, seated on the bed of a Śūdra, leads to a residence of his departed manes among excrements; for a month. Hence, one should practise *Brahmacaryayam* on the day of the celebration of *a Śrāddha* ceremony. Oblations of boiled-rice looked at by a dog, *Cāṇḍāla* or by a degraded person (after a *Śrāddha* ceremony) become defiled, hence such boiled-rice should be given away or strewn over with sesame seeds. Brāhmaṇas, who are sanctifiers of rows (Paṅktipāvanās), guard against the soiling of such oblations. Persons, well-versed in the Vedas with six sub-divisions, who are elderly *Snātakas* as well, and have a thorough knowledge of the *Sāma* Veda, *Trinaciretas, Trimadhus, Trisaparṇas,* and of *Mantras* and laws of virtue, and teach the Vedas to their disciples, are called *Paṅktipāvanās* (sanctifiers of a row of Brāhmaṇas, seated down to a meal). In competent Brāhmaṇas should not be engaged for performing *Homas.* According to a certain authority such men should not be engaged in performing *Śrāddhas* only.

इति गौतमीये धर्मशास्त्रे पञ्चदशोऽध्यायः॥१५॥

Chapter 16

श्रवणादिवार्षिकीं प्रोष्ठपदीं वोपाकृत्याधीयीतच्छन्दांस्यर्द्धपञ्चममासान् पञ्चदक्षिणायनं वा ब्रह्मचार्युत्सृष्टलोमा न मांसं भुञ्जीत द्वैमास्यो वा नियमः। नाधीयीत वायौ दिवा पांशुहरे कर्णश्राविणि नक्तं बाणभेरीमृदङ्गगजनर्त्तशब्देषु च श्वशृगालगर्दभसंह्लादे लोहितेन्द्रधनुनीहारेष्वभ्रदर्शने चापत्तौ मूत्रित उच्चरिते निशासन्ध्योदकेषु वर्षति चैके वल्मीकसन्तानमाचार्यपरिवेषणे ज्योतिषोश्च भीतो यानस्थः शयानः प्रौढपादः श्मशानग्रामांतमहापथाशौचेषु पूतिगंधांतः-शवदिवाकीर्त्तिशूद्रसन्निधाने शुल्कके चोद्रावे ऋग्यजुषञ्च सामशब्दो यावदाकालिका निर्घातभूमिकम्पराहुदर्शनोल्काः स्तनयित्नुवर्षविद्युतः प्रादुष्कृताग्निष्वनृतौ विद्युति नक्तञ्चापररात्रात् त्रिभागादिप्रवृत्तौ सर्वम्। उल्का विद्युत्समेत्येकेषां स्तनयितुरपराह्नेऽपि प्रदोषे सर्वं नक्तमर्द्धरात्रादहश्चेत् सज्योतिर्विषयस्थे च राज्ञि प्रेते विप्रोष्य चान्योऽन्येन सह संकुलोपाहितवेद-

समाप्तिच्छर्द्दिश्राद्धमनुष्ययज्ञभोजनेष्वहोरात्रममावास्यायाञ्च द्व्यहं वा कार्त्तिको फाल्गुन्याषाढ़ी पौर्णमासी तिस्रोऽष्टकास्त्रिरात्रमन्त्यामेके अभितो वार्षिकं सर्वे वर्षविद्युतस्तनयित्नुसन्निपाते प्रस्पन्दिन्यूर्ध्वं भोजनाद्युत्सवे प्राधीतस्य च निशायां चतुर्मुहूर्तं नित्यमेके नगरे मानसमप्यशुचि श्राद्धिनामाकालिक-मकृतान्नश्राद्धिकसंयोगे च प्रतिविद्यञ्च यावत् स्मरन्ति प्रतिविद्यञ्च यावत् स्मरन्ति॥

Observing perfect continence, and with all the hairs of his body shaved, one should read the Vedas *in* the months of *Śrāvaṇa* and *Bhādhra,* or during the five months the sun follows the southern, course. One should not eat cooked meat during the time. These vows should be observed for two months or mare. The Vedas should not be studied, on days when the soaring winds raise up clouds of dust from the ground, nor on nights when claps of thunder, or peals of trumpets, or sounds of drums, or barks of dogs, or brayings of asses, or howlings of jackals are heard, nor when thick mists enshroud the earth, in an unnatural season of the year, nor when purple rainbows are observed to span the firmament.

One should not study the Vedas while attending to a call of nature. Several authorities aver that the Vedas should not be studied an rainy evenings; nor on days or nights, when the sun or the moon is founded to be surrounded by rings of haloe, nor while seating on ant-hills. One should not study the Vedas while in a state of fright; nor while riding a carriage, nor while seated with a leg cocked up. One should not study the Vedas during the term of a birth-, or death uncleanness, nor at a cremation ground, nor by the side of a high road. Similarly, the Vedas should not be read near a Śūdra or a *Cāṇḍāla* (Divākīrti), not at places exhaling a fetid smell or containing carcasses. One should not study the Vedas during the term of a birth-uncleanness, nor having had *(lit.* after the rising of) eructations. The Vedas should not be read on the happening, in an unnatural season, of such physical phenomena as roarings of rain clouds, earth-quakes, meteor-falls, down-pours of rain and flashes of lightning. Likewise the Vedas should not be read during conflagrations of fire, or on descents of thunder-bolts in unnatural seasons of the year. The *Ṛk* and *Yajur* Vedas should not be read after having heard the chantings of *Śāman*. Similarly, roars of rain-clouds, heard in the small hours of the night and before the expiry of the third watch; interdicts the study of the Vedas *on* (the next morning). Several authorities aver that flashes of lightning seen in the morning should be likewise considered as prohibitive of the study of the Vedas. No part or portion of the Vedas should be read on evenings; marked by claps of thunder, or roars of rain clouds. Roars of rain clouds, heard after the mid-night, prohibit the study of the Vedas on the next morning. Similarly, roars of rain clouds heard on the morning interdict the study of the Vedas during the entire day. The death of the king of one's country, as well as interviews of friends on returning from a foreign, country, should be regarded as instances on which the study of the Vedas is prohibited. On the day on which the reading of a Veda, commenced before, is fmished, all further studies should be regarded as interdicted by law. The Vedas should not be studied on the occasion of *a Śrāddha* ceremony, or friendly feast, nor on the reader haying suffered from vomiting that day. Non-study for two days has been enjoined from the day of the new moon, each month, and the Vedas should not be studied on days of the full moon, in the months of *Kārtika, Phālguna,* and *Āṣāḍa.* For three nights one should refrain from studying the Vedas on the advent of the three *Aṣṭakas.* According to certain authorities, such prohibition exists only in respect of the last *Aṣṭakā.* One should not study the Vedas on the occasion of friendly dinners. Several authorities aver that the study of the Vedas *is* prohibited during the first three hours and a half of each night. That portion of *a* Veda, which has once been studied, should not be read over again. One should refrain from studying the Vedas in a town, nor they should be read near the performer of *a Śrāddha* ceremony who has not fed the Brāhmaṇas with boiled rice, nor till one can recollect them.

इति गौतमीये धर्मशास्त्रे षोड़शोऽध्याय:॥ १६॥

Chapter 17

प्रशस्तानां स्वकर्मसु द्विजातीनां ब्राह्मणो भुञ्जीत प्रतिगृह्णीयाच्चैधोदकयवसमूलफलमध्वभयाभ्युद्यतशय्यासनयानपयोदधिधानाशफरिप्रियङ्गुस्रङ्मार्गशाकान्यप्रणोद्यानि। सर्वेषां पितृदेवगुरुभृत्यभरणे चान्यवृत्तिश्चेन्नान्तरेण शूद्रात् पशुपालक्षेत्रकर्षककुलसंगतकारपितृपरिचारका भोज्यान्ना वणिक्चाशिल्पी नित्यमभोज्यं केशकीटावपन्नं रजस्वलाकृष्टशकुनिपदोपहतं भ्रूणघ्नप्रेक्षितं गवोपघ्रातं भावदुष्टं शुक्तं केवलमदधि पुनःसिद्धं पर्युषितमशाकभक्ष्यस्नेहमांसमधुन्युत्सृष्टपुंश्चल्यभिशस्तानपदेश्यदन्तिकतक्षकदर्यबन्धनिकचिकित्सकमृगयुकारुच्छिष्टभोजिगणविद्विपाषाणमपाङ्क्त्यानां प्रागदुर्बलाद्वृथान्नाचमनोनीत्थानव्यपेतानि। समासमाभ्यां विषमसमे पूजान्तरानर्ष्टितञ्च। गोश्च क्षीरमनिर्द्दशायाः सूतके चाजामहिष्योश्च नित्यमाविकमपयेमौष्ट्रमैकशफञ्च स्यन्दिनीयमसूसन्धिनीनाञ्च याश्च व्यपेतवत्साः। पञ्चनखाश्चाशल्यकशशकश्चाविद्गोधाखड्गकच्छपाः उभयतोदत्केशलोमैकशफकलविङ्कल्पलवचक्रवाकहंसाः काककङ्कगृध्नश्येना जलजा रक्तपादतुण्डा ग्राम्यकुक्कुटशूकरौ धेन्वनडुहौ, चापन्नदावसन्नवृथामांसानि किसलयक्यांकुलशुननिर्यासलोहितव्रश्चनाश्चनिचिदारुवकलाकटिट्रिभमांधातृनक्तञ्चरा अभक्ष्याः। भक्ष्याः प्रतुदाविष्किरा जालपादा मत्स्याश्चाविकृता वध्याश्च धर्मार्थे व्यालहता दृष्टदोषवाक्प्रशस्तान्यभ्युक्ष्योपयुंजीतोपयुंजीत॥

Brāhmaṇas should eat in the houses of twice-born ones, true to their proper duties in life, and boldly receive, for the performance of their *Daiva* and *Pitṛ Śrāddha* ceremonies, as well as for the support of their preceptors and servants, the unsolicited gifts of commendable water, barley, fruits, honey, edible roots, beds, cushions, milk, paddy, milk-curd, fish, *Priyaṅgus* (a kind of creeper) flowers, *Kuśa* grass and vegetables. Even Brāhmaṇas, who have abjured their own vocations, should receive those gifts from all except the Śūdras. Brāhmaṇas may safely partake of boiled rice, belonging to the keepers of their own domestic animals, or to tillers of their own lands, or to their own paternal servants, or to hereditary friends of their families, even if such keepers of animals, tillers of lands, servants, and hereditary friends be Śūdras; but they cannot eat boiled-rice belonging to

Śūdras, not falling under any of the foregoing categories. Boiled-rice of traders other than actual artisans may be safely partaken of by Brāhmaṇas. Boiled rice, defiled by the touch of hairs or insects, should never be eaten. Boiled rice, touched by a woman in her menses, or trampled down by a bird, or looked at by a destroyer of human fetus.(procurer of abortion), ox smelled by a cow, or having an offensive look, or served without any curries, salads, or milk-curd, as well as that which is stale, and twice-cooked should not be eaten. Boiled rice served without cooked edible leaves (Śakas) or saturated with unwholesome fatty matters, offensive to taste, as well as putrid meat or honey should not be eaten. Boiled rice, collected from the refuge of other men's plates, or cooked by a prostitute, or belonging be an accursed individual, or to a man of low parentage, or to one under the ban of law or punished by a royal court (of justice,) or to a carpenter, miser, hunter, captive, artisan, or a professional physician, as well as that given by one's enemy, or by *Uchchishta Bhoji,* or by a Brāhmaṇa, falling under the category of one supposed to defile a row of Brāhmaṇas seated down to a dinner *(Apankteya)* should not be partaken of. Eating before the weaklings (of one's family) have taken their meals should be regarded as prohibited. Boiled rice, not formally dedicated to *a* deity, or in respect of which the rite of *Ācamanam* has not been performed, as well as the one which one can not leave at will, should not be eaten. Pure and impure boiled rice should not be promiscuously mixed together. Boiled rice, which has not been consecrated by having been offered unto a deity in the course of a *Pujā,* should not be partaken of. The milk of a parturient cow should not be used till before the expiry of ten days from the date of her parturition. Similarly, the milk of a she-goat, or of a she-buffalo should not be used till before the expiry of ten days from the date of her delivery. The milk of an ewe or of a she-camel, or of a female animal with un-bifurcated hoofs should not be used at all. The milk of a cow in heat, or of one showing inclination to be impregnated, as well as that of one whose calf is dead, should never be used. The flesh of all five-nailed animals except that of a porcupine, hare, *Ghodā* (a genus of large lizards) rhinoceros, or a tortoise should be rejected as unfit for human consumption. The flesh of an animal possessing two rows of teeth, or of one possessing both *wool* and hair, or of one with unbifurcated hoops, as well as that of *Kalavinka* (sparrow), diver, crane *(Chakravāka),* swan, crow, valture, hawk, or domestic cock, or of a bird whose head and legs are red, together with the flesh of a boar, Cow, or bullock, should never be eaten. Boiled rice (food) not prepared for, and offered unto, a deity, as well as the flesh of an animal, not slaughtered in connection with a religious sacrifice, should never be eater. Garlic's, tender shoots of trees, as well as milky exudations and red saps of plants or trees should be regarded as unfit for human use. The flesh of a wood-pecker, heron, *Tittibha, Māndhātri* and such like birds, as well as that of birds that fly by night, should not be eaten. The flesh of *Pratudas* (birds that dart upon their prey), of *Vishikeras* (birds that scatter their food with legs before eating), of web-footed birds, wholesome fish, as well as flesh of those enjoined to be slaughtered in connection with a religious sacrifice, or of those not killed by any poisnous beast or reptile, and wholesome flesh in general may be eaten.

इति गौतमीये धर्मशास्त्रे सप्तदशोऽध्याय:॥ १७॥

Chapter 18

अस्वतंत्रा धर्मे स्त्री नातिचरेद्धर्तारं वाक्चक्षु:कर्मसंयता पतिरपत्यलिप्सुर्देवराद् गुरुप्रसूता नर्त्तुमतीयात् पिण्डगोत्रऋषिसम्बन्धिभ्यो योनिमात्राद्वा। नादेवरादित्येके। नातिद्वितीयं जनयितुरपत्यं समयादन्यत्र जीवतश्च क्षेत्रे परस्मात् तस्य द्वयोर्वा रक्षणाद्धर्त्तुरिव नष्टे भर्त्तरि षाड्वार्षिकं क्षपणं श्रूयमाणेऽभिगमनं प्रव्रजिते तु निवृत्ति: प्रसङ्गात् तस्य द्वादशवर्षाणि ब्राह्मणस्य विद्यासम्बन्धे भ्रातरि चैवं ज्यायसि यवीयान् कन्याग्न्युपयमनेषु षडित्येके। त्रीन् कुमार्युतूनतीत्य स्वयं युज्येतानिन्दितेनोत्सृज्य पित्र्यानलङ्कारान् प्रदानं प्रागृतोरप्रयच्छन् दोषो प्राग्वासस: प्रतिपत्तेरित्येके द्रव्यादानं विवाहसिद्ध्यर्थं धर्मतन्त्रसंयोगे च शूद्रादन्यत्रापि शूद्राद्बहुपशोर्हीनकर्मण: शतगोरनाहिताग्नि:

सहस्त्रगोश्च सोमपात् ससमीक्षाभुक्त्वा निचयायाप्यहीनकर्मभ्य आचक्षीत राज्ञा पृष्टस्तने हि भर्त्तव्यः श्रुतशीलसम्पन्नश्चेद्धर्मतन्त्रपीडायां तस्याकरणे दोषोऽदोषः।

A woman (wife) is subservient to her lord even in respect of doing religious acts, and she should never supersede him (act independently of him) in these matters. Controlled in her speech, mind, and senses, during her menstrual period, she, after the death of her husband, should evince her desire to be the mother of a mate child by her husbands younger brother, In the absence of such an uterine brother of her deceased husband, she should yet herself impregnated, for giving birth to a male child, by a *Sapinda* or a cognate relation, standing in the same category even through ties of spiritual clanship (*Ṛ-is*), or bearing her the same relationship through the female line. Under no circumstances, she should let her menstrual period pass unfruitful. The causation of the birth of a male child in the womb of a widow by any one, not related to her a her husband's younger brother (or cousin), is interdicted according to the opinion of certain authorities. A widow, under the circumstance, will not be competent to get herself more than twice impregnated by her dead husband's brother. In the absence of any express stipulation, sons, begotten on her person, shall belong to their progenitor. Sons, begotten on the field (wife) of a person, who is alive, shall belong to the legitimate husband of the wife, or they shall be regarded as belonging both to their progenitor and the husband of their mother. In fact the father ship in these cases shall belong to either of these two persons (progenitor *or* mother's husband) who shall maintain the children.

A wife is bound to wait for six years for a husband who is unheard of, and to go to him on hearing of him. A wife shall refrain from even talking about her husband in the event of his taking to asceticism. Similarly, a Brāhmaṇa shall wait for twelve years, or for six years, according to several authorities, for an elder brother, considered in the relationship of fellow students of the Vedas, in matters of keeping the sacred fire, or of marrying his daughters, etc.

After her three successive menstrual periods, an unmarried girl, happened to be not given away in marriage by her father or paternal kinsmen, shall renounce the ornaments given her by her parents, and shall be competent thereafter to marry a commendable bride-groom in express defiance of her father, or father's friends. A girl should be given in marriage before she menstruates-, and her guardians commit sin by not marrying her before that time. According to certain authorities, a daughter should be married before having her age of girlhood.

Money (gifts) may be taken from Śūdras for the purpose of celebrating a nuptial or sacrificial ceremony. For other acts as well, money gifts may be received from Śūdras, possessing a large number of cattle, from Brāhmaṇas, not keepers of the sacred fire, who are respectively masters of a hundred heads of cattle and are given to low pursuits, and from *Somapas,* who are respectively masters of a thousand heads of cattle. Articles of fare should be taken by one from persons of noble pursuit, in the event of one remaining without food up to the seventh part of the day. Every body is duly bound to speak the truth to his sovereign. A king is bound to support Brāhmaṇas of good conduct who are well-versed in the Vedas, in the event of their practice of virtues being interfered with by thoughts of maintenance; otherwise he shall acquire demerit.

इति गौतमीये धर्मशास्त्रेऽष्टादशोऽध्याय:॥ १८॥

Chapter 19

उक्तो वर्णधर्मश्चाश्रमधर्मश्चाथ खल्वयं पुरुषो कर्मणा लिप्यतेऽथैतदयाज्ययाजनमभक्ष्यभक्षणवद्यवदनं शिष्टस्याक्रिया प्रतिषिद्ध-सेवनमिति च तत्र प्रायश्चित्तं कुर्यान्न कुर्यादिति मीमांसन्ते न कुर्यादित्याहुर्नहि कर्म क्षीयत इति कुर्यादित्यपरे पुन: स्तोमेनेष्ट्वा पुन: सवनमायातीति विज्ञायते व्रात्यस्तोमेनेष्ट्वा तरति सर्वं पाप्मानं तरति ब्रह्महत्यां योऽश्वमेधेन यजतेऽग्निष्टुतामिशस्यमानं याजयेदिति च। तस्य निष्क्रयणानि जपस्तपो होम उपवासो दानमुपनिषदो वेदान्ता: सर्वच्छन्द:सु संहिता मधून्यघमर्षणमथर्वशिरोरुद्रा: पुरुषसूक्तं राजनरौहिणे सामनी बृहद्रथन्तरे पुरुषगतिर्महानाम्न्यो महावैराजं महादिवाकीर्त्त्यं ज्येष्ठसाम्नामन्यतमद्बहिष्पवमानं कूष्माण्डानि पावमान्य: सावित्री चेति पावनानि। पयोव्रतता शाकभक्षता फलभक्षता प्रसृतयावको हिरण्यप्राशनं घृतप्राशनं सोमपानमिति च मेध्यानि।

सर्वे शिलोच्चयाः सर्वाः स्रवन्त्यः पुण्या ह्रदास्तीर्थानि ऋषिनिवासगोष्ठपरिस्कन्दा इति देशाः। ब्रह्मचर्यं सत्यवचनं सवनेषूदकोपस्पर्शनमार्द्रवस्त्रताधःशायिताऽनाशक इति तपांसि। हिरण्यं गौर्वासोऽश्वो भूमिस्तिला घृतमन्नमिति देयानि। संवत्सरः षण्मासाश्चत्वारस्त्रयो द्वावेकश्चतुर्विंशत्यहो द्वादशाहः षडहस्त्र्यहोऽहोरात्र इति कालाः। एतान्येवानादेशे विकल्पेन क्रियेरन् एनःसु गुरुषु गुरूणि लघुषु लघुनि कृच्छ्रातिकृच्छ्रं चान्द्रायणमिति सर्वप्रायश्चित्तं सर्वप्रायश्चित्तम्।

Duties appertaining to (different) castes and orders of society have been described. Now I shall describe the acts by doing which a person becomes sinful. Now we shall discuss about the necessity of (atoning for the sin of) officiating as priests at the religious sacrifices of those who should not be thus served, of eating interdicted articles of fare, of omitting to do the proper acts, of speaking falsehood or that which should not be spoken, and of enjoying forbidden things. Several authorities aver that atonement is of no avail, since (our) acts are indestructible; while others opine that atonement *(Prāyascittam) is* necessary. The Vedic aphorism that " by performing an *Agniṣṭoma* sacrifice over again, one gets progeny" predicates the necessity of one's making atonement for one's sin, "A vow breaker, or a person not initiated with the holy thread (*Vrātya)* becomes absolved of his sin by celebrating an *:Agniṣṭoma* sacrifice." "A Brahmanicide is exonerated from his sin by celebrating a horse-sacrifice." A penitent should be caused to celebrate an *Agnishtuta* sacrifice." These Vedic aphorisms emphatically demonstrate the necessity of atoning for one's sin. For the expiation of his sin, a sinner should practise penitential austerities, observe fasts, practise charities, perform *Homas,* and read the *Upaniṣads,* the *Vedānta,* the *Saṁhitās* forming the sub-divisions of the Vedas, and the *Madhūvata, Aghamarṣaṇam, Atharvaśiras, Rudrādhyāyam, Puruṣa-Sūktam, Rajan-Rahin Sāman, Rathāntaram, Puruṣagatim, Mahānāmnim, Mahā-Yairājam, Mahādivātkirtyam, Mahiṣyavamānam, Kuṣmānāam, Pāvamānim, Sāvitrim,* and any of the *Yeṣiya Sāma Mantras.* One's sins may be absolved by one's living simply on water, by abjuring all food except leaves of edible plants or trees, by living only on barley diet, by licking gold, by drinking melted butter or Soma-juice, or by eating only fruits.

A pilgrimage to any of the sacred pools or rivers, or a sojourn to a hermitage, mountain, or pasturage is purifying in its effect. Observance of perfect continence, truthfulness, touching of water, fasting and lying down on the ground in wet cloths, are what constitute *Tapasyā.* Gifts of gold, cows, clothes, horses, lands, sesame seeds, melted butter, and food should be made. Twelve months, six months, four months, three months, two months, one month, or twenty-four days, twelve days, six days, three days, or one entire day and night should be respectively understood as terms of penitential penances. Any of the aforesaid measures of atonement should be adopted according to the nature of the place at which a person atones for his guilt. The austerity of these penances should be proportionate to the heinousness of one's sin. The practice of a *Kṛccham, Ati-kṛccham, Kṛcchati-Kṛccham,* or *Cāndrāyaṇam* penance should be regarded as a sufficient atonement for all kinds of sin.

इति गौतमीये धर्मशास्त्रे एकोनविंशोऽध्यायः॥ १९॥

Chapter 20

अथ चतुःषष्टिषु यातनास्थानेषु दुःखान्यनुभूय तत्रेमानि लक्षणानि भवन्ति ब्रह्महार्द्रकुष्ठी सुरापः श्यावदन्तो, गुरुतल्पगः, पङ्गवन्धः, स्वर्णहारी, कुनखी, श्वित्री, वस्त्रापहारी, हिरण्यहारी, दर्दुरी, तेजोऽपहारी मण्डली, स्नेहापहारी क्षयी, तथाजीर्णवानन्नापहारी, ज्ञानापहारी मूकः, प्रतिहन्ता गुरोरपस्मारी, गोघ्नो जात्यन्धा, पिशुनः पूतिनासः, पूतिवक्त्रस्तु सूचकः शूद्रोपाध्यायः श्वपाकस्त्रपुसौसचामरविक्रयी मद्यप, एकशफविक्रयी मृगव्याधः कुण्डाशी मृतकश्चैलिको वा नक्षत्री चार्बुदी नास्तिको रङ्गोपजीव्यभक्ष्यभक्षी गण्डरी, ब्रह्मपुरुष तस्कराणां देशिकः पिण्डितः षण्ढो महापथिक गण्डिकश्चण्डालो पुक्कसी गोष्ववकीर्णो मध्वामेही, धर्मपत्नीषु स्यान्मैथुनप्रवर्त्तकः खल्वाटगोत्रसमयस्त्र्यभिगामी पितृमातृभगिनीस्त्र्यभिगाम्या-

वीजितस्तेषां कुब्जकुण्डमण्डव्याधितव्यङ्गदरिद्राल्पायुषोऽल्पबुद्ध्यश्चण्डपण्ड-शैलूषतस्करपरपुरुषप्रेष्यपरकर्मकराः खल्वाटचक्राङ्गसङ्कीर्णाः क्रूरकर्माणः क्रमशश्चान्त्याश्चोपपद्यन्ते तस्मात् कर्त्तव्यमेवेह प्रायश्चित्तं विशुद्धैर्लक्षणैर्जायन्ते धर्मस्य धारणादिति धारणादिति।

Sinners, after suffering torments at sixty four different places of torture, are respectively reborn with the following physical deformities, or diseases. A Brahmanicide is reborn as a phagedenic lepor, a drunkard is reborn with black teeth, and a defiler of his preceptor's bed is reborn as a congenital blind or maimed person. A gold-stcaler suffers from bad nails at his next incarnation, a cloth-stealer is punished with psoriasis, a fire-stealer is punished with ring-like patches of eruptions on his skin, an oil-stealer is punished with pthisis, a gold-stealer is afflicted with ring-worm, a stealer of edible things is afflicted with indigestion, and a knowledge-stealer is punished with dumbness at their next birth. A man who kills his own preceptor is tormented with epileptic fits at his next incarnation. A cow-killer is reborn as a blind individual, a tell-tale is reborn as one with putrid nose, and a poisoner of other men's ears is tormented with fetour in his mouth at his next birth. A teacher of Śūdra students is reborn as a *Cāṇḍāla.* A seller of lead, of brass, or of Chowries is afflicted with the vice of drunkness at his next rebirth. A seller of animals with unbifurcated hoops is sure to be born in the womb of a female huntress at his next incarnation. A partaker of *a Kunda's* boiled rice is reborn in a family of menial servants. An astronomer suffers from tumours at his next birth, an atheist is reborn as a professional actor, an eater of interdicted articles of fare is tormented with boils and tumours at his next birth, a guide to a stealer of men or of the Vedas *is* reborn as an eunuch, and a carnal knower of a cow, or of *a. Caṇḍāli* or *Pukkasa* woman is afflicted with diabetes at his next birth. A husband, who induces his own virtuous wife to lie with another man, is reborn as a blind individual. A person who carnally knows a courtesan or a woman of his own *Gotra,* as well as he who holds incest with, his own father's or mother's sister, is successively reborn as a haunch back, dwarf, insane, diseased, deformed, indigent, short-lived, foolish, irascible, worthless, thievish, carrying out other men's behests, baldpated, and miscreant person in low and vulgar families. Hence one should atone for one's sin. Atonement preserves one's virtues intact and helps one to be reborn with commendable attributes and physical traits.

इति गौतमीये धर्मशास्त्रे विंशोऽध्याय:॥ २०॥

Chapter 21

त्यजेत् पितरं राजघातकं शूद्रायाजकं वेदविप्लावकं भ्रूणहनं यश्चान्त्यावसायिभि: सह संवसेदन्त्यावसायिन्या वा तस्य विद्यागुरून् योनिसम्बन्धांश्च सन्निपात्य सर्वाण्युदकादीनि प्रेतकर्माणि कुर्यु पात्रञ्चास्य विपर्यस्येयु:। दास: कर्मकरो वावकरादमेध्यपात्रमानीय दासी घटान् पूरयित्वा दक्षिणामुख: पदा विपर्यस्येदमनुदकं करोमिति नामग्राहस्तं सर्वेऽन्वालभेरन् प्राचीनावीतिनो मुक्तिशिखा विद्यागुरवो योनिसम्बन्धाश्च वीक्षेरन्नप उपस्पृश्य ग्रामं प्रविशन्ति। अत ऊर्ध्वं तेन सम्भाष्य तिष्ठेदेकरात्रं जपन् सावित्रीमज्ञानपूर्वं ज्ञानपूर्वञ्चेत् त्रिरात्रम्।

यस्तु प्रायश्चित्तेन शुध्येत तस्मिन् शुद्धे शातकुम्भमयं पात्रं पुण्यतमात् ह्रदात् पूरयित्वा स्रवन्तीभ्यो वा तत एनमप उपस्पर्शेयु:। अथास्मै तत्पात्रं दद्युस्तत् सम्प्रतिगृह्य जपेच्छान्ता द्यौ: शान्ता पृथिवी शान्तं शिवमन्तरीक्षं यो रोचनस्तमिह गृह्णामीत्येतैर्यजुभि: पावमानीभिस्तरत्समन्दीभि: कुष्माण्डैश्चाज्यं जुहुयाद्धिरण्यं ब्राह्मणाय वा दद्यात् गां चाचार्याय। यस्य तु प्राणान्तिकं प्रायश्चित्तं स मृत: शुध्येत्। तस्य सर्वाण्युदकादीनि प्रेतकर्माणिकुर्युरेतदेव शान्त्युदकं सर्वेषूपपातकेषूपपातकेषु।

A man should renounce a father who is a regicide, or an insulter of the Vedas, or attends on Śūdras as a priest, or procures abortions. Teachers and marriage-relations of a man, who mixes freely with Śūdra men and women of *Antyāvasāyin* class, should assemble together to interdict the offering of libations of water unto his spirit, after death No funeral rites should be done unto him after his death, and the vessels to be used in the course of this interdicting rite should be of a defiling character. Slaves or servants should be sent to a town for fetching such polluted vessels. Then a slave girl should be ordered to fetch a pitcher full of water, and the man to be interdicted should be caused to stand with his legs apart, and with his face turned towards the south. Then the congregated persons shall loudly utter, "let us interdict the offering of libations of water unto this man." So saying they will mention the name of the interdicted individual and catch hold of one another's arms. His teachers and marriage relations, after having performed *Ācamanam* in the manner of *Prācināvali,* shall cast a look at his face and enter the village by a separate path.

He, who unknowingly speaks to such a person after the ceremony of formal interdiction, should regain his purity by repeating the *Sāvitri Mantra* for a whole night in a standing posture, while having knowingly conversed with him, he should repeat standing the *Sāvitri Mantram* for three consecutive nights. In the event of his agreeing to do the necessary expiating penance, a golden pitcher should be caused to be filled with the water of a holy lake, and the interdicted person should be sprinkled over with water out of that. After that, the same pitcher should be successively made over to, and taken back from, the penitent, and the attending priest should recite the *Śāntam Dau, Śāntā Pṛthivi, etc., Mantram* from the Yajur Veda. After that, libations of melted butter should be cast in the sacred fire by reciting the *Pāvaminim, Taratsamandi* and *Kūṣmāṇḍī Mantras.* As an alternative gold should be gifted to a Brāhmaṇa and a cow to an *Ācārya.* He, in respect of whom expiation by death has been laid down, should do the proper penance and atone for his sin with his life. All funeral rites should be duly done unto his spirit after his death. Sprinkling of bliss-giving water over the penitent is laid down in respect of all minor delinquencies.

इति गौतमीये धर्मशास्त्रे एकविंशोऽध्यायः॥ २१॥

Chapter 22

ब्रह्मह-सुराप-गुरुतल्पगमातृपितृयोनिसम्बन्धगस्तेन-नास्तिक-निन्दितकर्माभ्यासिपतितात्यागयपतिता-त्यागिनः पातकसंयोजकाश्च तैश्चाब्दं समाचरन्। द्विजातिकर्मभ्यो हानिः पतनं परत्र चासिद्धिस्तामेके नरकं त्रीणि प्रथमान्यनिर्देश्यानि मनुः। न स्त्रीष्वगुरुतल्पगः पततीत्येके भ्रूणहनि हीनवर्णसेवायाञ्च स्त्री पतति कौटसाक्ष्यं राजगामिपैशुनं गुरोरनृताभिशंसनं महापातकसमानि अपांक्त्यानां प्राग्दुर्बलाद्गोहन्तृब्रह्मोज्झतन्मंत्रकृदवकीर्ण-पतितसावित्रिकेषूपपातकं याजनाध्यापनादृत्विगाचार्यौ पतनीयसेवायाञ्च-हेयौवन्यत्र हानात् पतति। तस्य च परतिग्रहीतेत्येके। न कर्हिचिन्मातापित्रोरवृत्तिदायन्तु न भजेरन्। ब्राह्मणाभिशंसने दोषस्तावान् द्विरनेनसि दुर्बलहिंसायामपि मोचने शक्तश्चेत्। अभिक्रध्यावगीरणं ब्राह्मणस्यवर्षशतमस्वर्ग्यं, निर्घाते सहस्रं, लोहितदर्शने यावतस्तत्प्रस्कन्द्य पांशून् संगृह्णीयात्।

Brahmanicides, drunkards, men who defile the bed of their own *Gurus,* as well as persons who carnally know any female relations on their father's or mother's side, atheists, miscreants, and men, who do not renounce, the degraded or keep their company, should be regarded as degraded persons.

Those, who associate with these (degraded) persons for a year, become themselves degraded. Degradation or fall in these instances means deprivation of the rights and privileges of a Brāhmaṇas, and a degraded status in the next world. According to certain authorities. "Degradation" spells as hell. Manu has not included the first three of these heinous sins regarding woman within his list of sinful acts. Several authorities aver that a procurer of abortions, even if he does not defile the bed of his preceptor, should be regarded as a *Mahāpātakin.* A woman, by carnally knowing a man, inferior to her in caste, becomes degraded. Bearing false witness, malice shown towards one's own king, and speaking falsehood to one's preceptor, should be regarded as acts equal to *Mahāpātakas* in their atrociousness. Of Brāhmaṇas who are not competent to sit in the same row with other good Brāhmanas *(Apaṅkteyas),* beef eaters, denouncers of the Vedas, *Avakīrṇas* and those who have renounced the use of vedic *Mantras* or of the sacred *Gāyatrī,* should be regarded as *Upapātakins* (minor sinners) *Ṛtviks* or teachers, attending as priests at any religious ceremony undertaken by any of these individuals, or giving instructions to any of them in scriptural knowledge, should be looked down upon by the society, and they should be held as degraded under certain circumstances. According to certain authorities, people who receive gifts from any of these people should be regarded as degraded. But no sin appertains to parents in receiving gifts from degraded sons, but degraded sons are disqualified from inheriting properties coming down from their parents. By falsely caluminating a Brāhmaṇa in society, one becomes equally degraded (as any of the aforementioned persons). By casting a false obloquy upon an innocent Brāhmaṇas, one acquires twice as much demerit as a calumniator of the foregoing type. A capable man that looks with indifference at the oppression of a weak person by a strong one, when he can fully succour such a distressed person, becomes doubly sinful. For rudely attacking or insulting a Brāhmaṇa, one is punished with a residence for a hundred years in hell. By thus assaulting a Brāhmaṇa one resides for a thousand years in hell, By drawing blood on his person one resides in hell for as many number of years as the number of dusts with which he dusts his wound.

इति गौतमीये धर्मशास्त्रे द्वाविंशोऽध्याय:॥ २२॥

Chapter 23

प्रायश्चित्तमग्नौ शक्तिर्ब्रह्मघ्नस्त्रिरवच्छादितस्य लक्ष्यं वा स्याज्जन्ये शस्त्रभृताम्। खट्वाङ्गकपालपाणिर्वा द्वादशसंवत्सरान् ब्रह्मचारी भैक्षाय ग्रामं प्रविशेत् स्वकर्माचक्षाण:, पथोपक्रामेत् सन्दर्शनादार्यस्य। स्नानासनाभ्यां विहरन् सवनेषूदकोपस्पर्शी शुध्येत्। प्राणलाभे वा तन्निमित्ते ब्राह्मणस्य द्रव्यापचये वा त्र्यवरं प्रति राज्ञोऽश्वमेधावभृथे वान्ययज्ञेऽप्य-ग्निष्टुदन्तश्चोत्सृष्टश्चेद्ब्राह्मणवधे। हत्वापि आत्रेयाश्चैवं गर्भे चाविज्ञाते वा। ब्राह्मणस्य राजन्यवधे षड्वार्षिकं प्राकृतं ब्रह्मचर्यं ऋषभैकसहस्राश्च गा दद्यात्।

वैश्ये त्रैवार्षिकं ऋषभैकशताश्च गा दद्यात्। शूद्रे संवत्सरमृषभैकदशाश्च गा दद्यादनात्रेयाञ्चैव गाञ्च। वैश्यवत्मण्डूकनकुलकाकविवरचरमूषिकाश्च। हिंसासु चास्थिमतां सहस्रं हत्वानस्थिमतामनडुद्धारे च। अपि वास्थिमतामेकैकस्मिन् किञ्चिद्दद्यात् षण्ढे च पलालभारः सीसमाषश्च वराहे घृतघटः, सर्पे लौहदण्डो, ब्रह्मबन्ध्वाञ्च ललनायां जीवोवैशिकेन किंचित् तल्पान्नधनलाभवधेषु पृथग्वर्षाणि द्वे, परदारे त्रीणि। श्रोत्रियस्य द्रव्यलाभे चोत्सर्गो यथास्थानं वा गमयेत्। प्रतिसिद्धमन्त्रसंयोगे सहस्रवाक् चेदग्न्युत्सादिनिराकृत्युपपातकेषु, चैव स्त्री चातिचारिणी गुप्ता पिण्डन्तु लभेत। अमानुषीषु गोवर्जस्त्रीकृते कुष्माण्डैर्घृतहोमो घृतहोमः।

A Brahmanicide, without in any .way covering or shielding his body, shall thrice pass through a blazing fire, or shall make himself the target of a soldier in battle, or shall roam about begging for twelve years in the garb of a *Brahmacārin,* carrying a *Khaṭvaṅga (club)* and a human skull in his hands, confessing his guilt to the world. He shall turn away from the sight of an Ārya. A Brahmanicide, by duly performing three ablutions, and by practising the *Āsanas* (postures of *Yoga)* at morning, noon, and evening, each day, shall perform the rite of *Ācamanam,* whereby he will regain his personal purity. As an alternative he shall thrice combat with a man, who has stolen all the possessions of a Brāhmaṇa, for the recovery thereof; and he shall be adjudged pure even if he dies in his attempt at recovering the goods of such a Brāhmaṇa; or under the circumstance, he shall give to a Brāhmaṇas that much money for the loss of which he contemplates to put an end to his life. A king, having killed a Brāhmaṇa, should regain his personal purity by performing an *Avabhṛtha* ablution after the celebration of a horse-sacrifice, or he should perform any0 other *Agnistut* sacrifice by Way of atonement. Having killed a woman in- her menses or a pregnant woman in whom signs of pregnancy have not been fully patent, one should practise the foregoing kind of expiatory penance. A Brāhmaṇa, having killed a Kṣatriya; should practise, for six years, the most austere of penances, and at the close of that he should make the gift of a bullock and a thousand kine. Having killed a

Vaiśya, he should practise, for three years, the same austerities, and make the gift of bullock and a hundred kine. Having killed a Śūdra, a Brāhmaṇa should practise, for a year, the same austere *Brahmacaryayam,* and make the gift of a bullock together with ten cows. The same expiatory penance should be practised for atoning the sin of killing a cow or a woman who has not menstruated.

Having killed a frog, ichneumon crow, she-mouse, or a hole-dwelling animal, one should practise the same expiatory penance as laid down in respect of atoning the sin of a Vaiśya-killing. Having killed a thousand of such vertebrate animals as lizards etc., or a cart-load of such invertebrate vermins as bugs, leeches, lice, etc., one should practise the same expiatory penance as the foregoing one. As an alternative a small gift should be made to a Brāhmaṇa for each animal destroyed. Having killed a eunuch, or a man with rudimentary (undeveloped) genitals, one should make the gift of a *Palāla* weight of lead and *Masha* pulse to a Brāhmaṇa. Having killed a boar, one should make the gift of a pitcherful of clarified butter to a Brāhmaṇa. Having killed a serpent, one should make the gift of an iron rod to a Brāhmaṇa. Having killed a *Brahmavandhu* (nominal Brāhmaṇa) woman, one should make the gift of an animal to a Brāhmaṇa, whereas no such expiatory gifts should be made after having killed *a Venujivin* (one who lives by making bamboo-made articles). Having committed homicides out of greed for wealth, food, or beddings, one should practise *Brahmacaryayam* for a couple of years for each act of man killing. Having killed an individual, attached to another man's wife, one should practise *Brahmacaryayam* for three years in succession. Having picked up an article belonging to a *Śrotriya,* one should return it to its owner, or renounce its possession. Having uttered a thousand words in combination with an interdicted *Mantra,* one should perform an *Agnyutsāde or Nirākṛti* penance, which is the atonement for all *Upapātakas* (minor sins). A false wife should be kept imprisoned in a room, on an allowance of daily sustenance. Having held incest with a female beast, other than a cow, one should recite the *Kūṣmāṇḍa Mantram,* and perform a *Homa* with libations of melted butter.

इति गौतमीये धर्मशास्त्रे त्रयोविंशोऽध्याय:॥ २ ३॥

Chapter 24

सुरापस्य ब्राह्मणस्योष्णामासिञ्चेयु: सुरामास्ये मृत: शुध्येदमत्या पाने पयोघृतमुदकं वायुं प्रतित्र्यहं तप्तानि सकृच्छ्रस्ततोऽस्य संस्कार:। मूत्रपरीषरेतसाञ्च प्राशने श्वापदोष्ट्रखराणाञ्चाङ्गस्य ग्राम्यकुक्कुटशूकरयोश्च गन्धाघ्राणे सुरापस्य प्राणायामो घृतप्राशनञ्च पूर्वैश्च दष्टस्य (दृष्टस्य)। तल्पे लोहशयने गुरुतल्पग: शयीत सूर्मीं वा ज्वलन्तीं श्लिष्येल्लिङ्गं वा सवृषणमुत्कृत्याञ्जलावाधाय दक्षिणाप्रतीचीं (दिशं) व्रजेदजिह्ममा-शरीरनिपातान्मृत: शुध्येत्। सखीसयोनिसगोत्राशिष्यभार्यासु स्नुषायां गवि च तल्पसमोऽवकर इत्येके श्वभिरादयेद्राजा निहीनवर्णगमने स्त्रियं प्रकाशं पुमांसं खादयेद्यथोक्तां वा गर्द्दभेनावकीर्णी निर्ऋतिं चतुष्पथे यजते तस्याजिनमूर्ध्ववालं परिधाय लोहितपात्र: सप्तगृहान् भैक्षं चरेत् कर्माचक्षाण: संवत्सरेण शुध्येत्। रेतस्कन्दने भये रोगे सुप्तेऽग्नीन्धनभैक्षचरणानि सप्तरात्रं कृत्वाज्यहोम: साभिसन्धेर्वा रेतस्याभ्यां सूर्याभ्युदिते ब्रह्मचारी तिष्ठेदहरहर्भुञ्जानोऽभ्यस्तमिते च रात्रिं जपन् सावित्रीमशुचिं दृष्ट्वादित्यमीक्षेत प्राणायामं कृत्वा भोज्यभोजनेऽमेध्यप्राशने वा निष्पुरीषीभावस्त्रिरात्रावरमभोजनं सप्तरात्रं वा स्वयं शीर्णान्युपयुंजान: फलान्यनतिक्रामन् प्राक्पञ्चनखेभ्यश्छर्द्दिनो घृतप्राशन-ञ्चाक्रोशामृतहिंसासु त्रिरात्रं परमन्तप: सत्यवाक्ये चेद्वारुणीपावमानीभिर्होमो विवाहमैथुननिर्मातृसंयोगेष्वदोषमेकेऽनृतं न तु खलु गुर्वर्थेषु यत: सप्त पुरुषानितश्च परतश्च हन्ति मनसापि गुरोरनृतं वदन्नल्पेष्व-प्यर्थेष्वन्त्यावसायिनीगमने कृच्छ्राब्दोऽमत्या द्वादशरात्रमुदक्यागमने त्रिरात्रं त्रिरात्रम्।

Hot wine should be poured into the mouth of a Brāhmaṇa, addicted to wine, until he dies; such a death is the only atonement for his sin. Having unknowingly taken wine, a Brāhmaṇa should practise a *Tapta-Kṛccham* penance by living for three days on each of the following substances, viz., milk, melted butter, water and air; and after that, he should be again initiated with the thread. Having eaten any excrementitious matter, or semen, or the flesh of a camel, ass, domesticated pig or cock, or of a wild beast, or having smelled the smell of wine coming out of the mouth of a drunkard, one should live on melted butter (for a day) and practise *Prāṇāyāma.* The same expiatory penance should be practised for taking anything bitten by any of the foregoing animals. A man, who has defiled the bed of his elder or preceptor, should lie down on a red- hot bed of iron, or he should be made to embrace a hot iron image of a female, or he should cut his genitals, and holding them in his united palms, should walk towards the south-west quarter, until he drops down dead from bleeding. Such a death absolves him of his sin. This penance should be likewise practised by one after having carnally known one's son's wife, or the wife of a friend disciple or cognate, or after having held incest with a cow. According to several authorities, the atonement in these cases is same as what has been laid down in respect of an *Avakīrṇi. A* woman of a superior caste, having been found guilty of illicit intercourse with a man of an inferior caste, the king of the country shall cause her to be torn alive by dogs at a public place, or the guilty man should be dealt with in the same manner. An *Avakīrṇi* (vow-breaker) should worship the deity *Niriti* at a crossing of two roads by sacrificing an ass; then clad in the skin of that ass from the surface of which hairs have not been removed and carrying a red alms-bowl, he should live by daily begging alms at the doors of seven men, confessing his guilt to the world, all the time. After thus living for a year, he should be judged pure again. An emission of one's semen during sleep, or out of fright, or on account of a disease should be atoned for by begging for seven days in the manner of an *Agnindhan,* and by performing a *Homa* with libations of melted butter. An act of masturbation should be atoned for in the two following ways. Observing perfect continence, a masturbator should stand up from sunrise to sunset and take a single meal, each day, and mentally repeat the *Gāyatrī Mantra,* all night long. Having seen any impure thing, one should look at the sun and practise a *Prāṇāyāma.* Having eaten any inpure or interdicted article of fare, one should take a good purgative, and after the cleansing of his stomach he should fast for three days; or without striving to come by any food he should live on ripe fruits, just of them selves fallen [from trees], and before they are sized by any five-nailed animal.

After vomiting, one should drink clarified butter Having used any angry word, or behaved falsely and maliciously to any body, one should practise severe austerities, for three days. Having spoken a falsehood, one should perform *a Hama* by reciting the *Vāruṇī, Pāvamāni Mantram.* Certain authorities aver that, a lie is no lie if spoken for bringing about a matrimonial alliance, or the union of a man and a woman. But the slightest false-hood should not be spoken to a preceptor, in as much as a small lie in such a case leads the seven generations of the speaker to hell. For one year *a Kṛccha Vratam* penance should be practised for atoning the sin of one's going unto an *Antyāvasāya* woman. An unwitting intercourse, under the circumstance, calls for a practice of the same penance for twelve days. Having visited a woman in her menses, one should practise a *Kṛccha Vratam,* for three days.

इति गौतमीये धर्मशास्त्रे चतुर्विंशोऽध्याय:।२४॥

Chapter 25

रहस्यं प्रायश्चित्तमविख्यातदोषस्य चतुर्ऋचं तरत्समंदीत्यप्सु, जपेदप्रतिग्राह्य प्रतिजिघृक्षन् प्रतिगृह्य वाभोज्यं बुभुक्षमाण: पृथिवीमावपेदृत्वन्तरारमण उदकोपम्पर्शनाच्छुद्धिमेके स्त्रीषु पयोव्रतो वा दशरात्रं घृतेन द्वितीयमद्भिस्तृतीयं दिवादिष्वेकभक्तको जलक्लिन्नवासा लोमानि नखानि त्वचं मांसं शोणितं स्नाय्वस्थिमज्जानमिति होम आत्मनो मुखे मृत्योरास्ये जुहोमीत्यंतत: सर्वेषामेतत् प्रायश्चित्तं भ्रूणहत्याया:। तथान्य उक्तो नियमोऽग्ने त्वं वारयेति महाव्याहृतिभिर्जुहुयात् कुष्माण्डैश्चाज्यं तद्व्रत एव वा ब्रह्महत्यासुरापानस्तेयगुरुतल्पेषु प्राणायामै: स्नातोऽघमर्षणं जपेत् सममश्वमेधावभृथेन सावित्रीं वा सहस्रकृत्व आवर्त्तयन् पुनीतेहैवात्मानमन्तर्जले वाघमर्षणं त्रिरावर्त्तयन् पापेभ्यो मुच्येत मुच्यते।

A person, who has got no notoriety as a sinner, should

practise an expiatory penance in secret. Having received the gift of an interdicted article, or having felt a desire for accepting such a gift, one should recite, standing in water, the four *Ṛks* beginning as *Tarat Samādhi,* etc. Having felt a desire for eating an interdicted article of fare, one should make a gift of land. Having visited a woman in her menses, a mart should recover his purity by simply bathing. Several authorities aver that, the penitent, under the circumstance, should live on milk regimen for ten days, or live on simple 'water for two or three days. A procurer of abortions should take a light meal in the forepart of the day, and then clad in wet clothes, should perform a *Homa,* saying that, "I offer oblations unto hairs, nails, skin, flesh, blood, ligaments and bones (of the destroyed fetus) and unto the mouth of death and myself." According to several authorities, drunkards, Brahmanicides, gold-stealers and defilers of their preceptors' beds should perform *a Mahā Vyāhriti Homa* by reciting the *Mantra,* " extinguish my sin, O fire," or by casting libations of melted butter in the sacrificial fire by reciting the *Kūṣmāṇḍa Mantram,* or practise the aforesaid expiatory penance, or practise *Prāṇāyāma,* and thereafter bathe and recite the *Aghamarṣaṇam Sūktām.* The last named measure is equally purifying as an *Avabhṛtha* ablution made after the celebration of a horse-sacrifice. As an alternative, those individuals (drunkards, etc.,) should recite the *Gāyatrī* a thousand times. Sunk in water, a sinner should thrice repeat the *Aghamarshanam Suktam, which* tends to extinguish all sin.

इति गौतमीये धर्मशास्त्रे पञ्चविंशोऽध्याय:॥ २५॥

Chapter 26

तदाहु: कतिधावकीर्णो प्रविशतीति मरुत: प्राणेनेन्द्रं बलेन बृहस्पतिं ब्रह्मवर्च्चसेनाग्निमेवेतरेण सर्व्येणेति सोऽमावास्यायां निश्यग्निमुपसमाधाय प्रायश्चित्ताज्याहुतीर्जुहोति कामावकीर्णोऽस्म्यकीर्णोऽस्मि कामकामाय स्वाहा कामातिमुग्धोऽस्म्याभिमुग्धोऽस्मि कामकामाय स्वाहेति समिधमाधायानुपर्युक्ष्य यज्ञवास्तुं कृत्वोपस्थाय सन्मासिञ्चत्वित्येतया त्रिरुपतिष्ठेत त्रय इमे लोको एषां

लोकानामभिजित्या अभिक्रान्त्या इत्येतदेवैकेषां कर्माधिकृत्ययोः पूत इव स्यात् स इत्थं जुहुयादित्थमनुमन्त्रयेद्वरो दक्षिणेति। प्रायश्चित्तमविशेषादनार्ज्जवपैशुनप्रतिषिद्धाचारानाद्य प्राशनेषु। शूद्रायाञ्च रेतः सिक्त्वा योनौ च दोषवति कर्मण्यभिसन्धिपूर्वेष्वविङ्गभिरप उपस्पृशेद्वारुणीभिरन्यैर्वा पवित्रैः प्रतिषिद्धवाङ्गनसयोरपचारे व्याहृतयः सङ्ख्याताः पञ्च सर्वास्वपो वाचामेदहश्च आदित्यश्च पुनातु स्वाहेति प्रातः रात्रिश्च मा वरुणश्च पुनात्विति सायमष्टौ वा समिधमादध्याद्देवकृतस्येति हुत्वैवं सर्वस्मादेनसो मुच्यते मुच्यते॥

Then they discoursed on the places where the different portions of the vow of an *Avakīrṇi* merges itself in the Maruts, his strength enters the self of Indra, his Brahmanic energy resorts to *Bṛhaspati*, and the rest lie concealed in Agni. Hence he should install the sacred fire on the night of the new moon, and cast libations of clarified butter in it by way of expiation (saying as follows) : Out of lust I have broken this vow, out of lust I have carnally known a woman while practising *Brahmacaryayam, (lit.* become an *Avakirṇī)* I offer these libations unto *Kāma-Kāma,* I was overwhelmed, by lust, my reason was overclouded. I offer these libations of melted butter unto *Kāma-Kāma.* Passion got the upper-hand of my soul, I was overwhelmed, I offer these libations of melted butter unto *Kāma-Kāma.* He should lay down the sacrificial twigs by reciting these *Mantras,* and having sprinkled water over them, he should construct the sacrificial platform *(lit.* places) and stand by it. Then he should thrice recite the *Ṛk,* running as *Sanmāsiñcata.* Then having recited the *Ṛk,* (commencing as) *Traya Ime Lokā* (These three regions) he should regain his purity and religious privileges through the purity and privileges of every one residing therein. Thus one should perform the *Homa,* and thus these *Mantras* should be recited, after which a cow should be gifted to a Brāhmaṇa. This penance should, be likewise practised by one who has acted in a crooked or miserly way; or has done any of the interdicted acts, or has eaten any of the interdicted food. Having cast one's seed in a Śūdra woman, or having eaten any interdicted food, one should take an ablution by reciting the *Vāruṇi Mantra* or any other sacred *Mantra* of the

Vedas. Having sinned with tongue or mind, one should, after reading the five *Maha Vyāhṛtis* in the morning, read the *Sarva Svāpa Vāca,* etc., and the *Ṛk* running as *Ratriśca mā varuṇaśca,* etc., in the evening, or perform *a Homa* by casting eight sacrificial twigs in the fire with the recitation of *Devākṛtasya,* etc., *Mantra;* whereby one would be absolved of all sin.

इति गौतमीये धर्मशास्त्रे षड्विंशोऽध्याय:॥ २६॥

Chapter 27

अथात: कृच्छ्रान् व्याख्यास्याम:। हविष्यान् प्रातराशान् भुक्त्वा तिस्रो रात्रीर्नाश्नीयादथापरं त्र्यहं नक्तं भुञ्जीत। अथापरं त्र्यहं न कञ्चन याचेदथापरं त्र्यहमुपवसेत् तिष्ठेदहनि रात्रावासीत। क्षिप्रकाम: सत्यं वदेदनार्यैर्न सम्भाषेत, रौरवयौधाजिने नित्यं प्रयुञ्जीतानुसवनमुदकोपस्पर्शनमापोहिष्ठेति तिसृभि: पवित्रवतीभिर्मर्जयेत् हिरण्यवर्णा: शुचय: पावका इत्यष्टाभि:। अथोदकतर्पणम्। ॐ नमो हमाय मोहमाय संहमाय धुन्वते तापसाय पुनर्वसवे नमो नमो मौञ्ज्यायौर्म्याय वसुविंदाय सर्वविन्दाय नमो नम: पाराय सुपाराय महापाराय पारयिष्णवे नमो नमो, रुद्राय पशुपतये महते देवाय त्रम्बकायैकचराधिपतये हवाय शर्वायेशानायोग्राय वज्रिणे घृणिने कपर्द्दिने नमो नम: सूर्यायादित्याय नमो नमो, नीलग्रीवाय शितिकण्ठाय नमो नम:, कृष्णाय पिङ्गलाय नमो नम:, ज्येष्ठाय श्रेष्ठाय वृद्धायेन्द्राय हरिकेशायोर्ध्वरेतसे नमो नम:, सत्याय पावकाय पावकवर्णाय कामरूपिणे नमो नमो, दीप्ताय, दीप्तरूपिणे नमो नमस्तीक्ष्णरूपिणे नमो नम: सौम्याय सुपुरुषाय महापुरुषाय मध्यमपुरुषायोत्तमपुरुषाय ब्रह्मचारिणे नमो नामश्चन्द्रललाटाय कृत्तिवाससे पिनाकहस्ताश्च नमो नम इति। एतदेवादित्योपस्थानमेता एवाज्याहुतयो; द्वादशरात्रेस्यान्ते चरुं श्रपयित्वैताभ्यो देवताभ्यो जुहुयात् अग्नये स्वाहा सोमाय स्वाहाग्नीषोमाभ्यामिद्राग्निभ्यामिन्द्राश्च विश्वेभ्यो देवेभ्यो ब्रह्मणे प्रजापतये अग्नये स्विष्टिकृत इति ततो ब्राह्मणतर्पणम्। एतेनैवातिकृच्छ्रो व्याख्यातो यावत् सकृदाददीत तावदश्नीयादब्भक्षस्तृतीय: सकृच्छ्रातिकृच्छ्र: प्रथमं चरित्वा शुचि: पूत: कर्मण्यो भवति। द्वितीयं चरित्वा यत्किञ्चिदन्यन्महापातकेभ्य: पापं कुरुते तस्मात् प्रमुच्यते। तृतीयं चरित्वा सर्वस्मादेनसो मुच्यते। अथैतांस्त्रीन् कृच्छ्रान् चरित्वा सर्वेषु वेदेषु स्नातो भवति। सर्वैर्द्देवैर्ज्ञातो भवति यश्चैवं वेद यश्चैवं वेद।

Now I shall dicourse on the mode of practising the *Kṛccha* (most austere) penances. Take *a Haviṣya* meal in the morning on the first day, then fast for three successive days. After that, take a single meal at night and do this for three successive nights, then for three days live on what is obtained without solicitation, and after that fast, for three days more. A penitent shall remain standing in days, and pass the nights sitting, during the entire term of the penance. He shall content himself with little, speak nothing but perfect truth, abjure the compariy of the uncivilised *(Anāryas)* and use the skin of a *Ruru* or *Yaudha* deer. At each bath he should consecrate and touch the water by reciting the *Āpohiṣṭhā Mantra* and thereafter perform the *Tarpaṇa* by offering libations of water to the following deities, as obeisance to *Homa,* to *Mohama,* and to the bow-wielding one *(Pināka-hasta),* etc. These Mantras should be likewise used in connection with rites of *Homa* and *Sūryopasthāna* (invocation of the sun). Then after the expiry of twelve days, penitent shall cause the sacrificial porridge *(Caru)* to be cocked, and perform a *Homa* by offering oblations of that *Caru* to several deities. The mantras to be recited at the time of offering these oblations are, "obeisance to Agni, obeisance to Soma, obeisance to Agni and Soma, obeisance to Agni and Indra, obeisance to Indra, obeisance to Vaiśvadevas, obeisance to Brāhmaṇa obeisance to Prajāpati, obeisance to Agni, and obeisance to *Sviṣṭikṛt.* After that, he should perform the rite of *Brahma-tarpaṇam.* By this we have described the process of practising the severest form of expiatory penances and austerities.

The second form of practising a *Kṛccha Vratam,* consists in one's living on articles, obtained without begging or solicitation. The third form consists in living on water. By practising the first form of penance one becomes pure, holy and competent to perform religious rites. A practice of the second form extinguishes all forms of sin, except the *Mahāpātakas,* whereas that of one of the third form grants absolute absolution. A practice of any of these three forms of expiatory penances ranks equal in merit with an ablution made after the study of all the Vedas. He, who is cognisant of this fact, becomes favoured of the gods.

इति गौतमीय धर्मशास्त्रीये सप्तविंशोऽध्याय:॥ २७॥

Chapter 28

अथातश्चान्द्रायणं तस्योक्तो विधिः कृच्छ्रे वपनं व्रतं चरेत्। श्वोभूतां पौर्णमासीमुपवसेदाप्यायस्व सन्ते पयांसि नवो नव इति चैताभिस्तर्पणमाज्यहोमौ हविषश्चानुमंत्रणमुपस्थानं चन्द्रमसो यद्देवा देवहेडनमिति चतसृभिराज्यं जुहुयाद्देवकृतस्येति चान्ते समिद्भिः। ॐ भूर्भुवः स्वस्तपः सत्यं यशः श्रीः रूपं गिरोजस्तेजः पुरुषो धर्मः शिवः शिव इत्यतैर्ग्रासानुमन्त्रणम्। प्रतिमंत्रं मनसा नमः स्वाहेति वा। सर्वग्रासप्रमाणस्याविकारेण चरुभैक्षशक्तुकणयावशाकपयोदधिघृतमूलफलोदकानि हवींषि। उत्तरोत्तरं प्रशस्तानि। पौर्णमास्यां पञ्चदश ग्रासान् भुक्त्वैकापचयेन परपक्षमश्नीयादमावास्यायामुपोष्यैकोपचयेन पूर्वपक्षं विपरीतमेकेषाम्। एष चान्द्रायणो मासो मासमेतमाप्त्वा विपापो विपाप्मा सर्वमनो हति द्वितीयमाप्त्वा दश पूर्वान् दशापरानात्मानञ्चैकविंशं पंक्तीश्च पुनाति। संवत्सरञ्चाप्त्वा चन्द्रमसः सलोकतामाप्नोत्याप्नोति॥

Now I shall describe the process of practising *Cāndrāyaṇam.* Rules to be observed in practising this penance have been already set forth. In the *Kṛccha* form of *Cāndrāyaṇam,* a penitent should have his head cleanly shaved, and observe a fast on the day of the full moon. The *rites* of *Tarpaṇam, Ājya-Homa (Homa* done with libations of melted butter), consecration of the clarified butter and invocation of the moon should be done by reciting the Mantra, running as *Āpyāyasva sante, etc.* Libations of clarified butter, should be cast in the sacred fire by reciting the four *Mantras* running as– *Yaddevā devahelanam, etc.* Then *a Homa* should be performed by tasting twigs of sacrificial trees in the fire with the accompaniment of *Deva Kṛtasya,* etc., *Mantra.* The morsels of food should be consecrated by reciting the Oṁ, *Bhūr, bhuvaḥ, Svastapaḥ Satyam Yaśaḥ Śrirūpam Giraujastejaḥ Puruṣa Dharma Śivaḥ Śiva.* Then *Namas Svāhā* should be mentally recited. The morsels of food should be made of a size as to admit of being easily introduced into the cavity of the mouth. These morsals should be made either of *Caru* (sacrificial porridge), or of articles obtained by begging, fried barley-powder, barley, leaves of - edible plants, milk, melted butter, fruits, edible roots, bulbs, or of simple water; each preceding substance being held more meritorious than the one immediately following it in the order of enumeration. Such fifteen morsels of food should be taken on the day of the full moon, and a penitent shall daily decrease the number of morsels by one during the dark fortnight, observing a perfect fast on the day of the new moon, and thereafter increasing the number of morsels by one, each day, till the day of the full moon. According to certain authorities this penance of *Cāndrāyaṇa* is completed in a single month. By practising it for a month, a penitent is absolved of all sin, by practising it for *a* couple of months he purifies his own spirit together with those of his ten immediate ancestors and descendants, and consecrates the row *(Paṅkti)* of Brāhmaṇas in which he sits down. By practising it continuously for a year, one ascends to the region of the moon.

इति गौतमीये धर्मशास्त्रेऽष्टाविंशोऽध्याय:॥ २८॥

Chapter 29

ऊर्ध्वं पितु: पुत्रा ऋक्थं भजेरन्। निवृत्ते रजसि मातुर्जीवति चेच्छति सर्वं वा पूर्वजस्येतरान् बिभृयात्। पूर्ववद्बिभागे तु धर्मवृद्धि:। विंशतिभागो ज्येष्ठस्य मिथुनमुभयतोद्युक्तो रथो गोवृष:। काणखोरकूटषण्डा मध्यमस्य। अनेकश्चेदविर्धान्यायसी गृहमनोयुक्तं चतुष्पदाञ्चैकैकं यवीयस: समञ्चेतरत् सर्वं द्व्यंशी वा पूर्वज: स्यादेकैकमितरेषामेकैकं वा धनरूपं काम्यं पूर्व: पूर्वो लभेत। दशत: पशूनां नैकशफ: नैकशफानां वृषभोऽधिको ज्येष्ठस्य। वृषभषोडशा ज्यैष्ठिनेयस्य समं वा। ज्यैष्ठिने येन यवीयसां प्रतिमातृ वा स्ववर्गे भागविशेष:। पितात्सृजेत् पुत्रिकामनपत्येऽग्निं प्रजापतिञ्चेष्ट्वास्मदर्थमपत्यमिति संवाद्याभिसन्धिमात्रात् पुत्रिकेत्येकेषाम्। तत्संशयान्नोपयच्छेदभ्रातृकाम्। पिण्डगोत्रऋषिसम्बन्धा ऋक्थं भजेरन्, स्त्री चानपत्यस्य। बीजं वा लिप्सेत देवरवन्त्यन्यतो जातमभागम्। स्त्रीधनं दुहितृणामप्रत्तानामप्रतिष्ठितानाञ्च। भगिनीशुल्कं सोदार्यणामूर्ध्वं मातु: पूर्वञ्चैके। संसृष्टविभाग: प्रेतानां ज्येष्ठस्य संसृष्टिनि प्रेते असंसृष्टो ऋक्थभाक्, विभक्तज: पित्र्यमेव। स्वमर्ज्जितं वैद्योऽवैद्येभ्य: कामं भजेरन्। पुत्रा औरसक्षेत्रजदत्तकृत्तिमगूढोत्पन्नापविद्धा

ऋक्थभाजः कानीनसहोढपौनर्भवपुत्रिकापुत्रस्वयन्दत्तक्रीता गोत्रभाजश्चतुर्थांश-भागिनश्चौरसाद्यभावे। ब्राह्मणस्य राजन्यापुत्रो ज्येष्ठो गुणसम्पन्नस्तुल्यांशभाक् ज्येष्ठांशहीनमन्यत्; राजन्यावैश्यापुत्रसमवाये स यथा ब्राह्मणीपुत्रेण। क्षत्रियाच्चेत शूद्रापुत्रोऽप्यनपत्यस्य शुश्रूषुश्चेल्लभेत वृत्तिमूलमन्तेवासविधिना। सवर्णपुत्रोऽप्यन्यायवृत्तो न लभेतैकेषाम्। श्रोत्रियो ब्राह्मणस्यानपत्यस्य ऋक्थं भजेरन्, राजेतरेषां जडक्लीबौ भर्त्तव्यावपत्यं जडस्य भागार्हं शूद्रापुत्रवत्। प्रतिलोमासूदकयोगक्षेमकृतान्नेष्वविभागः स्त्रीषु च। संयुक्तास्वनाज्ञाते दशावरैः शिष्टैरूहवद्भिरलुब्धः प्रसस्तं कार्यम्। चत्वारश्चतुर्णां पारगा वेदानां, प्रागुत्तमास्त्रय आश्रमिणः, पृथग्धर्मविदस्त्रय, एतान् दशवरान् परिषदित्याचक्षते। असम्भवे त्वेतेषामश्रोत्रियो वेदविच्छिष्टो विप्रतिपत्तौ यदाह, यतोऽयमप्रभावो भूतानां हिंसानुग्रहयोगेषु धर्मिणं विशेषेण स्वर्गं लोकं धर्मविदाप्नोति ज्ञानभिनिवेशाभ्यामिति धर्मो धर्मः।

Sons shall divide among themselves the estates of their father, after his death. A father, on the cessation of the menstrual function of his son's mother, may divide his properties, in his life-time, among his sons, if he so desires it. A father may bequeath his whole estate to his eldest son, providing mere maintenance to other sons, or leaving to them only properties enough to defray the costs of their subsistence. The merit of a divisioner of estates is increased by making such a partition. Twenty parts of a partitioned (paternal) estate, together with male and female slaves, domestic animals each possessing two rows of teeth, cars, cows and bullocks, should form the portion of an eldest son; blind, maimed, castrated animals, as well as those, that are deprived of the power of locomotion, should fall to the portion of a second, (lit. middle) son. In the event of his father dieing, possessed of a large number of sheep, a sheep, cart, paddy, iron (implements), together with a house and a quadruped should fall to the portion of a youngest son, and the rest of the property should be equally divided among all the sons. As an alternative, an eldest son shall take two parts, and the remaining sons shall take one part, each, of a partitioned paternal estate; or each successive son shall take one part less than a brother immediately his elder. An eldest son shall take ten parts of animals, one animal with bifurcated hoops, and a bullock. A son of an eldest son shall take a sixteenth part of the number of animals, or he shall take an equal share with his youngest uncle, or sons of different mothers (by a common father) shall take specific shares according to the difference of their mothers.

A sonless father shall give away his daughter in marriage, saying "her sons shall be my sons." Several authorities hold that mere entertainment of such a thought by a father in his mind will create the right of *Putrikā*. Hence, there is a prohibition regarding marrying a brotherless bride, inasmuch as the existence of *Putrikāskip* in such a case may not be easily discovered. Persons related to a (deceased) individual by ties of *Gotra, Piṇḍa,* or spiritual clanship *(Ṛṣis),* may inherit the estates left by him. The estates of a childless person shall go to his wife after his death, or his widow shall seek for a son from his uterine brother. A son begotten on such a widow by any one except her deceased husband's brother shall not be competent to inherit the property of his mother's deceased husband. Unmarried daughters, not well-settled in life, shall inherit the *Strīdhanam* of their mother. Money-dowries obtained at the time of a sister's marriage shall go to her brothers after her mother's demise, or according to several authorities, they may take the money even during their mother's life-time. Estates left by a deceased individual should be first divided among persons living in commensality. On the death of an elder brother who had been living in commensality, a brother of his, living separate, shall inherit his property. A brother born after the partition (of his paternal estate) shall be an heir to his father's portion only, (and not to any subsequent accretions made thereto by his brothers.) Of brothers living in commensality and belonging to a joint-family, one happening to be a practising physician, while others are not physicians *(Avaidyas),* the physician brother shall be the owner of all the properties earned by him.

Aurasa (1), Kṣetraja: (2), Datta (3), Kṛtrima (4) Gūḍhotpanna

(5) and Apaviddha (6) all these (six) kinds of sons are competent to inherit their paternal properties. Kānīna (7), Sahoḍha (8), Paunarbhava (9), Putrikāputra (10), Svayamdatta (11), and Kṛta (12) sons inherit only the Gotra of their fathers, but they, in the absence of any Aurasa, etc., sons of their father, shall be deemed competent to inherit a quarter part of the estate left by him.

A good and eldest born son of a Brāhmaṇa father by a Kṣatriya mother shall take equal shares with a son begotten by his father on a Brāhmaṇa wife, but a son of a Kṣatriya mother, under the circumstances, not possessed of the foregoing qualifications, shall not take the preference of an eldest born. Sons born of Vaiśya and Kṣatriya wives of a Brāhmaṇa testator, *(Dhani)* shall inherit his property according to shares and principles laid down before in connection with sons of Brāhmaṇa and Kṣatriya wives of a Brāhmaṇa. A son, begotten by a Kṣatriya on a Śūdra wife, shall inherit his property in the manner of a disciple, in the event of there being no other kinds of sons of his father, and on the proof his nursing him at his deathbed. A son begotten by a man on a wife belonging to the same caste with him *(Savarṇā)* shall be debarred from inheriting his paternal estates on his happening to lead an improper life. *Śrotriyas* should be regarded as heirs to estates left by childless Brāhmaṇas, while estates left by members of any other caste shall vest in the sovereign of a country. Idiots and eunuchs are entitled to maintenance only. A son of an idiotic father shall take a share like a son begotten on a Śūdra mother. Water, articles of confectionary or of culinary art, slave girls, and articles necessary for the purpose of practising *yoga* can never be partitioned. All matters of doubt should be submitted to the deliberations of at least ten honest, greedless, impartial men of wisdom of the following type, for settlement. Four of them must be Brāhmaṇas well-versed in the Vedas, one member of good conduct from each of the following under viz., *Brahmacārins,* house-holders and *Vānaprasthas* (forest dwelling hermits,) and three several Jurists, well read in the regulations (Law). A council consisting of ten members of the aforesaid types is called a *Pariṣad.* In the absence of *a Pariṣad,* all matters of dispute should be adjudicated according to the decisions of good *Śrotriyas,* well versed in the Vedas, inasmuch as they are above all feelings of partiality or unjust oppression. By practising special virtues the virtuous go to heaven, culture of knowledge being the highest of them all.

इति गौतमीये धर्मशास्त्रे एकोनत्रिंशोऽध्यायः॥ २९॥

॥ गौतमस्मृतिः समाप्ता ॥

१६. वसिष्ठस्मृतिः

16. Vasiṣṭha Smṛti

Chapter 1

अथातः पुरुषनिःश्रेयसार्थं धर्मजिज्ञासा। ज्ञात्वा चानुतिष्ठन् धार्मिकः प्रशस्ततमो भवति लोके प्रेत्य वा विहितो धर्मः। तदलाभे शिष्टाचारः प्रमाणम्। दक्षिणेन हिमवते उत्तरेण विन्ध्यस्य ये धर्मा ये चाचारास्ते सर्वे प्रत्येतव्या, न त्वन्ये, प्रतिलोमकल्पधर्माः।

Now therefore[1] [is] the enquiry into the sacred law for the welfare of men. Knowing and following [it i.e., the sacred law] a religious man becomes most worthy of praise in this world and after death. The sacred law [has been settled by] the revealed texts. On failure of this, the practice of the Śiṣṭas[2] (has) authority. Religious practices and customs [which prevail in the country lying] to the south of the Himālaya and to the north of the Vindhya, must be every where acknowledged, but not different ones [are to be considered] as sacred laws.

एतदार्यावर्त्तमित्याचक्षते। गङ्गायमुनयोरन्तराप्येके। यावद्वा कृष्णमृगो विचरति तावद्ब्रह्मवर्च्चसमिति। अथापि भाल्लविनो निदाने गाथामुदाहरन्ति।

[People] say that this (tract of the country) is Āryāvarta. Some [say that the country of the Āryas is situated] between [the rivers] Gaṅgā and Yamunā; [others say] as an alternative that so far as the black antelope grazes [the country is full of] Brahma effulgence.[3] Now the Bhāllavins[4] quote [the following) verse in

---

1. Kṛṣna Paṇḍit, the commentator, holds that the word *atas* (therefore) is used to indicate that one, after initiation, is to be taught prescribed rules.
2. One whose heart is free from desire. The definition occurs in the body of the text of the Benares edition.
3. The text is *Brahmavarchasam* : Brahma effulgence is the literal rendering : it means spiritual pre-eminence as adopted by Buhler.
4. See Max-Muller's History of Sanskrit literature, p.193.

the Nidāna.[1]

पश्चात् सिन्धुविहरिणी सूर्यस्योदयने पुरा।
यावत् कृष्णोऽभिधावति तावद्वै ब्रह्मवर्चसम्।।

In the west the river rambling into the ocean[2], in the east the region where the sun rises as far as the black antelope wanders so far [is found] Brahma effulgence.

त्रैविद्यवृद्धा यं ब्रुयुर्द्धर्मं धर्मविदो जनाः।
पवने पावने चैव स धर्मो नात्र संशयः।।

The religious instructions which men, deeply versed in the three Vedas and acquainted with the sacred law; declare for purifying one's self and others are Dharma (sacred laws); there is not the least doubt in it.

देशधर्मजातिधर्मकुलधर्मान् श्रुत्यभावादब्रवीन्मनुः। सूर्याभ्युदितः सूर्याभिनिर्मुक्तः कुनखी श्यावदन्तः परिवित्तिः परिवेत्ता अग्रेदिधिषुः दिधिषुपतिर्वीजहा ब्रह्मघ्न इत्येत एनस्विनः।

In the absence of (express) revealed texts Manu has declared the laws of countries, castes and families. He who sleep, at sunrise or sunset, he who has deformed nails or black teeth, he whose younger brother is married first, he who has espoused before his elder brother, the husband of a younger sister married before the elder, the husband of an elder sister, whose younger sister is married before, he who kills (*i.e.*; neglects the recitation of) the *Mantra,* he who slays a Brāhmaṇa, these all are sinful men.

पञ्च महापातकान्याचक्षते। गुरुतुल्यं सुरापानं भ्रूणहत्यां ब्राह्मणसुवर्णहरणं पततिसम्प्रयोगञ्च ब्राह्मेण वा यौनेन वा।

They say that there are five heinous crimes (Mahāpātaka)

1. It is a section of law dealing with the disquisition of the countries.
2. Another text is *Sindhurvidharani* : The commentator Kṛṣna Paṇḍit means it ocean. Buhler translates it as boundary-river which is probably the Saraswati. We have followed the text *Sindhurviharani*. *Viharani* can never be an adjective of *Sindhu* which is masculine.

viz., violating a preceptor's[1] bed, drinking spirituous liquor, killing an embryo, stealing the gold of a Brāhmaṇa, associating with out-castes either by [holding) spiritual or matrimonial [alliances with them.)

अथाप्युदाहरन्ति।

Now they quote the example :

संवत्सरेण पतति पतितेन सहाचरन्।

याजनाध्यापनाद्यौनादन्नपानासनादपि।।

He; who during a year associates with an outcast; becomes outcasted by sacrificing for him, by teaching him, by a matrimonial alliance [with him] and by using the same carriage or seat.

अथाप्युदाहरन्ति।

Now they quote the example :-

विद्याविनाशे पुनरभ्युपैति
जाति प्रणाशे त्विह सर्वनाश:।
कुलापदेशेन ह्वयोऽपि पूज्य-
स्तस्मात् कुलीनां स्त्रियमुद्वहन्ति।। इति

On learning being destroyed [one] may again acquire it : but all is destroyed with the loss of caste. By virtue of pedigree even a horse becomes estimable therefore [men] should wed wives from a respectable family.

त्रयो वर्णा ब्राह्मणस्य वशे वर्त्तेरन्, तेषां ब्राह्मणो धर्मं यद्ब्रूयात् तत् राजा चानुतिष्ठेत्। राजा तु धर्मेणानुशासन् षष्ठं षष्ठं धनस्य हरेदन्यत्र ब्राह्मणात्। इष्टापूर्त्तस्य तु षष्ठमंशं भजति। इति ह ब्राह्मणा वेदमाद्यं करोति, ब्राह्मण आपद उद्धरति तस्मादब्राह्मणोऽनाद्य:, सामोऽस्य राजा भवतीतीह प्रेत्य चाभ्युदयिकमिति ह विज्ञायते।।

The three castes shall remain under a Brāhmaṇas control. The

1. The term *Guru* may also mean father, meaning 'Knowing one's own step-mother.'

Brāhmaṇa shall declare their duties and the king shall carry them into practice. And a king, who rules in accordance with the sacred law, may take the sixth part of the riches, (of his subjects), except from Brāhmaṇas. He [also], obtains the sixth part [of merit] of *Iṣṭa* (sacrifices) and *Pūrta* (charitable works). It is said that the Brāhmaṇa first made the Vedas known. The Brāhmaṇa saves [one] from misfortune. Therefore a Brāhmaṇa shall not be made to pay taxes. Soma is his king. It is declared that it (*i.e.*, such conduct) brings on well-being both in this world and in the next.

इति वासिष्ठे धर्मशास्त्रे प्रथमोऽध्यायः॥१॥

Chapter 2

चत्वारो वर्णा ब्राह्मणक्षत्रियवैश्यशूद्राः। त्रयो वर्णा द्विजातयो ब्राह्मणक्षत्रियवैश्याः। तेषां मातुरग्रेऽधिजननं, द्वितीयं मौञ्जिबन्धने। तत्रास्य माता सावित्री पिता त्वाचार्य्य उच्यते। वेदप्रदानात् पितेत्याचार्यमाचक्षते।

There are four castes (Varṇa), Brāhmaṇas, Kṣatriyas, Vaiśyas and Śūdras. Three castes; Brāhmaṇas, *Kṣatriya*s, and Vaiśyas (are called) the twice-born. Their first birth is from their mother and the second from the investure with the sacred girdle. There (*i.e.*, in the second birth) Sāvitri is the mother and the preceptor is said to be the father. They call, the preceptor father because he gives instructions in the Veda.

अथाप्युदाहरन्ति।

द्वयमिह वै पुरुषस्य रेतो ब्राह्मणस्योर्ध्वं नाभेरर्वाचीनं मन्येत। तद्यदूर्ध्वं नाभेस्तेनास्यानौरसी प्रजा जायते। यदुपनयति यत् साधु करोति। अथ यदर्वाचीनं नाभेस्तेनास्योरसी प्रजा जायते, जनन्यां जनयति, तस्माच्छ्रोत्रियमनूचानसपुत्रोऽसीति न वदन्तीति।

They quote the following example :- Indeed the virile energy of a man, learned in spiritual science, is of two sorts, that which is above the navel and the other such is situated below; through that which is above the navel his offspring is produced when he invests one with the sacred thread and makes him holy; By that which resides below the navel the children of his body are produced on their mother. Therefore they [should] never say to *a Śrotriya,* who teaches, the Veda "You are destitute of a son."[1]

हारीता: अथाप्युदाहरन्ति।

Hārita quotes the following verse -

न त्वस्य विद्यते कर्म किञ्चदामौञ्जिबन्धनात्।

वृत्त्या शूद्रसमो ज्ञेयो यावद्वेदे न जायते।।

अन्यत्रादकर्मस्वधापितृसंयुक्तेभ्य:।

There is no religious rite for a [child of the twice born] before he has been invested with the sacred girdle. His conduct shall be known as equal [to that of] a Śūdra before his new birth from the Veda. [The above prohibition relates to all rites] except those connected with libations of water, (the exclamation] Svadhā, and the departed manes.

विद्या ह वै ब्राह्मणमाजगाम

गोपाय मा शेवधिस्तेऽहमस्मि।

असूयकायानृजवेऽव्रताय

न मा ब्रूया वीर्यवती तथा स्याम।।

[Sacred] learning approached a Brāhmaṇa [also said} "Preserve me, I am your treasure, reveal me not to an envious person, nor to a wily man, nor to one who has broken his vow. I shall then remain powerful.

न आवृणात्यवितथेन कर्मणा

बहुदु:खं कुर्वंस्त्वमृतं वा संप्रयच्छन्।

तन्मन्यत पितरं मातरञ्च

तस्मै न द्रुहेत कतमच्च नाहम्।।

He, who covers [him], with great difficulty, with truthful deeds, confers on him immortality; [the pupil] shall consider [such a preceptor] as his father and mother; he must not grieve him [by saying] I am indebted to none.

---

1. Some texts read *apujya* (unworthy of adoration) for *aputro*.

अध्यापिता ये गुरु नाद्रियन्ते

विप्रा वाचा मनसा कर्मणा वा।

यथैव ते न गुरुर्भोजनीया-

स्तथैव तान् न युनक्ति श्रुतं तत्।।

As those Vipras, who after being instructed do not non or their preceptor by their speech, in their hearts, or by their acts, will not be profitable to their teacher so the sacred learning will not profit them.

यमेव विद्याच्छुचिमप्रमत्तं

मेधाविनं ब्रह्मचर्योपपन्नम्।

यस्त्वेतदद्रुह्येत कतमच्च नाहं

तस्मै मां ब्रूयान्निधिपाय ब्रह्मन्।।

Reveal me, O Brāhmaṇa, as to the keeper of your treasure, to him whom you shall know as pure, attentive, intelligent and celebate and who will not grieve or revile thee.

दहत्यग्निर्यथा कक्षं ब्रह्म त्वब्दमनादृतम्।

न ब्रह्म तस्मै प्रब्रूयाच्छक्यमानमकृन्तत।।

As fire consumes a room so, Brahma (Veda), not honoured [destroys the enquirer}: One shall not proclaim the Veda to him who does not show him honour according to his ability.

षट् कर्माणि ब्राह्मणस्याध्ययनमध्यापनं यजनं याजनं दानं प्रतिग्रहश्चेति।

The duties of a Brāhmaṇa, are six viz., studying the Veda, teaching, sacrificing, officiating as a priest for others, giving alms and accepting gifts.

त्रीणि राजन्यस्याध्ययनं यजनं दानं शस्त्रेण च प्रजापालनं स्वधर्मस्तेन जीवेत्।

The duties of a Kṣatriya are three viz., studying, sacrificing for himself, and giving alms. His own [special duty is also] to protect his subjects according to spiritual injunctions[1] : let him gain his livelihood thereby.

एतान्येव त्रीणि वैश्यस्य कृषिवाणिज्यपशुपाल्यकुसीदञ्च।

Those three [are also the occupation] of a Vaiśya besides agriculture, trading, tending cattle, and lending money at interest.

एतेषां परिचर्या शूद्रस्य।

To serve these (*i.e.* the three superior castes is the occupation) of a Śūdra.

अनियता वृत्तिरनियतकेशवेशाः सर्वेषां मुक्तशिखावर्ज्जम्।

These (*i.e.*, the Śūdras) have no fixed regulation; about their means of livelihood, [arrangement of? hairs and dresses; but they must not allow the lock on the crown to remain untied.

अजीवतः स्वधर्मणान्यतरामपापीयसीं वृत्तिमातिष्ठेरन् न तु कदाचित् पापीयसीम्। वैश्यजीविकामास्थाय पण्येन जीवतोऽश्मलवणमपण्यं पाषाणकौषक्षौमाजिनानि च तान्तवञ्च रक्तं सर्वञ्च कृतान्नं पुष्पमूलफलानि च गन्धरसा उदकञ्चौषधीनां रसः सोमश्च शस्त्रं विषं मांसञ्च क्षीरं सविकारं अपस्त्रपु जतुसीसञ्च।

Those, who are unable to live by their own lawful occupation, may adopt one which is not sinful but never one which is sinful. Having resorted to a Vaiśya's mode of living a Brāhmaṇa and a *Kṣatriya*, while maintaining themselves by trade [shall not sell] stones, salt, hempen [cloth], silk, linen [cloth], skins, a dyed woven cloth, prepared food, fruits, roots, perfumes, treacle's, water, We juice extracted from medicinal herbs, Soma, weapon, poisons, milk, preparations from milk, iron, tin, lac and lead.

अथाप्यदारहन्ति।

Now they quote the following verse as an example :-

सद्यः पतति मांसेन लाक्षया लवणेन च।
त्र्यहेण शूद्रो भवति ब्राह्मणः क्षीरविक्रयात्।।

---

1. There are two readings *Śāstreṇa* and *Śastreṇa*. The latter mean 'with his weapons.'

By [selling] meat, lac and salt, a Brāhmaṇa becomes directly outcasted; by selling milk he becomes (equal to] a Śūdra after three days.

ग्राम्यपशूनामेकशफाः केशिनश्च सर्वे, चारण्याः पशवो वयांसि दंष्ट्रिणश्च। धान्यानां तिलानाहुः।

Among domesticated animals, those with uncloven hoofs and those that have an abundance of hair, any wild animals, birds, tusked animals [must not be sold]; of grains they declare sesamum [as forbidden.]

अथाप्युदाहरन्ति।

Now they quote the following verse as an example.

भोजनाभ्यञ्जनाद्दानाद्यद्वान्यत् कुरुते तिलैः।
कृमिभूतः स विष्टायां पितृभिः सह मज्जति॥

If one applies sesamum to any other purpose save food, anointing and gifts he will be born again as a worm and together with his departed manes be plunged into excreta.

कामं वा स्वयं कृष्योत्पाद्य तिलान् विक्रीणीरन्। अन्यत्र धान्यविक्रयात्। रसारसैः समतो हानतो वा निमातव्या न त्वेव लवणं रसैस्तिलतण्डूलपक्वान्नं विद्यान्मनुष्याश्च विहिताः। परिवर्त्तकेन ब्राह्मणराजन्यौ वार्द्धुषान्न नाद्याताम्।

If they fail to gain their livelihood by selling rice they may sell sesamum at pleasure if they have themselves produced it by tillage. *Rasa* (substance for flavouring food) may be given either in an equal quantity or less in exchange for a *Rasa,* but never salt. It is permitted to barter sesamum, rice, cooked food, learning and men (*i.e.*, slaves). Even by exchange a Brāhmaṇa shall not take boiled rice from a Kṣatriya who lends [money] at an exhorbitant rate of interest.

अथाप्युदाहरन्ति।

Now they quote the following verses as an example :

समर्घं धान्यमुद्धृत्य महार्घं यः प्रयच्छति।

स वै वार्द्धुषिको नाम ब्रह्मवादिषु गर्हितः॥

He who purchasing rice at a fair price, sells it for a higher price, is called a *Vārdhūṣika* (usurer) and is blamed amongst those who recite the Veda.

वार्धूषिं भ्रूणहत्याञ्च तुलया समतोलयत्।

अतिष्ठद् भ्रूणहा कोट्यां वार्द्धुषि न्र्यक्पपात ह॥

Usury and killing an embryo when weighed in the scales the destroyer of an embryo remains at the top and the usurer sinks downwards.

कामं वा परिलुप्तकृत्याय पापीयसे दद्यद् द्विगुणैहिरण्यं त्रिगुणं धान्यं, धान्यनैव रसा व्याख्याताः। पुष्पमूलफलानि च तुलावृतमष्टगुणम्।

One should give at pleasure gold double and grain treble [its value on repayment] unto a sinful [usurer] destitute of all religious deeds; [the case of flavouring substances] has been explained by [the regulation about] grain. Similar is. [the case of] flowers, roots and fruits: [They may lend] what is sold by weight [taking] eight times [the original value at the time of re-payment].

अथाप्युदाहरन्ति।

Now they quote the following verses as an example.

राजानुमतभावेन द्रव्यवृद्धिं विनाशयेत्।

पुनः राजाभिषेकेण द्रव्यवृद्धिञ्च वर्जयेत्॥

By the king's will[1] shall stop the interest on articles. And after the coronation of [a new] king the capital grows again.

द्विकं त्रिकं चतुष्कञ्च पञ्चकञ्च शतं स्मृतम्।

मासंस्य वृद्धिं गृह्णीयाद्वर्णानामनुपूर्वशः॥

Two in the hundred, three, four and five, as has been laid

---

1. There are two readings *rājānumatabhāvena* and *rājatu-mṛta-bhavena*. We have followed the first. Dr. Buhler has followed the second and translated "the king's death shall stop etc." The succeeding passage tactily indicates that interest is stopped on the death of a king. In that case it is merely a tautology. The one, that we have followed, clearly lays down a law that a king can stop the accumulation of interest at any time he likes.

down in the *Smṛti* one may take interest monthly according to the order of the castes.

वसिष्ठवचनप्रोक्तां वृद्धिं वार्द्धुषिके शृणु।
पञ्चमाषांस्तु विंशत्या एवं धर्मो न हीयते।।

Hear the interest for a money-lender declared by the words of Vasiṣtha, five Māṣās for twenty in this the law is not violated.

इति वासिष्ठे धर्मशास्त्रे द्वितीयोऽध्यायः।।२।।

Chapter 3

अश्रोत्रियाननुवाका अनग्नयः शूद्रधर्माणो भवन्ति नानृग्ब्राह्मणो भवति। मानवञ्चात्र श्लोकमुदाहरन्ति।

सोऽनधीत्य द्विजो वेदमन्यत्र कुरुते श्रमम्।
स जीवन्नेव शूद्रत्वमाशु गच्छति सान्वयः।।

[The Brāhmaṇas] who neither study nor teach the Veda, nor maintain sacred fires, become of the conduct of a Śūdra. Without studying the *Ṛk,* one does not be come a Brāhmaṇa. They quote a śloka from, Manu on this subject. A twice-born person, who not having studied the *Pāda,* spends his labour on another [subject], soon falls, even while living, to the condition of a Śūdra and his descendants after him.

न वणिक् न कुसीदजीवी। ये च शूद्रप्रेषणं कुर्वन्ति। स स्तेनो न चिकित्सकः।

He who lives by trade [does not become a Brāhmaṇa]; nor he who lives by usury; not those who obey a Śūdra's commands, nor a thief, nor a physician.

अव्रतो ह्यनधीयाना यत्र भैक्षचरा द्विजाः।
न ग्रामं दण्डयेद्राजा चौरभुक्तपदो हि सः।।

The king shall punish the village where Brāhmaṇas, failing to observe their sacred duties and study the Veda, live by begging, for it feeds the thieves.

चत्वारोऽपि त्रयो वापि यं ब्रूयुर्वेदपारगाः।
स धर्म इति विज्ञेयो नेतरेषां सहस्रशः॥

What four or three (Brāhmaṇas), who have mastered the Vedas, proclaim must be recognized as the sacred law, not [the determination] of a thousand inferior persons.

अव्रतानाममन्त्राणां जातिमात्रोपजीविनाम्।
सहस्रशः समेतानां पर्षत्त्वं नैव विद्यते॥

Many thousands [of Brāhmaṇas], who do not observe their sacred duties, who are not acquainted with the Mantra and who subsist only by the name of their caste, cannot form a Synod.

यद्वदन्त्यन्यथा भूत्वा मूर्खा धर्ममतद्विदः।
तत्पापं शतधा भूत्वा तद्वक्तॄष्वनुगच्छति॥

That sin, which ignorant persons, unacquainted with the sacred law, preaches, shall fall, multiplied a hundredfold, on the speakers.

श्रोत्रियायैव देयानि हव्यकव्यानि नित्यशः।
अश्रोत्रियाय दत्तानि तृप्तिं नायान्ति देवताः॥

Offerings to the celestials and the departed manes must daily be given to a Śrotriya alone. Gifts made to a person who has not read the Veda do not gratify the celestials.

यस्य चैव गृहे मूर्खा दूरे चैव बहुश्रुतः।
बहुश्रुताय दातव्यं नास्ति मूर्खे व्यतिक्रमः॥

If an ignorant person lives in one's own house and a man vastly read in the Śruti at a distance, gifts should be given unto the learned : there is no sin in neglecting an ignorant weight.

ब्राह्मणातिक्रमो नास्ति विप्रे वेदविवर्जिते।
ज्वलन्तमग्निमुत्सृज्य न हि भस्मनि हूयते॥

The sin of neglecting a Brāhmaṇa is not committed against a twice-born person who is ignorant of the Veda. Passing by a burning fire one does not offer libations into ashes.

यश्च काष्ठमयो हस्ती यश्च चर्ममयो मृगः।
यश्च विप्रोऽनधीयानस्त्रयस्ते नामधारकाः।।

An elephant made of wood, an antelope made of leather, and a Brāhmaṇa indisposed to the study of the Veda these three have nothing but the name.

विद्वद्भोज्यानि चान्नानि मूर्खा राष्ट्रेषु भुञ्जते।
तदन्नं नाशमायाति महद्वा जायते भयम्।।

In those kingdom, where ignorant men eat the food of the learned, food meets with destruction and a great evil appears.

अप्रज्ञायमानवृत्तं योऽधिगच्छेद्राजा तद्धरेत् अधिगन्त्रे षष्ठमंशं प्रदाय। ब्राह्मणश्चेदधिगच्छेत् षट्कर्म्मसु वर्त्तमाना न राजा हरेत्।

If any one finds treasure [the owner] of which is not known the king shall take it giving one sixth to the finder. If a Brāhmaṇa, who is given to the performance of six fold sacred duties, finds it the king shall not take it.

आततायिनं हत्वा नात्र त्राणमिच्छोः किञ्चित् किल्विषमाहुः।
षड्विधास्त्वाततायिनः।

They say that by killing an assassin with a view to personal safety one commits no sin. There are six Classes of assassins *(ātatāyins)*

अथाप्युदाहरन्ति।

Now they quote the following verses on the subject :-

अग्निदो गरदश्चैव शस्त्रपाणिर्धनापहः।
क्षेत्रदारहरश्चैव षडेत आततायिनः।।

An incendiary, a poisoner, one holding a weapon in his hand, a robber, the taker away of lands, the seducer of another man's wife these six are called assassins *(ātatāyins)*.

आततायिनमायान्तमपि वेदान्तपारगम्।
जिघांसन्तं जिघांसीयान्न तेन ब्रह्महा भवेत्।।

One does not become guilty of Brahmanicide; if he kills an assassin who comes with the intention of slaying; even if he is a master of the entire Veda together with the Upanishads.

स्वाध्यायिनं कुले जातं यो हन्यादाततायिनम्।

न तेन भ्रूणहा स स्यान्मन्युस्तन्मन्युमृच्छति।।

He; who kills an assassin well-read in the Veda and hailing from a good family, is not visited, by that deed, by the guilt of the murderer of a learned Brāhmaṇa; [in] that [case] fury recoils upon fury.

त्रिणाचिकेतः पञ्चाग्निस्त्रिसुपर्णवान् चतुर्मेधा वाजसनेयी षडङ्गविद् ब्रह्मदेयानुसन्तान्दोगो ज्येष्ठसामगो मन्त्रब्राह्मणविद यस्य धर्मानधीते यस्य च पुरुषमातृपितृवंशः श्रात्रियो विज्ञायते विद्वांसः स्नातकाश्चेति पङ्क्तिपावनाः।

A Triṇāciketa, one who keeps five fires, a Trisuparṇa, one who [knows the texts of] the four sacrifices (*Aśvamedha*, *Puruṣamedha*, *Sarvamedha* and *Pitṛmedha*), one who knows Vājasaneya [branch of the White Yajur Veda], one who knows the six Aṅgas, the son of a woman married according to the Brahma rife, one who knows *Chandas* (Vedic metre), one who sings *Jyesthasāman,* one who knows the *Mantra* and the Brāhmaṇa, one who studies the sacred law treatises, one whose ancestors, both on the mother's and on the father's side, are known to have been Śrotriyas and learned men and Snātakas are the sanctifiers of the row.

चातुर्विद्यो विकल्पी च अङ्गविद्धर्मपाठकः।

आश्रमस्थास्त्रयो मुख्याः परिषत् स्याद्दशावरा।।

[Four students of) the four Vedas, one who knows *Mīmaṁsā,* one who, knows the Aṅgas a preceptor of the sacred law, three leading men of the three *Āsramas* (orders) constitute a *pariṣad* (a legal assembly) consisting, at least, of ten [members].

उपनीय तु यः कृतश्च वेदमध्यापयेत् च आचार्यो, यस्त्वेकदेशं स उपाध्यायश्च वेदाङ्गानि।

He, who after having invested a pupil with the sacred thread teaches him the Veda, is called an *Ācārya.*

He, who teaches a portion of the Veda, is called am *Upādhyāya* (sub-teacher); similarly one who [teaches] the. Aṅgas (subsidiary subjects) [of the Vedas].

आत्मत्राणे वर्णसंकरे वा ब्राह्मणवेश्यौ शस्त्रमाददीयाताम्। क्षत्रियस्य तु तान्नत्यमेव रक्षणाधिकारात्।

A Brāhmaṇa and a Vaiśya may take up arms in self-defence, or in [order to prevent] a confusion of the castes. That (*i.e.*, to take up arms) however is the daily [occupation] of a Kṣatriya on account of his privilege for protecting

प्राग्वोदग्वासीनः प्रक्ष्याल्य पादौ पाणी चामणिबन्धनात्। अङ्गुष्ठमूलस्योत्तरतो रेखा ब्राह्मं तीर्थं तेन त्रिराचामेदशब्दवत्। द्विः परिमृज्यात् खान्यद्भिः संस्पृशेत् मूर्द्धन्यपो निनयेत्। सव्ये च पाणौ। व्रजंस्तिष्ठन् शयानः प्रणतो वा नाचामेत्।

Having washed his feet and hands up to the wrist and sitting with his face directed towards the east or the north he shall thrice rinse his mouth with water out *of Brahmatīrtha,* the part of the hand above the root of the thumb, without uttering any sound. He shall, twice wipe [the mouth]. He shall touch with water, the cavities [of the head] He shall pour water on his head and on the left hand: lie shall not sip water walking, standing, lying down or bending low.

हृदयङ्गमाभिरद्भिरबुदबुदाभिरफेनाभिर्ब्राह्मणः, कण्ठगामिः क्षत्रियः शुचिः। वैश्योऽद्भिः प्राशिताभिस्तु, स्त्रीशूद्रौ स्पष्टाभिरेव च।

A Brāhmaṇa [becomes pure by sipping] water, free from bubbles and foamy that reaches his heart. A Kṣatriya [becomes] pure [by sipping water reaching his throat; a Vaiśya by water that wets his palate; a woman and a Śūdra by merely touching water [with the lips.]

पुत्रद्वारापि यागास्तर्पणानि स्युः। न वर्णगन्धरसदुष्टाभिः। याश्च स्युरशुभागमाः। न मुख्या विप्रुष उच्छिष्टं कुर्वन्त्यनङ्गश्लिष्टाः।

The offering of water may be performed by a son. [One shall not purify himself with water] that has been defiled with colours, perfumes, or flavouring substances, nor with what is collected from unclean places. Drops [of saliva], falling from the mouth, which do not touch a limb of the body, do not make [one] impure,

सुप्त्वा भुक्त्वा पीत्वा स्नात्वा चाचान्तः पुनराचामेत्। वासश्च परिधाय चोष्ठौ संस्पृश्य यावलोमकौ न श्मश्रुगता लेपः दन्तवद्दन्तसक्तेषु यच्चान्तर्मुखे भवेदाचान्तस्यावशिष्टं स्यान्निगिरन्नेव तच्छुचिः॥

If after having sipped water one sleeps, eats, drinks, or bathes he must again rinse his mouth with water. Similarly if [one] puts on a cloth, or touches the lips on which no hair grows. No defilement is caused by the hair of the moustache [entering the mouth]. If [remnants of food] adhere to the feeth [they are pure] like, the teeth; and one is purified by swallowing those which [become detached] in the mouth.

परानथाचामयतः पादौ या विप्रुषो गताः।
भूम्यां तास्तु समाः प्रोक्तास्ताभिर्नोच्छिष्टभाग् भवेत्॥

One is not made impure by the drops which fall on his feet while some body gives to others water for rinsing mouth; they are said to be equally [clean] as the ground.

अचरन्नभ्यवहार्य्येषु उच्छिष्टं यदि संस्पृशेत्।
भूमौ निक्षिप्य तद्द्रव्यमाचान्तः प्रचरेत् पुनः॥

If while moving about in an eating house one touches the residue of food he shall then place that thing on the ground, sip water and afterwards move on again.

यद्यन्मीमांस्यं स्यात् तत्तदद्भिस्तु संस्पृशेत्।
श्वहताश्च मृगा वन्या घातितश्च खगैः पलम्॥
बालैरनुपविद्धान्तः स्त्रीभिराचरितश्च यत्।
परिसङ्ख्याय तान् सर्वान् शुचीनाह प्रजापतिः॥
प्रसारितञ्च यत् पण्यं न दोषाः स्त्रीमुखानि च।

मशकैर्मक्षिकाभिश्च विलीनो नोपहन्यते।।
क्षितिस्थाश्चैव या आपो गवां प्रीतिकराश्च याः।
परिसङ्ख्याय तान् सर्वान् शुचीनाह प्रजापतिरिति।।

One should sprinkle with water all objects [the purity of which] may be doubtful.

Wild animals killed by dogs, a fruit thrown by a bird [from the tree], what has been spoiled by children, and what has been done by women, enumerating all these Prajāpati (the Lord of all created beings) has declared them to be pure. A vendible article tendered for sale, and the faces of women are never impure. What has been dirtied by gnats and flies is never impure. Similarly [is]; water collected on the ground and what satisfies the thirst of cows-- enumerating all these Prajāpati has declared them pure.

लेपगन्धापकर्षणं शौचममेध्यलिप्तस्याद्भिमृदा च। तैजसमृण्मयदारवतान्तवानां भस्मपरिमार्जनं प्रदाहतक्षणनिर्णेजनानि। तैजसवदुपलमणीनां मणिवच्छङ्खशुक्तीनां दारुवदस्थ्नां रज्जुविदलचर्मणा चैलवच्छौचम्। गोवालैः फलचमसानां गौरसर्षपकल्केन क्षौमजानाम्। भूम्यास्तु सम्मार्ज्जनप्रोक्षणोपलेपनोल्लेखनैर्यथास्थाने दोषविशेषात् प्राजापत्यमुपैति।

Any thing contaminated by unclean [substances] becomes pure when the stains and the smell have been removed by water and earth. Objects made of metal, those made of clay, those made of wood and a cloth made of thread shall be [severally] scoured with ashes, heated by fire, planed and washed. Stones and gems [should be treated] like objects made of metal conch-shells and pearl-shells like gems; objects made of bone like wood. Ropes, chips [of bamboo] and leather become pure [if treated like clothes; fruits and *Camasa* (a vessel for drinking *Soma* juice at a sacrifice) [if rubbed] with [a brush of] cow-hairs; a linen cloth [if smeared] with a paste of yellow mustard [and washed afterwards with water]. A land becomes pure, proportionate to the degree of defilement, by sweeping [the spot], by besmearing with cow-dung, by scraping it, by sprinkling [water] or by heaping [pure earth on [it].

अथाप्युदाहरन्ति।

Now they quote [the following verses] as an example.

खननाद्दहनाद्वर्षाद्गोभिराक्रमणादपि।
चतुर्भिः शुध्यते भूमिः पञ्चमाच्चोपलेपनात्॥

Land is purified by these four ways, (viz.,) by digging; burning, scraping, being trodden by cows, and fifthly by being besmeared with cow-dung.

रजसा शुध्यते नारी नदी वेगेन शुध्यति।
भस्मना शुध्यते कांस्यं ताम्रमम्लेन शुध्यति॥

A woman becomes purified by her monthly course; a river becomes purified by its current; a bell-metal becomes purified by ashes and a copper by acid [substances.]

मद्यैर्मूत्रैः पुरीषैर्वा श्लेष्मपूयाश्रुशोणितैः।
संस्पृष्टं नैव शुध्येत पुनः पाकेन मृण्मयम्।

But an earthen vessel, that has been defiled by spirituous liquor, urine, excreta, phlegm, pus, :fears or blood, is not purified even by another burning.

अद्भिर्गात्राणि शुध्यन्ति मनः सत्येन शुध्यति।
विद्यातपोभ्यां भूतात्मा बुद्धिर्ज्ञानेन शुध्यति॥

The body is purified by water, the mind is purified by truth, the soul by learning and austerities and the understanding is purified by knowledge.

अद्भिरेव काञ्चनं पूयेत तथा राजतम्। अङ्गुलिकनिष्ठिकामूले दैवं तीर्थम्। अङ्गुल्यग्रे मानुषम्। पाणिमध्य आग्नेयम्। प्रदेशिन्यङ्गुष्ठयोरन्तरा पित्र्यम्।

Gold is purified by water only, similarly silver. The *Tīrtha,* sacred to the deities, lies at the base of the little finger. That sacred to human beings is at the tip of the fingers. That sacred to the fire is in the middle of the band. That sacred to the departed manes [lies] between the fore-finger and the thumb.

रोचन्त इति सायं प्रातरशनान्यभिपूजयेत्। स्वदितमिति पित्र्येषु। सम्पन्नमित्याभ्युदयिकेषु।

One shall honour his morning and evening meals [saying) "they please me." [In the offerings of food to] the departed manes [one should say] "[have dined well." [On the occasion of dinners given for attaining prosperity [one should say]. " It is perfect:"

इति वासिष्ठे धर्मशास्त्रे तृतीयोऽध्याय:॥३॥

Chapter 4

प्रकृतिविशिष्टं चातुर्वर्ण्यं संस्कारविशेषाच्च। ब्राह्मणोऽस्य सुखमासीद्बाहू राजन्य: कृत:। ऊरू तदस्य यद्वैश्य, पद्भ्यां शूद्रो अजायतेति। गायत्र्या छन्दसा ब्राह्मणमसृजत्, त्रिष्टुभा राजन्यं, जगत्या वैश्यं न केनचिच्छन्दसा शूद्रमित्यसंस्कार्यो विज्ञायते। त्रिष्वेव निवास: स्यात् सर्वेषां सत्यमक्रोधो दानमहिंसा प्रजननञ्च। पितृदेवतातिथिपूजायां पशु हिंस्यात्।

मधूपर्के च यज्ञे च पितृदैवतकर्मणि।
अत्रैव च पशुं हिंस्यान्नान्यथेत्यब्रवीन्मनु:॥

The four castes are marked out by their origin and particular initiatory rites. The Brāhmaṇa was his mouth, the Kṣatriya formed his arms, the Vaiśya his thighs, the Śūdra was born from his feet. He created the Brāhmaṇa with the *Gāyatrī,* the Kṣatriya with the Triṣṭubh, the Vaiśya with the Jagatī and the Śūdra without any metre. This indicates [that a Śūdra] shall not receive the sacraments. [His] refuge shall be in the [first] three [castes). Truthfulness, absence of anger, liberality, abstention from injuring living creatures and the procreation of the offspring [are duties common] to all. One may slay an animal When he worships the manes, the deities and the guests. On [offering] a Madhuparka [to a guest], at a sacrifice, in all rites for the deities and manes, on all these occasions only one may slay an animal; so hath Manu said.

नाकृत्वा प्राणिनां हिंसां मांसमुत्पद्यते क्वचित्।
न च प्राणिवध: स्वर्ग्यस्तस्माद्यागे वधोऽवध:॥

[One can] never procure meat without injuring living creatures, and to injure living creatures does not procure heavenly bliss. Therefore destruction [of animals] at a sacrifice is no destruction.

अथापि ब्राह्मणाय राजन्याय वा अभ्यागताय वा महोक्षं वा महाजं वा पचेदेवमस्यातिथ्यं कुर्वन्तीति। उदकक्रियामशौचे च द्विवर्षात् प्रभृति मृत उभयं कुर्यात्। दन्तजननादित्येके शरीरमग्निना संयोज्यानवेक्षमाण आपोऽभ्यवयन्ति।

One may cook a full-grown ox or a full-grown be-goat for a Brāhmaṇa or a Kṣatriya guest. In this way they offer hospitality. One should perform both watery rites and [the assumption of] impurity on the death [of a relative] who completed the second year. Some say that [this rule applies also to children] that died after teething. After having burnt the body [the relatives] shall enter water without looking at [the place of cremation].

ततस्तत्रस्था एव सव्योत्तराभ्यां पाणिभ्यामुदकक्रियां कुर्वन्ति। अयुग्मा दक्षिणामुखाः। पितॄणां वा एषा दिग् या दक्षिणा। गृहान् व्रजित्वा स्वस्तरे त्र्यहमनश्नन्त आसीरन्। अशक्तौ क्रीतोत्पन्नेन वर्त्तेरन्।

Thereupon they, stationed there, of odd numbers and facing the south, perform the watery rites with both hands, right and left. That which is south is the region of the departed manes. Having gone home they shall sit fasting, for three days, on mats. If unable [to fast so long] they shall live on food bought or given unsolicited.

दशाहं मरणाशौचं सपिण्डेषु विधीयते। मरणात् प्रभृति दिवसगणना। सपण्डिता सप्तपुरुषं विज्ञायते। अप्रत्तानां स्त्रीणां त्रिपुरुषं त्रिदिनं विज्ञायते। प्रत्तानामितरे कुर्वीरन्। तांश्च तेषां जननेऽप्यवमेव निपुणां शुद्धिमिच्छतां मातापित्रोर्बीजनिमित्तत्वात्।

It is laid down that death impurity lasts for ten days in [case of] *Sapiṇḍa* [relatives]. The counting of days shall begin with that of death. It has been ordained that *Sapiṇḍa* relationship extends to the seventh generation. It has been declared that [impurity on the death of] an unmarried woman [extends] to the third generation and [lasts] for three days. Others[1] [than the blood relations] shall perform [obsequies] for married women. They *i.e.*, married women, too [shall observer impurity] for them *(i.e.,* their husband's relatives) [The rule of impurity] shall be exactly the same on the birth of a child for those men who long for complete, purity or for the mother or father on account of their (supplying the] said.

अथाप्युदाहरन्ति।

Now they quote the following verses as an example :

नाशौचं सूतके पुंसः संसर्गञ्चेन्न गच्छति।
रजस्तत्राशुचिर्ज्ञेयं तच्च पुंसि न विद्यते॥

On the birth [of a child] the male does not become impure if he does not touch [the mother], for there menstrual blood is known to be pure which does not exist in males.

ब्राह्मणो दशरात्रेण पञ्चदशरात्रेण भूमिपः।
विंशतिरात्रेण वैश्यः शूद्रो मासेन शुध्यति॥

A Brāhmaṇas becomes purified after ten nights, a Kṣatriya after fifteen nights, a Vaiśya after twenty nights and a Śūdra after a month.

अशौचे यस्तु शूद्रस्य सूतके वापि भुक्तवान्।
स गच्छेन्नरकं घोरं तिर्यग्योनिषु जायते॥

If [a twice-born person] eats [the food of] a Śūdra during a birth or death impurity he shall enter into a dreadful hell and be born in the womb of an animal.

अनिर्दशाहे पक्वान्नं नियोगाद् यस्तु भुक्तवान्।
कृमिर्भूत्वा स देहान्ते तद्विष्ठामुपजीवति॥

[A twice-born person], who eats, by appointment, cooked food [from a Śūdra's house] during the period of impurity, shall

---

1. The text has *Itara.* We have given the literal rendering– it means that her husband's relatives shall perform the obsequies.

become a worm after death and lead his life.

द्वादशमासान् द्वादशार्द्धमासान् वा अनश्नन् संहितामधीयान: पूतो भवतीति विज्ञायते। ऊनद्विवर्षे प्रेते गर्भपतने वा सपिण्डानां त्रिरात्रमशौचं सद्य: शौचमिति गौतम:। देशान्तरस्थे प्रेते ऊर्ध्वं दशाहाच्चैकरात्रमशौचम्। आहिताग्निश्चेत् प्रवसन् म्रियते, पुन:संस्कारं कृत्वा शववच्छौचमिति गौतम:। यूपयतिश्मशानरजस्वलासूतिकाशुचीनुपस्पृश्य सशिरा अभ्युपेयादप:।

It has been declared that [such a sinner], becomes pure by reciting the Saṁhitā for twelve months[1] or twelve half months[2] while fasting. On the death of a child of less than two years, or on a miscarriage, the impurity of the *Sapiṇḍas* lasts three nights.[3] Purification is immediate [according to Gautama] If (a person) dies in a foreign land and ((his *Sapiṇḍas*] hear (of his death) after ten days the impurity lasts for one night. If one, who has killed the sacred fire, dies on a journey [his *Sapiṇḍas*] shall perform his obsequies[4] and shall duly observe the impurity of death. So Gautama [says]. Touching a sacrificial post, an ascetic, a cremation ground, a woman in menses one who has lately given birth to a child and other a impure men one shall bathe his head after sipping water.

इति वासिष्ठे धर्मशास्त्रे चतुर्थोऽध्याय:।।४।।

Chapter 5

अस्वतन्त्रा स्त्री पुरुषप्रधाना अनग्निरुदक्या च अनृतमिति विज्ञायते।

A woman is never independent; she has males tar her masters. That she has no fire or watery rite, is known to be untrue.

अथाप्युदाहरन्ति।

Now they quote the following verses as an example :

---

1. This is the penance when one commits the sin knowingly.
2. This is the penance when one commits the sin unknowingly.
3. *i.e.*, Three days and nights.
4. Shall make a dummy with the Kuśa grass and then burn it. This is also the practice when nothing is heard of a person gone to a foreign country.

पिता रक्षति कौमारे भर्त्ता रक्षति यौवने।
पुत्राश्च स्थविरे भावे न स्त्री स्वातन्त्र्यमर्हति।।

[Her] father protects [a woman] in child-hood, her husband in her youth and her sons protect her in old age; a woman is never fit for independence.

तस्या भर्त्तुरभिचार उक्तः प्रायश्चित्तरहस्येषु। मासि मासि रजो ह्यासां दुष्कृतान्यपकर्षति।।

Her penance for being unfaithful to her husband has been spoken of in the [section on] secret penances: Month after month menstrual discharge dissipates her sins.

त्रिरात्रं रजस्वलाशुचिर्भवति, सा नाञ्ज्यात् नाप्सु स्नायात्, अधः शयीत, दिवा न स्वप्यात्, नाग्निं स्पृशेत्, न रज्जुं प्रमृजेत्, न दन्तान् धावयेत्, न मांसमश्नीयात् न ग्रहान् निरीक्षेत, न हसेत, न किञ्चिदाचरेत्, नाञ्जलिना जलं पिबेत्, न खर्परेण न लोहितायसेन वा। विज्ञायते हीन्द्रस्त्रिशीर्षाणं ताष्ट्रं हत्वा पाप्मना गृहीतो मन्युत इति। तं सर्वाणि भूतान्यभ्याक्रोशन् भ्रूणहन् भ्रूणहन्निति। स स्त्रिय उपाधावत्। अस्यै मे ब्रह्महत्यायै तृतीयं भागं गृह्णीतेति गत्वैवमुवाच। ता अब्रुवन् किं नो भूदिति। सोऽब्रवीद्वरं वृणीध्वमिति। ता अब्रुवन्नृतौ प्रजां विन्दामह इति, कामं मा विजानीमोऽलम्भवाम इति, यथेच्छया आ प्रसवकालात् पुरुषेण सह मैथुनभावेन सम्भवाम इति चैषोऽस्माकं वरस्तथेन्द्रेणोक्तास्ताः प्रतिजगृहुस्तृतीयं भ्रूणहत्यायाः। सैषा भ्रूणहत्या मासि मास्याविर्भवति। तस्माद्रजस्वलान्नं नाश्नीयात्। अतश्च भ्रूणहत्याया एवैतद्रूपं प्रतिमास्यान्ते कञ्चुकमिव। तदाहुर्ब्रह्मवादिनः। अञ्जनाभ्यञ्जनमेवास्या न प्रतिग्राह्यं तद्धि स्त्रियोऽन्नमिति, तस्मात् तस्यास्तत्र न च मन्यन्ते आचारा याश्च योषित इति। सेयमुपयाति।

उदक्यास्त्वासते तेषां ये च केचिदनग्नयः।
गृहस्थाः श्रोत्रियाः पापाः सर्वे ते शूद्रधर्मिणाः।।

A woman, in her course, remains impure for three nights. [During that time] she shall not apply collyrium to her eyes, bathe in the water, sleep on the ground, sleep during the day time, touch fire, make a rope, clean her teeth, eat meat, look at the planets, laugh, do any work, drink water, out of her joined palms or out of a bell-metal, copper or iron vessel. It has been declared; that Indra having killed the three headed son of Tvaṣṭā was seized by sin and considered [himself so affected]. All beings tried out against him [saying] "O you slayer of a learned Brāhmaṇas! O you slayer of a learned Brāhmaṇa!!" He tan to women [and said] "Take upon yourselves the third part of this my sin of Brahmanicide." They said, "What shall we have [for doing your wish]?" He said, "Choose a boon." They said "May we obtain offspring during our season and may we live at pleasure with our husbands till the time of giving birth to children." They having obtained the boon and being replied 'So be it' took upon themselves the third part [of the sin] of Brahmanicide. Therefore the murder of a learned Brāhmaṇa takes place every month [with their menstrual discharge]. Therefore one shall not take food from a woman in her courses for such one puts on; every mouth, the shape of the guilt of Brahmanicide. The Brahmavādins [the reciters of the Veda] say : "Collyrium and ointment must not be accepted from her, for that is the food of women. They do not like the conduct of those women in that condition and say "She shall not approach me." Those [Brāhmaṇas in] whose [houses] menstruating women sit, those who preserve no sacred fire, and those in whose family there is ho Śrotriya are all sinful and equal td Śūdras.

इति वासिष्ठे धर्मशास्त्रे पञ्चमोऽध्याय:॥५॥

Chapter 6

आचार: परमो धर्म: सर्वेषामिति निश्चय:।

हीनाचारपरीतात्मा प्रेत्य चेह विनश्यति॥

To live; according to regulations; is undoubtedly the highest duty of all men. One, whose soul is lot contaminated by vile conduct, perishes in this world and in the next.

नैनं तपांसि न ब्रह्म नाग्निहोत्रं न दक्षिणा।

हीनाचाराश्रितं भ्रष्टं तारयन्ति कथञ्चन॥

Neither austerities, nor the Veda, nor the Agnihotra, nor gift of sacrificial presents can save one who has, resorted to low conduct and deviated [from the path of duty.]

आचारहीनं न पुनन्ति वेदा
यद्यप्यधीताः सह षड्भिरङ्गैः।
छन्दांस्येन मृत्युकाले त्यजन्ति
नीडं शकुन्ता इव जातपक्षाः॥

The Vedas do not purify him who is devoid of good conduct, though he may have studied them together, with the six Aṅgas; the metres leave this man, at death as full-pledged birds leave their nest.

आचारहीनस्य तु ब्राह्मणस्य
वेदाः षडङ्गा अखिलाः सपक्षाः।
कां प्रीतिमुत्थापयितुं समर्था
अन्धस्य दारा इव दर्शनीयाः॥

Like unto beautiful doors[1] [unable to please] a blind man how can all the Vedas with the six Aṅgas and esoteric sciences please a Brāhmaṇa who is devoid of good conduct?

नैनं छन्दांसि वृजिनात् तारयन्ति
मायाविनं मायया वर्त्तमानम्।
तत्राक्षरे सम्यगधीयमाने
पुनाति तद्ब्रह्म यथावदिष्टम्॥

The sacred metres do not save, from sin, the deceitful man who behaves deceitfully. If one syllable is studied completely that Veda purifies duly.[2]

---

1. The Benares text reads *dāra* which Buhler has translated as wife; in that case *darśaniyas* must be in the singular.
2. The Benares text differs which Buhler, differing with the commentator, translates as follows:– ''But that Veda, two syllables of which are studied in the right manner, purifies, just as the clouds give beneficient rain in the month of Isha.'' Isha is another name of Aśvina, the month of September.

दुराचारो हि पुरुषो लोके भवति निन्दितः।
दुःखभागी च सततं व्याधितोऽल्पायुरेव च॥

A man of bad conduct is blamed, in this, world, suffers from misery, is always, affected by diseases and becomes short-lived.

आचारात् फलते धर्ममाचारात् फलते धनम्।
आचाराच्छ्रियमाप्नोति आचारो हन्त्यलक्षणम्॥

From good conduct proceeds spiritual merit, from good conduct proceeds wealth, through good conduct one acquires prosperity and good conduct destroys inauspicious marks.

सर्वलक्षणहीनोऽपि यः सदाचारवान् नरः।
श्रद्दधानोऽनसूयश्च शतं वर्षाणि जीवति॥

Although: destitute of all, good marks a mat? who follows good conduct, has faith and is free from envy, lives a hundred years:

आहारनिर्हारविहारयोगाः
सुसंवृता धर्मविदा तु कार्याः।
वाग्बुद्धिवीर्याणि तपस्तथैव
धनायुषी गुप्ततमे च कार्ये॥

Eating, acts of evacuation, dalliance and practice of austerities shall be performed secretly by one who is conversant with the sacred law; speech, intellect, energy, austerities, wealth and age must be most carefully concealed.

उभे मूत्रपुरीषे तु दिवा कुर्यादुदङ्मुखः।
रात्रौ कुर्याद्दक्षिणस्थ एवं ह्यायुर्न रिच्यते॥

A man shall world urine and faces facing the north in the day-time; but in the night he shall do it facing the south; doing so his life will not be injured.

प्रत्यग्निं प्रतिसूर्यञ्च प्रतिगां प्रति च द्विजम्।
प्रति सोमोदकं सन्ध्यां प्रज्ञा नश्यति मेहतः॥

The understanding, of that man perishes who passes urine against a fire, the sun, a cow, a Brāhmaṇa, the moon, water and the twilights.

न नद्यां मेहनं कार्यं न पथि न च भस्मनि।
न गोमये न वा कृष्टे नोप्ते क्षेत्रे न शाद्वले॥

One shall not pass urine in a river, nor on a path, nor on ashes, nor on a cow-dung, nor on a ploughed field, nor on one that has been sown, nor on a grass plot.

छायायामन्धकारे वा रात्रावहनि वा द्विजः।
यथासुखमुखः कुर्यात् प्राणबाधभयेषु च॥

Either in the shade or in darkness, either in the night or in the day a twice-born person may pass urine in any position he pleases when he fears for his life.

उद्धृताभिरद्भिः कार्यं कुर्यान्न स्नानमनुद्धृताभिरपि।
आहरेन् मृत्तिकां विप्रः कूलात् ससिकतां तथा॥

One shall perform [the purification] with water fetched [for the purpose] : he shall perform bath with [what is] not fetched [for the purpose] [for purification] a Brāhmaṇa shall take earth that is mixed with gravel, from the bank [of a river.]

अन्तर्जले देवगृहे वल्मीके मूषिकस्थले।
कृतशौचावशिष्टे च न ग्राह्याः पञ्च मृत्तिकाः॥

Five sorts of earth must not be used, *viz.,* such as lies in the water, such as lies in a temple, what is on an ant-hell, on a hillock, thrown up by rats and left by one after cleaning himself.

एका लिङ्गे करे तिस्र उभाभ्यां द्वे तु मृत्तिके।
पञ्चापाने दशैकस्मिन्नुभयोः सप्तमृत्तिकाः॥

The organ must be cleaned by one [application of] earth, the [right] hand by three, both [feet] by two, the anus by five, the one *(i e, the* left hand) by ten and both (*i.e.*, hands and feet) by seven [applications.]

एतच्छौचं गृहस्थस्य द्विगुणं ब्रह्मचारिण:।
वानप्रस्थस्य त्रिगुणं यतीनान्तु चतुर्गुणम्॥

Such is the purification for a house-balder, it is double for religious students, treble for hermits and quadruple for ascetics.

अष्टौ ग्रासा मुनेर्भक्तं वानप्रस्थस्य षोडश।
द्वात्रिंशत् तु गृहस्थस्य अमितं ब्रह्मचारिण:॥

Eight mouthfuls form the meal of an ascetic, sixteen that of a hermit, thirty-two that of a house-holder and, an unlimited quantity that of a religious student.

अनड्वान् ब्रह्मचारी च आहिताग्निश्च ते त्रय:।
भुञ्जाना एव सिध्यन्ति नैषां सिद्धिरनश्नताम्।

An ox, a student, and a Brāhmaṇa who has kindled the sacred fire, can do their work if they eat; without eating [much] they cannot do it.

तपोदानोपहारेषु व्रतेषु नियमेषु च।
इज्याध्ययनधर्मेषु यो नासक्त: स निष्क्रिय:॥

He is said to be destitute of action who is not attached to penances, charities, offerings to a deity, religious observance self-imposed restraint, sacrifices and sacred duties.

योगस्तपो दमो दानं सत्यं शौचं दया श्रुतम्।
विद्या विज्ञानमास्तिक्यमेतद्ब्राह्मणलक्षणम्॥

The concentration of the mind, austerities, subjugation of the senses, charity, truthfulness, purity, compassion, sacred learning, temporal learning, discriminating knowledge, and faith in the existence of God are the characteristic marks of a Brāhmaṇa.

सर्वत्र दान्ता: श्रुतपूर्णकर्णा
जितेन्द्रिया: प्राणिवधे निवृत्ता:।
प्रतिगृहे शङ्कुचिताग्रहस्ता-
स्तेब्राह्मणास्तारयितुं समर्था:॥

Those Brāhmaṇas can save [from evil] who are, perfectly self controlled, whose ears are filled with spiritual texts, who have subdued organs of sense and action, who have ceased to injure living beings, and who close their hands when gifts are given.

असूयकः पिशुनश्चैव कृतघ्नो दीर्घरोषकः।
चत्वारः कर्मचाण्डाला जन्मतश्चापि पञ्चमः॥

One who is envious., one who is wicked, one who is ungrateful, and one whose anger lasts long, these (our are *Cāṇḍāla* by deeds; the fifth is one birth.

दीर्घवैरमसूयाञ्च असत्यं ब्रह्मदूषणम्।
पैशुन्यं निर्दयत्वञ्च जानीयाच्छूद्रलक्षण्॥

Bearing enmity for a long time, envy, speaking untruth, vilifying Brāhmaṇas, wickedness. And cruelty know [them], as the characteristics of a Śūdra.

किञ्चिद्वेदमयं पात्रं किञ्चित् पात्रं तपोमयम्।
पात्राणामपि तत् पात्रं शूद्रान्नं यस्य नोदरे॥

Some become worthy recipients of gifts, on account of their proficiency in the Veda and some through the practice of austerities. But that Brāhmaṇa, whose stomach does not contain the food of a Śūdra, is even the worthiest of all recipients

शूद्रान्नरसपुष्टाङ्गो ह्यधीयानोऽपि नित्यशः।
जुह्वित्वापि यजित्वापि गतिमूर्ध्वां न विन्दति॥

[A Brāhmaṇa, whose] limbs are nourished by the food and flavouring substances (given by a] Śūdra, does not meet the path leading upwards, even if he daily studies [the Veda*]*, offers oblations to the fire and performs sacrifices.

शूद्रोन्नेनोदरस्थेन यः कश्चिन् म्रियते द्विजः।
स भवेच्छूकरो ग्राम्यस्तस्य वा जायते कुले॥

If a twice-born person dies with the food of a Śūdra in his stomach he will become a village-pig [in the next birth] or be born in [that Śūdra's] family.

शूद्रान्नेन तु भुक्तेन मैथुनं योऽधिगच्छति।
यस्यान्नं तस्य ते पुत्रा न च स्वर्गार्हको भवेत्।।

If after being fed with a Śūdra's food he holds sexual intercourse his sons will belong to the giver of the food and he shall not ascend the celestial region.

स्वाध्यायाढ्यं योनिमित्रं प्रशान्तं
चैतन्यस्थं पापभीरुं बहुज्ञम्।
स्त्रीयुक्तान्नं धार्मिकं गोशरण्यं
व्रतैः क्षान्तं तादृशं पात्रमाहुः।।

[The learned] declare him as the worthy recipient who is ended with Vedic studies, who is of goad family, who is of subdued passions, who is stationed in the All-intelligent, who fears sin, who knows much, who is beloved of the females [of his family], who is religious, who is a refuge of cows, and who is forgiving by the practice of penances.

आमपात्रे यथा न्यस्तं क्षीरं दधि घृतं मधु।
विनश्येत् पात्रदौर्बल्यात्तच्च पात्रं रसाश्च ते।।
एवं गांच हिरण्यश्च वस्त्रमश्वं महीं तिलान्।
अविद्वान् प्रतिगृह्णानो भस्मीभवति दारुवत्।।

Just as milk, curd, clarified butter and honey, poured into an unburnt earthen vessel, perish on account of the weakness of the vessel, and neither the vessel no; those liquids [remain], so a man, devoid of learning, who accepts cows or gold, clothes, a horse, land and sesamum,- becomes ashes like a wood.

नाङ्गं नखञ्च वादित्रं कुर्यात्। न वापोऽञ्जलिना पिबेत्। न पादेन पाणिना वा राजानमपि हन्यात्, न जलेन जलम्। नेष्टकाभिः फलानि पातयेत् न फलेन फलम्। न कल्कपुटको भवेत्। न म्लेच्छभाषां शिक्षेत्।

One shall not make his joints or his nails crack. He shall not drink water with folded palms. We shall not strike along with his foot or his hand. He shall not strike water with water. One shall not strike down fruits with brick bats, nor a fruit by throwing another fruit at it. He shall not take sesamum paste with folded palms. He shall not learn a language spoken by Mlechhas,

अथाप्युदाहरन्ति।

Now they quote the following verses as an example :

न पाणिपादचपलो न नेत्रचलपो भवेत्।
न चाङ्गचपलो विप्र इति शिष्टस्य गोचर:।।

The opinion of the *Śiṣṭas* is that a man shall not be unusually active with his hands, nor with his feet, nor with his eyes, nor with his tongue and limbs.

पारम्पर्यागतो येषां वेद: सपरिबृंहण:।
ते शिष्टा ब्राह्मणा ज्ञेया: श्रुतिप्रत्यक्षहेतव:।।

Those Brāhmaṇas, in whose families the study of the Vedas, with all the subsidiary subjects, is hereditary, are to be known as *Śiṣṭas* on account of their seeing perceptibly the revealed texts.

यत्र सन्तं न चासन्तं नाश्रुतं न बहुश्रुतम्।
न सुवृत्तं न दुर्वृत्तं वेद कश्चित् स ब्राह्मण इति।।

He, indeed, is a Brāhmaṇa of whom no one knows if he is good or bad, if he is ignorant or deeply learned, if he is of good or bad conduct.

इति वासिष्ठे धर्मशास्त्रे षष्ठोऽध्याय:।।६।।

Chapter 7

चत्वार आश्रमा ब्रह्मचारिगृहस्थवानप्रस्थपरिव्राजका:। तेषां वेदमधीत्य वेदो वा वेदान् वा अविशीर्णब्रह्मचर्योऽपनिक्षेप्सुमावसेत्। ब्रह्मचर्याचार्य्यं परिचरेदाशरीरविमोक्षणात्। आचार्य प्रमीतेऽग्निं परिचरेत् विज्ञायते हि चाहवाग्निराचार्य्य इति। संयतवाक् चतुर्थषष्ठाष्टमकालभोजी भैक्षमाचरेत्। गुर्वधीनो जटिल: शिखाजटो वा गुरुं गच्छन्तमनुगच्छेदासीनञ्चानुतिष्ठेत शयानञ्चासीन उपवसेदाहूताध्यायी सर्वभैक्षं निवेद्यं तदनुज्ञया भुञ्जीत। खट्वाशयनदन्तप्रक्षालनाभ्यञ्जनवर्जी तिष्ठेदहनि

रात्रावासीत्। त्रिः कृत्वोऽभ्युपेयादापः।

There are four Āśramas or orders, *viz.,* the student, the householder, the hermit and the ascetic. Of them a man, who has studied one, two or three Vedas without violating the rules of studentship, may enter any of these which so ever he pleases. A[perpetual] student shall serve his preceptor until death; in case the preceptor dies he shall serve the sacred fire. It is known [in the Veda] that a preceptor is the sacred fire. [A religious student) shall be of controlled speech, eat in the fourth, sixth or eighth hour of the day and go out a-begging. He shall remain under his preceptor, wear either matted locks or one on the crown of his head, follow the teacher while walking, stand while he is;(seated and remain seated while he lies down. He shall study on being called by the preceptor to do so. Having dedicated [unto the preceptor] all that he has received by begging he shall eat with his permission. He shall avoid to sleep on a cot, to, clean teeth, to rub oil on the body and to, apply collyrium. He shall remain standing during the day and seated during he might. He shall bathe thrice a day.

इति वासिष्ठे धर्मशास्त्रे सप्तमोऽध्याय:॥७॥

Chapter 8

गृहस्थो विनीतक्रोधहर्षो गुरुणानुज्ञातः स्नात्वा असमानार्षामस्पृष्टमैथुनां यवीयसीं सदृशीं भार्यां विन्देत्। पञ्चमीं मातृबन्धुभ्यः सप्तमीं पितृबन्धुभ्यः वैवाह्यमग्निमिन्ध्यात्। सायमागतमतिथिं नावरुन्ध्यात्। नास्यानश्नन् गृहे वसेत्।

A house-holder shall be of suppressed anger and joy. Having bathed he shall, commanded by the preceptor, take for a wife a young female of his own caste who does not belong to the same Gotra or Pravara, and who has not had intercourse [with another man], who is not related within five degree on the mother's side nor within seven degrees on the father's side. He shall offer oblations to the nuptial fire. He shall not send away elsewhere a guest who comes in the evening. A [guest] shall not live in 'his house without receiving food.

यस्य नाश्नाति वासार्थी ब्राह्मणो गृहमागतः।
सुकृतं तस्य यत् किञ्चित् सर्वमादाय गच्छति।।

If a Brāhmaṇa, coming to his (*i.e.* a house-holder's) house for residence, does not take food he shall go, away taking with him all, the spiritual merit [of that, house-holder].

एकरात्रन्तु निवसन्नतिथिर्ब्राह्मणः स्मृतः।
अनित्यं हि स्थितिर्यस्मात् तस्मादतिथिरुच्यते।।

A Brāhmaṇa, who lives for one night only is called a guest *(atithi)* in the Smṛti, for *atithi* is he who lives for a short time only.

नैकग्रामीणमतिथिं विप्र साङ्गतिकं तथा।
काले प्राप्ते अकाले वा नास्यानश्नन् गृहे वसेत्।।

A Brāhmaṇa, who lives in the same village or one- who comes on pleasure or business, is not [called] an *atithi,* [But a guest], whether he comes at the proper time or an improper hour, must not live in the house [of a house-holder] without taking his food.

श्रद्धाशीलोऽस्पृहयालुः अलमग्न्याधेयाय नानाहिताग्निः स्यादलञ्च सोमपानाय नासोमयाजी स्यात्। युक्तः स्वाध्याये प्रजनने यज्ञे च गृहेष्वभ्यागतं प्रत्युत्थानासनशयनवाक्सुनृताभिर्मानयेत्। यथाशक्ति चान्नेन सर्वभूतानि।

[A householder] must have faith and be free from covetousness; [if he is] capable of maintaining sacred fires he must not fail to kindle them; if lie is capable of drinking Soma juice he must not abstain from performing a Soma sacrifice.

[A house-holder] must be busy with reciting the Veda; procreating children and performing sacrifices. He shall honour visitors to his house by rising to meet them, by [offering them] seats, by speaking to there kindly and extolling their virtues. He shall [entertain] all creatures with food according to his ability.

गृहस्थ एव यजते गृहस्थस्तप्यते तपः।
चतुर्णामाश्रमाणान्तु गृहस्थस्तु विशिष्यते।।

A house-holder alone celebrates sacrifices, a house-holder alone practices austerities, therefore the order of house-holders is the most distinguished among the four:

यथा नदीनदाः सर्वे समुद्रे यान्ति संस्थितिम्।
एवमाश्रमिणः सर्वे गृहस्थे यान्ति संस्थितिम्॥

As all rivers and rivulets go id the ocean to be United so all orders are to associate with the house-holders:

यथा मातरमाश्रित्य सर्वे जीवन्ति जन्तवः।
एवं गृहस्थमाश्रित्य सर्वे जीवन्ति भिक्षुकाः॥

As all creatures live depending upon their mother to all the mendicants live depending upon' [the protection of]'the householders.

नित्योदकी नित्ययज्ञोपवीती नित्यस्वाध्यायी पतितान्नवर्जी।
ऋतौ गच्छन् विधिवच्च जुह्वन् न ब्राह्मणश्च्यवते ब्रह्मलोकात्॥

A Brāhmaṇas, who daily carries water, who always wears, the sacred thread, who daily studies the Veda, Who avoids the food of outcasts; who' visits his wife in the proper season, who celebrates sacrifices according to rules; does not fall from the region of Brāhmaṇa.

इति वासिष्ठे धर्मशास्त्रेऽष्टमोऽध्यायः॥८॥

Chapter 9

वानप्रस्थो जटिलश्चीराजिनवासा ग्रामञ्च न प्रविशेत्। न फालकृष्टमधितिष्ठेत्। अकृष्टं मूलफलं सञ्चिन्वीत। ऊर्ध्वरेताः क्षमाशयः। मूलफलभैक्षेणाश्रमागतमतिथिमर्च्चयेत्। दद्यादेव च प्रतिगृह्णीयात्। त्रिषवणमुदकमुपस्पृशेत्। श्रावणकेनाग्निमाधायाहिताग्निः स्याद् वृक्षमूलिकः ऊर्ध्वषड्भ्यो मासेभ्योऽनग्निरनिकेतः। दद्याद्देवपितृमनुष्येभ्यः। स गच्छेत् स्वर्गमानन्त्यम्।

A Vānaprastha (hermit, shall wear matted locks and put on bark and deer skin. He shall not enter a Village. He shall not tread a ploughed land. He shall gather wild-growing roots and fruits.

He shall draw up his virile power and be forgiving. He shall honour guests coming to his hermitage with alms of roots and fruit. He shall only give but never receive [presents.] He shall bathe thrice (morning, noon, and evening). Kindling fire according to the regulation of *Śrāvaṇaka* (Sūtra) he shall preserve the sacred Fire. He shall live at the root of a tree. Living thus for over six months he shall keep no fire and have no house. He who [thus] gives [their due] to the deities, departed manes and men, shall attain to the endless celestial region.

इति वासिष्ठे धर्मशास्त्रे नवमोऽध्याय:॥९॥

Chapter 10

परिव्राजक: सर्वभूताभयदक्षिणां दत्त्वा प्रतिष्ठेत्।

A religious mendicant shall depart giving a present of the promise of safety from injury to all creatures.

अथाप्युदाहरन्ति।

Now they quote the following verses as an example :

अभयं सर्वभूतेभ्यो दत्त्वा चरति यो द्विज:।
तस्यापि सर्वभूतेभ्यो न भयं जातु विद्यते॥
अभयं सर्वभूतेभ्यो दत्त्वा यद्भुवि वर्त्तते।
हन्ति जातानजातांश्च प्रतिगृह्णाति यस्य च॥
सन्न्यसेत् सर्वकर्माणि वेदमेकं न सन्न्यसेत्।
वेदसन्न्यासत: शूद्रस्तस्माद्वेदं न संन्यसेत्॥

A twice-born person; who having given a promise of safety to all creatures wanders about; has clothing to fear from all creatures. He who lives in this world without giving *a* promise of safety to all living creatures, destroys the born and the unborn likewise does one who accepts presents. Let one renounce all the religious rites but not [the recitation of] the Veda. By discarding the Veda one becomes a Śūdra *and* therefore one shall not r6nounce the Veda.

एकाक्षरं परं ब्रह्म प्राणायामः परन्तपः।
उपवासात् परं भैक्षं दया दानाद्विशिष्यते।।

[To recite] one syllable (Om) is the highest [method oil reciting Brahmā (Veda); to suppress vital airs is the highest form of penance; to live on alms is better than fasting and compassion is preferable to liberality.

मुण्डोऽममत्वपरिग्रहः सप्तागाराण्यसङ्कल्पिता न चरेद्भैक्ष्यं विधूमे सन्नमुषले एकशाटोपरिवृतोऽजिनेन वा गोप्रलूनैस्तृणैर्वेष्टितशरीरः स्थण्डिलशाय्यनित्यां वसतिं वसेत् ग्रामान्ते देवगृहे शून्यागारे वृक्षमूले वा मनसा ज्ञानमधीयान्। अरण्यनित्यो न ग्राम्यपशूनां सन्दर्शने विहरेत्।

[An ascetic] shall shave his head, shall own nothing avid no home. He shall beg food at seven-houses not selected before, when it is smokeless and when the pestle lies motionless. He shall wear a single garment, or cover his body with deer-skin or with grass that has been nibbled at by a cow. He shall live on the naked ground and shall not live long at one place:. [He shall live] at the outskirts of a village, in a temple, in an empty house or at the root of a tree. He shall seek knowledge by the mind. Living always in the forest he shall not walk about within sight of the village cattle.

अथाप्युदाहरन्ति।

Now they quote the following verses as an example:

अरण्यनित्यस्य जितेन्द्रियस्य सर्वेन्द्रियप्रीतिनिवर्त्तकस्य।
अध्यात्मचिन्तागतमानसस्य ध्रुवा ह्यनावृत्तिरुपेक्षकस्य।।
अव्यक्तलिङ्गोऽव्यक्ताचारोऽनुन्मत्त उन्मत्तवेशः।

Freedom from re-births is certain for him who always lives in the forest, who has conquered the sense organs, who has renounced all sensual gratification, whose mind is devoted to the meditation of the Supreme Self and who is [perfectly] indifferent. He shall be of no visible mark or rule of conduct. Though not mad he shall appear like a maniac.

अथाप्युदाहरन्ति।

Now they quote the following verses as an example :

न शब्दशास्त्राभिरतस्य मोक्षो
न चापि लोके ग्रहणे रतस्य।
न भोजनाच्छादनतत्परस्य
न चापि रम्यावसथप्रियस्य।।

There is no salvation for him, who is addicted to the study of the science of words, nor for him who is given to the acceptance of presents in this world, nor for him who is fond of eating and clothing, nor for him who loves a charming residence.

न चोत्पातनिमित्ताभ्यां न नक्षत्राङ्गविद्यया।
अनुशासनवादाभ्यां भिक्षां लिप्सेत कर्हिचित्।।

One shall not seek to obtain alms by [explaining] evil portends and omens, nor by skill in astrology and palmistry, nor by [the exposition of] the scriptural injunctions, nor by casuistry.

अलाभे न विषादी स्याल्लाभे चैव न हर्षयेत्।
प्राणयात्रिकमात्रः स्यान्मात्रासङ्गा द्विनिर्गतः।।

He shall not be dejected when he gets nothing nor glad when he receives something. Renouncing all attachment for earthly possessions he shall seek only as much as will sustain life.

न कुट्यां नोदके सङ्गे न चैले न त्रिपुष्करे।
नागारे नासने नान्ने यस्य वै मोक्षवित्तमः।।

He alone is the foremost of those conversant with (the road of] emancipation who cares neither for a hut, nor for water, nor for clothes, nor for the three Puṣkaras[1], nor for a dwelling, nor for a seat, nor for food.

ब्राह्मणकुले वा यल्लभेत् तद्भुञ्जीत सायं मधुमांससर्पिर्वर्जम्। यतीन् साधून् वा गृहस्थान् सायंप्रातश्च तृप्येत्। ग्रामे वसेदजिह्मोऽशरणोसङ्कसुकः।

1. Three sacred tanks at the holy shrine of Puṣkara.

He shall eat in the evening what he shall get in the house of a Brāhmaṇa except honey, meat and clarified butter. Evening and morning the ascetics and pious house-holders shall derive satiation [from eating]. [An ascetic] shall live [at his option] in a village, should not be crooked, shall not have a house and be of concentrated mind. He shall not join his senses with their objects. By avoiding injury and kindness he shall be indifferent to all living creatures.

न चेन्द्रियसंयोगं कुर्वीत केनचित्, उपेक्षकः सर्वभूतानां हिंसानुग्रहपरिहारेण। पैशुन्यमत्सराभिमानाहङ्काराश्रद्धानार्जवात्मस्त्वपरगर्हादम्भ-लोभमोहक्रोधासूयाविवर्जनं सर्वाश्रमिणां धर्म्मिष्ठो यज्ञोपवीत्युदककमण्डलुहस्तः शुचिर्ब्राह्मणो वृषलान्नपानवर्जी न हीयते ब्रह्मलोकात्॥

To renounce back-biting, envy, pride, conceit, unbelief, crookedness, self-praise, slandering, egoism, avarice, stupefaction, anger, and jealousy is the duty of all orders. A Brāhmaṇa, who is pious, who wears the sacred thread, who holds in his hand a pitcher filled with water, who is pure and who renounces a Śūdra's food and drink, shall not fall from the region of Brahma.

इति वासिष्ठे धर्मशास्त्रे दशमोऽध्यायः॥१०॥

Chapter 11

षट्कर्मा गृहदेवताभ्यो बलिं हरेत्। श्रोत्रियायान्नं दत्त्वा ब्रह्मचारिणे वानन्तरं पितृभ्यो दद्यात्, ततोऽतिथिं भोजयेत् श्रेष्ठासमानुपूर्वेण स्वगृह्याणां कुमारीबालवृद्धतरुणप्रभृतींस्ततोऽपरान् गृह्यान्। श्वचाण्डालपतितवायसेभ्यो भूमौ निर्वपेत्। शूद्रेभ्य उच्छिष्टं वा दद्याच्छेषं यती भुञ्जीत।

[A Brāhmaṇa] of six rites shall give Bali-offerings to the [presiding] deities of the house. Having offered food unto a Śrotriya [one shall] offer [it] unto a student and then unto the departed manes, he shall then feed his guests in due order, the worthiest first, then the maidens. The infants, the aged and the advanced [in age] members of his family and then the other members and dependants. He shall throw some food on the ground for the dogs, Cāṇḍālas, outcasts and crows. He may give to a Śūdra the residue [of the food]. The self-controlled [householder] shall eat what remains.

सर्वोपयोगेन पुनः पाको यदि निवृत्ते वैश्वदेवेऽतिथिरागच्छे-द्विशेषेणास्मा अन्नं कारयेद्विजायतेऽह्नि वैश्वानरः प्रविशत्यतिथिर्ब्राह्मणो गृहम्।

A fresh meal, with all the materials Las for the first shall be [made] if a guest comes after the Vaiśvadeva has been offered; for such a guest he shall have a particular food made. It is known [in the Veda] that Vaiśvānara fire enters the house [in the shape of a] Brāhmaṇa guest. Through him they get rain and food through rain. Therefore people know that the [the [reception of a guest] is a ceremony averting evil.

तस्मादुपवानमन्यत्र वर्षाभ्यस्तां हि शान्तिजनाविद्धिरिति तं भोजयित्वोपासीतासीमान्तादनुव्रजेदनुज्ञाताद्वा। परपक्ष ऊर्ध्वं चतुर्थ्यां पितृभ्यो दद्यात्, पूर्वेद्युर्ब्राह्मणान् सन्निपात्य यतीन् गृहस्थान् साधून् वा परिणतवयसोऽविकर्मस्थान् क्षोत्रियान् शिष्यानन्तेवासिनः शिष्यानपि गुणवतो भोजयेद्विलग्नशुक्लविगृधिश्यावदन्तकुष्ठिकुनखिवर्जम्।

Having fed him one shall honour him, shall accompany him to the outskirt or until he gets permission [to return]. One shall offer oblations unto the manes during the dark fort-night after the fourth [day]. Having invited the Brāhmaṇas an the day previous [to the Śrāddha] one shall feed the ascetics, virtuous householders who are Śrotriyas, who are of advanced years, who do not follow forbidden occupations, pupils living in the house, and qualified pupils. One shall feed all except those who neglect their duties, those suffering from white leprosy, eunuchs, those who have black teeth, those who suffer from black leprosy, and those who have deform nails.

अथाप्युदाहरन्ति।

अथ चेन्मन्त्रविद्युक्तः शारीरैः पंक्तिदूषणैः।
अदूष्यन्तं यमः प्राह पंक्तिपावन एव सः॥

Now they quote the following verses as an example if one,

conversant with the Mantras, is afflicted with bodily [defects] which desecrate a row, Yama calls him, irreproachable.

श्राद्धेनोद्वासनी यानि उच्छिष्टान्या दिनक्षयात्।
खे पतन्ति हि या धारास्ता: पिबन्त्यकृतोदका:॥

And he too, is a sanctifier of the row, At a Śrāddha, the remnants [of a meal] shall not be cleared away, until the end of the day. They (*i.e.* the manes] for whom no watery libations have been offered) drink streams flowing from the sky.

उच्छिष्टेन प्रपुष्टास्ते यावन्नास्तमितो रवि:।
क्षीरधारास्ततो यान्त्यक्षया: सञ्चरभागिन:॥

They are nourished by the remnants till the sun is not set. The streams of mill become kin-ending and movable.

प्राक्संस्कारप्रमीतानां प्रवेशनमिति श्रुति:।
भागधेयं मनु: प्राह उच्छिष्टोच्छेषणे उभे॥

Manu has said that both the remainder [in the vessels) and the fragments are the share of those members of the family who died before receiving the sacraments.

उच्छेषणं भूमिगतं विकिरेल्लेपसोंदकम्।
अनुप्रेतेषु विसृजेदप्रजानामनायुषाम्॥

One shall give the residue, that has fallen on the ground, consisting of the wipings and water to the manes of those who died without offspring and of those who died young.

उभयो: शाखयोर्युक्तं पितृभ्योऽन्नं निवेदितम्।
तदन्तरं प्रतीक्षन्ते ह्यसुरा दुष्टचेतस:॥

Food shall be dedicated unto the manes supported by both the hands. The wicked-minded *Asuras* always seek holes therein.

तस्मादशून्यहस्तेन कुर्यादन्नमुपागतम्।
भोजनं वा समालभ्य तिष्ठतोच्छेषणे उभे॥

Therefore one shall not offer food in empty hands; or he shall stand holding the dish [until] leavings of both kinds have been produced.

द्वौ दैवे पितृकृत्ये त्रीन्नेकैकमुभयत्र वा।
भोजयेत् सुसमृद्धोऽपि न प्रसृज्येत विस्तरे।।

One shall feed two [Brāhmaṇas] at the offering to the deities, three at the offering to the manes or one on either occasion; even a very rich man shall not be anxious to [feed] a very large number.

सत्क्रिया देशकालौ च शौचं ब्राह्मण-सम्पदः।
पञ्चैतान् विस्तरो हन्ति तस्मात् तं परिवर्जयेत्।।

Good treatment, [consideration of] time and place, purity and [selection of] virtuous Brāhmaṇas [as guests] a large company destroys these five; therefore one shall not invite a large number.

अपि वा भोजयेदेकं ब्राह्मणं वेदपारगम्।
शुभशीलोपसम्पन्नं सर्वालक्षणवर्जितम्।।

Or one may feed even one Brāhmaṇa who ha: studied the whole Veda, who is endued with good conduct and who is free from all evil marks.

यद्येकं भोजयेच्छ्राद्धे दैवं तत्र कथं भवेत्।
अन्नं पात्रे समुद्धृत्य सर्वस्य प्रकृतस्य तु।।
देवतायतने कृत्वा ततः श्राद्धं प्रवर्त्तते।
प्राश्येदग्नौ तदन्नन्तु दद्याद्वा ब्रह्मचारिणे।।

How can oblation to the deities be made if one feeds a single Brāhmaṇa at a Śrāddha. Having collected *in* a vessel [a portion of) all sorts of food, placed it in, a temple one shall then begin the performance of a Śrāddha. He shall throw into the fire [a portion of that) food or shall give it to a Brahmacārin.

यावदुष्णं भवत्यन्नः यावदश्नन्ति वाग्यताः।
तावद्धि पितरोऽश्नन्ति यावन्नोक्ता हविर्गुणाः।।

They shall, controlling the speech, eat the food so long it continues warm; the manes eat it so long the qualities of the food are not spoken of.

हविर्गुणा न वक्तव्याः पितरो भावतर्पिताः।
पितृभिस्तर्पितैः पश्चाद्वक्तव्यं शोभनं हविः।।

The qualities of the food must not be spoken of as long as the manes *(i.e.,* the Brāhmaṇas representing them) are not satiated. Afterwards when the Pitṛs are satisfied they may say, Beautiful is the sacrificial food:

नियुक्तस्तु यदा श्राद्धे दैवे तन्तु समुत्सृजेत्।
यावन्ति पशुरोमानि तावन्नरकमृच्छति।।

But one, who being invited at a Śrāddha or a sacrifice rejects it *i.e.,* meat) shall go to hell for as many years as the beast has hairs.

त्रीणि श्राद्धे पवित्राणि दौहित्रः कुतपस्तिलाः।
त्रीणि चात्रं प्रशंसन्ति शौचमक्रोधमत्वराम्।।

Three are sanctifying in a Śrāddha, a daughter's son, the eighth Muhūrtta of the day and sesamum and three, [others] purify more the food, *viz.,* purity, freedom from anger and from precipitation.

दिवसस्याष्टमे भागे मन्दीभवति भास्करः।
स कालः कुतपो नाम पितृणां दत्तमक्षयम्।।

The eighth part of the day, when the Sun's progress becomes slow, that period is named *Kutapas;* what is then] given to the manes endures for ever.

श्राद्धं दत्त्वा य भुक्त्वा च मैथुनं योऽधिगच्छति।
भवन्ति पितरस्तस्य तन्मासं रेतसो भुजः।।

The departed manes of that man, who holds sexual intercourse with a woman after offering or having dined at a Śrāddha, feed for a month on his semen.

यतस्ततो जायते च दत्त्वा भुक्त्वा च पैतृकम्।
न स विद्यामवाप्नोति क्षीणायुश्चैव जायते।।

One who studies after offering food at a Śrāddha or partaking of funeral food, is born in this or that (i. e., indifferent) family; he does not acquire sacred learning and becomes short-lived [in that birth].

पिता पितामहश्चैव तथैव प्रपितामहः।
उपासते सुतं जातं शकुन्ता इव पिप्पलम्॥

The father, the grand father and the great grandfather adore a son born to them as the birds [become hopeful on seeing] a Pippala tree.

मधुमांसैश्च शाकैश्च पयसा पायसेन वा।
अधनो दास्यति श्राद्धं वर्षासु च मघासु च॥

Even a poor man makes funeral offerings with honey, meat, vegetables, milk and porridge both in the rainy season and under the constellation of Maghā.

सन्तानवर्द्धनं पुत्रं तृप्यन्तं पितृकर्मणि।
देवब्राह्मणसम्पन्नमभिनन्दन्ति पूर्वजाः॥

The ancestors always welcome a descendant who lengthens, the line, who finds pleasure in performing funeral sacrifices and who is rich in idols and good Brāhmaṇas.

नन्दन्ति पितरस्तस्य सुवृष्टैरिव कर्षकाः।
यद्गयास्थो ददात्यन्नं पितरस्तेन पुत्रिणः॥

The manes rejoice at him as husbandmen at good rain. The manes possess a descendant in him who offers them food at Gayā.

श्रावणयाग्रहायण्योश्चान्वष्टकायाञ्च पितृभ्यो दद्याद् द्रव्यदेशब्राह्मण-सन्निधाने वा कालनियमोऽवश्यम्। यो ब्राह्मणोऽग्निमादधीत, दर्शपूर्णमासाग्रयणेष्टिचातुर्मास्यपशुसोमैश्च यजते। नैयमिकं ह्येतदृणं संस्तुतञ्च विज्ञायते हि त्रिभिरृणैरृणवान् ब्राह्मणा जायते; यज्ञेन देवेभ्यः, प्रजया पितृभ्यो, ब्रह्मचर्य्येण ऋषिभ्यः इत्येष वा अनृणो यज्वा यः पुत्री ब्रह्मचर्यवानिति। गर्भाष्टमेषु ब्राह्मणमुपनयीत, गर्भैकादशेषु राजन्यं, गर्भद्वादशेषु

वैश्यम्। पालाशो दण्डो बैल्वो वा ब्राह्मणस्य, नैयग्रोध: क्षत्रियस्य, वा औडम्बुरो वा वैश्यस्य। कृष्णाजिनमुत्तरीयं ब्राह्मणस्य, रौरवं क्षत्रियस्य, गव्यं वस्ताजिनं वैश्यस्य। शुक्लमाहतं वासा ब्राह्मणस्य, माञ्जिष्ठं क्षत्रियस्य, हारिद्रं कौशेयं वैश्यस्य सर्वेषां वा तान्तवमरक्तम्। भवत्पूर्वां ब्राह्मणो भिक्षां याचेत, भवन्मध्यां राजन्यो, भवदन्त्यां वैश्यश्च। आषोडशाद्ब्राह्मणस्यानतीत: काल, आद्वाविंशात् क्षत्रियस्याचतुर्विंशाद्वैश्यस्यात ऊर्ध्वं पतितसावित्रीका भवन्ति। नैनानुपनयेन्नाध्यापयेन्न याजयेन्नैभिर्विवाहयेयु:। पतितसावित्रीक उद्दालकव्रतं चरेत्।

One shall make offerings to the manes both on the full moon days of the month of Śrāvaṇa (July August) and Agrahāyaṇa (November and December) and on the Anvaṣṭakā.[1] There is no necessity of restriction about time if materials, [sacred] place and [good] Brāhmaṇas are near at hand. A Brāhmaṇa, who kindles the sacred fires, shall perform the full and new moon sacrifices, the (half-yearly] Agrahāyaṇa Iṣṭhi, the Cāturmāsya sacrifice, the sacrifices in which animals are killed and the Soma sacrifices. All this is enjoined in the Veda and is spoken highly of as a debt. A Brāhmaṇa is born loaded with three debts. He owes sacrifices to the deities, descendants to the departed manes and religious studentship to the *Ṛṣis*. One becomes free from debt who celebrates sacrifices, who begets a son, and who leads the life of a religious student. One shall invest a Brāhmaṇa with the sacred thread in the eighth year after conception, a Kṣatriya in the eleventh year after conception and a Vaiśya in the twelfth year after conception. The staff of a Brāhmaṇa [student] may be [made] of Palāśa wood or Bel wood; that of a Kṣatriya of the wood of Nyagrodha, and that of a Vaiśya of Udumbara wood. The upper garment of a Brāhmaṇa [shall be] the skin of a black antelope; that of a Kṣatriya the skin of a spotted deer; that of a Vaiśya a cow-skin or that of a he-goat. The wearing cloth of a Brāhmaṇa shall be white [and] spotless; that of a Kṣatriya dyed with madder that of a Vaiśya dyed with turmeric or made of [raw]

1. The day following the Aṣṭaka or the eigth day i.e., the ninth day of the dark halves of Māргasiras, Pauṣa, Māgha and Phālguna.

silk. The undyed cotton cloth [is] for all [religious students]. A Brāhmaṇa shall beg alms Placing (the word] *Bhavad* (Lord) first; a Kṣatriya placing [the word] *Bhavad* in the middle and a Vaiśya placing [the word] *Bhavad* at the end. The time for the initiation of a Brāhmaṇa does not expire until the completion of the sixteenth year, for that of a Kṣatriya until the completion of the twenty second year and for that of a Vaiśya until the completion of the twenty-fourth. After that they become men whose Sāvitrī has been neglected: One shall not initiate such men, teach them nor officiate as priests at their sacrifices; one shall not contract matrimonial alliances with them. A man; who we Sāvitrī has been neglected, may perform the *Uddālaka* penance.

द्वौ मासौ यावकेन वर्त्तयेन्मासं माक्षिकेनाष्टरात्रं घृतेन षड्रात्रमयाचितं त्रिरात्रमब्भक्षोऽहोरात्रमेवोपवसेत्। अश्वमेधावभृथं गच्छेद्व्रात्यस्तोमेन वा यजेत्।

He shall live for two months on barley-gruel for one month on honey collected by bees, for eight nights on clarified butter, for six nights on unsolicited food, for three nights on water and shall fast for a day and night. Or he may go to bathe at the terminating bath of a horse-sacrifice or he may offer a Vrātyastoma.

इति वासिष्ठे धर्मशास्त्रे एकादशोऽध्याय:॥११॥

Chapter 12

अथात: स्नातकव्रतानि। स न कञ्चिद्याचेतान्यत्र राजान्तेवासिभ्य: क्षुधापरीतस्तु किञ्चिदेव याचेत कृतमकृतं वा क्षेत्रं गामजाविकं सन्ततं हिरण्यं धान्यमन्नं वा, न तु स्नातक: क्षुधावसीदेदित्युपदेशो। न नद्याम् सहसा संविशेन्न रजस्वलायामयोग्यायाम्। न कुलं-कुलं स्याद्वसन्ती विततां नातिक्रमेन्नोद्यन्तमादित्यं पश्येन्नादित्यं तपन्तं नास्तं, मूत्रपुरीषे कुर्यान्न निष्ठीवेत्, परिवेष्टितशिरा भूमिमयज्ञियैस्तृणैरन्तर्द्धाय मूत्रपुरीषे कुर्यादुदङ्मुखश्चाहनि नक्तं दक्षिणामुख: सन्ध्यामासीतीत्तरामुदाहरन्ति।

Now [are] the duties of a Snātaka. He shall not beg from any body except a king.' and a pupil. Bat stricken with hunger lie may ask foe some [small gift,] cultivated or uncultivated field, a cow, a goat or a sheep; or for gold, grain or food. But the injunction is that a Snātaka shall not be exhausted with hunger. He shall not be !a stay-at-home. He shall not cross a rope to which a calf is tied. He shall not look at the sun when he rises or sets or sheds-heat. One shall not pats urine or excreta in water, nor spit into it. He shall pass urine or excreta after wrapping up his head, covering the ground with grass that is not used in a sacrifice, facing the north in the day time, the south at night, and the north in the twilight.

Now they quote the following verses as an example :

स्नातकानान्तु नित्यं स्यादन्तर्वासस्तथोत्तरम्।
यज्ञापवीते द्वे यष्टिः सोदकश्च कमण्डलुः।।

The Snātakas shall always put on a lower and an upper garment, [wear] two sacrificial threads [and shall carry] a staff and a pitcher filled with water.

अप्सु पाणौ च काष्ठे च कथितं पावकं शुचिम्।
तस्मादुदकपाणिभ्यां परिमृज्यात् कमण्डलुम्।।

[A vessel is being spoken of [as] pure with water, or with a stick, or with fire. Therefore [a Snātaka] shall clean [his] vessel with water and with his [right] hand.

पर्यग्निकरणं ह्येतन्मनुराह प्रजापतिः।
कृत्वा चावश्यकार्याणि आचामेच्छौचवित्ततः।।

Manu, the lord of created beings, designates it as encircling it with fire. Having performed the obligatory rites one, perfectly acquainted with the rules of purification, shall sip water.

प्राङ्मुखोऽन्नानि भुञ्जीत, तूष्णीं साङ्गुष्ठं कृशग्रासं ग्रसेत, न च मुखशब्दं कुर्यादृतुकालाभिगामी स्यात्। पर्ववर्जं स्वदारे वा। तीर्थमुपेयात्।

He shall eat food, facing the east. He shall silently swallow the entire mouthful with the four fingers and with the thumb. He shall not make a sound with his mouth. He may know his wife in the proper season or at any other time except on the Parva days. He shall drink sacred waler,

अथाप्युदाहरन्ति।

Now they quote .the following verses as an example :

यस्तु पाणिगृहीताया आस्ये कुर्वीत मैथुनम्।
भवन्ति पितरस्तस्य तन्मांसरेतसो भुजः।
य स्यादनतिचारेण रतिसाधर्मसंश्रिता।।

The ancestors of a man, who commits intercourse through the mouth of his wedded wife, feed, that month, on his semen, for all unnatural intercourse is against the sacred law.

अपि च पावकोऽपि ज्ञायते। अद्य श्वो वा विजनिष्यमाणाः पतिभिः सह शयन्त इति स्त्रीणामिन्द्रदत्तो वरः। उन्नतवृक्षमारोहेण कूपमवरोहेन्नाग्निं मुखेनापधमेन्नाग्निं ब्राह्मणञ्चान्तरेण व्यपेयान्नाग्न्योर्ब्राह्मणयोरनुज्ञाप्य वा। भार्या सह नाश्नीयादवीर्यवदपत्यं भवतीति वाजसनेयके विज्ञायते। नेन्द्रधनुर्नाम्ना निर्द्दिशेन्मणिधनुरिति ब्रूयात्। पालाशमासनपादुके दन्तधावनमिति वर्जयेत्। नोत्सङ्गे भक्षयेदधो न भुञ्जीत। वैणवं दण्डं धारयेद्रुक्मकुण्डले च। न बहिर्माला धारयेदन्यत्र रुक्ममय्याः सभासमवायांश्च वर्जयेत्।

It is known that Indra conferred upon women the sanctifying boon that even those [among them], who are to be mothers either to-day or to-morrow, *may* cohabit with their husbands. He (*i.e.*, *a* Snātaka) shall not ascend a lofty tree, shall not descend into a well shall not blow the fire with his mouth, and shall not pass between a fire and a Brāhmaṇa; nor between two fires; nor between two Brāhmaṇas; or he may do so after having obtained permission. He shall not take meals with his wife, for it is said in the Vājasaneyaka, "His children shall be shorn of manly vigour." He shall not point out a rain-bow by its [true] name], Indras bow." He shall call it a jewelled bow. He shall avoid seats, dogs and sticks for cleansing teeth made of Palāśa wood. He shall not eat [food placed] in his lap he shall not eat [food placed] in a chair. Let him carry a bamboo-staff and wear two golden ear-rings. He shall not wear any visible garland save a golden one. He shall avoid assemblies and crowds.

अथाप्युदाहरन्ति।

Now they quote the following verses as an example:

अप्रामाण्यञ्च वेदानामार्षाणाञ्चैव दर्शनम्।

अव्यवस्था च सर्वत्र एतन्नाशनमात्मनः॥

To deny the authority of the Vedas, to doubt the injunctions of the Ṛṣis and to consider one's own argument as directly authoritative destroys one's soul.

नानाहूतो यज्ञं गच्छेद्, यदि व्रजेदधिवृक्षसूर्यमध्वनि न प्रतिपद्येत, नावञ्च सांशयिकीम्। बाहुभ्यां न नदीन्तरेदुत्थायापररात्रमधीत्य न पुनः प्रतिसंविशेत्। प्राजापत्ये मुहूर्त्ते ब्राह्मणः स्वनियमाननुतिष्ठेदिति।

One shall not go to a sacrifice without being invited. If he goes, he must not go by the door covered with trees or facing the sun. He shall not ascend an unsafe boat. He shall not cross a river by swimming with his arms. Having risen up in the last part [of the night] and, recited [the Veda] he shall not lie down again. In the Muhūrta sacred to Prajāpati a Brāhmaṇa shall perform, some sacred duties.

इति वासिष्ठे धर्मशास्त्रे द्वादशोऽध्यायः॥१२॥

Chapter 13

अथातः स्वाध्यायश्चोपाकर्म श्रावण्यां पौर्णमास्यां प्रौष्ठपद्यां वाग्नि-मुपसमाधाय कृताधानो जुहोति देवेभ्यश्छन्दोभ्यश्चेति। ब्राह्मणान् स्वस्ति वाच्य दधि प्राश्य तत् उपांशु कुर्वीत। अर्द्धपञ्चममासानर्द्धषष्ठानत ऊर्ध्वं शुक्लपक्षेष्वधीयीत। कामन्तु वेदाङ्गानि। तस्यानध्यायाः सन्ध्यास्तमिते स्युस्तत्र शवे दिवाकीर्त्ये नगरेषु कामं गोमयपर्युषिते परिलिखिते वा श्मशानान्ते शयानस्य श्राद्धिकस्य।

Now therefore the Upākarman [the rite preparatory to] Vedic study [shall be done] on the full-moon day of the month of Śrāvaṇa or Prauṣṭhapada. Having kindled the sacred fire he shall offer oblations to the deities and the sacred metres. Having made oblations to the sacred metres, having made the Brāhmaṇas utter words of well-being and after having fed them with curd he shall continue the Vedic study for four months and a half, or six-months and a half, and then perform the dedicatory rite. Thereafter he shall study the Veda during the light fortnight and the Aṅgas (supplementary subjects) of the Veda at pleasure. [The Veda] shall not be studied during the period of conjunction (twilight) in towns where a corpse [lies] or Cāṇḍālas [live] [He may study] at pleasure [in a place], which has been besmeared with cow-dung, and around which a line has been drawn. [He shall not, study] near a cremation-ground, lying down, or after he has eaten or taken a present at a funeral rite.

मानवं चात्र श्लोकमुदाहरन्ति–

Now they quote a verse as an example from Manu:-

फलान्यापस्तिलान् भक्ष्यमथान्यच्छ्राद्धिकं भवेत्।
प्रतिगृह्याप्यनध्याय: पाण्यास्या ब्राह्मणा: स्मृता: इति।।

Whether be it fruit, water, sesamum, food, or any gift at a Śrāddha, one shall not, having just accepted it, recite the Veda; for it is said in the *Smṛti* that, the hand of a Brāhmaṇa is his mouth.

धावत: पूतिगन्धिप्रसृतेरितवृक्षमारूढस्य नावि सेनायाञ्च, भुक्त्वा, चार्धघ्राणे, बाणशब्दे, चतुर्दश्याममावास्यायामष्टम्यामष्टकासु, प्रसारित-पादोपस्थस्योपाश्रितस्य गुरुसमीपे, मिथुनव्यपेतायां वाससा, मिथुनव्यपेतेनानिर्मुक्ते। न ग्रामान्ते, च्छर्दितस्य, मूत्रितस्योच्चरितस्य यजुषाञ्च, सामशब्दे, वा जीर्णे, निर्घातभूमौ च। न चन्द्रसूर्योपरागेषु, दिङ्नादपर्वतनादकम्पनप्रपातेषूपलरुधिरपांशुवर्षेष्वाकालिकम्। उल्काविद्युत् सज्योतिषमपर्त्त्वाकालिकं वा। आचार्य्ये च प्रेते त्रिरात्रमाचार्य्या पुत्रशिष्यभार्यास्वहोरात्रम्। ऋत्विक्श्वशुरपितृव्यमातुलानवरवयस: प्रत्यत्यायाभिवदेद् ये चैव पादग्राह्यास्तेषां भार्य्या गुरीश्च मातापितरौ। यो विद्यादभिवन्दितुमहमयम्भो इतिब्रूयाद, यश्च न विद्यात् प्रत्यभिवादं नाभिवदेत्। पतित: पिता परित्याज्यो माता तु पुत्रे न पतति।

[One shall not recite the Veda] while running, while a foul

smell comes, ascending a tree, in a boat or in a camp, after meals, while his hinds are moist, while the sound of an arrow [is heard], on the fourteenth day of each fortnight, on the new moon-day, on the either day of a fortnight and on an Aṣṭaki [day], while he stretches his feet out, while he makes leap, leaning against [some thing), on a bed that had been used in a conjugal intercourse, in a dress that he leap used during a sexual intercourse except it has been washed at the outskirts of a village, after vomiting, while passing urine or excreta. One shall not recite the Ṛgveda or the Yajur-Veda while the sound [of the chanting] of the Sāman [is audible] nor when a thunderbolt falls, nor when an earth-quake happens, nor during the solar and lunar eclipses, nor when a sound is heard in the sky or in the mountains, nor during an earth-quake or muttering of clouds, nor when showers of stones, blood and sand [fall from the sky], nor during twenty-four hours [after the event]. If meteors, lightnings and other luminous bodies appear (the study of the Veda shall be stopped] for twenty-four hours. If the teacher dies [one shall not study the Who] for three nights; and if teacher's son, pupil or wife [dies], during a day and a night; likewise [on the death of] a priest or any relation made by a marriage. The feet of a preceptor must be embraced; one shall honour an officiating priest, a father-in-law, paternal and maternal uncles, younger than himself, by rising and saluting them, Similarly, [he shall honour] the wives of those persons whose feet must be embraced, and the teacher's [wives] and his parents. One shall say "I am such and such", to one who is acquainted [with the meaning of the salute.], But he shall not salute .him, who does not know the meaning of a salute. The father, when out-casted, must be forsaken, but the mother is never forsakable unto a son.

अथाप्युदाहरन्ति।

Now they quote the following verses as an example :

उपाध्यायाद्दशाचार्य आचार्याणां शतं पिता।
पितुर्दशशतं गावा गौरवेणातिरिच्यते।।

An Ācarya is ten times more venerable than an *Upādhyāya;* the father, a hundred times more than the *Ācārya;* and the mother, a thousand times more than the father.

भार्याः पुत्राश्च शिष्याश्च संस्पृष्टाः पापकर्मभिः।
परिभाष्य परित्याज्याः पतितो योऽन्यथा भवेत्।।

A wife, sons, and pupils, who are contaminated by sinful deeds, must first be admonished [by being pointed out] and then forsaken. He, who, forsakes them in any other way, becomes [himself] an out-cast.

ऋत्विगाचार्यावयाजकानध्यापकौ हेयावन्यत्र हानात् पतितो नान्यत्र पतितो भवतीत्याहुरन्यत्र स्त्रियाः, सा हि परगमिता, तद्भिन्नामक्षुण्णामुपेयात्।

An officiating priest or a preceptor, who neglects to perform sacrifices, or to teach [the Veda] shall, be, forsaken. The wife must not take that husband, who, though not really in outcast, appears like one. She shall never speak of him. A woman, by holding intercourse with a person other [than her husband], become an outcast. The husband may, therefore, take another wife, who has never been enjoyed by another man.

गुरौर्गुरो सन्निहिते गुरुवद्वृत्तिरिष्यते।
गुरूवद्गुरुपुत्रस्य वर्त्तितव्यमिति श्रुतिः।।

If the preceptor's preceptor is near he must, be treated like the preceptor himself. The Śruti says that, one must treat a teacher's son just as the teacher himself.

शास्त्रं वस्त्रं तथान्नानि प्रतिग्राह्याणि ब्राह्मणस्य। विद्या वित्तं वयः सम्बन्धः कर्म च मान्यं पूर्वः पूर्वो गरीयान्। स्थविरबालातुरभारिकचक्रवतां पन्थाः समागमे परस्मै देयः, राजस्नातकयोः समागमे राज्ञा स्नातकाय देयः सर्वैरिव वा उच्चतमाय। तृणभूम्यग्न्युदकवाक्सूनृतानसूयाः सप्त, गृहे नोच्छिद्यन्ते कदाचनेति।।

Scriptural works, raiments and food shall be accepted [as presents] by a Brāhmaṇa. Learning, wealth, age, relationship, and occupation must be respected. But each preceding one is more venerable [than the succeeding one]: If one meets aged men, infants, sick men, load-carriers, and persons riding on wheels, he must give way to each of the latter. If a king and a Snātaka meet, the king must make *way* for the Snātaka. All must make way for the greatest [man among them.] Grass, land, fire, water, truth and absence of envy none of these is found wanting in the houses of good men.

इति वासिष्ठे धर्मशास्त्रे त्रयोदशोऽध्यायः॥१३॥

Chapter 14

अथातो भोज्याभोज्यञ्च वर्णयिष्यामः। चिकित्सकमृगयुपुंश्चलीदण्डिकस्ते नाभिशस्तषण्डपतितानामभोज्यं, कदर्येक्षितबद्धातुरसोमविक्रयितक्षकरजकशौण्डिकसूचकतवार्द्धुषिकचर्मावकृत्तानां, शूद्रस्य, चायज्ञस्योपयज्ञे, यश्चोपपतिं मन्यते यश्च गृहीततद्धेतुर्यश्च वधार्हं नोपहन्यात्, कौ बन्धमोक्षौ इति चाभिक्रुश्येत्, गणान्नं गणिकान्नमथाप्युदारहन्ति।

I shall now describe what may be eaten and what may not be eaten. Food given by a hunter, a woman of immoral character, a mace-bearer, a thief, one under the ban of an imprecation, a eunuch, or by an out-caste must not be eaten; nor that given by a miser, by one who has performed the initiatory rite of a Śrauta sacrifice, by one fettered with a chain, by a sick person, by a seller of *Soma*-plants, by a carpenter or a washerman, by a seller of spirituous liquor or a spy, by a usurer, or a cobbler; [nor that given] by a Śūdra, nor at an inferior sacrifice [performed by one who is] devoid of five sacrifices, [nor that] given by the paramour of a married woman, or a husband, who procures a paramour [to his wife], or by one *(i.e.,* a king) who does not slay a person deserving destruction, or by one who cries out whether bound or freed; food given by a multitude of men or by harlots should not be eaten.

Now they quote the following verses as an example :

नाश्नन्ति श्वपतेर्देवा नाश्नन्ति वृषलीपतेः।
भार्याजितस्य नाश्नन्ति यस्य चोपपतिर्गृहे॥

The celestials do not partake of [the offerings) by a man, who keeps dogs, nor by him whose [only] wife is a Śūdra woman, nor by him who is hen-pecked, nor by him in whose house [lives] the paramour [of his wife.]

एधोदकसवत्सकुशलाभ्युद्यतपानावसथशफरिप्रियङ्गुस्तरजमधुमांसानि नैतेषां प्रतिगृह्णीयादथाप्युदारहन्ति।

One shall not accept from such [people even] fuel, water, fruits, fodder, *Kuśa* grass, parched grain, unsolicited drink, house, small fish, millet, perfumes, honey and meat.

Now they quote the following verses as an example :

गुर्वर्थदारमुज्जिहीर्षन्नर्च्चिष्यन् देवतातिथीन्।
सर्वत: प्रतिगृह्णीयान्न तु तृप्येत् स्वयं तत:।।

For the sake of a Guru (religious guide) when he wishes to save his wife [and family from starvation,] when he wishes to honour the deities or guests, one may accept [presents] from anybody; but he shall never satisfy himself (*i.e.*, convert to his own use) [with them].

न मृगयोरिषुचारिण: परिवर्जमन्नं विज्ञायते ह्यगस्त्यो वर्षसाहस्त्रिके सत्रे मृगयां चचार, तस्यासंस्तु रसमया: पुरोडाशा मृगपक्षिणां प्रशस्तानामपि ह्यन्नम्। प्राजापत्यान् श्लोकानुदाहरन्ति।

उद्यतामाहृतां भिक्षां पुरस्तादप्रचोदिताम्।
भोज्या प्रजापतिर्मेने अपि दुष्कृतकारिण:।।

Food, given by a hunter using the bow, shall not be rejected. It is said [in the Veda] that at a sacrifice extending over one thousand years, Agastya went out to hunt. He had delicious cakes made with the meat of beasts and fowls. They quote some verses made by Prajāpati. Prajāpati has ordained that, food, freely offered and brought, may be eaten although [the giver] may be a sinful person, provided it has not been asked as alms beforehand.

श्रद्धधानैर्न भोक्तव्यं चौरस्यापि विशेषत:।
नत्वेव बहुधा तस्य यावानपहृता भवेत्।।

Particularly a thief's food must not be eaten by one who has faith,[1] nor that given by a Brāhmaṇa, who sacrifices for many and initiates many.

न तस्य पितरोऽश्नन्ति दश वर्षाणि पञ्च च।
न च हव्यं वहत्यग्निर्यस्तामभ्यवमन्यते॥

The manes do not eat for fifteen years [the food] of that man who rejects food [offered voluntarily], nor does the fire carry his offerings.

चिकित्सकस्य मृगया: शल्यहस्तस्य पाशिन:।
षण्ढस्य कुलटायाश्च उद्यतापि न गृह्यते॥

But alms, albeit offered voluntarily, must not be accepted from a physician, from a hunter, from a surgeon, from one who uses a noose, from a eunuch or a faithless woman.

उच्छिष्टमगुरोरभोज्यं स्वमुच्छिष्टमुच्छिष्टोपहतञ्च॥ यदर्शनं केशकीटोपहतञ्च, कामन्तु केशकीटानुद्धृत्याद्भिः प्रोक्ष्य भस्मनावकीर्य वाचा च प्रशस्तमुपयुञ्जीतापि ह्यन्नम्।

Residue of food left by other persons than the preceptor must not be eaten, nor the residue of one's own meal and food sullied by leavings; nor food sullied by contact with a dress, hair, or with insects. But if he likes he may use [such food], after taking out the hair and the insects, sprinkling it with water, and throwing ashes on it, and after it has been declared by words as fit [for taking].

प्राजापत्यान् श्लोकानुदाहरन्ति।

Now they quote the following verses by Prajāpati, as an example :–

त्रीणि देवा: पवित्राणि ब्राह्मणानामकल्पयन्।
अदृष्टमद्भिर्निर्णिक्तं यच्च वाचा प्रशस्यते॥

---

1. There is another reading which Buhler has followed, "offered by a man who has faith, must certainly be eaten even though the giver be a thief." This seems to be a better reading, but we have followed the Bengali edition.

The deities created for Brāhmaṇas three instruments of purification, namely, ignorance, sprinkling them with water and commending [them] by word of mouth.

देवद्रोण्यां विवाहेषु यज्ञेषु प्रकृतेषु च।
काकैः श्वभिश्च संस्पृष्टमन्नं तन्न विसर्जयेत्।।

One shall not cast away the food, which, at a procession with images of deities; at a nuptial ceremony, or at a sacrifice, is touched by crows or dogs.

तस्मात् तदन्नमुद्धृत्य शेषं संस्कारमर्हति।
द्रवाणां प्लावनेनैव घनानां क्षरणेन तु।।
पाकेन सुखसंस्पृष्टं शुचिरेव हि तद्भवेत्।।

Having taken out thereof [the defiled portion of] food one shall purify the remainder, the liquids by straining them and the solid food by sprinkling it with water. Some [articles] become pure when they are looked at, if not defiled by touch.

अन्नं पर्युषितं भावदुष्टं हल्लेखं पुनः सिद्धमाममृजीषपक्कञ्च कामन्तु दध्यादघृतेन चाभिधारितमुपयुञ्जीतापि ह्यन्नम्।

Stale food, what is naturally bad, what has been placed once only in the dish, what has been cooked again, raw food and [that] insufficiently cooked [must not be eaten]; but one may take it, if one likes, after pouring over it milk, curd and clarified butter.

प्राजापत्यान् श्लोकानुदाहरन्ति।

Now they quote the following verses by Prajāpati as an example:–

हस्तदत्तास्तु ये स्नेहा लवणं व्यञ्जनानि च।
दातारं नोपतिष्ठन्ति भोक्ता भुङ्क्ते च किल्विषम्।।

Oily substances, salt and curries, offered with the hand, do not benefit the giver, and he, who partakes of them, will eat sin.

लशुनपलाण्डुक्रमूकगृञ्जनश्लेष्मांतवृक्षनिर्यासलोहितावृश्चनाश्वश्वकाकावलीढशूद्रोच्छिष्टभोजनेषु कृच्छातिकृच्छ्र इतरेऽप्यन्यत्र मधुमांसफल-

विकर्षेष्वग्राम्यपश्वविषयः सन्धिनीक्षीरमवत्साक्षीरं गोमहिष्यजातरोमा-निर्दशाहानामनामन्त्र्यं नाव्युदकमपूपधानाकरम्भशक्तुचरक-तैलपायसशाकानिल-शुक्तानि वर्जयेदन्यांश्च क्षीरयवपिष्टवीरान्।

For eating garlic, onions, mushrooms, turnips, Śleṣmātaka, exudations from trees, red sap of trees flowing from incisions, food eaten by horses, dogs and crows, and leavings of a Śūdra, a *Kṛcchātikṛccha* [penance must be performed]. Elsewhere [the penance is ordained] by others for taking meat, honey and particular kinds of fruits, and flesh of some wild animals. One shall not drink the milk of cow that is in heat, or of one whose calf has died, or that which a cow-buffalo or a she goat gives during the first ten days [after giving birth to young ones], or water collected at the bottom of a boat. One shall avoid wheat-cakes, fried grain, porridge, barley-meal, stale and other sorts of [bad] food prepared with milk and barley-flour.

श्वाविच्छल्लकशशकच्छपगोधाः पञ्चनखा नाभक्ष्याः, अनुष्ट्राः पशूनामन्यतोदतश्च मत्स्यानां वा वेहगवयशिशुमारनक्रकुलीरा विकृतरूपाः सर्पशीर्षाश्च, गौरगवयशलभाश्चानुदिष्टास्तथा धेन्वनड्वाहौ मेध्यौ वाजसनेयने। खड्गे तु विवदन्त्यग्रामशूकरे च, शकुनानाञ्च विशुविविष्किरजालपादाः कलविङ्कप्लवहंसचक्रकाकभासमद्गुटिट्टिभाटवाध्नक्तञ्चरा दार्वाघाटाश्चटक-वैलातकहारितखञ्जरीटग्राम्यकुक्कुटशुकसारिकाकोकिलक्रव्यादा ग्रासाचारिणाश्च

Of five-toed animals, the porcupine, the hedge-hog, the hare, the tortoise and the iguana may be eaten, of [domestic] animals those having one jaw only save camels; of aquatic animals the alligator and the crab [must not be eaten]; nor those which are mis-shaped like snakes; nor kine, Gavayas and Śarabhas, nor those that have not been [specially] mentioned. It is said in the, Vājasaneya [Saṁhitā] that, the meat of] milch cows and oxen is fit for sacrificial offerings. They make conflicting statements about the rhinoceros and the wild boar. Among birds those which seek food by scratching with their feet, the webb-footed one, the Kalaviṅka, the water-hen, the flamingo, the Brāhmaṇi duck, the Bhāsa, the crow, the blue pigeon, the osprey, the Cātaka, the dove, the crane, the black partridge, the grey heron, the vulture, the falcon, the white egret, the ibis, the cormorant, the peewit, the flying-fox, those flying about at night, the wood-pecker, the-the Vailātaka, the green pigeon, the wagtail, the village-sparrow, the village-cock, the parrot, the starling, the cuckoo, those living on flesh, and those moving about villages [must not be eaten].

इति वासिष्ठे धर्मशास्त्रे चतुर्दशोऽध्यायः॥१४॥

Chapter 15

शोणितशुक्रसम्भवः पुरुषो मातापितृनिमित्तकः। तस्य प्रदानविक्रयत्यागेषु मातापितरो प्रभवतः। न त्वेकं पुत्रं दद्यात् प्रतिगृहीयाद्वा, स हि सन्तानाय पूर्वेषाम्। न स्त्री दद्यात् प्रतिगृह्णीयाद्वान्यत्रानुज्ञानाद्भर्त्तुः। पुत्रं प्रतिग्रहीष्यन् बन्धूनाहूय राजनि चावेद्य निवेशनस्य मध्ये व्याहृतीर्हुत्वा दूरेबान्धवसन्निकृष्टमेव। सन्देहे चोत्पन्ने दूरेबान्धवं शूद्रमिव स्थापयेत्। विज्ञायते ह्येकेन बहु जायते इति तस्मिंश्चेत् प्रतिगृहीते औरसः पुत्र उत्पद्यते, चतुर्थभागभागी स्यात्।

Man formed of blood and semen, proceeds from his mother and his father as his cause. Therefore the parents have power to give, to sell, and to abandon their [son]. But one shall not give, or receive [in adoption] an only son, for he must live to continue the line of his ancestors. A woman shall neither give nor receive a son save with the permission of her husband. He, who wishes to adopt a son, shall collect his kinsmen, announce his desire to the king, shall make offerings in the middle of the house, reciting the Mahāvyāhṛti, and take as a son, a not-remote kinsman, just the nearest among his relatives. But if a doubt arises about this remote kinsman, [the adopter] shall set him apart with a Śūdra. It is said in the Veda that, through one he saves many. If after adoption, a son of one's *own loins* is born, [the adopted son] shall obtain a fourth part, if he is not engaged in rites, procuring prosperity.

यदि नाभ्युदयिके युक्तः स्याद्वेदविप्लविनः सव्येन पादेन प्रवृत्ताग्रान् दर्भान् लोहितान् वोपस्तीर्य पूर्णं पात्रमस्मै निनयेन्निनेतारश्चास्य प्रकीर्य केशान्

ज्ञातयोऽन्वारभेरन्नपसव्यं कृत्वा गृहेषु स्वैरमापाद्येरन्नत ऊर्द्ध्वं तेन सह धर्ममीयुस्तद्धर्माणस्तद्धर्मापन्नाः। पतितानान्तु चरितव्रतानां प्रत्युद्धारः।

He, who divulges the Veda [to unworthy persons, shall be excommunicated] by spreading red Kuśa grass having tips with left foot and placing the water-vessel thereon. Allowing their hair to hang down, and with their sacred threads on the right side, his relatives shall touch him who empties [the pot]. Then turning their left hands towards [that spot] they may go and come at pleasure. They shall not afterwards admit the outcast to sacred rites. Those, who admit him to religious rites, become his equals. But outcasts, if they have performed the [necessary] penitential rite, [may be] re-admitted.

अथाप्युदाहरन्ति।

Now they quote the following verses as an example :

अग्न्यभ्युद्धरतां गच्छेत् क्रीडन्ति च हसन्ति च। यश्चोत्पातयतां गच्छेच्छ्रौचमित्याचार्य-मातृपितृहन्तारस्तत्प्रसादाद्भयाद्वा। एषां प्रत्यापत्तिः पूर्णाब्दात् प्रवृत्ताद्वा काञ्चनं पात्रं माहेयं वा पूरयित्वापोहिष्ठाभिरेव षड्भिर्ऋग्भिः सर्वत्र व्यतिरिक्तस्य प्रत्युद्धीरपुत्रजन्मना व्याख्यातः।

[Some] shall come by redemption by [entering] into fire. [People] shall play and laugh [with such a person]. He shall walk behind those, who excommunicate him, like one weeping and sorrowing. Those, who kill their teachers, their mothers, or their fathers, may be readmitted either after being pardoned, or after expiating their sin. Having filled a golden or an earthen pot [with water] from a sacred lake or river, they pour [the water] over him, [reciting] "ye waters are, etc." All [other rites relating to the] readmission of one, who has [thus] bathed, have been explained by [those laid down for] the birth of a son.

इति वासिष्ठे धर्मशास्त्रे पञ्चदशोऽध्यायः॥१५॥

Chapter 16

अथ व्यवहाराः राजमन्त्री सदःकार्याणि · कुर्यात्। द्वयोर्विवदमानयोरत्र पक्षान्तरं न गच्छेद्। यथासनमपराधो ह्यन्तेनापराधः। समः सर्वेषु भूतेषु यथासनमपराधो ह्याद्यवर्णयोर्विधानतः सम्पन्नतामाचरेत्। राजा बालानामप्राप्तव्यवहाराणां प्राप्तकाले तु तद्वत्।

Now [are] the laws. Let the minister of the king transact business on the bench. When there is a dispute between two parties, if he sides with one of them, their guilt will be considered as [the king's] own. [A king] shall be equitable to all created beings. If he commits any crime, it shall be rectified by the regulations of [the first two] castes. The king [shall administer the property of] the infants, who are not of age for legal actions. [A minor] shall be [treated] as others when he comes of age.

लिखितं साक्षिणो भुक्तिः प्रमाणं त्रिविधं स्मृतम्।
धनस्वीकररणं पूर्वं धनी धनमवाप्नुयात्।। इति

There are three kinds of proofs, it is declared in the Smṛti, which give title to a property, namely documents, witnesses, and possession; [by these] an owner may recover his former property.

मार्गक्षेत्रयोर्विसर्गे तथा परिवर्त्तनेन ऋणग्रहेष्वर्थान्तरेषु त्रिपादमात्रम्। गृहक्षेत्रविरोधे सामन्तविरोधेऽपि लेख्य प्रत्ययः, प्रत्यभिलेख्यविरोधे ग्रामनगरवृद्धश्रोणिप्रत्ययः।

[In all disputes] about roads, fields, different interpretations of gifts, and debts on mortgage, the legal procedure is of three feet (*i.e.* requires three kinds of evidence).[1] In a dispute about a

---

1. There is a difference of reading : Buhler has followed the Benares text and translated the passage thus : "From fields through which (there is a right of) road (a space sufficient for the road) must be set apart, likewise a space "for turning (a cart, and for) other things (of the same description there shall be) a passage three feet about." We have translated *Arthantareṣu* as different interpretations i.e., of the terms of agreements. Buhler has translated it as near other things. The commentator Kṛṣna Paṇḍit means "near pleasure-gardens and the like."

house or a field reliance [may be placed on the evidence] of neighbours. If the statements of the neighbours disagree, reliance [shall be placed on the statement of] the aged villagers or citizens, and of guilds and corporations.

अथाप्युदाहरन्ति।

Now they quote the following verses as an example :–

य एकं क्रीतमाधेयमन्वाधेयं प्रतिग्रहम्।
यज्ञादुपगमा बोनैस्तथा धूमशिखा ह्यमी।
तत्र भुक्ते दशवर्षमेवोदाहरन्ति।

What is bought, a pledge, property given to a wife after marriage by her husband's family, and what is obtained from a sacrifice– know all this as burning fire. Whatever has been continuously enjoyed [by another person] for ten years [is lost to the owner.]

आधिः सीमाधिकश्चैव निक्षेपोपनिधिः स्त्रियः।
राजस्वं श्रोत्रियद्रव्यं न राजा दातुमर्हतीति॥

A king is not justified to make a gift of a pledge, a boundary, the property of minors, a deposit, a sealed deposit, women, the property of a king, and the property of a Śrotriya.

तच्च सम्भोगे न गृहीतव्यम्। गृहिणां द्रव्याणि राजगामीनि भवन्ति, तथा राजा मन्त्रिभिः सह नागरैश्च कार्याणि कुर्यादसौ वा राजा श्रेयान् वसुपरिवारः स्यादगृध्रं परिवारं वा राजा श्रेयानगृध्रपरिवारः स्यान्न गृध्री गृध्रपरिवारः स्यान्न, परिवाराद्दोषाः प्रादुर्भवन्ति स्तेयहारविनाशनं, तस्मात् पूर्वमेव परिवारं पृच्छेत्।

They are not lost by being enjoyed [by others]. The properties of house-holders [given up by them] go to the king. With ministers and citizens a king shall administer affairs. Whether is a king, who is surrounded by many servants, superior to one who has servants, [keen-eyed] like vultures ? A king, who has servants like vultures, is not superior. A king shall not be like a vulture, nor shall he have servants like vultures. Through his servants originate crimes such as theft, robbery, murder etc.. Therefore let him question his servants beforehand.

अथ साक्षिण:।

Now about witnesses :

क्षात्रियो रूपवान् शीलवान् पुण्यवान् सत्यवान् साक्षिण: सर्व एव वा, स्त्रीणान्तु साक्षिण: स्त्रिय: कुर्यात्, द्विजानां सदृशा: द्विजा:, शूद्राणां सन्त: शूद्राश्च, अन्त्यानामन्त्या:।

Persons, well-read in the Śruti, beautiful, possessed of good character, and truthful, are to be witnesses. All men may [be witnesses of all men]. One shall make women witnesses about women; twice-born persons shall be fitting [witnesses for] twice-born men; Śūdras for Śūdras, and low castes for low castes.

अथाप्युदाहरन्ति।

Now they quote the following verses as an example :

प्रातिभाव्यं वृथादानमाक्षिकं सौरिकञ्च यत्।
दण्डशुल्कावशिष्टञ्च न पुत्रो दातुमर्हतीति।।

A son shall not pay money owing [by his father] for a surety, a money promised for a worthless object, money due for losses at play, or for spirituous liquor, nor what remains unpaid [on account] of a fine or toll.

ब्रूहि साक्षिन् यथातत्त्वं लम्बन्ते पितरस्तव।
तव वाक्यमुदीर्यन्तमुत्पतन्ति पतन्ति च।।

Speak out, O witness, every thing truly; your departed manes hang [in suspense depending on your answer] with the utterance of your words they will rise [into heaven], or fall [into hell].

नग्नो मुण्ड: कपाली च भिक्षाय क्षुत्पिपासित:।
अन्ध: शत्रुकुले गच्छद्यस्तु साक्ष्यनृतं वदेत्।।

Naked, with head, shaven, stricken with hunger and thirst, and blind shall go the man, who gives false evidence, with a potsherd to beg food at the door of his enemy.

पञ्च कन्यानृते हन्ति दश हन्ति गवानृते।
शतमश्वानृते हन्ति सहस्त्रं पुरुषानृते॥

One kills five by [giving] false [evidence] about a maiden; one kills, ten by [giving] false [evidence] about kine; one kills a hundred by giving false evidence about a horse, and a thousand, by giving false evidence about a man.

उद्वाहकाले रतिसम्प्रयोगे प्राणात्यये सर्वधनापहारे।
विप्रस्य चार्थे ह्यनृतं वदेयु: पञ्चानृतान्याहुरपातकानि॥

People may speak untruth at the time of marriage, while holding sexual intercourse, when their lives are in danger, while their entire property is at stake, and for the sake of a Brāhmaṇa. These five falsehoods are not sinful.

स्वजनस्यार्थे यदि वार्थहेतो:
पक्षाश्रयेणैव वदन्ति कार्यम्।
वैशब्दवादं स्वकुलानुपूर्वान्
स्वर्गस्थितांस्तानपि पातयन्ति॥

If for the sake of a relative, or for money, men give partial evidence in a law-suit, they bring down [into hell] their own ancestors, although stationed in the celestial region.

इति वासिष्ठे धर्मशास्त्रे षोड़शोऽध्याय:॥१६॥

Chapter 17

ऋणमस्मिन् सन्नयति अमृतत्वञ्च गच्छति।
पिता पुत्रस्य जातस्य पश्यच्च जीवतो मुखम्॥

The father throws his debts on [the son] and acquires immortality, if he sees the face of a living son.

अनन्ता: पुत्रिणां लोका, नापुत्रस्य लोकोऽस्तीति श्रूयते, प्रजा: सन्त्वपुत्रिण इत्यपि शाप:। प्रजाभिरग्नेस्त्वमृतत्वमश्नुयामित्यपि निगमो भवति।

It is said in the Śruti that, endless are the regions for those, who have sons; there is no region for him, who has no son. There is a curse that men (*i.e.*, enemies) may have no male offspring. Through offspring Agni acquired immortality. In this there is the rule :

पुत्रेण लोकान् जयति पौत्रेणानन्त्यमश्नुते।
अथ पुत्रस्य पौत्रेण व्रध्नस्याप्नोति विष्टपमिति।।

Through a son one conquers the world; through a grandson one acquires immortality; but through his son's grand-son he acquires the solar region.

क्षेत्रिण: पुत्रो जनयितु: पुत्र इति विवदन्ते।

There is a dispute [among the learned; some say] 'the son belongs to the husband of the wife; [and some say,] the son belongs to the begetter.'

तत्रोभयथाप्युदाहरन्ति।

They quote on both sides the following verses as an example:

यद्यन्यगोषु वृषभो वत्सान् जनयते सुतान्।
गोमिनामेव ते वत्सा मोघं स्यन्दनमोक्षणमिति।।

अप्रमत्ता रक्षन्तु वैनं मा च क्षेत्रे परे बीजानि वासौ जनयितु: पुत्रो भवति। सम्परायो मोघं रेतोऽकुरूत तन्तुमेतमिति।

If [one man's] bull were to procreant a hundred calves on another man's cows, they would belong to the owner of the cows; useless is the spending of his power. [Some say,] 'vigilantly watch the pro-creation of your offspring lest strangers might sow seed on your soil.' The son belongs to the begetter. The adage is that, one of successful virile power has created this offspring.

बहूनामेकजातानामेकश्चेत् पुत्रवान् नर:।
सर्वेते तेन पुत्रेण पुत्रवन्त इति श्रुति:।।

If amongst many begotten by one [father] one has a son, they all have offspring through that son, thus says the Veda.

बह्वीनां द्वादश ह्येव पुत्रा: पुराणदृष्टा: स्वयमुत्पादित: स्वक्षेत्रे संस्कृतायां प्रथम: तदलाभे नियुक्तायां क्षेत्रजो द्वितीय: तृतीय: पुत्रिका

विज्ञायते, अभ्रातृका पुंस: पितृलभ्येति प्रतिचीनं गच्छति पुत्रत्वम्। श्लोक:।

Twelve kinds of sons only are recognised by the ancients. The first is the son begotten [by the husband] himself on his own married wife. In his absence the second begotten on one's own wife or widow [by another man] on being authorized. The third is an appointed daughter.[1] A brotherless maiden comes back to her male ancestors; returning she becomes their son. [There is a] verse.

अभ्रातृकां प्रदास्यामि तुभ्यं कन्यामलङ्कृताम्।
अस्यां यो जायते पुत्र: स मे पुत्रो भवेदिति।।

"I shall confer on you a brotherless damsel adorned with ornaments. The son to whom she may give birth shall be my son."

पौनर्भवश्चतुर्थ: पुनर्भू: कौमारं भर्त्तारमुत्सृज्यान्यै: सह चरित्वा तस्यैव कुटुम्बमाश्रयति।

The fourth is the son of a re-married woman. She is called *Punarbhu* (re-married), who leaving the husband of her youth and having lived with others seeks the protection of his relatives.

सा पुनर्भूर्भवति या च क्लीबं पतितमुन्मत्तं वा भर्त्तारसुत्सृज्यान्यं पतिं विन्दते मृते वा सा पुनर्भूर्भवति। कानीन: पञ्चमो, या पितृगृहेऽसंस्कृता कामादुत्पादयेन्मातामहस्य पुत्रो भवतीत्याहु:।

And she [too] is called *Punarbhū,* who leaving an impotent, outcast, or mad husband, or after the demise of her husband, takes another lord. The fifth is the son of an unmarried maiden. [The learned say] that, the son whom an unmarried woman gives birth

---

1. This is a curious fact but the practice is still prevalent in Kashmir. Buhler quotes an historical incident from *Rajatarañginī* "Where it is stated Kalyandevī, princess of Ganda, and wife of king Gayapida, was called by her father Kalyanamalla." He says in the same note:– "When I collated the passage with the help of a Kashmirian, I was told that a certain Brāhmaṇa, still living in Srinagar, has changed the name of his only child, a daughter called Amri, to the corresponding masculine form Amirgu in order to secure to himself through her the same spiritual benefits as if he had a son."

to through lust in her father's residence is the son of his maternal grand-father.

अथाप्युदाहरन्ति।

Now they quote the following verses as an example :

अप्रत्ता दुहिता यस्य पुत्रं विन्दति तुल्यत:।
पुत्रो मातामहस्तेन दद्यात् पिण्डं हरेद्धनमिति।।

If an unmarried daughter gives birth to a son begotten by a man of equal caste, the maternal grandfather gets a son through him; he shall offer *piṇḍa* and steal (inherit) the property [of his grand-father.]

गूढे च गूढोत्पन्न: षष्ठ इत्येते। दायादा बान्धवास्त्रातारो महतो भयादित्याहु:। अथादायादास्तत्र सहोढ एव प्रथमो या गर्भिणी संस्क्रियते तस्यां जात: सहोढ: पुत्रो भवति। दत्तको द्वितीयो यं मातापितरौ दद्याताम्। क्रीतस्तृतीयस्तच्छुन:शेफेन व्याख्यातं हरिश्चन्द्रो ह वै राजा सोऽजीगर्त्तस्य सोपवत्सै: पुत्रं विक्राय्य स्वयं क्रीतवान्। स्वयमुपागतश्चतुर्थस्तच्छुन:शेफेन व्याख्यातं शुन:शेफो ह वै यूपे नियुक्तो देवतास्तुष्टाव तस्येह देवता: पाशं विमुमुचुस्तमृत्विज ऊचुर्ममैवाय पुत्रोऽस्त्विति तानाह न सम्पेदे ते सम्पादयामासुरेष एव यं कामयेत तस्य पुत्रोऽस्त्विति तस्येह विश्वामित्रो होतासीत् तस्य पुत्रत्वमियाय। अपविद्ध: पञ्चमो यं मातापितृभ्यामपास्तं प्रतिगृह्णीयात्। शूद्रापुत्र एव षष्ठो भवतीत्याहुरित्येतेऽदायादा बान्धवा:।

[A son] born secretly in the house is the sixth. (The learned declare that these all (*i.e.,* six) are heirs and kinsmen and preservers from great danger. Now amongst those, who are not heirs, the first is he, who is received with a pregnant bride. [The son of a maiden] who is married pregnant, [is called] a *Sahoḍha* (a son received with the bride). The second is the adopted son whom his father and mother give [in adoption.] The third is the son bought. That is explained by [the story of] Sunaḥśepa. Hariścandra indeed was a king. He himself bought the son of Ajigartha by [giving him] young animals [and wealth.] The fourth is the son himself arrived. This is explained by [the story of]

Sunaḥśepa. Sunaḥśepa, forsooth, [when] tied to the sacrificial stake, lauded the celestials. Then the deities liberated him from the fetters. The sacrificial priests said, "He shall be our son." He did not comply with their request. [Then] they made him make [this] compact. "He shall be the son of him whom he chooses." Visvāmitra was the Hotā and he became his son. The fifth is an *Apaviddha* (cast off son.) [He is called so] who, renounced by his father and mother, is received as a son]. The sixth is the son of a Śūdra woman. These six are kinsmen but not heirs.

अथाप्युदाहरन्ति।

Now they quote the following verses as an example :

यस्य पूर्वेषां वर्णानां न कश्चिद्दायादः स्यादेते तस्यापहरन्ति।

These (i.e. the last-mentioned six sons) shall inherit the property of him, who has no heir belonging to the first-mentioned [six classes]. Now about the partition [of paternal property] amongst brothers.

अथ भ्रातृणां दायविभागो द्व्यंशं ज्येष्ठो हरेद्गवाश्वस्य चानुसदृशमजावयो गृहं च कनिष्ठस्य काष्ठं गां यवसं गृहोपकरणाणि च मध्यमस्य मातुः पारिणेयं स्त्रियो विभजेरन्। यदि ब्राह्मणस्य ब्राह्मणीक्षत्रियावैश्यासु पुत्राः स्युस्त्र्यंशं ब्राह्मण्याः पुत्रो हरेद् द्व्यंशं राजन्यायाः पुत्रः सममितरे विभजेरन्नन्येन चैषां स्वयमुत्पादितः स्यात् द्व्यंशमेव हरेदन्येषान्त्वाश्रमान्तरगताः क्लीबोन्मत्तपतिताश्च भरणम्। क्लीबोन्मत्तान्यं प्रेतपत्नी षण्मासं व्रतचारिण्यक्षारलवणं भुञ्जानां शयीतोर्ध्वं षड्भ्यो मासेभ्यः स्नात्वा श्राद्धं च पत्ये दत्त्वा विद्याकर्मगुरुयोनिसम्बन्धात् सन्निपात्य पिता भ्राता वा नियोगं कारयेत् तपसे वोन्मत्तामवशां व्याधितां वा नियुञ्जात् ज्यायसीमपि षोडशवर्षां न चेदामयाविन स्यात्। प्राजापत्ये मुहूर्त्ते पाणिग्रहणवदुपचारोऽन्यत्र संस्थाप्य वाक्पारुष्याद्दण्डपारुष्याच्च ग्रासाच्छादनस्नानलेपनेषु प्राग्यामिनी स्यादनियुक्तायामुत्पन्न उत्पादयितुः पुत्रो भवतीत्याहुः स्याच्चेन्नियोगिनी दृष्ट्वा लोभान्नास्ति नियोगः। प्रायश्चित्तं वाप्युपनियुञ्ज्यादित्येके। कुमार्युतुमती त्रिवर्षाण्युपासीतोर्ध्वं त्रिभ्यो वर्षेभ्यः पतिं विन्देत तुल्यम्।

The eldest shall take two shares, and a tithe of the kine and horses. The goats, the sheep and the house belong to the youngest; black iron, the utensils and the furniture, to the middle-most. The daughter shall divide the nuptial presents of their mother. If a Brāhmaṇa has sons by wives of the Brāhmaṇa, Kṣatriya and Vaiśya castes, the son of the Brāhmaṇa wife shall receive three shares; the son of the Kṣatriya wife, two shares, and the other sons shall inherit equal shares. And if one of the brothers has earned something by his own [endeavour1] he shall get two shares. But those who have entered a different order, those, who are eunuchs, insane and out-cast, shall receive no share but [they] are entitled to maintenance.

The widow of an eunuch or mad man, deceased, shall sleep on the ground, for six months, practising religious virtues and abstaining from taking pungent food and salt. Having bathed after six months, she shall offer the Śrāddha to her husband. Then her father, or her brother shall assemble his *(i.e.,* deceased person's) preceptors, who taught him or officiated at his sacrifices and his kinsmen, and shall appoint her [to raise offspring for her deceased husband]. One shall not appoint a woman; who is insane, not under control, and diseased, nor one who is very aged; sixteen years [is the age for appointing a woman] and she must be healthy.

[The male appointed] shall approach [the widow] in the *muhūrta,* sacred to Prajāpati, like a husband, without dallying with her, and without abusing or ill: treating her. She shall get food; dress, baths and unguents from [the estate of] her former [husband]. The [learned] say that, sons begotten on a woman, not appointed, belong to the begetter. A woman shall not be appointed for the man, who had seen her with lustful eyes. Others say that if (a widow] is to be appointed [under these

---

1. Kṛṣṇa Paṇḍit thinks that, the Sutra forbids an appointment which is made with the intention to secure the estate, or a share of the estate of the natural father from whom the Kṣatriya son inherits also. But it seems equally probable that it is intended to prevent a widow from agreeing to an appointment in order to obtain control over her husband's estate,– Buhler.

circumstances] she shall have to perform a penance. A maiden, who has attained puberty, shall wait for three years. After three years she may take a husband of the same caste.

अथाप्युदाहरन्ति।

Now they quote as an example,

पितुः प्रदानात् तु यदा हि पूर्वं
कन्यावयो यः समतीत्य दीयते।
सा हन्ति दातारमपीक्षमाणा
कालातिरिक्ता गुरुदक्षिणे च॥

If the suitable age of a maiden expires before she is given away by her father, she, who has been waiting [for a husband] destroys him, who gives her away, just as the fee that is paid too late to the teacher [kills the pupil]

प्रयच्छेन्नग्निकां कन्यामृतुकालभयात् पिता।
ऋतुमत्यां हि तिष्ठन्त्यां दोषः पितरमृच्छति॥

Fearing the appearance of the menses, the father shall marry his daughter while she still runs about naked. If she stays (in her father's house) after menstruating, sin visits the father.

यावच्च कन्यामृतवः स्पृशन्ति
तुल्यैः सकामामभियाच्यमानाम्।
भ्रूणानि तावन्ति हतानि ताभ्याम्।
मातापितृभ्यामिति धर्मवादः॥

As often as are the menstrual courses of a maiden, who is desirous of, and is solicited in marriage by, a qualified bridegroom of the same caste, so often her father and mother are guilty of [the crime of] killing an embryo such is the sacred law.

अद्भिर्वाचा च दत्तायां म्रियेताथो वरो यदि।
न च मन्त्रोपनीता स्यात् कुमारी पितुरेव सा॥

If the betrothed of a maiden dies after she has been given away to him by words and water but before she was married with

Mantras, she belongs to her father alone.

यावच्चेदाहृता कन्या मन्त्रैर्यदि न संस्कृता।
अन्यस्मै विधिवद्देया यथा कन्या तथैव सा।।

If a maiden has been carried away by force and not married with *Mantras,* she may be lawfully given away to another man. She is like a maiden.

पाणिग्रहे मृते बाला केवलं मन्त्रसंस्कृता।
सा च त्वक्षतयोनिः स्यात् पुनः संस्कारमर्हतीति।।

If a damsel has merely been married, at the death of her husband, by Mantras, and if the marriage has not been consummated she may be married again.

प्रोषितपत्नी पञ्चवर्षा प्रवसेद्यद्यकामा यथा प्रेतस्य एवञ्च वर्त्तितव्यं स्यात्, एवं पञ्च ब्राह्मणीप्रजाता, चत्वारि राजन्या प्रजाता, त्रीणि वैश्या प्रजाता, द्वे शूद्रा प्रजाता, अत ऊर्ध्वं समानोदकपिण्डजन्मर्षिगोत्राणां पूर्वः पूर्वो गरीयान् न खलु कुलीने विद्यमाने परगामिनी स्यात्। यस्य पूर्वेषां षण्णां न कश्चिद्दायदः स्यात् सपिण्डाः पुत्रस्थानीया वा तस्य धनं विभजेरंस्तेषामलाभे आचार्यान्तेवासिनौ हरेयातां, तयोरलाभे राजा हरेत्, न तु ब्राह्मणस्य राजा हरेद् ब्रह्मस्वन्तु विषं घोरम्।

A wife whose husband is in a foreign country, [and who has not given birth to a son], shall wait for five years without cherishing any desire. She shall live and behave like a widow. A wife of the Brāhmaṇa caste, who has issue, [shall wait] for five years; and one who has no issue, four years; the wife of a Kṣatriya who has issue, five years; and one who has no issue, three years; a wife of the Vaiśya caste who has ring, four years; and one who has none, two years; a wife of the Śūdra caste who has offspring, three years; and who has none, one year. Of those who are connected [with her husband by libations of water. Funeral cake, birth and *by gotra* (family), each preceding person is more preferable. But if a member of her family survives, she shall certainly not go to a stranger. The *Sapiṇḍas,* or those who are of the status of a son to him, shall divide the heritage of him who has no heir of the first-mentioned six sorts. On failure of them the preceptor and the pupil shall inherit the property. On failure of these two the king inherits. But a king shall never take the property of a Brāhmaṇa, for it is a dreadful poison.

न विषं विषमित्याहुर्ब्रह्मस्वं विषमुच्यते।
विषमेकाकिनं हन्ति ब्रह्मस्वं पुत्रपौत्रकमिति॥

They do not call poison, poison; the property of a Brāhmaṇa is called poison. Poison kills only one man but the property of a Brāhmaṇa kills (him, who takes it), together with his sons and grandsons.

त्रिविद्यसाधुभ्यः संप्रयच्छेदिति।

He should make it over to pious men, who are well versed in the three Vedas.

इति वासिष्ठे धर्मशास्त्रे सप्तदशोऽध्यायः॥१७॥

Chapter 18

शूद्रेण ब्राह्मण्यामुत्पन्नश्चाण्डालो भवतीत्याहुः, राजन्यायां वैश्यायामन्त्यावसायी। वैश्येन ब्राह्मस्यामुत्पन्नो रामको भवति इत्याहुः, राजन्येन ब्राह्मण्यामुत्पन्न सूतो भवतीत्याहुः।

They say that, the offspring of a Śūdra by a Brāhmaṇa woman is a Cāṇḍāla. That of a Kṣatriya by a Vaiśya woman is Anta-Vyavasāyin. That of a Vaiśya, by a Brāhmaṇa woman becomes a Rāmaka.[1] [That of a Vaiśya] by a Kṣatriya woman [is called] Pukkasa. That begotten on a Brāhmaṇa woman by a Kṣatriya becomes a Sūta. So [the learned] declare.

अथाप्युदाहरन्ति।

---

1. Kṛṣṇa Paṇḍit, the commentator, reads *Ronaki* for Rāmaka. This indicates, according to some, that the Hindus, of the period, to which the Vasiṣṭha Dharma Śāstra belongs, had become aware of the existence of the Roman empire. Buhler holds, and so do we, that there is no reason to make such an assumption. ''On the other hand,'' says Buhler, ''Romaka is a correction which would easily suggest itself to a Paṇḍit, who was unable to find a parallel passage in which the word Rāmaka occurs.''

Now they quote the following verse as an example :

छिन्नोत्पन्नास्तु ये केचित् प्रातिलोम्यगुणाश्रिताः।
गुणाचारपरिभ्रंशात् कर्मभिस्तान् विजानीयुरिति॥

One may know by their deeds those, who have been born secretly and are stigmatised for being begotten from unions in the inverse order of castes, because they are shorn of virtue and good conduct.

एकान्तरद्व्यन्तरत्र्यन्तरानुजाता ब्राह्मणक्षत्रियवैश्यैरवच्छिन्ना निषादा भवन्ति। शूद्रायां पारशवः पारयन्नेव जीवन्नेव शवो भवतीत्याहुः शव इति मृताख्या। एतच्छावं यच्छूद्रस्तस्माच्छूद्रसमीपे तु नाध्येतव्यम्।

[Children] begotten by Brāhmaṇas, Kṣatriyas and Vaiśyas on women of the next lower, second lower and third lower castes become Niṣādas. [The son of a Brāhmaṇa] by a Śūdra woman [is] a Pāraśava. They say that the condition of a Pāraśava is that of one, who, albeit living, is a corpse. The designation of a dead body is *Śava*. Some say that a Śūdra is a corpse; therefore, the Veda must not be recited near a Śūdra.

अथापि यमगीतान् श्लोकानुदारहरन्ति।
श्मानमेतत् प्रत्यक्षं ये शूद्राः पापचारिणः।
तस्माच्छूद्रसमीपे च नाध्येतव्यं कदाचन॥

Now they quote the following verses as an example from Yama-Gītā. These Śūdras, who are of sinful deeds, are manifestly a cremation ground. Therefore, the Veda shall never be recited near a Śūdra.

न शूद्राय मतिं दद्यान्नोच्छिष्टं न हविस्कृतम्।
न चास्योपदिशेद्धर्मं न चास्य व्रतमादिशेत्॥

One shall not give advice unto a Śūdra, nor the residue of his food, nor [the residue of] the offerings [to the deities]; nor shall he explain the sacred law to him, nor shall he order him to perform a religious rite.

यश्चास्योपदिशेद्धर्मं यश्चास्य व्रतमादिशेत्।

सोऽसंवृतं तमो घोरं सह तेन प्रपद्येत इति।।

He, who explains the sacred law to him, he, who orders him to perform a religious rite, goes, together with that very man, into the dreadful hell [called] Asaṁvṛta.

व्रणद्वारे कृमिर्यस्य सम्भवेत कदाचन।
प्राजापत्येन शुध्येत हिरण्यं गौर्वासो दक्षिणेति।।

If ever a worm is produced in an wound [on his body] he shall purify himself by performing Prājāpatyam and give cow, gold and a raimant as sacrificial present.

नाग्निचित् शूद्रामुपेयात्, कृष्णवर्णा सा सरमाया इव, न धर्माय, न धर्मायेति।

One, who has placed the sacred fire, shall never approach a Śūdra woman; for she, belonging to the black race, is like a bitch, not for religious rites [but for pleasure].[1]

इति वासिष्ठे धर्मशास्त्रेऽष्टादशोऽध्याय:।।१८।।

Chapter 19

धर्मो राज्ञ: पालनं भूतानां तस्यानुष्ठानात् सिद्धि:। भयकारणं ह्यपालनं तै एतत् सूत्रमाहुर्तिद्वांसस्तस्मादगार्हस्थ्यनैयमिकेषु। पुरोहिते दद्याद् विज्ञायते ब्राह्मण: पुरोहितो राष्ट्रं दधातीति। तस्य भयमपालनादसामर्थ्याच्च। देशधर्मजातिधर्मकुलधर्मान् सर्वान् वैताननुप्रविश्य राजा चतुरो वर्णान् स्वधर्मे स्थापयेत् तेष्वधर्मपरेषु दण्डन्तु देशकालधर्माधर्मवयोविद्यास्थानविशेषैर्दिशेत्। आगमादुष्टाभावात् पुष्पफलोपगान्यदेयानि हिंस्यात् कर्षणकरणार्थञ्चोप-हत्यागार्हस्थ्यं गाञ्च मानोन्माने रक्षिते स्यातां, अधिष्ठानान्नो नीहारसार्थानामस्मान्न मूल्यमात्रं नैहारिकं स्यान्महामहस्थ: स्यात्, सम्मानयेदवाहवाहनीयद्विगुणकारिणी स्यात् प्रत्येकं प्रयास्य: पुमान्। शतं वा राद्धर्यं वा तदेतप्यर्था: स्त्रिय: कराष्टौ मानधारमध्यमा: पाद: कार्षापणस्य निरुक्तोऽन्तरो मानाकर: श्रोत्रियो राजपुमानथ प्रव्रजितबालवृद्धतरुणप्रदाता प्रागामिका: कुमार्यो मृतापत्यश्च बाहुभ्यामुत्तरं शतगुणं दद्यान्नदीकक्षवन-

1. The Bengal text is faulty.

शैलोपमाङ्ग निष्करा: स्युस्तदुपजीविनो वा दद्युः प्रतिमासमुद्वाहकरैस्तवागमयेद्राजनि च प्रेते दद्यात्। प्रासङ्गिकं तेन मातृवृत्तिर्व्याख्याता राजमहिष्या: पितृव्यमातुलांशजा पितृव्यान् राजा बिभृयात् तद्बन्धुंश्चान्यांश्च राजपत्न्यो ग्रासाच्छादनं लभेरन्। अनिच्छन्तो वा प्रव्रजेरन् क्लीबोन्मत्तांशजा वापि। मानवं श्लोकमुदारहन्ति।

The duty of a king is to protect all beings; by fulfilling it he attains success. Not to protect [them] is a source of fear; the learned have spoken of this rule. It is said [in the Veda] that a Brāhmaṇa priest upholds the kingdom, therefore, one shall make gifts to a priest in all the rites obligatory on a house-holder. His (king's) fear arises also from non-protection and want of capacity. Paying attention to all the laws of the countries, duties of castes and of families, a king shall make the four castes (Varṇa) follow their respective duties. He shall punish those, who deviate from the path of duty. He shall award [punishment] after due consideration of the place, time, the duties, learning etc., (of the delinquent) and the seat [of occurrence]. For the purpose of extending cultivation, one may cut down trees, that do not bear fruits or flowers, for it is not prohibited by the Śruti. The measures and weights of objects necessary for domestic purposes must be protected [from being falsified]. He *(i.e.* king) shall not take property for his own use from [the inhabitants of] his kingdom. The measures and price [of property] only shall be subject to taxes. On an expedition against the enemy, companies, consisting of ten, shall be able to perform a double duty. There shall be places for distributing water. [The king] shall make one hundred men at the least, engage in battle. The wives [of soldiers killed] shall, be provided for. Duties shall be levied on goods sold :in the market. A ferry shall be taken away from a river in which there is no water. A Śrotriya is free from taxes, likewise, a servant of the king, one who has no protector, one who has become a religious mendicant, an infant, an extremely aged man, a young man (who studies), and one, who makes gifts, are exempted so are widows, who return to their former (family), maidens and those women whose children are dead. He, who swims with his arms across a river in order to avoid payment of toll], shall pay one hundred times [the amount due]. No tax shall be paid for rivers, dry grass, forests places of cremation and mountains. Those, who secure their livelihood from them, may pay [something]. But he shall take a monthly tax from artisans. On the death 04 a king, one shall give what is necessary for the occasion. It is hereby explained that his mother shall receive a maintenance. The king shall maintain the paternal and maternal uncles of the principal queen, as well as her other relatives. The wives of [the deceased] king shall receive food and raiment, or if they are reluctant, they may depart. [The king shall maintain] eunuchs and mad men, [since) their shares [go to him]

मानवं श्लोकमुदाहरन्ति।

Now they quote the following verses of Manu as an example:

न रिक्तकार्षापणमस्ति शुल्कं
न शिल्पवृत्तौ न शिशौ न धर्म्मे।
न भैक्षवृत्तौ न हुतावशेषे
न श्रोत्रिये प्रव्रजिते न यज्ञे॥

No duty is paid on a sum less than a Karṣāpaṇa; [there is no tax) on livelihood gained by wit, nor on an infant, nor on an emissary, nor on what is gained by begging, nor on the residue of a property left after a robbery, nor on a Śrotriya, nor on a religious mendicant, nor on a religious sacrifice.

स्तेनाभिशस्तदुष्टशस्त्रधारिसहोढव्रणसम्पन्नव्यपदेष्ट्रेष्वेकेषां दण्डोत्सर्गे राजैकरात्रमुपवसेत् त्रिरात्रं पुरोहितः कृच्छ्रमदण्ड्यदण्डने पुरोहितस्त्रिरात्रं वा।

By failing to inflict punishment on a thief, on a cursed weight, on a wicked person, on one [caught] with weapons in his hands, on a thief caught with stolen property in his possession, on one covered with wounds and a cheat, a king shall fast for one night; and the priest, for three nights. If an innocent man is punished [the king shall perform] a *Krccha* penance, and the priest [shall fast] for three nights.

अथाप्युदाहरन्ति।

Now they quote the following verses as an example :

अन्नादे भ्रूणहा मार्ष्टि पतौ भार्यापचारिणी।
गुरौ शिष्यस्तु याज्यश्च स्तेनो राजनि किल्विषम्॥

The destroyer of a learned Brāhmaṇa throws his guilt on him, who takes his food; an adulterous wife, on her husband; a disciple and a sacrificer, on an [ignorant] teacher [and officiating priest); and a thief, on the king [who pardons him].

राजभिर्धृतदण्डास्तु कृत्वा पापानि मानवाः।
निर्मलाः स्वर्गमायान्ति सन्तः सुकृतिनो यथा॥

If having committed crimes, men are purified by the king, they go pure to the celestial region and [become] as holy as the virtuous.

एनो राजानमृच्छन्त्यप्युत्सृजन्तं सकिल्विषम्।
तश्चेन्न घातयेद्राजा राजधर्मेण दुष्यतीति॥

The sin visits the king, who pardons an offender. If he does not cause him to be killed, he becomes guilty in accordance with the regal laws.

राज्ञामन्येषु कार्येषु सद्यः शौचं विधीयते।
तथा तान्यपि नित्यानि काल एवात्र कारणमिति॥

Immediate purification is laid down in respect of (the violation of) all royal duties. They are always pure, and Yama is the authority (for this statement.)

यमगीतश्चात्र श्लोकमुदाहरन्ति।

Now they quote a verse proclaimed by Yama.

नात्र दोषोऽस्ति राज्ञां वै व्रतिनां न च मन्त्रिणाम्।
ऐन्द्रस्थानमुपासीना ब्रह्मभूता हि ते सदेति॥

In this, no sin attaches to kings, to those who are engaged in religious observances and to the ministers, for they are seated on the throne of Indra, and are always equal to Brahma.

इति वासिष्ठे धर्मशास्त्रे एकोनविंशोऽध्यायः॥१९॥

Chapter 20

अनभिसन्धिकृते प्रायश्चित्तमपराधे सविकृतेऽप्येके।
गुरुरात्मवतां शास्ता राजा शास्ता दुरात्मनाम्।
इह प्रच्छन्नपापानां शास्ता वैवस्वतो यम इति।।

There is penance for a crime committed unwittingly; some [say] also for [a crime] committed intentionally. The spiritual teacher corrects the learned; the king corrects the evil-minded, but Yama, the son of Vivaśvat, indeed punishes those, who commit sins secretly.

तत्र च सूर्याभ्युदयिकः सन्नहस्तिष्ठेत् सावित्रीञ्च जपेदेवं सूर्याभिनिर्मुक्तो रात्रावासीत्।

Of men one, who has slept at sun-rise, shall stand during the day and recite Sāvitrī, and one, who has slept at sun-set, shall sit whole night [reciting the *Gāyatrī*.]

कुनखी श्यावदन्तस्तु कृच्छ्रद्वादशरात्रं चरित्वा पुनर्निर्विशेत्। अथ दिधिषूपतिः कृच्छ्रं द्वादशरात्रं चरित्वा निर्विशेत्। ताञ्चैवोपयच्छेद्दिधिषूपतिः कृच्छ्रातिकृच्छ्रौ चरित्वा निर्विशेत्।

One with deformed nails or black teeth shall perform a *Kṛccha* penance, extending over twelve days, and then again enter the domestic mode of life flaying performed *a Kṛccha* penance for twelve days, one, whose younger brother has first married, may again enter the domestic mode of life and take to himself even that woman whom his younger brother married.] He, who has taken a wife before his elder brother, shall perform a *Kṛccha* penance and an *Atikṛccha* penance, and then marry.

चरणमहरहस्तद्वक्ष्यामो ब्रह्माघ्नः कृच्छ्रं द्वादशरात्रं चरित्वा पुनरुपनीतो वेदमाचार्यात्। गुरुतल्पगः सवृषणं शिश्नमुत्कृत्याञ्जलावाधाय दक्षिणामुखो गच्छेत् यत्रैव प्रतिहन्यात् तत्र तिष्ठेदाप्रलयान्निष्कालको वा घृताक्तस्तप्तां सूर्मिं परिष्वजेन्मरणान्मुक्तो भवतीति विज्ञायते। आचार्यपुत्रशिष्यभार्य्यासु चैवं योनिषु च गुर्वीं सखीं गुरुसखीञ्च गत्वा कृच्छ्राब्दं चरेत्। एतदेव चाण्डालपतितान्नभोजनेषु ततः पुनरुपनयनं वपनादीनान्तु निवृत्तिः।

We now declare [the necessity of] daily performing a penance. Having performed a *Kṛccha* penance for twelve [days and] nights, one, who has killed (*i.e.*, forgotten) Brahma (*i.e.*, Veda, after being again initiated with the sacred thread, shall receive the Veda from his teacher. The violator of a step-mother shall cut off his organ together with the testes, take them in his joined-hands and proceed towards the south; wherever he meets with an impediment there he shall stand till he dies; or having shaved his hair and smeared his body with clarified butter he shall embrace the heated iron image [of a woman.] It is said [in the Veda] he becomes liberated [from the sin] after death. The same [penance is laid down for him, who commits the offence] with the wife of a teacher, of a son, or of a pupil. By knowing a venerable woman, or a female friend or wife of a Guru, one shall perform *a Kṛccha* penance for a year. The same penance [is laid down] for taking food of a Cāṇḍāla, or of an out-cast. After wards initiation, [must be performed once more] but the tonsure and the rest may be omitted.

मानवञ्चात्र श्लोकानुदाहरन्ति।

Now they quote a verse from Manu as an example;

वपनं मेखला दण्डो भैक्षचर्या व्रतानि च।
निवर्त्तन्ते द्विजातीनां पुनः संस्कारकर्मणीति।।

The tonsure, [the wearing, of] a sacred girdle, [the holding of a] staff and the begging of alms-these religious rites may be omitted on second initiative rites of the twice-born.

सर्वमद्यपाने क्लीबव्यवहारेषु विण्मूत्ररेतोऽभ्यवहारेषु चैवम्। मद्यभाण्डे स्थिता अपो यदि कश्चिद् द्विजोऽर्थवित्। पद्मोडुम्बरविल्वपलाशानामुदकं पीत्वा त्रिरात्रेणैव शुध्यति। अभ्यासे सुराया अग्निवर्णां तां द्विजः पिबेत्। भ्रूणहनञ्च वक्ष्यामो ब्राह्मणं हत्वा भ्रूणहा भवत्यविज्ञातञ्च गर्भम्। अविज्ञाता हि गर्भाः पुमांसो भवन्ति तस्मात् पुंस्कृत्य जुहुयात् लोमानि मृत्योर्जुहोमि लोमभिर्मृत्य वासय इति।

Such [is the penance in respect of those] drinking spirituous liquor and associating with eunuchs. If any twice-born person, conversant with the meaning [of the sacred literature], drinks water lying in a liquor vessel, he shall, after drinking the juice of lotus; *Udumbara*, *Bel*, and *Palāśa* leaves, for three nights, attain to purification. For habitually drinking spirituous liquor, a twice-born person shall drink one [liquor] of the colour of fire. We shall describe Bhrūṇahā (the destroyer of a learned Brāhmaṇa, or of an embryo.) He is called a Bhrūṇahā, who slays a Brāhmaṇa, or destroys an embryo [the sex of] which is unknown. The embryos of which the sex is unknown become males; therefore, they should offer oblations unto the fire for the production of males. The destroyer of a learned Brāhmaṇa shall kindle a fire, and offer [the following eight oblations,]

प्रथमां त्वचं मृतोर्जुहोमि त्वचा मृत्युं वासय इति द्वितीयां लोहितं मृत्योर्जुहोमि लोहतेन वासय इति तृतीयां त्वचं मृत्योर्जुहोमि तावति मृत्युं वासय इति चतुर्थीं मांसानि मृत्योर्जुहोमि मांसैर्मृत्युं वासय इति पञ्चमीं मेदोन मृत्योर्जुहोमि मेदसा मृत्युं वासय इति षष्ठीम् अस्थीनि मृत्योर्जुहोमि अस्थिभिर्मृत्युं वासय इति सप्तमीं मज्ञानं मृत्योर्जुहोमि मज्ञभिर्मुत्युं वासय इति अष्टमीं राजार्थे ब्राह्मणार्थे वा संग्रामेऽभिमुखमात्मानं घातयेत् त्रिरञ्जितो वापराद्धः पूतो भवतीति विज्ञायते। द्विरुक्तं कृतः कनीयो भवतीति।

The first, [by saying] I offer my hair to Death, I feed Death with my hair;' the second, [by saying] I offer my skin to Death, I feed Death with my skin; the third, [by saying] `I offer my blood to Death, I feed Death with my blood;' the fourth, [by saying] `I offer my flesh to Death, I feed Death with my flesh;' the fifth, [by saying] `I offer my sinews to Death, I feed Death with my sinews;' the sixth, [by saying] `I offer my bones to Death, I feed Death with my bones;' the eighth, [by saying] `I offer my marrow to Death, I feed Death with my marrow.' For the sake of the king, or for the sake of Brāhmaṇas, one shall cause oneself to be slain in battle with one's face divested towards [the enemy.] It is declared in the Veda (A murderer), who is thrice undefeated, or is thrice defeated [in battle], becomes pure. A sin, which is twice proclaimed, becomes smaller.

तदाप्युदाहरन्ति।

Now they quote the following verses as an example .

पतितं पतितं त्यक्त्वा चौरं चौरेति वा पुनः।

वचसा तुल्यदोषः स्यान्मिथ्यादिदोषता व्रजेदिति॥

By saying to an out-cast, "O you, out-cast," or to a thief, "O you thief," a person commits a sin as great as [that of the offender]. [If he] falsely [charges any body with such an offence], his sin will be twice as great.

एवं राजन्यं हत्वाष्टौ वर्षाणि चरेत्। षड्वैश्यं त्रीणि शूद्रं ब्राह्मणीञ्चात्रेयीं हत्वा सवनगतौ च राजन्यवैश्यौ चात्रेयीं वक्ष्यामो रजस्वलामृतुस्नातामात्रेय्याहुः। अत्रेत्येषामपत्यं भवतीति चात्रेयी। राजन्यहिंसायां वैश्यहिंसायां शूद्रं हत्वा संवत्सरम्। ब्राह्मणसुवर्णहरात् प्रकीर्य केशान् राजानमभिधावेत् स्तेनोऽस्मि भोः शास्तु भवानिति तस्मै राजादुम्बरं शस्त्रं दध्यात् तेनात्मानं प्रमापयेन्मरणात् पूतो भवतीति विज्ञायते। निष्कालको वा घृताक्तो गोमयाग्निना पादप्रभृत्यामानमतिदाहयेन्मरणात् पूतो भवतीति विज्ञायते।

Likewise, having killed a Kṣatriya, he shall perform a penance extending over eight years; for killing a Vaiśya, six years; for killing a Śūdra, three. For slaying a Brāhmaṇa woman, who is an Ātreyī, or a Kṣatriya or Vaiśya engaged in a sacrifice, [the same penance shall be performed.] We shall explain [the term] Ātreyī. [The learned] say that, she, who has bathed after the menses, is an Ātreyī; she too is called an Ātreyī, who is descended from [the family of] Atri. By slaying a *Kṣatriya*, by killing a Vaiśya, and by destroying a Śūdra, [one shall perform penance] for a year. By robbing a Brāhmaṇa, one shall run with flying hair to the king, [declaring] I am a thief, Sir, punish me." The king shall then give him a weapon made of Udumbara wood; with that weapon he shall kill himself. It is said in the Veda that, he becomes pure after death, or [the thief] shall shave off all his hair, smear his body with clarified butter, and cause himself to be burnt from the feet upwards in a fire of dry cow-dung. It is said in the Veda that, he becomes pure after death.

अथाप्युदाहरन्ति।

Now they quote the following verses as an example :

पुराकालात् प्रमीतानामानाकविधिकर्मणाम्।
पुनरापन्नदेहानामङ्गं भवति तच्छृणु॥

Hear, now, the limbs of those, who having committed various crimes died a long time ago and were afterwards re-born, are [marked].

स्तेन: कुनखी भवति श्वित्री भवति ब्रह्महा।
सुराप: श्यावदन्तस्तु दुश्चर्मा गुरुतल्पग:॥ इति

A thief will have deformed nails, a slayer of Brāhmaṇas will suffer from white leprosy; a drinker of spirituous liquor will have black teeth, and a violator of his Guru's bed will suffer from bad skin.

पतितै: सम्प्रयोगे च ब्राह्मेण यौनेन वा तेभ्य: सकाशान्मात्रा उपलब्धास्तासां परित्यागस्तैश्च न संवसेदुदीचीं दिशं गत्वानश्नन् संहिताध्ययनमधीयान: पूतो भवतीति विज्ञायते।

Property obtained from the out-cast, after contracting alliances with them either by [teaching] the Veda, or by marriage, shall be relinquished. One shall not associate with such [men]. It is said in the Veda that, [he, who mixes with the out-cast], shall regain his purity by reciting the Saṁhitā while proceeding in a northerly direction and fasting.

अथाप्युदाहरन्ति।

They quote the following verse as an example :

शरीरपातनाच्चैव तपसाध्ययनेन च।
मुच्यते पापकृत् पापाद्दानाच्चापि प्रमुच्यते। इति विज्ञायते।

A sinner is freed from his sin by tormenting his body, by practising austerities, and by Vedic studies; he becomes also liberated by making gifts. This is said in the Veda.

इति वासिष्ठे धर्मशास्त्रे विंशोऽध्याय:॥२०॥

Chapter 21

शूद्रश्चेद्ब्राह्मणीमभिगच्छेद्वीरणैर्वेष्टयित्वा शूद्रमग्नौ प्रास्येद्ब्राह्मण्याः शिरसि वापनं कारयित्वा सर्पिषाभ्यज्यनग्नां खरमारोप्य महापथमनुव्राजयेत् पूता भवतीति विज्ञायते।

If a Śūdra knows a Brāhmaṇa woman, [the king] shall cause the Śūdra to be packed up in *Vīraṇa* grass and thrown into a fire. Having caused the head of the Brāhmaṇi to be shaved and her body to be smeared with clarified butter, he shall cause her to be placed naked on the back of a donkey and conducted along the high-road. It is said that, she becomes pure [thereby].

वैश्यश्चेद्ब्राह्मणीमभिगच्छेल्लोहितदर्भैर्वेष्टयित्वा वैश्यमग्नौ प्रास्येद्ब्राह्मण्याः शिरसि वापनं कारयित्वा सर्पिषाभ्यज्य नग्नां गोरथमारोप्य महापथमनुसंव्राजयेत् पूता भवतीति विज्ञायते।

If a Vaiśya knows a Brāhmaṇa woman, [the king] shall cause the Vaiśya to be tied up with Lohita grass, and he shall throw him into a fire. Having caused the head of the Brāhmaṇi to be shaved and her body to be smeared with clarified butter, he shall cause her to be placed naked on a yellowish donkey and conducted along the high road. It is said in the Veda that, she becomes pure [thereby].

राजन्यश्चेद्ब्राह्मणीमभिगच्छेच्छरपत्रैर्वेष्टयित्वा राजन्यमग्नौ प्रास्येद्ब्राह्मण्याः शिरोवापनं कारयित्वा सर्पिषाभ्यज्य नग्नां रक्तखरमारोप्य महापथमनुव्राजयेत्।

If a Kṣatriya knows a Brāhmaṇa woman, [the king] shall cause the Kṣatriya to be tied up with blades of Sara grass and shall throw him into a fire. Having caused the head of the Brāhmaṇi to be shaved and her body to be smeared with clarified butter, he shall cause her to be placed naked on a white donkey and conducted along the high road. It is said in the Veda that, she becomes pure [thereby].

एवं वैश्यो राजन्यायां शूद्रश्च राजन्यावैश्ययोर्मनसा भर्तुरतिचारे त्रिरात्रं यावकं क्षीरं भुञ्जानाधःशयाना त्रिरात्रमप्सु निम्नगायाः सावित्र्यष्टशतेन शिरोभिर्वा जुहुयात् पूता भवतीति विज्ञायते।

A Vaiśya, [who commits lachery] with a Kṣatriya woman, [shall be treated] in the same manner; so shall a Śūdra [who holds incest] with a Kṣatriya or a Vaiśya woman. If [a wife] has been mentally faithless to her husband, she shall live on barley or rice boiled with milk, for three days, and sleep on the bare ground. After [the expiration of] three days, [the husband] shall offer eight hundred Homas, [reciting] the Sāvitrī [and the Siras] Mantra, while she is immersed in water. It is said in the Veda that, she becomes pure [thereby].

इति वासिष्ठे धर्मशास्त्रे एकविंशोऽध्यायः॥२१॥

॥ वसिष्ठस्मृतिः समाप्ता ॥